LOVING V. VIRGINIA IN A POST-RACIAL WORLD
RETHINKING RACE, SEX, AND MARRIAGE

In 1967, the U.S. Supreme Court ruled that laws prohibiting interracial marriage were unconstitutional in *Loving v. Virginia*. Although this case promotes marital freedom and racial equality, there are still significant legal and social barriers to the free formation of intimate relationships. Marriage continues to be the sole measure of commitment, mixed relationships continue to be rare, and same-sex marriage is legal in only seven out of fifty states. Most discussion of *Loving* celebrates the symbolic dismantling of marital racial discrimination. This book, however, takes a more critical approach to ask how *Loving* has influenced the "loving" of America. How far have we come since then, and what effect did the case have on individual lives?

Kevin Noble Maillard is Professor of Law at Syracuse University where he teaches family law, trusts and estates, and on the subjects of children and the law, adoption, and popular culture and the law. He has written about and lectured on nontraditional families, racial intermixture, the role of marriage in America, civil liberties within the family, and popular culture and the law. His work has been published in the *New York Times, Cardozo Law Review, SMU Law Review, Fordham Law Review*, and *Law & Inequality*. He is a frequent presenter at legal and interdisciplinary conferences.

Rose Cuison Villazor is an Associate Professor of Law at Hofstra Law School. She teaches and writes in the areas of race, citizenship, property, and immigration law. Her articles have appeared in the *New York University Law Review, California Law Review, Washington University Law Review*, and *Southern California Law Review*. In 2011, she received the AALS Minority Section Derrick A. Bell, Jr., Award, which is given to a junior faculty member who, through activism, mentoring, teaching, and scholarship, has made an extraordinary contribution to legal education, the legal system, or social justice.

Loving v. Virginia in a Post-Racial World

RETHINKING RACE, SEX, AND MARRIAGE

Edited by

KEVIN NOBLE MAILLARD

Syracuse University, College of Law

ROSE CUISON VILLAZOR

Hofstra University, School of Law

CAMBRIDGE
UNIVERSITY PRESS

University Printing House, Cambridge CB2 8BS, United Kingdom

One Liberty Plaza, 20th Floor, New York, NY 10006, USA

477 Williamstown Road, Port Melbourne, VIC 3207, Australia

314-321, 3rd Floor, Plot 3, Splendor Forum, Jasola District Centre, New Delhi - 110025, India

79 Anson Road, #06-04/06, Singapore 079906

Cambridge University Press is part of the University of Cambridge.

It furthers the University's mission by disseminating knowledge in the pursuit of education, learning and research at the highest international levels of excellence.

www.cambridge.org
Information on this title: www.cambridge.org/9780521147989

First published 2012
Reprinted 2013

A catalogue record for this publication is available from the British Library

Library of Congress Cataloging in Publication data
Loving v. Virginia in a post-racial world : rethinking race, sex, and marriage /
Kevin Noble Maillard, Rose Cuison Villazor.
    p.   cm.
Includes bibliographical references and index.
ISBN 978-0-521-19858-5 (hardback) – ISBN 978-0-521-14798-9 (pbk.)
    1. Interracial marriage–Law and legislation–United States.   2. Loving, Richard Perry–Trials,
litigation, etc.   I. Villazor, Rose Cuison.   II. Maillard, Kevin Noble.
KF517.L68   2012
346.7301´63–dc23   2012012290

ISBN 978-0-521-19858-5 Hardback
ISBN 978-0-521-14798-9 Paperback

Contents

About the Contributors

Taunya Lovell Banks is the Jacob A. France Professor of Equality Jurisprudence and the Francis & Harriet Iglehart Research Professor of Law at the University of Maryland School of Law, where she teaches constitutional law, torts, and seminars on popular culture, citizenship, and critical race theory. Prior to entering legal education in 1976, Professor Banks worked as a civil rights lawyer in Mississippi, litigating voting rights and housing discrimination cases and providing technical assistance to black elected officials. Her scholarship has appeared in the *Asian Law Journal*, *Harvard Civil Rights–Civil Liberties Law Review*, *Michigan Law Review*, and *UCLA Law Review*.

Jacquelyn L. Bridgeman is Professor of Law and Associate Dean for Academic Affairs on the University of Wyoming's College of Law faculty. Her work focuses on African Americans and the American legal system. She teaches in the areas of family law, torts, and legal writing. Before joining the College of Law faculty, Professor Bridgeman was an associate attorney at the Los Angeles, California, law firms of Curiale, Dellaverson, Hirschfeld, Kraemer & Sloan and Loeb & Loeb. Her work has been published in the *Boston College Third World Law Journal*, *Seattle Journal for Social Studies*, and *Seton Hall Law Review*.

I. Bennett Capers joined the faculty of the Maurice A. Deane School of Law at Hofstra University as an Associate Professor of Law in 2005. Prior to teaching, Professor Capers served as an assistant U.S. attorney in the Southern District of New York and as an associate at Willkie Farr & Gallagher. Professor Capers teaches Criminal Law, Criminal Procedure, Evidence, Law and Literature, and Race and the Law. His scholarship explores the dialogic relationship between culture and law and has appeared in the *California Law Review*, *Columbia Law Review*, *Michigan Law Review*, and the *UCLA Law Review*.

Rose Cuison Villazor is an Associate Professor of Law at the Maurice A. Deane School of Law at Hofstra University. She teaches and writes in the areas of race, citizenship, property, and immigration law. In 2011, she received the Association of American Law Schools Minority Section Derrick A. Bell, Jr., Award. Her articles have appeared in the *New York University Law Review*, *California Law Review*, *Washington University Law Review*, and *Southern California Law Review*.

Tucker B. Culbertson is Assistant Professor of Law and LGBT Studies at Syracuse University. Before joining the faculty at Syracuse, Professor Culbertson was a Fellow with the Center for the Study of Law and Culture at Columbia Law School and a Lecturer in Political Science at San Francisco State University and UC-Berkeley. Professor Culbertson's research and writing presently focus on counterterrorism, color-blindness, marriage, and the extraterritorial application of the U.S. the Constitution. His recent and forthcoming works appear, among other places, in the *Washington University Law Review*, *University of Miami Law Review*, *Stanford Journal of Civil Rights and Civil Liberties*, *Journal of Animal Law*, *Women's Studies Quarterly*, and two anthologies of critical legal theory.

Angelique Davis is Assistant Professor of Women and Gender Studies and Political Science at Seattle University. She is the Director of the Pre-law Program for the College of Arts and Sciences and is a frequent writer and presenter of issues of race, reparations, and the multiracial category. Professor Davis teaches Civil Rights, Citizenship/Civic Engagement, Constitutional Law, Law, Politics and Society, and Gender and the Law. Prior to entering academia, Professor Davis was an Assistant City Attorney for the City of Seattle and a Senior Associate at the Seattle law firm of Williams, Kastner & Gibbs. Her work has been published in the *Berkeley La Raza Law Journal* and *Thomas Jefferson Law Review*.

Jason A. Gillmer is the John J. Hemmingson Chair in Civil Liberties at the Gonzaga University School of Law. Prior to teaching, Professor Gillmer clerked for Judge Donald Alsop on the District Court of Minnesota and for Judge Kim Wardlaw on the U.S. Court of Appeals for the Ninth Circuit. He was also an associate in the law firm of Robins, Kaplan, Miller & Ciresi. Professor Gillmer is a legal historian whose scholarship focuses on race, slavery, and civil rights, including issues of interracial intimacy, racial identity, and racial and class ideology. His articles have been published in the *Alabama Law Review*, *North Carolina Law Review*, and *Southern California Law Review*.

John DeWitt Gregory is the Sidney and Walter Siben Distinguished Professor of law at the Maurice A. Deane School of Law at Hofstra University. He teaches primarily in the areas of matrimonial and family law. He is an elected member of the American Law Institute, a Fellow of the American and New York Bar Foundations, and a member of the board of editors of the *Family Law Quarterly*. He has co-authored numerous books, including *The Law of Equitable Distribution*, *Property*

Division in Divorce Proceedings, and *Understanding Family Law*. His scholarship has appeared in the *Family Law Quarterly, Florida Law Review, Howard Law Journal,* and *Santa Clara Law Review.*

Joanna L. Grossman is Professor of Law and Hofstra Research Fellow at the Maurice A. Deane School of Law at Hofstra University. She writes extensively about family law, especially state regulation of marriage. Professor Grossman has served on the editorial board of *Perspectives,* the magazine of the ABA's Commission on Women in the Profession. She was elected to membership in the American Law Institute in 2009. She is the co-author, with Lawrence M. Friedman, of *Inside the Castle: Law and the Family in 20th Century America,* and the coeditor, with Linda McClain, of *Gender the Equality: Dimensions of Women's Equal Citizenship.* She has published articles in the *Stanford Law Review, Georgetown Law Journal,* and the *Yale Journal on Law and Feminism,* among other publications.

Angela P. Harris is Professor of Law at the University of California at Davis School of Law. She writes widely in the field of critical legal theory, examining how law sometimes reinforces and sometimes challenges subordination on the basis of race, gender, sexuality, class, and other dimensions of power and identity. She is the coauthor *of A Woman's Place Is in the Marketplace: Gender and Economics, Cultural Economics: Markets and Culture,* and *When Markets Fail: Race and Economics,* as well as numerous textbooks on race, economics, and equality. She has published articles in the *California Law Review, Cornell Law Review, Fordham Law Review,* and *Stanford Law Review.*

Renée M. Landers is Professor of Law at Suffolk University School of Law. She previously served as counsel to the Boston law firm of Ropes & Gray for five years and as an attorney for the U.S. Department of Health and Human Services and the U.S. Department of Justice. In 1985, she served as a law clerk to former Chief Justice Edward F. Hennessey of the Connecticut Supreme Judicial Court. Professor Landers' scholarship has appeared in the *DePaul Law Review, New England Law Review,* and the *University of California at Hastings Law Journal.*

Robin A. Lenhardt is an Associate Professor of Law at Fordham University, where she specializes in matters pertaining to race, civil rights, family law, and constitutional law. A former law clerk to U.S. Supreme Court Justice Stephen G. Breyer and Judge Hugh Bownes of the U.S. Court of Appeals for the First Circuit, Professor Lenhardt was of Counsel in the Washington, DC office of Wilmer, Cutler & Pickering, where she was a member of the litigation team that defended the University of Michigan in the *Gratz v. Bollinger* and *Grutter v. Bollinger* affirmative action lawsuits. Her scholarship has appeared in the *California Law Review, Fordham Law Review, New York University Law Review,* and *UCLA Law Review.*

Rachel F. Moran is Dean and Michael J. Connell Distinguished Professor of Law at the University of California at Los Angeles School of Law. Prior to her appointment at UCLA, Professor Moran was the Robert D. and Leslie-Kay Raven Professor of Law at the University of California at Berkeley School of Law. From July 2008 to June 2010, Dean Moran served as a founding faculty member of the University of California at Irvine Law School. She is the author of *Interracial Intimacy: The Regulation of Race and Romance*. Her law review articles have been published in the *California Law Review*, *Howard Law Journal*, *Northwestern Law Review*, and *Stanford Law Review*.

Adele M. Morrison is an Associate Professor of Law at Wayne State University Law School, where she teaches courses in Criminal Law, Family Law, and Child, Family, and State. She most recently served as visiting professor of law and acting director of the Civil Justice Clinic at Washington University in St. Louis School of Law. She was a Remington Hastie Fellow at the University of Wisconsin Law School and has taught at Western New England University, the University of Denver, and Northern Illinois University. Her research interests are family law, domestic violence, critical race theory, and LGBT studies. Her work has appeared in the *Harvard Journal of Law and Gender*, *UC Davis Law Review*, and *Wisconsin Law Review*.

Camille A. Nelson is Dean and Professor of Law at Suffolk University. Before joining Suffolk Law, Dean Nelson served as Professor of Law at the Maurice A. Deane School of Law at Hofstra University. From 2000 to 2009, she was a member of the faculty of St. Louis University School of Law. She also was a visiting professor at Washington University in St. Louis School of Law, where she became the Dean's Scholar in Residence. Dean Nelson is a member of the American Law Institute and is widely recognized for her writings and lectures, which have focused on the intersection of critical race theory and cultural studies with particular focus on criminal law and procedure, health law, and comparative law. She has published in the *Denver University Law Review*, *Florida Law Review*, *Iowa Law Review*, and *Wisconsin Law Review*.

Kevin Noble Maillard is Professor of Law at Syracuse University where he teaches family law, trusts and estates, and popular culture and the law. He has written about and lectured on nontraditional families, racial intermixture, the role of marriage in America, civil liberties within the family, and popular culture and the law. His work has been published in the *New York Times*, *Cardozo Law Review*, *SMU Law Review*, *Fordham Law Review*, and *Law & Inequality*.

Angela Onwuachi-Willig is the Charles M. and Marion J. Kierscht Professor of Law at the University of Iowa. She previously taught at the University of California at Davis School of Law (King Hall). Her research and teaching interests include family law, employment discrimination, critical race theory, feminist legal theory, and evidence. In 2006, Professor Onwuachi-Willig was honored for her service by the Minority Groups Section of the Association of American Law Schools with the Derrick A. Bell, Jr., Award. Since 2011, she has been a Fellow of the American Bar Foundation. She is the author of the forthcoming book *According to Our Hearts: Lessons on Race, Family, and Law from* Rhinelander v. Rhinelander. Her recent publications have appeared in the *Michigan Law Review, California Law Review, Wisconsin Law Review, Minnesota Law Review,* and *Iowa Law Review.*

Nancy K. Ota is Professor of Law at Albany Law School. Professor Ota previously taught at the University of Toledo College of Law. Before attending law school, she worked as a commercial banker in international trade and corporate finance in New Orleans and San Francisco. Professor Ota writes in the areas of race, sexuality, gender, class, and national identity in social history. Her scholarship has been published in the *Albany Law Review, DePaul University Law Review,* and the *Washington and Lee Race and Ethnic Ancestry Law Journal.*

Carla D. Pratt is Associate Dean for Academic Affairs and Professor of Law at the Penn State University, Dickinson School of Law. She teaches and writes in the area of race and the law, with particular emphasis on the role of law in constructing American Indian and African-American identity. Another aspect of her scholarship examines the role of race in the legal profession. She teaches Constitutional Law, Federal Indian Law, Race and American Law, and Professional Responsibility. She is the coauthor of *The End of the Pipeline: A Journey of Recognition for African Americans Entering the Profession of Law.* Her scholarship has appeared in the *Fordham Law Review, Houston Law Journal,* and *Wisconsin Law Review.*

Victor C. Romero is the Maureen B. Cavanaugh Distinguished Faculty Scholar and Professor of Law at the Penn State University, Dickinson School of Law. He teaches and writes in the area of immigrant and minority rights. Professor Romero has served as president of both the South Central Pennsylvania Chapter of the ACLU and the NAACP of the Greater Carlisle Area. An elected member of the American Law Institute, Professor Romero is the coeditor of the anthology *Immigration and the Constitution,* and author of *Alienated: Immigrant Rights, the Constitution, and Equality in America.* He has also published in the *Georgetown Immigration Law Journal, Howard Law Journal,* and *Villanova Law Review.*

Leti Volpp is Professor of Law at University of California at Berkeley School of Law. She writes about citizenship, migration, culture, and identity. Her numerous honors include two Rockefeller Foundation Humanities Fellowships, a MacArthur Foundation Individual Research and Writing Grant, and the Association of American Law Schools Minority Section Derrick A. Bell, Jr., Award. Her articles have been published in the *Columbia Law Review, Michigan Law Review, UCLA Law Review,* and numerous edited collections.

Peter Wallenstein is a Professor of History in the History Department at Virginia Tech. His research emphasizes the American South, the history of racial identity in the United States, and the history of U.S. higher education. In 2004, he received the Hughes-Gosset Prize from the Supreme Court Historical Society for his article "To Sit or Not to Sit: The Supreme Court of the United States and the Civil Rights Movement in the Upper South." He is the author of the influential book *Tell the Court I Love My Wife: Race, Marriage, and Law–An American History,* for which he received the Sturm Award for Excellence in Faculty Research. His other published books include *From Slave South to New South: Public Policy in Nineteenth-Century Georgia* and *Blue Laws and Black Codes: Conflict, Courts, and Change in Twentieth-Century Virginia.*

Jacob Willig-Onwuachi is Associate Professor of Physics at Grinnell College, where he has served as a Harris Fellow. He previously taught in the Departments of Radiology and Biomedical Engineering at the University of California at Davis and completed a postdoctoral fellowship at Beth Israel Deaconess Medical Center/Harvard Medical School. His primary research and teaching interests include medical physics, magnetic resonance imaging, electromagnetic theory, and "workshop" physics. He has also taught and written in the areas of race, law, gender, and society. Some of his recent publications have appeared in *Magnetic Resonance in Medicine, Physics in Medicine and Biology,* and the *Harvard Civil Rights–Civil Liberties Law Review.*

Acknowledgments

This book would not have been possible without the help of a number of people during the last several years. We first thank our contributors for the work that they put in writing, editing, and revising their work.

We are indebted to Robert Chang, Matthew Fletcher, Kate Fort, Katherine Franke, Deborah Gershenowitz, Kevin Johnson, Sonia Katyal, Randall Kennedy, Janis McDonald, Melissa Murray, Melynda Price, Ediberto Roman, and Wenona Siegel, who offered feedback, raised criticisms, and asked difficult questions. Additionally, Phil Hirschkop, counsel for Richard and Mildred Loving, provided valuable insight.

We are grateful to Dean John Attanasio of Southern Methodist University Dedman School of Law, Dean Hannah Arterian of Syracuse University College of Law, and Dean Nora Demleitner of the Maurice A. Deane School of Law at Hofstra University for providing financial support to this project.

Finally, we thank our families for their love, patience, and support.

Foreword

Angela Harris

On or about June 12 each year since 2004, Loving Day – "an educational campaign and a global network of annual celebrations" – holds a "Flagship Celebration" in New York City to commemorate the anniversary of the Supreme Court's ruling in *Loving v. Virginia*.[1] In 2009, according to the website Blended People of America, the sixth annual Loving Day celebration in New York City "saw the gathering of about 1,100 people.... From 3 to 7 pm, guests mingled, heard and exchanged stories, danced to music, looked over the riverfront, created artwork, or gathered as families in a warm and welcoming environment."[2]

Loving Day presents itself as a quintessentially post-racial celebration. The Loving Day organizers, and their website, look back respectfully and gratefully to the Lovings, whose legal struggle made it possible for Americans of different racial identities to dance, marry, kiss, form families, and celebrate beauty, pleasure, and desire without fear of police or prisons. Now, in the new fluid reality that Loving Day celebrates, even the concept of "miscegenation" has begun to seem bizarre and antiquated. The very idea of race mixing assumes that there is purity to be lost. The "blended people" who come together for Loving Day, however, represent themselves as already various – each a tapestry of ethnicities, religions, racial identities, and cultures. Mixing, in this new context, does not represent a falling-away from purity and strength. Instead, mixing takes on a postmodern meaning. Loving Day celebrants see their mixed backgrounds as making possible deep, complex, rich identities layered with history, custom, and meaning, in the way that a deejay mixes beats, melodies, and rhythms to make deep, rich, funkier layers of sound.

The personal testimonials that Loving Day collects and displays on its website applaud the beauty and power of "love."[3] Couples describe how their attraction

[1]   388 U.S. 1 (1967).
[2]   *See*   http://blendedpeopleamerica.com/component/content/article/50-featured/88-loving-day.html (last visited November 3, 2010).
[3]   Loving Day, http://www.lovingday.org/ (last visited February 25, 2010).

transcended their fear of difference. Individuals describe the strength and beauty of their "blended" backgrounds, or the circumstances that drew them to people different from themselves. The decision in *Loving v. Virginia*, with its apt name, represents for this group the transformation from fear and hatred into love. For the Loving Day organization, moreover, *Loving* is a triumph not only of love, but of law. The Loving Day logo, designed by one of the group's founders, is a red shield containing a heart. The heart represents love, but the shield, the group's website explains, represents law. Visitors to the website are accordingly encouraged to learn about the case and to be thankful for the Lovings' struggle, knowing that love and the rich beauty that it makes possible are now safely protected by the state.

Other kinds of stories, however, also float around the website, beneath and between the stories of love victorious. One contributor to the "couples" page – a white woman named Amy, married to a black man – writes cheerfully, "No matter what 'mix' your relationship might be, there will always be ups and downs ... just be sure to live your life in love, because at the end of the day that is what truly matters!"[4] But Amy's blog about her relationship, "The Many Shades of Love," paints a more complicated picture. For example, one of Amy's clients, a white woman, intermittently feels compelled to share her racist thoughts. Amy reports:

> Yesterday it went a little like this ... somehow the topic of her children came up, who by the way she does not speak to, and she said the reason she doesn't to speak to one of her sons is because "He is married to a black." Yes "a black." Wow ... really!? What year are we in? What century is she from? Oh wait, it gets much worse. Then she proceeds to share her "lovely" feelings about black people and how much she hates them. Oh I'm not done yet. It just keeps going downhill from there! Then she starts talking about the grandbaby in the equation, and she says, "Yes, and my son has a monkey baby from her too." Are you kidding me!!!!!!!??? That comment made me sick to my stomach. How on earth do you feel this way about your own grandchild? How, how, how!!??[5]

What is the opposite of love? Not hate, as the convention goes; nor indifference, as some have suggested. If love is a set of practices through and by which we build connections to others, its opposite is the process by which connection is denied. Critical theorists use the word "abjection" to describe how bodily products that teeter on the line between self and not-self – sputum, saliva, waste – are cast out and treated as foreign. That which is abject inspires feelings of revulsion and horror because it is neither this nor that; it reminds us with a shiver that the line between me and not-me is permeable.[6] Abjection, the act of casting out in disgust, redraws the boundary again.

4 http://www.lovingday.org/couples-stories/amy-o (last visited February 25, 2010).
5 http://themanyshadesoflove.blogspot.com/2009/11/seeing-beneath-skin.html (last visited October 3, 2011).
6 *See* Martha C. Nussbaum, HIDING FROM HUMANITY: DISGUST, SHAME, AND THE LAW (2004) (arguing that laws and policies should not be built on feelings of disgust, because disgust embodies "magical

Just as individuals patrol the borders of their bodies, keeping the self in and the other out, human social groups patrol their borders. From day to day, humans grant or deny one another small courtesies and recognitions in rituals that confer person-hood.[7] We acknowledge that the people standing in line with us or sharing an eleva-tor with us are deserving of dignity and equal treatment. Philip Zimbardo and others have demonstrated, however, how readily humans, especially when seeking accep-tance or praise from one another, are willing to withdraw this acknowledgment from others.[8] When denied treatment as a person, a human becomes abject: something carrying the form of a person but not the substance of a person. This uncanniness inspires disgust and forms a basis for cruelty and casting-out.

As the high incidence of child abuse attests, individual humans idiosyncrati-cally and spontaneously "dehumanize" each other all the time.[9] But some kinds of dehumanization are organized, systematic, and group-based. Sometimes dehu-manization is state-sponsored, as in war and torture, when the rules under which we acknowledge others' personhood are officially suspended. Sometimes subnational groups undertake a campaign to dehumanize other subnational groups, resulting in campaigns of extermination. The twentieth century saw the birth of technologies that facilitated the horrors of genocide: killing an entire cohesive human group. But the most effective and crucial technology is a story that explains why certain humans are not persons and thus can be tortured or killed with impunity. Race – a symbolic system within which visible bodily marks betray invisible inherent cultural, mental, and moral differences that divide humans into fixed and enduring subspecies – has, since its invention and elaboration, been one of the most efficient devices for the abjection of human groups.

What does law have to do with all this? The essays in this book complicate Loving Day's picture of the law as a sturdy shield that surrounds and protects love. The fact

ideas of contamination, and impossible aspirations to purity that are just not in line with human life as we know it").

[7] Here I am using "human" to denote a biological, species connection, and "person" to denote the social subject, a human who is recognized by other humans as possessed of dignity and requiring equal treatment and respect. The sociologist Erving Goffman used the metaphor of dramaturgy to describe the labor humans put in every day to present themselves to one another as worthy of per-sonhood, and described in detail the small slippages and failings that can result in "stigma" – person-hood partially denied by others. See Erving Goffman, THE PRESENTATION OF SELF IN EVERYDAY LIFE (1959); STIGMA: NOTES ON THE MANAGEMENT OF SPOILED IDENTITY (1963).

[8] Philip Zimbardo, THE LUCIFER EFFECT: UNDERSTANDING HOW GOOD PEOPLE TURN EVIL (2007); see also Stanley Milgram, OBEDIENCE TO AUTHORITY: AN EXPERIMENTAL VIEW (reprinted 2009).

[9] "Depersonalization" might be a better term given my distinction between the human and the person. However, I will stick with the more familiar term. On the incidence of child abuse, see the Fourth National Incidence Study of Child Abuse and Neglect (NIS-4): Report to Congress, Executive Summary, January 2010, available at http://www.acf.hhs.gov/programs/opre/abuse_neglect/natl_incid/index.html (estimating that in 2005–2006, 1.25 million children experienced "maltreatment" (including neglect), with 44% of that number, or about 553,300 children, being abused. For a sad and vivid example of the dehumanization of a child within a family, see Dave Pelzer, A CHILD CALLED IT (1995).

that *Loving v. Virginia* had to be brought at all, of course, recognizes the law's past complicity with dehumanization. Law's concern with maintaining the social order has meant a commitment to maintaining, and sometimes extending, the color line, from Virginia's first statute connecting the condition of slavery with one's ancestry to the Supreme Court's decision in 1967. When the Court in *Loving v. Virginia* finally overturned Virginia's miscegenation laws, the majority opinion contained a critical phrase that signaled the justices' awareness of the link between marriage and racial domination: "White Supremacy."

The law speaks endlessly of relations between persons, but rarely speaks of its own role in creating, or destroying, personhood itself. *Loving's* mention of white supremacy broke this silence, yet the Court's opinion provides no explanation or definition of the concept. This book fills the gap, investigating the law's role in regulating and intervening in the social process by which humans are made into persons or non-persons. Marriage is a function of the "police power," a broad and amorphous power that permits the law to regulate and control bodies and populations. And the regulation of marriage, like the regulation of immigration, has been used not only to prevent certain unions from being legally recognized, but to protect the racial purity of the nation itself. In the early days of the republic, as Matthew Jacobson argues, a white person was a person willing to take up arms against Indians and slaves.[10] Whiteness later evolved to exclude Asians (too "foreign" to be assimilated), Mexicans (racial "mongrels" lacking the mental and moral strength to assimilate), Italians, Jews, and many other groups. In purportedly protecting the purity of whiteness, miscegenation law – and the case that overturned it – speaks not only to the recognition of personal bonds, but of national ones; not only the conferral of individual personhood, but the consolidation of citizenship.

Loving's dominant legacy has been the simple narrative sketched by the founders of Loving Day: a story about prejudice overcome. The essays in this book go further. They describe how state power can be used in the "private" sphere to make some human bodies unintelligible as persons. In the process, they reveal what is at stake in marriage law – not only love and beauty, but power and privilege; not only private celebration, but public order. They reveal how "love" is made possible or impossible by law: through geographical restrictions keeping bodies away from one another; through legal restrictions meant to do the same (including miscegenation law and immigration law); through legal doctrines that distribute personhood unequally; and through legal rules that refuse the right to sex and family to some persons and relationships, but not to others. This powerful collection thus revises what *Loving*, and "loving," signify.

---

[10] *See, generally,* Matthew Jacobson, WHITENESS OF A DIFFERENT COLOR: EUROPEAN IMMIGRANTS AND THE ALCHEMY OF RACE (1998).

Introduction

Loving v. Virginia in a Post-Racial World: Rethinking Race, Sex, and Marriage

Kevin Noble Maillard and Rose Cuison Villazor

On June 16, 1967, the U.S. Supreme Court unanimously ruled that state laws prohibiting interracial marriage were unconstitutional. In this landmark case, *Loving v. Virginia*,[1] the Court championed the rightful place of Fourteenth Amendment guarantees of equal protection and due process in the realm of marriage and family. As a result of the Court's opinion, petitioners Richard Loving, a White man, and Mildred Jeter, a woman of color, could finally live in Virginia as a legally married couple. No longer would they – and other interracial couples who wanted to marry – be subject to the discriminatory regulations of the state that sought to maintain and police racial boundaries.

For most of American history, law not only placed restrictions on the selection of a marital partner, but also forged a collective definition of the legitimate family. At most, forty-one states enacted laws preventing interracial marriage, with the majority of jurisdictions banning Black-White unions.[2] In a minority of other states, intermarriages between Whites and Asians, Latinos/as, or Native Americans were also prohibited.[3] Racial classifications differed from state to state, thus allowing a "Black" person to cross state lines to find themselves categorized differently according to their blood quantum.[4]

---

[1] 388 U.S. 1 (1967).

[2] Peggy Pascoe, *Miscegenation Law, Court Cases, and Ideologies of "Race" in Twentieth-Century America*, 83 J. AM. HIST. 44, 49 (1996).

[3] *See*, Note *Constitutionality of Anti-Miscegenation Statutes*, 58 YALE L.J. 472, 480 (1949); Leti Volpp, *American Mestizo: Filipinos and Antimiscegenation Laws in California*, 33 U.C. DAVIS L. REV. 795, 798–99 (stating that while antimiscegenation laws were originally intended with a focus on Black-White relationships, some states also prohibited marriages between Whites and Native Americans, Asians, and/or Filipinos).

[4] *See generally*, Kevin Noble Maillard and Janis McDonald, *The Anatomy of Grey: a Theory of Interracial Convergence*, 26 LAW & INEQ. 305 (2008) (for a discussion on traditional "racial passing" and the inherent difficulties of rigid racial categorization); Kevin Noble Maillard, *The Pocahontas Exception: The Exemption of American Indians from Racial Purity Laws*, 12 MICH. J. RACE & L. 351 (2007) (for a

The law at issue in *Loving*, Virginia's Racial Integrity Act, made it "unlawful for any white person in this State to marry any save a white person, or a person with no other admixture of blood than white and American Indian."[5] Because of Virginia's antimiscegenation law, the Lovings traveled to Washington, DC to get married. They returned to Virginia as a married couple yet they were unable to live openly as an interracial family. Within months, they were arrested in the middle of the night and sentenced to one year in prison. Offered the possibility of avoiding imprisonment if they left Virginia for twenty-five years, the Lovings moved to Washington, DC. However, longing for home, the Lovings paired with the American Civil Liberties Union to challenge the constitutionality of the Racial Integrity Act.

The case reached the Supreme Court. Using forceful language, the Court recognized that the antimiscegenation law constituted "measures designed to maintain White Supremacy."[6] Notably, the Supreme Court expressed that "restricting the freedom to marry solely because of racial classifications violates the central meaning of the Equal Protection Clause."[7] Additionally, the Court viewed marriage as "implicit in the concept of ordered liberty,"[8] a freedom that should have included interracial unions.

The moral and legal arguments in *Loving* underscored the importance of equality and freedom in the selection of a marital partner. According to the Supreme Court, constitutional doctrine prohibits the state from denying a person's decision to marry a person of another race. With few exceptions, equal protection means that the government must treat similarly situated people the same way. If a law discriminates against one group, offering preferential treatment for another, equal-protection law affords the disadvantaged class a judicial remedy. Thus, classifications that draw sharp distinctions between groups must withstand constitutional review. In the context of discrimination based on race, such governmental distinction must be subject to the "most rigid scrutiny."[9]

Additionally, in *Loving*, the Supreme Court emphasized that due process protects individuals from arbitrary governmental intrusions upon their intimate lives. This includes an individual's freedom to marry the person of his or her own choosing. Thus, the *Loving* Court viewed interracial marriage as a valid and protected matter of equal treatment and individual liberty.

---

discussion on the racial identification of Native Americans based on blood quantum). *See, supra* n.3, at 480 (for a list of the antimiscegenation laws of each state and how the prohibited race is defined).

[5] *Loving*, 388 U.S. at 5 n.4. This exception for Native-American ancestry was written to accommodate the descendants of Pocahontas and John Rolfe, who identified as White. *See,* Maillard, *The Pocahontas Exception, supra,* n.4, at 354. 1924, 12 MICH. J. RACE & L. 107 (2007).

[6] *Loving*, 388 U.S. at 11.

[7] *Id.* at 12.

[8] Palko v. Connecticut, 302 U.S. 319, 324–25 (1937).

[9] *Loving*, 388 U.S. at 11 (internal quotations omitted).

Theoretically, *Loving*'s principle of constitutional freedom in marital choice should have transformed the racial composition of the American family. Yet more than forty years later, interracial marriage and mixed-race people remain out of the mainstream. According to the 2010 census, only 8 percent of married couples were classified as interracial,[10] up from 2 percent in 1970.[11] Analysis by the Pew Research Center indicates that, for Asians and Latinos/as, interracial marriages are actually on the decline.[12] Examined from a gender lens, interracial marriages reveal a gap in mixed-race relationships as well: Black men are more likely to enter an exogamous union than Black women.[13]

As these statistics demonstrate, legal and social barriers to interracial marriage persist. Indeed, in the last few years, an interracial couple in Louisiana reported that they were prohibited from marrying. On October 6, 2009, Beth Humphrey, who is White, and Terence McKay, who is Black, contacted Keith Bardwell, a justice of the peace, to obtain a marriage license.[14] Mr. Bardwell's wife answered the phone and asked several questions, including whether Beth and Terence were forming an "interracial marriage."[15] Upon discovering the couple's interracial status, Mrs. Bardwell informed Beth that she and Terence would have to find another justice of the peace. According to Beth, Mrs. Bardwell told them, "well, we don't do interracial marriages."[16] In an interview, Mr. Bardwell explained that, "I have one problem with marrying mixed marriages, and that is the offspring."[17]

Without doubt, part of what many found troubling about the Louisiana couple's rejection of marriage was Mr. Bardwell's blatant disregard of principles of racial equality. In our so-called "post-racial" world, where the current American president

[10] Pew Research Center, *Marrying Out: One-in-Seven New U.S. Marriages Is Interracial or Interethnic*, June 4, 2010, at 11, *available at* http://pewsocialtrends.org/files/2010/10/755-marrying-out.pdf (last visited June 22, 2011).

[11] U.S. Bureau of the Census, Table 1: Race of Wife by Race of Husband: 1960, 1970, 1980, 1991, and 1992 (1994), *available at* http://www.census.gov/population/socdemo/race/interractab1.txt (last visited June 22, 2011).

[12] Pew Research Center, *supra* n.10, at 8 (see chart, *Intermarriage Trends, 1980 and 2008*).

[13] *Id.*, at 11 ("One-in-eight (12.5%) married black men have a non-black spouse, compared with 5.5% of married black women.").

[14] Associated Press, *Interracial Couple Denied Marriage License by Louisiana Justice of the Peace*, October 15, 2009, *available at* http://www.huffingtonpost.com/2009/10/15/interracial-couple-denied_n_322784.html (last updated March 15, 2009).

[15] Samira Simone, *Governor Calls for Firing of Justice in Interracial Marriage Case*, CNN.COM, October 17, 2009, *at* http://edition.cnn.com/2009/US/10/16/louisiana.interracial.marriage/index.html (last visited June 23, 2011).

[16] *Louisiana Newlyweds Want Justice of Peace Fired*, CNN.COM, October 19, 2009, *at* http://articles.cnn.com/2009-10-19/us/interracial.marriage_1_keith-bardwell-interracial-marriages-social-justice (last visited June 23, 2011).

[17] Transcripts: American Morning (October 19, 2009), CNN.COM, *available at* http://transcripts.cnn.com/TRANSCRIPTS/0910/19/ltm.02.html (last visited June 23, 2011).

is himself the child of an interracial family, such action counters the social and legal gains achieved from the civil rights movement. At minimum, Bardwell's discriminatory conduct reveals what many interracial couples already know: ongoing barriers and prejudices to family formation continue. More generally, it requires a closer examination of how law and society affect intimate choices and a deeper look at *Loving* itself.

This anthology takes *Loving v. Virginia* to task for its influence on the "loving" of America. First, the book underscores *Loving's* promise to challenge the legal definition and cultural expectations of the traditional family. Yet, there is an ongoing struggle to eradicate the divisive legacies of the past. Second, in a "post-racial" world, *Loving's* pronouncements of equality and liberty are limited at a time when our employment of race is changing. Third, this book explores *Loving's* role in the current debate on the changing definition of marriage. Fourth, it examines its untapped potential to transform the legal recognition of intimacy beyond marriage. Overall, this anthology interrogates *Loving's* impact on race, sex, and family in a "post-racial" world.

Despite its monumental impact on civil liberties, *Loving* is generally overlooked as an important case in constitutional law and legal history. In comparison to its more famous cousin, *Brown v. Board of Education*,[18] *Loving*, on its own merits, is woefully neglected as a landmark case involving equal protection and civil liberties. What was seen as the biggest fear of racial separatists – the integration of the home – is treated as an afterthought to the civil rights movement of the 1960s. If *Brown* dismantled systems of racial supremacy at the institutional and public level, *Loving* enables a transformation at the most domestic and private. This leaves *Loving* as one of the most underexamined cases in the modern era.[19] This book gives *Loving* the attention it deserves.

Marriage, the contested institution that it is, remains the most visible and recognized referent for legitimate families.[20] Today, perhaps the most contested restriction

[18] 347 U.S. 483 (1954), *supplemented by* 349 U.S. 294 (1954).
[19] In the last few years, a number of law reviews held symposia to celebrate the fortieth anniversary of *Loving v. Virginia*: Wisconsin Law Review (2006), California Law Review (2006), Fordham Law Review (2007).
[20] Nancy F. Cott, who has written extensively on the history of marriage, has sworn that:
   Marriage thus is a bundle of rights, obligations, and benefits, but it also is more than that. It has a legitimacy earned through many years of validation and institutionalization in law and society. Enhanced by government recognition for so long, being legally married in the United States is, and has been for hundreds of years, a privileged status. The idea that marriage is the happy ending, *the marker of a relationship's legitimacy*, the sign of adult belonging, and the definitive expression of love and commitment, is deeply ingrained in our society. It is reflected in and perpetuated through law, custom, literature, and even folk tales.
   Affidavit of Nancy F. Cott, Varnum v. Brien, 2007 WL 2461202 (D. Iowa, 2007) (No. CV5965) (emphasis added); *see also* R. A. Lenhardt, *Beyond Analogy: Perez v. Sharp, Antimiscegenation Law, and the Fight for Same-Sex Marriage*, 96 CAL. L. REV. 839, 889–94 (2008).

is sex-based. The fight for marriage equality for gays and lesbians is being waged on both the state and federal levels. In California, for example, a state ballot initiative, Proposition 8, which defined marriage as a union between "one man and one woman," successfully passed in 2008. Although it has been successfully challenged in both the state and federal courts, Proposition 8's goal of defining the "traditional family" continues to gain support from many. Currently, only seven states – Connecticut, Iowa, Massachusetts, New Hampshire, New York, Vermont and Washington – and the District of Columbia allow same-sex marriage.[21] On the federal level, Congress enacted the Defense of Marriage Act (DOMA),[22] which ensured that states that prohibit same-sex marriages do not have to recognize same-sex marriages validly entered elsewhere. Even at the time this book goes to press, the status of same-sex marriage remains unsettled. Choosing a partner regardless of race has an ideological parallel to choosing a partner regardless of sexual orientation. Accordingly, *Loving* is most often referenced in constitutional arguments about same-sex marriage, in what has become known as the "*Loving* Analogy."

This book covers five sections that analyze, critique, and reconsider the lasting effects of antimiscegenation law on marital and family unions in the twenty-first century. Part One analyzes the case itself and the quiet revolution begun by Mildred Jeter and Richard Loving. As John DeWitt Gregory and Joanna L. Grossman wrote in their chapter, *Loving* marked the first time that the Supreme Court invoked the Fourteenth Amendment in marriage law, an area normally regulated by states. Although the case dismantled formal barriers to marriage, they point out that cultural norms have been slow to change.

Part Two of the volume includes five chapters that examine the regulation of interracial marriage, intimacy, and sexual relations at different points in U.S. history before 1967. Collectively, the chapters in this part highlight that prohibitions against interracial marriages affected all racial groups. Recognizing that antimiscegenation laws had a significant impact on Black-White relationships, these chapters also question the legitimacy of the Black-White binary by addressing racial restrictions on other groups, including Latinos, Asian Americans, and Native Americans.

To begin, Jason Gillmer demonstrates that Black-White intimacy and affection occurred despite legal prohibitions against it. In the shadow of antimiscegenation laws, interracial couples and families faced challenges in obtaining legal and societal recognition. His essay reminds us that antimiscegenation laws were just that: formal restrictions on interracial intimacy that did not always stop Black and White individuals from having consensual and long-term intimate relationships. Next, Carla

---

[21] Note that several other states recognize same-sex marriages entered elsewhere but do not allow same-sex couples to get married within their state.

[22] Defense of Marriage Act (D.O.M.A.), 1 U.S.C.A. § 7 (1996).

Pratt examines antimiscegenation law within an indigenous context by looking at tribal restrictions against Black-Native interracial marriage. Mirroring the separatist hegemony that surrounded their territory, tribes employed similar racial restrictions in an effort to maintain purity of blood. In a different context, Leti Volpp explores California's ban against marriages between Filipino men and White women. Her chapter illuminates how colonialism and immigration law played important roles in restricting intimacy between groups conceived of as "foreign" and those recognized as "American." In restricting sexual relations between Filipino men and White women, Volpp argues, antimiscegenation law functioned to deny Filipino men membership in the polity. Finally, Robin A. Lenhardt's chapter considers the 1947 California Supreme Court case of *Perez v. Sharp*. Prior to *Loving*, this case stood as the lone case in the twentieth century that invalidated antimiscegenation laws. Lenhardt argues that *Perez*, long ignored by courts and scholars, offers a more robust support of substantive due process and denunciation of race discrimination in marriage. Specifically, *Perez* underscored that the right to choose one's partner constituted an important part of an individual's fundamental liberty.

Part Three moves from past problems of racial crossings to present conflicts in "post-racial" America. Just as *Brown*'s integrationist mandate failed to be applied "with all deliberate speed," swiftness in racial acceptance has not neatly materialized in the aftermath of a court order. More specifically, the universal constitutionality of color-blind marriage laws has not led to widespread racial intermingling. Monoracialism – people partnering with and marrying others in their racial group – continues to be the norm. As chapters in this part demonstrate, with a presumption of homogeneity firmly in place, interracial couples face denials and exclusions because of their legally legitimate existence.

Nevertheless, this part of the book delights in experience. As an alternative to this restricted homogenous assumption, the authors argue for a paradigm shift that dispels notions of their families as deviant or abnormal. The shocking and enriching stories offered by the authors depict legal conflicts based on everyday experience. Following the robust tradition of critical race theory, these essays offer first-person accounts of housing discrimination, family confrontations, and social exclusion that provide individual and unique analyses of the effect of *Loving* on daily life.

This section begins with Kevin Noble Maillard's essay on the lasting effects of antimiscegenation law. Even though more than four decades have passed since *Loving*, prohibitions against interracial marriage create a presumption of illegitimacy for historical claims of mixed race. When the claim involves American political figures, interracial denial heavily relies on legal presumptions rather than actual proximity. Next, Camille A. Nelson addresses sexual stereotypes in interracial relationships. In her analysis of the "racialization of sex and the sexualization of race," she offers legal and anecdotal accounts of collective views of the politicization of sex in interracial relationships. Couples in mixed unions face disparate impacts, and she calls for a "critical consciousness" to combat such pressures. In I. Bennett Capers's chapter on the lingering stigma of race mixing, he explains that counterintuitive yet enduring informal systems of law coexist alongside formal ones. In comparison to articulated and codified "black letter law," invisible, unwritten norms of "white letter law" continue to police Black-White interactions. In the next essay, Renée Landers offers a first-person account of growing up in a mixed-race family, and questions the affect of *Loving* on the everyday lives of families, using a number of statistics to demonstrate the slow rate of racial change. Even though courts have protected the right of persons to choose partners without regard to race, simple statistics demonstrate that people's minds are hard to change. Jacquelyne Bridgeman also offers a personal account of her life in an interracial family, noting the importance of defining oneself beyond a Black-White race-based identity. In this approach to personhood, she asks for a release of racial boundaries and entrenchments to make room for a free variety of self-identifications.

Part Four of this volume offers a more critical and less celebratory look at *Loving v. Virginia*. Collectively, the essays reveal that *Loving*'s promise of equal protection and due process in the context of race, sex, and marriage needs to be situated within the greater context of post-racialism. Yet, claims of race no longer being relevant have been largely exaggerated. Indeed, our ideas of race and racism have become more complex. It is unclear whether contemporary equal-protection laws and cases, including *Loving*, are best equipped to address the evolving understanding of race.

The essays in this part explore the impact of *Loving* on the legal and political meaning of Blackness. Taunya Lovell Banks highlights that the Black community is more diverse as a result, in part, of increased interracial marriage and migration from the Carribean, Latin America, and Africa. Thus, there is no unitary Black community. Indeed, individuals within the Black community have had varied discriminatory experiences. This chapter calls for the development of more flexible and realistic legal theories and doctrines that will more adequately address the subtle yet compelling differences between the experiences of people within the Black community. Angelique Davis focuses her analysis of Blackness on examining the Multiracial Category Movement (MCM). Her chapter advocates for the concept of "political Blackness" to unify the legal and political goals of those with Black ancestry who desire redress for slavery and Jim Crow. Under this theory, an individual's desire to classify oneself as multiracial does not mean dissociation, or renouncement, of one's Black ancestry. Instead, Davis contends that the MCM could strengthen Black racial justice efforts. Even though *Loving* protects marital freedom, it is still limited in protecting the civil liberties of interracial couples and families in their everyday lives. Angela Onwuachi-Willig and Jacob Willig-Onwuachi's chapter demonstrates the specific ways in which interracial families encounter discrimination in gaining equal access to housing. Drawing on their own experiences, they note that traditional protections afforded by contemporary antidiscrimination laws fail to cover interracial families.

Part Five considers the regulation of interracial marriage beyond the boundaries of the United States. The traditional understanding of the policing of mixed-race unions has focused on state antimiscegenation laws. Yet, contrary to the familiar story, restrictions on marriage and intimacy between races have also occurred outside of the United States. By introducing immigration law, these chapters highlight the limitations on marriage and sexual relations that have been imposed by the U.S. military and the federal government. As a whole, this part calls for greater scrutiny of the role of federal laws and regulations in shaping racial relationships in our country.

First, Rose Cuison Villazor's chapter conducts a close exploration of the complex web of laws that led to the federal government's regulation of interracial marriages in Japan after World War II. Unlike state prohibitions on mixed marriages, the federal antimiscegenation framework that Villazor identifies comprises three separate laws – immigration, citizenship, and military, which worked together to ban mainly Whites from marrying Japanese nationals. Nancy K. Ota demonstrates in her chapter that the military aimed not only to limit interracial marriages – including those between Black soldiers and White European brides – but it also sought to police private conduct and sexual relations between interracial couples. As she points out, the military's regulations regarding marriage and sexual relationships were part of a broad array of disciplining measures designed to promote the heterosexual, nuclear family. Lastly, Victor Romero's chapter analogizes the story of Richard and Mildred Loving to the struggle of American-noncitizen same-sex partners today. Because immigration law does not consider a marriage between same-sex partners as a valid marriage, thousands of binational married couples are forced to travel outside of the United States to live together where their unions are recognized. By restricting the ability of married couples to stay together, immigration law functions in some ways like Virginia's Racial Integrity Act, which forced the Lovings to temporarily leave their home state.

Part Six of this volume questions the centrality of marriage in defining family and relationships. Additionally, this part looks to alternative methods beyond marriage for desegregating the family. The traditional notion of the family is changing, in part because of same-sex marriage and nonmarital cohabitation.

Adele Morrison begins this section by drawing a link between race and sexual orientation, to conclude that rights for the LGBTQIA (lesbian, gay, bisexual, transexual, queer, intersex, and asexual) community are civil rights. At the intersection of these constituencies is the Black LGBTQIA community. Morrison views interracial same-sex couples as the crucial yet underexamined catalyst in the transformation of a traditional, monoracial, heterosexual definition of marriage. Rachel F. Moran's chapter calls for an autonomous look at boundaries to equality in caregiving relationships, which goes beyond what is known as the *Loving* Analogy. In asking for an independent assessment of sexual orientation discrimination, she questions the traditional analogy that views all claims of inequality and discrimination through a racial lens. Finally, Tucker Culbertson confronts *Loving* for its inability to recognize alternatives to marriage. In upholding marital freedom for some, the case underscores the nuclear paradigm of family life and intimate association that excludes others. His chapter points out an irony of *Loving*: a case about freedom of choice that in fact narrows the options for legally recognized expressions of intimacy.

As a whole, this volume reinstates the contemporary and timely importance of *Loving v. Virginia* during an era when intimate decisions about race and sexuality have, once again, become a central subject of contemporary political and social discourse. We hope that our collection opens a critical dialogue between interracialism and contemporary fears about same-sex marriage..

PART ONE

Explaining *Loving v. Virginia*

1

The Legacy of *Loving*

John DeWitt Gregory and Joanna L. Grossman

What has *Loving v. Virginia* meant in American law? *Loving's* legal and doctrinal legacy is threefold. *Loving* has been used to define and affirm the fundamental right to marry, to enforce federal constitutional limits on domestic relations, and to invalidate racial classifications and other practices that perpetuate racial subordination. Before *Loving*, the Supreme Court's role with respect to marriage law was limited to refereeing conflicts among the states, who had long differed over the substantive restrictions on marriage, and, even more stridently, about the accessibility of divorce.[1] Increasing mobility and the rise of divorce mills made conflicts between states about the proper regulation of marriage and divorce a common occurrence, disputes that reached the Supreme Court's doorstep on occasion.[2] Through those decisions, the Supreme Court – and, to a greater extent, lower federal and state courts – developed an approach to interstate recognition that drew on notions of comity, pragmatic considerations about the need for portable personal status, and, where applicable, principles of the Full Faith and Credit Clause.[3]

There was no federal law norm about the right approach to regulating marriage and divorce before *Loving*, and thus no substantive principles for the Supreme Court to bring to bear on the few family law cases it heard.[4] This limited involvement

---

[1]   On the history of marriage and divorce, *see* Joanna L. Grossman & Lawrence M. Friedman, INSIDE THE CASTLE: LAW AND THE FAMILY IN 20th CENTURY AMERICA (2011). *See also*, Joanna L. Grossman, *Fear and Loathing in Massachusetts: Same-Sex Marriage and Some Lessons from the History of Marriage and Divorce*, 14 B.U. PUB. INT. L.J. 87 (2004) (considering history of interstate conflict over marriage and divorce).

[2]   *See, e.g.*, Williams v. North Carolina, 317 U.S. 287 (1942) (ruling that North Carolina must give Full Faith and Credit to a Nevada divorce granted to North Carolina residents); Estin v. Estin, 334 U.S. 541 (1948) (ruling that a Nevada divorce court had no authority to terminate a husband's obligation to provide support established under a New York decree of legal separation).

[3]   *See generally* Joanna L. Grossman, *Resurrecting Comity: Revisiting the Problem of Non-Uniform Marriage Laws*, 84 OR. L. REV. 433 (2005) (describing history of interstate conflicts over marriage).

[4]   The Court occasionally made pronouncements about the importance of marriage while elaborating on the meaning of a fundamental right for constitutional purposes, but all of these mentions were

was thus consistent with the long-standing belief that domestic relations law was reserved to the states.[5] Indeed, prior to *Loving*, the Supreme Court had invalidated not a single state marriage or divorce law,[6] despite significant variations among state codes,[7] and had often made clear its belief that marriage was a matter for the states to regulate. As Justice Field wrote in *Maynard v. Hill*, an 1888 case involving the validity of a legislative divorce granted by the Oregon Territory to a Vermont husband, "Marriage ... *has always been subject to the control of the legislature.*"[8] Pre-*Loving*, then, the Supreme Court's deference to state substantive norms regarding marriage was essentially complete. Thus, by invalidating under the U.S. Constitution a state law that restricted marriage based on race, *Loving* heralded a new era for the Supreme Court by including federal constitutional norms within an area – domestic relations – that traditionally fell within state domain.

THE RULING

Mildred Jeter, a part-African, part-Cherokee woman, and Richard Loving, a white man, crossed the border in 1958 from their home state of Virginia to neighboring Washington, DC, to marry.[9] They returned to Virginia and set up house, but were indicted for violating Virginia's ban on interracial marriages. "Indicted" is perhaps too polite a description of how the Lovings became criminal defendants. Early one morning, three law enforcement officers entered their bedroom, shined a flashlight on them, and asked Richard, "What are you doing in bed with this lady?"[10] When he pointed to their District of Columbia marriage certificate hanging on the bedroom wall, Richard was told by Sheriff R. Garnett Brooks, "That's no good here."[11] The couple was hauled off to jail for unlawful cohabitation.

pure dicta. *See, e.g.,* Skinner v. Oklahoma, 316 U.S. 535, 541 (1942) (observing that marriage is "fundamental to the very existence and survival of the race"); Meyer v. Nebraska, 262 U.S. 390, 399 (1923).

[5] *See* Jill Elaine Hasday, *The Canon of Family Law*, 57 STAN. L. REV. 825, 831 (2004) ("The family law canon contends that family law is, and has always been, a matter of exclusively local jurisdiction.... Yet contesting the family law canon's construction reveals the existence and extent of federal family law.").

[6] The California Supreme Court had invalidated the state's antimiscegenation law on federal equal protection grounds in 1948, but that ruling was not appealed to the U.S. Supreme Court. *See* Perez v. Sharp, 198 P.2d 17 (Cal. 1948).

[7] *See* Grossman, *Resurrecting Comity, supra* n.3, at 437–43 (describing marriage law variations in the century prior to 1967).

[8] 125 U.S. 190, 205 (1888) (refusing to invalidate the legislative divorce) (emphasis added); *see also* Pennoyer v. Neff, 95 U.S. 714, 734–35 (1878) (noting that a state has an "absolute right to prescribe the conditions upon which the marriage relation between its own citizens shall be created, and the causes for which it may be dissolved").

[9] *Loving v. Virginia*, 388 U.S. 1, 2–3 (1967).

[10] *See* David Margolick, *A Mixed Marriage's 25th Anniversary of Legality*, N.Y. TIMES, June 12, 1992, at B20.

[11] *See id.*

   The Virginia law, under which the Lovings were charged and convicted, criminalized not only a marriage celebrated between a white person and a "colored person"
in Virginia, but also such a marriage conducted out of state if celebrated by Virginia
residents who left in order to evade the state's miscegenation ban.[12] (Nonwhites
could marry other nonwhites under the code.) The trial judge suspended the sen-
tences on the condition that the couple leave the state of Virginia and not return
together for twenty-five years.
   Pursuant to the court's order, the Lovings moved to the District of Columbia,
but returned to Virginia four years later and filed a motion to vacate their convictions on federal constitutional grounds.[13] They challenged the constitutionality
of the Virginia law under both the Equal Protection and Due Process Clauses of
the Fourteenth Amendment. In striking down the law, the Supreme Court reached
three important conclusions. First, the Court dispensed with the notion that state
power to regulate marriage was unlimited. Although earlier cases like *Maynard v.
Hill* used broad language to describe state legislative control over domestic relations, *Loving* made clear that state marriage laws must comply with federal constitutional norms. As the Court stated, Virginia "does not contend in its argument before
this Court that its powers to regulate marriage are unlimited notwithstanding the
commands of the Fourteenth Amendment."[14] The Court thus established a role for
federal courts in hearing challenges to state marriage laws, and for the Constitution
in circumscribing them.
   Second, the Court concluded that Virginia's miscegenation ban violated the
Equal Protection Clause of the Fourteenth Amendment. As discussed in greater
detail later, it is the state's proffered defense to this particular challenge – and the
Supreme Court's repudiation of it – that has proved the most important aspect of
Loving's legacy. Virginia argued that "because its miscegenation statutes punish
equally both the white and the Negro participants in an interracial marriage, these
statutes, despite their reliance on racial classifications, do not constitute an invidious discrimination on the basis of race."[15] And if the classification is not invidious,
Virginia contended, the Court should consider only whether there was any "rational
basis" for the state to adopt and further a policy of discouraging interracial marriages.[16] The Supreme Court roundly rejected Virginia's approach, however, and put
the so-called equal-application theory to rest. Applying the "most rigid scrutiny,"[17]

---

[12] *Loving*, 388 U.S. at 4–5 (excerpting relevant Virginia statutes). Anti-evasion laws such as this one were
    common but not universal. *See* Grossman, *Fear and Loathing, supra* n.1, at 100–05 (discussing preva-
    lence and scope of marriage evasion laws at various points in American history).
[13] *Id.* at 3.
[14] *Id.* at 7.
[15] *Id.* at 8.
[16] *Id.*
[17] *Id.* at 11 (citing Korematsu v. United States, 323 U.S. 214, 216 (1944)).

the Court found no sufficiently compelling purpose to justify Virginia's racial classification. Rather, the Court ruled that the unilateral law violated Equal Protection
as a "measure[s] designed to maintain White Supremacy."[18]

The Court also concluded that Virginia's miscegenation ban violated the Due
Process Clause of the Fourteenth Amendment. "The freedom to marry has long
been recognized as one of the vital personal rights essential to the orderly pursuit
of happiness by free men. Marriage is one of the 'basic civil rights of man,' fundamental to our very existence and survival."[19] This aspect of the holding drew
primarily on *Skinner v. Oklahoma,* a case in which the Supreme Court struck
down as a violation of substantive due process a state law imposing compulsory
sterilization as a penalty for some forms of theft but not others. The Court viewed
the right to marry as akin to the right to avoid involuntary sterilization, and thus
deserving of due process protection. The Court also cited *Maynard v. Hill* in support of its due process analysis, but that case had only to do with the desirabil-
ity and importance of marriage as a social institution, and nothing to do with a
constitutional right to enter it. With little discussion, the Court concluded that
Virginia's law was inconsistent with due process protections for marriage. The
immediate import of *Loving* was clear: states no longer had the power to prohibit
interracial marriages.

THE RIGHT TO MARRY AFTER *LOVING*

Because of the inextricable link in *Loving* between the invidiousness of the racial
classification and the fundamental nature of marriage,[20] the impact of *Loving* on
other types of marriage restrictions was not predetermined. The ruling certainly
did not signify the Supreme Court's willingness to generally override state law with
respect to marriage, nor to view all marriage prohibitions as equally invidious. Just
five years later, the Court dismissed an appeal in *Baker v. Nelson,* one of the first cases
to challenge (unsuccessfully) a state's refusal to permit same-sex couples to marry,
"for want of substantial federal question."[21] Published dissents from the denial of
certiorari in several cases in the 1970s and 1980s perhaps reveal a broader dispute on

---

[18] *Id.* at 11–12. The Court found support in McLaughlin v. Florida, 379 U.S. 184 (1964), a little-discussed
case in which it had invalidated a Florida law banning cohabitation by interracial couples. *See also,*
id. at 198 (Stewart, J., concurring) (noting that they "cannot conceive of a valid legislative purpose …
which makes the color of a person's skin the test of whether his conduct is a criminal offense").

[19] *Loving,* 388 U.S. at 12.

[20] *See* Pamela S. Karlan, *Foreword: Loving Lawrence,* 102 MICH. L. REV. 1447, 1448 (2004) ("Today, most
courts and scholars see the Equal Protection and Due Process Clauses as discrete bases for strict scrutiny. But in *Loving,* the two clauses operated in tandem.").

[21] 409 U.S. 810 (1972).

the Court about the appropriateness of federal intervention into state laws regulating marriage and other intimate relationships.[22]

The Court did, however, revisit the scope of the federal constitutional right to marry in two important cases after *Loving*. In 1978, *Zablocki v. Redhail* struck down a Wisconsin statute that prohibited noncustodial parents who were behind on support obligations and whose children were on welfare from marrying without prior court approval.[23] The Court began its analysis with *Loving*, which, in the Court's words, was the "leading decision" on "the right to marry."[24] Truth be told, in 1978, *Loving* was the Court's only decision on the *right* to marry. Drawing on *Loving*, *Skinner*, and *Griswold v. Connecticut*,[25] and the Court's view of marriage's importance as espoused in *Maynard v. Hill*, the plurality in *Zablocki* characterized marriage as a right "of fundamental importance," the infringement of which warranted heightened scrutiny. Between the time of *Loving* and *Zablocki*, the right of privacy had been broadened to include a panoply of rights regarding marriage, family, intimate relationships, and reproduction.[26] In *Zablocki*, the Court found the importance of the right to marry sufficiently fundamental to justify "critical examination" of laws that significantly interfere with it.[27]

Zablocki was not, however, a due process case.[28] It was, instead, a case decided under the now moribund fundamental rights branch of the Equal Protection Clause. So *Zablocki* did not establish absolute protection for the right to marry; rather, it stands for the proposition that classifications that directly and substantially interfere with the fundamental interest in marriage must be subjected to heightened scrutiny. Although *Zablocki* was an equal protection case, and *Loving* stopped short of declaring marriage a fundamental right in its due process analysis, the two cases together have been understood to establish that "the right to marry counts as fundamental for constitutional purposes."[29]

---

[22] *See, e.g.*, Hollenbaugh v. Carnegie Free Library, 439 U.S. 1052, 1055 (1987) (Marshall, J., dissenting from the denial of certiorari) (refusing to review public library's decision to discharge two employees because of nonmarital coparenting and cohabitation); Whisenhunt v. Spradlin, 464 U.S. 965 (1983) (Brennan, J., dissenting from the denial of certiorari) (refusing to review police department policy disciplining two offers for nonmarital cohabitation).

[23] 434 U.S. 374 (1978).

[24] *Id.* at 383.

[25] 381 U.S. 479 (1965).

[26] *See, e.g.*, Moore v. City of E. Cleveland, 431 U.S. 494 (1977) (the right to live with nonnuclear family members); Cleveland Bd. of Educ. v. LaFleur, 414 U.S. 632 (1974) (the right to continue working while pregnant); Roe v. Wade, 410 U.S. 113 (1973) (the right to seek an abortion); Eisenstadt v. Baird, 405 U.S. 438 (1972) (the right of single people to obtain contraceptives).

[27] The precise standard adopted in *Zablocki* authorizes "rigorous scrutiny" for marriage regulations that "interfere directly and substantially with the right to marry." *Id.* at 386.

[28] For a helpful discussion of *Zablocki* and its relationship to *Loving*, see Laurence C. Nolan, *The Meaning of* Loving: *Marriage, Due Process, and Equal Protection (1967–1990) as Equality and Marriage, from* Loving *to* Zablocki, 41 How. L.J. 245 (1998).

[29] Cass R. Sunstein, *The Right to Marry*, 26 CARDOZO L. REV. 2081, 2087 (2005).

Zablocki, moreover, made clear that the Court's unwillingness to tolerate certain marriage restrictions was not limited to those drawn on the basis of race. The defendant in *Zablocki*, after all – a Caucasian, teenage father of an out-of-wedlock child with a new pregnant girlfriend – was part of no "suspect" class.[30] Justice Powell argued in his concurrence in *Zablocki* that the majority was overreading *Loving* by applying it outside of the race context, although he agreed with the majority that the Wisconsin statute must fall to the constitutional challenge.[31]

A decade later, the Court took up the right to marry again in *Turner v. Safley*,[32] a case challenging the constitutionality of a Missouri prison regulation that permitted inmates to marry only with permission of the prison superintendent, approval that was to be granted only for "compelling reasons."[33] There, *Loving* and *Zablocki* were cited together as precedent for the proposition that "the decision to marry is a fundamental right, a point so well-established it is conceded by the State of Missouri."[34] The question for the Court in *Turner* was only whether that fundamental right was shared, in whole or in part, by prison inmates. As with other rights, the Court held that prisoners retain the fundamental right to marry, which can be burdened only to the extent required by legitimate penological interests.[35] Here, the Court found insufficient justification for the marriage restriction and thus invalidated it.[36] *Turner* completed the right-to-marry trilogy, which provides robust constitutional protection for the right to marry against attempted governmental intrusions.[37]

LOVING, SUBSTANTIVE DUE PROCESS, AND THE LIMITS OF FEDERALISM

An important but sometimes overlooked aspect of *Loving* is its role in establishing the federal constitutional limits on state domestic relations laws. The validity of Virginia's antimiscegenation law had been litigated in an earlier case, *Naim v.*

[30] *See also* Mark Strasser, Loving *in the New Millennium: On Equal Protection and the Right to Marry*, 7 U. CHI. L. SCH. ROUNDTABLE 61 (2000) (noting that *Zablocki* "laid to rest the suggestion that only marital statutes discriminating on the basis of race will be held to violate the Equal Protection Clause").
[31] *See Zablocki*, 434 U.S. at 396 (Powell, J., concurring in the judgment).
[32] 482 U.S. 78 (1987).
[33] *Id.* at 82.
[34] *Id.* at 94.
[35] Thirteen years earlier, the Supreme Court denied certiorari in a case challenging the validity of a prison marriage regulation. *See In re* Goalen, 512 P.2d 1028 (Utah 1973), *cert. denied*, 414 U.S. 1148 (1974). Justice Stewart, joined by Justices Douglas and Brennan, dissented from the denial of certiorari, raising the question whether Utah's justification for the marriage restriction was sufficient to overcome the right to marry as articulated in *Loving*. *See In re* Goalen, 414 U.S. at 1150 (Stewart, J., dissenting).
[36] *Turner*, 482 U.S. at 97.
[37] For an interesting discussion of what the "right" to marry really consists of, see Sunstein, *supra* n.30.

Naim, in which a white woman sought to annul her marriage to a Chinese man, evasively contracted in North Carolina.[38] The Supreme Court of Appeals of Virginia upheld the law against the constitutional challenge, observing that "[m]arriage ... is subject to the control of the States. Nearly seventy years ago the [U.S.] Supreme Court said [so], and it has said nothing to the contrary since."[39] In rejecting the petitioner's challenge to the miscegenation law, the Virginia court relied squarely on the fact that marriage had traditionally been "subject to state regulation without federal intervention, and, consequently ... should be left to exclusive state control by the Tenth Amendment."[40] Even though the Supreme Court declined to review *Naim*,[41] it made clear in *Loving* that the Virginia court's ruling vastly overstated a state's power. The *Loving* majority wrote:

> While the state court is no doubt correct in asserting that marriage is a social relation subject to the State's police power, the State does not contend in its argument before this Court that its powers to regulate marriage are unlimited notwithstanding the commands of the Fourteenth Amendment. Nor could it.[42]

Loving thus cemented not only the right but also the practice of federal courts' reviewing state domestic relations laws for consistency with federal constitutional guarantees.[43] As the Tenth Circuit Court of Appeals noted in *Wise v. Bravo*, a case involving visitation interference, "The state's power to legislate, adjudicate and administer all aspects of family law ... is subject to scrutiny by the federal judiciary within the reach of the Due Process and/or Equal Protection Clauses of the Fourteenth Amendment."[44]

This repudiation of unlimited state power over domestic relations had implications beyond the right to marry and spurred an expansion of substantive due process rights more generally. Prior to *Loving*, there were only a handful of cases, mostly involving attempted intrusions into parental autonomy,[45] in which the Supreme

---

[38]   87 S.E.2d 749 (Va. 1955).

[39]   *Id.* at 751.

[40]   *Loving*, 388 U.S. at 7 (discussing *Naim*).

[41]   *See* Naim v. Naim, 87 S.E.2d 749 (Va. 1955), *vacated*, 350 U.S. 891 (1955), *on remand* 90 S.E.2d 849 (Va. 1956), *appeal dismissed*, 350 U.S. 985 (1956). According to Pamela Karlan, the Court "disingenuously" denied jurisdiction in order to avoid jeopardizing the effectiveness of its recent racial equality ruling in *Brown v. Board of Education* by tackling the "politically incendiary" question of interracial marriage.

[42]   *Loving*, 388 U.S. at 7 (citations omitted).

[43]   *See also* Robert A. Destro, *Loving v. Virginia after 30 Years: Introduction*, 47 CATH. U. L. REV. 1207, 1218 (1998) (noting *Loving*'s support for "federal oversight of State power to define, regulate, and order sexual, marital, and family relationships").

[44]   666 F.2d 1328, 1332 (10th Cir. 1982) (rejecting section 1983 claim based on police failure to enforce visitation order) (citing *Loving*, 388 U.S. at 1).

[45]   *See, e.g.*, Meyer v. Nebraska, 262 U.S. 390 (1923) (invalidating, on due process grounds, statute that banned teaching of foreign language to children who had not passed the eighth grade); Prince v.

Court considered overriding a state law regarding family status or operation based on constitutional constraints. But the body of constitutional family law grew dramatically beginning in the 1970s, an arc triggered in part by the Supreme Court's repudiation of Virginia's marriage law in *Loving*. According to Pamela Karlan, "*Loving* is seen today as a critical point in the revival of substantive due process."[46] The number of specific rights protected by that doctrine increased significantly in the two decades after *Loving* was decided.[47]

There is now a lengthy patchwork of cases that stand for the principle that individuals have "the right to be free, except in very limited circumstances, from unwanted governmental intrusions into one's privacy,"[48] and *Loving* is virtually always among those cited. *Loving* thus provides support for the right not to marry as well as the right to marry, and the related rights to make decisions over a "broad range of private choices involving family life and personal autonomy."[49] The Supreme Court includes *Loving* among the litany of cases collectively establishing the contours of the right to privacy: "Choices about marriage, family life, and the upbringing of children are among associational rights this Court has ranked as 'of basic importance in our society, rights sheltered by the Fourteenth Amendment against the State's unwarranted usurpation, disregard, or disrespect.'"[50]

LOVING AND THE HEIGHTENED SUSPICION
OF RACIAL CLASSIFICATION

As *Zablocki* made clear, *Loving* was not just a case about race. But other cases have made clear that *Loving* was also not just a case about marriage. *Loving v. Virginia*

Massachusetts, 321 U.S. 158 (1944) (affirming against Fourteenth Amendment challenge parent's conviction for violating child labor law by using child to distribute religious pamphlets).

[46] Karlan, *supra* n.21, at 1463 n.7.

[47] *See* cases cited *supra* n.27.

[48] Hollenbaugh v. Carnegie Free Library, 439 U.S. 1052, 1055 (1987) (Marshall, J., dissenting from the denial of certiorari) (citing, for example, *Loving, Zablocki, Skinner, Meyer*, and *Moore* to argue for the invalidation a public employer's prohibition on unmarried employees' living together in an intimate relationship).

[49] Whisenhunt v. Spradlin, 464 U.S. 965 (1983) (Brennan, J., dissenting) (arguing that the court should consider the validity of police department's antinepotism policy as applied to a nonmarried couple). Somewhat curiously, *Loving* is omitted from the litany of cases cited by the majority in *Lawrence v. Texas* to define the "substantive reach of liberty under the Due Process Clause." 539 U.S. 558, 564–66 (2003). This may have been deliberate, given Justice Kennedy's clear intent to avoid creating a precedent for invalidating same-sex marriage bans on substantive due process grounds. *See id.* at 578 ("The present case … does not involve whether the government must give formal recognition to any relationship that homosexual persons seek to enter.").

[50] M.L.B. v. S.L.J., 519 U.S. 102, 116 (1996) (invalidating a Mississippi statute requiring a woman to prepay record preparation fees in order to appeal an order terminating her parental rights). *Loving* is cited in pivotal privacy cases. *See, e.g., Michael H. v. Gerald D.*, 491 U.S. 110 (1989) (upholding conclusive presumption of husband's paternity over constitutional challenge from child's biological

has come to stand for the proposition that the Fourteenth Amendment should be used as a sword to stamp out vestiges of slavery. Because of the centrality of race to *Loving*, the opinion has had a robust life outside of the family law context. Indeed, some have come to understand *Loving* as first and foremost a "race" case.[51]

The *Loving* majority took a hard line on racial classifications, both rejecting the "equal application" theory the state had urged (that the law was valid because it punished whites and nonwhites equally for marrying in violation of the statute), and applying an unrelenting form of scrutiny to the law.[52] The equal application theory had been validated in an 1883 case, *Pace v. Alabama,* in which the Supreme Court upheld a law that punished illicit interracial sexual conduct more severely than illicit intraracial sexual conduct.[53] Because punishment was determined by the nature of the offense (intraracial versus interracial conduct) rather than the race of the defendant, the Court upheld the constitutionality of the statute against an equal protection challenge. Blacks and whites were both punished less severely for engaging in conduct with someone of the same race, and more severely for conduct with someone of a different race. This characterization enabled the Court to overlook the subordinating effect of the law under the guise of formal equality. *Pace* wreaked much havoc in lower courts, which could cite it to hold back challenges to their own miscegenation laws.

The Supreme Court officially repudiated the reasoning in *Pace* three years before the Lovings' case came before it. In *McLaughlin v. Florida*, the Court considered the constitutionality of a statute imposing a more severe penalty for interracial cohabitation than for intraracial cohabitation.[54] Florida defended its statute with *Pace*, but the Supreme Court rejected that view as too narrow a view of the Equal Protection Clause, although it expressly drew no conclusion about the validity of bans on interracial marriage.[55] The Court in *Loving* read *McLaughlin* to require

---

father); Harris v. McRae, 448 U.S. 297 (1980) (refusing to extend the right to privacy to include a right to Medicaid reimbursement for a medically necessary abortion); Carey v. Population Servs. Int'l, 431 U.S. 678 (1977) (striking down New York ban on distribution of nonprescription contraceptives); Moore v. City of E. Cleveland, 431 U.S. 494 (1977) (invalidating zoning ordinance that distinguished between nuclear and nonnuclear families for purposes of residential restrictions.).

[51] *See, e.g.,* Destro, *supra* n.44, at 1219 ("The first and most obvious way to characterize Loving is as a 'race' case.").

[52] *Loving*, 388 U.S. at 7–8.

[53] U.S. 583 (1883).

[54] 379 U.S. 184 (1964).

[55] *Id.* at 188 ("In our view, however, *Pace* represents a limited view of the Equal Protection Clause which has not withstood analysis in the subsequent decisions of this Court."). On the importance of *McLaughlin* to the question presented in Loving, see Wadlington, supra n.7, at 1213–14 ("Although the majority of the United States Supreme Court found it unnecessary to take the step of ruling on miscegenous marriage statutes when *McLaughlin* came before them, they eliminated one of the key grounds on which state courts had previously relied to uphold interracial marriage bans by delivering the coup de grace to the *Pace* rationale.").

"consideration of whether the classifications drawn by any statute constitute an arbitrary and invidious discrimination,"[56] regardless of whether they appeared to impose equal burdens on members of different races. *Loving* thus cemented the death of the equal application theory with its observation that "the fact of equal application does not immunize the statute from the very heavy burden of justification which the Fourteenth Amendment has traditionally required of state statutes drawn according to race."[57]

In the context of racial classifications, *Loving's* rejection of "equal application" discrimination has stood firm. In *Powers v. Ohio,* for example, the Supreme Court refused to accept the argument that race-based peremptory challenges should be permissible if used against members of all races.[58] As the Court observed, "[i]t is axiomatic that racial classifications do not become legitimate on the assumption that all persons suffer them in equal degree."[59]

Loving is also cited as precedent for the level of scrutiny to be applied to race-based classifications. Because of the "Fourteenth Amendment's proscription of all invidious racial discriminations," the majority in *Loving* demanded more than the "rational" and "legitimate" explanations the state tried to offer in defense of the statute.[60] Chief Justice Earl Warren demanded that the state satisfy the "very heavy burden of justification" required for race-based classifications in state laws.[61] *Loving* continues to be cited today for the proposition that racial classifications in a variety of contexts, including affirmative action,[62] voting rights,[63] school financing,[64] and even voluntary desegregation,[65] warrant the highest form of judicial scrutiny.

Loving also continues to represent the Supreme Court's efforts to put an end to racial subordination. The observation in *Loving* that the Supreme Court has "consistently repudiated 'distinctions between citizens solely because of their ancestry' as being 'odious to a free people whose institutions are founded upon the doctrine of equality,'" is often quoted. The Court also relied on *Loving* in *Palmore v. Sidoti,* a

---

[56] *Loving,* 388 U.S. at 10.

[57] *Id.* at 9.

[58] *See* 499 U.S. 400 (1991).

[59] *Id.* at 410.

[60] *Loving,* 388 U.S. at 8.

[61] *Id.* at 9.

[62] *See, e.g.,* Grutter v. Bollinger, 539 U.S. 306 (2003) (citing *Loving* and applying strict scrutiny to evaluate the constitutionality of a race-conscious law school admissions policy); Adarand Constructors, Inc. v. Pena, 515 U.S. 200 (1995); Wygant v. Jackson Bd. of Educ., 476 U.S. 267 (1986); Fullilove v. Klutznick, 448 U.S. 448 (1980); Regents v. Bakke, 438 U.S. 265 (1978).

[63] *See, e.g.,* Miller v. Johnson, 515 U.S. 900 (1995) (citing *Loving* for the proposition that racial distinctions are inherently suspect and that the Equal Protection Clause's "central mandate is racial neutrality in governmental decisionmaking"); Shaw v. Reno, 509 U.S. 630 (1993).

[64] *See* San Antonio Indep. Sch. Dist. v. Rodriguez, 411 U.S. 1 (1973).

[65] *See* Parents Involved in Cmty. Schs. v. Seattle Sch. Dist. No. 1, 551 U.S. 701 (2007).

case in which the trial court divested a white mother of custody because she remarried a black man.[66] Citing the Fourteenth Amendment, the Court concluded that private biases and the potential harm they might inflict were impermissible considerations for courts in custody cases. Most recently, in *Parents Involved in Community Schools v. Seattle School District No. 1*,[67] *Loving* was treated by both the concurrence and the dissent as a cornerstone in the Supreme Court's equal protection doctrine. In the concurrence, *Loving* was credited for first establishing the principle that race-based classifications must be subjected to strict scrutiny and cited in support of the claim that governmental entities are constitutionally obligated to remedy de jure segregation but not de facto segregation. These cases, far afield from the core right to marry, establish *Loving*'s importance to constitutional protection against race discrimination.

THE PERSONAL AND CULTURAL LEGACIES OF *LOVING*

For the Lovings, the Supreme Court's ruling paved the way for them to return to their families and friends in their home state of Virginia. This was the ultimate goal in their legal quest, according to a personal narrative by Robert Pratt, who knew both Richard and Mildred.[68] They had "not really been that interested in the civil rights movement," but contacted Attorney General Robert Kennedy to seek help with what they viewed as a personal struggle.[69] Kennedy referred their case to the American Civil Liberties Union, and two lawyers from Alexandria took up the cause.[70] They did not attend the argument in the Supreme Court, and, when asked afterward what the ruling meant for them, Richard noted only that: "For the first time, I could put my arm around her and publicly call her my wife."[71] The Lovings told reporters that they had the support of their hometown community. "Everyone here really wanted us to win the case. They were as happy as we were at the decision."[72] Richard told *Life* magazine in a profile before their case was heard by the Supreme Court that

---

[66] *See* 466 U.S. 429 (1984).

[67] 551 U.S. 701 (2007) (striking down voluntary desegregation efforts by school districts in Seattle and Louisville as unconstitutional).

[68] *See* Robert A. Pratt, *Crossing the Color Line: A Historical Assessment and Personal Narrative of Loving v. Virginia*, 41 How. L.J. 229 (1998).

[69] *See id.* at 237–38.

[70] The case certainly had an impact on the lawyers, Philip J. Hirschkop and Bernard S. Cohen, as well. As David Margolick describes, "[t]here were cold shoulders from some disapproving bar colleagues, nasty anonymous telephone calls, disparaging references to 'two Jew lawyers' in the Ku Klux Klan newspaper and sugar dumped into the gasoline tanks of family cars." *See* Margolick, *supra* n.10, at B20.

[71] *See* Simeon Booker, *The Couple That Rocked the Courts*, Ebony, Sept. 1967, at 78.

[72] *See State Couple 'Overjoyed' by Ruling*, Richmond Times-Dispatch, June 13, 1967, at B1.

they "encounter[ed] hostile stares only when they venture[d] away."[73] Although he always wanted to "ask them what the hell they are staring at," Richard vowed to wait until he and his wife "were allowed to live here legally" before confronting them.[74] The Lovings' marriage ended tragically in 1975 when Richard was killed by a drunk driver. Mildred lost an eye in the same accident, but lived several decades more without Richard.[75] She and Sheriff Brooks have "not exchanged a single word," although they saw each other occasionally in Central Point, Virginia, the small town where they both lived.[76] When interviewed on the twenty-fifth anniversary of the ruling in *Loving*, Brooks was unapologetic about his role in arresting the couple. "I was acting according to the law at the time, and I still think it should be on the books. I don't think a white person should marry a black person. I'm from the old school. The Lord made sparrows and robins, not to mix with one another."[77]

Mildred shied away from attention and press coverage, insisting, according to Pratt, that she never considered herself a celebrity.[78] And Mildred, according to Pratt, continued to shy away from celebrity status or efforts to recognize her contribution to the civil rights movement. As Pratt described Mildred, after meeting with her thirty years after the Supreme Court ruled on her case, "she still sees herself as an ordinary black woman who fell in love with an ordinary white man, and had they been allowed to marry without the state's interference, that would have been the end of it."[79] Peggy Loving Fortune, the youngest of the couple's three children, married a man of mixed race. Her parents never openly took credit for changing the world, but Peggy credited them with setting "the world free to be with whomever they want."[80]

During the decade of the *Loving* decision, and even before the case began wending its way to the High Court, opposition to interracial cohabitation and marriage had significantly diminished within secular institutions as it had within religious groups and congregations. In 1963, for example, the U.S. Air Force ended its practice of asking personnel whether they had married a person of another race during their overseas tours.[81] The same year, the resolution committee of the Young

---

[73] *The Crime of Being Married*, Life, Mar. 18, 1966, at 85.
[74] *Id.*
[75] *See* Pratt, *supra* n.73, at 241.
[76] *See* Margolick, *supra* n.10, at B20.
[77] *Id.*
[78] She did eventually agree to cooperate with an HBO movie made about the case, "Mr. and Mrs. Loving," which aired in 1996. *See* Pratt, *supra* n.73, at 242.
[79] *Id.* at 244; *see* Margolick, *supra* n.10, at B20 ("We have thought about other people, but we are not doing it just because somebody had to do it and we wanted to be the ones. We are doing it for us, because we want to live here.").
[80] *See* Margolick, *supra* n.10, at B20.
[81] *See* Warren Weaver, Jr., *Air Force Drops Marriage Query*, N.Y. Times, July 3, 1963, at 12. New York Senator Jacob Javits objected to the question, "Are you a member of an interracial marriage?" after

Democratic Clubs of America presented to its convention delegates a resolution that condemned state laws banning interracial marriage.[82]

It would be naive, of course, to think that opponents of interracial marriage were silent during the years leading up to *Loving*. Some four years before the decision, for example, Arthur Krock, a prominent *New York Times* writer, expressed his opinion, after the announcement that the first black woman ever admitted to the University of Georgia had married a white fellow student,[83] that "the future of race relations [had] reached an inflammatory stage," and that the Supreme Court might "find a greater opportunity to withhold indefinitely the firebrand that a decision on the constitutionality of [miscegenation] laws would be."[84]

Krock's alarms seem at best to have been overblown and grossly exaggerated. Indeed, two months after the Court handed down its *Loving* decision, Virginia's first interracial marriage was scarcely noted.[85] And months later, the first interracial marriage in Tennessee was celebrated on the steps of the Nashville City Hall and Courthouse.[86] As late as the year 2000, Alabama was the last of the states, by means of an amendment of the state's constitution, to repeal its prohibition against interracial marriage.[87] One writer observed on the eve of the vote on the constitutional amendment:

> In the state nicknamed "The Heart of Dixie," the land of Bill Connor and George Wallace, the movement to relinquish this searing symbol of the past has caused barely a ripple. There are no billboards on the highways, no marches for or against the repeal, no yard signs or bumper sticker. Articles about Amendment 2, as the ballot measure is known, are few and far between in the local press.[88]

In sum, if newspaper coverage reflects or even bears on popular opinion, during the period shortly prior to and after the *Loving* decision, concerns about interracial marriage seem not to have been near the forefront of American consciousness. Yet, these articles also suggest that cultural acceptance of interracial marriage was far from complete, even though laws banning the practice were on the wane.

We conclude with a caveat, perhaps an unnecessary one. The comments and observations that we make here relate solely to what we perceive as the societal view

---

receiving a letter from an airman who protested the inclusion of the question in connection with reassignment in the United States. *Id.*

[82] See *Democrats Asked to Oppose Antimiscegenation Laws*, N.Y. TIMES, Oct. 14, 1965, at 30.

[83] See *Georgia Calls Negro Coed's Wedding Illegal*, N.Y. Times, Sept. 4, 1963, at 27.

[84] *Id.*

[85] See *Virginia Ban Struck Down, Has an Interracial Wedding*, N.Y. TIMES, Aug. 13, 1967, at 31.

[86] See *Negro and White Wed in Nashville*, N.Y. TIMES, July 22, 1967, at 11.

[87] See Susie Parker, *Erasing A Remnant of Jim Crow South From Law Books*, CHRISTIAN SCI. MONITOR, Mar. 23, 1999, at 2.

[88] See Somini Sengupta, *Removing a Relic of the Old South*, N.Y. TIMES, Nov. 5, 2000, at D5.

of interracial marriage in the *Loving* era. We do not mean to draw conclusions about the general state of race relations in America at that time or now. Rather, many would agree with a recent observation – occasioned by the firing of controversial radio personality Don Imus for his racially charged description of the women's basketball team from Rutgers University – that "racism remains a central issue in our national life."[89]

CONCLUSION

Loving's declaration of marriage as a fundamental right has played an important role in defining the right to marry. The ruling was also central to the long line of cases in its wake that broadened and strengthened a right to privacy that encompassed decision making over virtually all aspects of family life without government interference. Its pronouncements about the constitution's intolerance for racial classifications and other vestiges of slavery have been invoked in a wide variety of contexts and serve as a potent reminder of the Fourteenth Amendment's purpose.

Legalizing interracial marriage was an essential step toward racial equality. For the government to deny individuals access to such an important institution of civil society for no reason other than the color of their skin is obviously inconsistent with notions of formal equality. The legacy of *Loving*, however, seems to stop there. Interracial marriages remain, forty years later, a relatively unusual occurrence, and the black-white cultural and marital divide is still deeply entrenched. That cultural change has lagged behind the legal change is no criticism of the Supreme Court's ruling in *Loving*, but simply a reflection of the limits of law. Had *Loving* come out the other way, we would certainly not come together to celebrate its impact.

---

[89] *See* Weston Kosova, *Imus: Race, Power and the Media*, NEWSWEEK, Apr. 23, 2007, at 29.

PART TWO

Historical Antecedents to *Loving*

2

Telling Stories of Love, Sex, and Race

Jason A. Gillmer

In 1662, more than 300 years before *Loving v. Virginia*, the Virginia colonial legislature enacted the first statute penalizing sex across the color line. In the years that followed, legislators, legal thinkers, and racial ideologues throughout the South condemned the practice, promising banishment, fines, and imprisonment for those who refused to obey. Interracial sex, the guardians of the social order reasoned, blurred the carefully drawn distinctions between black and white, slave and free. Yet few doubted then and no one doubts now that interracial sex, if not a frequent part of Southern life, was not uncommon either. The sheer number of people with light-brown skin and soft, wavy hair – 500,000 in the 1860 census, a number most agree was a gross underestimate – provided glaring evidence of interracial contacts for even those who were not personally involved in the practice.[1]

Yet, notwithstanding their regular occurrence, efforts to provide some content and character to these early relationships are fraught with difficulty. Sources are difficult to locate and sometimes even harder to interpret, leaving many simply to rely on stock characters and familiar storylines. Following the groundbreaking work of scholars like Deborah Gray White, most point out today how interracial sex in the years before *Loving* was used as a tool of oppression, reinforcing the bedrock principles of white supremacy and patriarchal privilege. Many white men of all social ranks regularly took advantage of black women, and white society in general was all too willing to greet accusations of black-on-white rape with violence and destruction.

This chapter seeks to revisit[2] these basic assumptions with detailed evidence from some early cases. The purpose is not so much to refute the underlying ideas

---

[1] II HENING'S STATUTES AT LARGE: BEING A COLLECTION OF ALL THE LAWS OF VIRGINIA FROM THE FIRST SESSION OF THE LEGISLATURE, IN THE YEAR 1615, at 170 (William Waller Hening ed., 1823); BUREAU OF THE CENSUS, U.S. DEP'T OF COMMERCE, NEGRO POPULATION IN THE UNITED STATES 1790–1915, at 220 (1918).

[2] Deborah Gray White, "AR'N'T I A WOMAN?" FEMALE SLAVES IN THE PLANTATION SOUTH (rev. ed. 1999); *see also* Angela Y. Davis, WOMEN, RACE, & CLASS (1981); Peter W. Bardaglio, *Rape and the Law*

behind these dominant narratives, but to broaden our understanding about the nature of interracial sex and intimate relations between individuals. To that end, this chapter revels in trial records rather than appellate decisions, and listens to the voices from the neighborhood rather than from the state capitols. By doing so – by recasting the debate to the community level – it becomes fairly evident that sex between the races in the nineteenth and early twentieth centuries did not necessarily fit a particular paradigm, but was instead filled with contradictions and beset with complications. Rapes and lynchings occurred more than anyone would like to admit; but along the back roads and country farms, blacks and whites also met on terms that were mutually negotiated and renegotiated to fit their individual circumstance and experience. The playing field was not always equal, but the records left behind reveal a world with much more fluidity and nuance than traditional accounts allow.[3]

With such an ambitious undertaking and yet with such limited space, this essay has settled on two stories from Texas, chosen in part because the location is both unique and typical. After all, most of the settlers who came to the Lone Star State were Southerners, and they brought with them their notions of what race meant and of what proper white women did. But the people who lived here also had to accept a more practical reality, one that was based on the vast spaces and underpopulated places where blacks and whites interacted on a daily basis. The first story involves a white man and black woman from the time of slavery; the second involves a black man and a white woman from the turn of the century. Neither one can properly be characterized as canonical in the traditional sense; the events were in many respects mundane and the holdings uneventful. Yet each is designed to challenge some of our assumptions, and to force us to look at these couplings for what they were: unique, complex, and yet filled with the stuff of everyday life.

in the Old South: "Calculated to Excite Indignation in Every Heart," 60 J.S. HIST. 749 (1994); Karen A. Getman, *Sexual Control in the Slaveholding South: The Implementation and Maintenance of a Racial Caste System*, 7 HARV. WOMEN'S L.J. 115 (1984); A. Leon Higginbotham, Jr. & Barbara K. Kopytoff, *Racial Purity and Interracial Sex in the Law of Colonial and Antebellum Virginia*, 77 GEO. L.J. 1967 (1989); Jennifer Wriggins, *Rape, Racism, and the Law*, 6 HARV. WOMEN'S L.J. 103 (1983).

3 A handful of scholars have begun to recast issues of interracial sex in a new light. See, e.g., Victoria E. Bynum, UNRULY WOMEN: THE POLITICS OF SOCIAL & SEXUAL CONTROL IN THE OLD SOUTH (1992); Lisa Lindquist Door, WHITE WOMEN, RAPE, & THE POWER OF RACE IN VIRGINIA 1900–1960 (2004); Martha Hodes, WHITE WOMEN, BLACK MEN: ILLICIT SEX IN THE 19th-CENTURY SOUTH (1997); Walter Johnson, *The Slave Trader, the White Slave, and the Politics of Racial Determination in the 1850s*, 87 J. AM. HIST. 13 (2000); Melton A. McLaurin, CELIA, A SLAVE: A TRUE STORY OF VIOLENCE AND RETRIBUTION IN ANTEBELLUM MISSOURI (1991); Joshua D. Rothman, NOTORIOUS IN THE NEIGHBORHOOD: SEX AND FAMILIES ACROSS THE COLOR LINE IN VIRGINIA, 1787–1861 (2003); Dianne Miller Sommerville, RAPE & RACE IN THE NINETEENTH-CENTURY SOUTH (2004).

JOHN CLARK AND SOBRINA

In 1861, with the country in the midst of a Civil War, John Clark died at his home in Wharton County, Texas. The inventory of his estate revealed a man of tremendous wealth: he was the owner of more than 8,500 acres of land, close to 2,000 head of cattle, and – perhaps the best indicator of his success in life – an astonishing 139 slaves.[4] What the inventory did not reveal, however, was that three of these slaves were his by a "dark mulatto" woman named Sobrina, Clark's longtime slave. The fact that Clark fathered children with a slave is not surprising. As one contemporary put it, there "was not a likely-looking black girl in this State that is not the concubine of a white man."[5] But what is surprising is what happened after the war. Filing suit in the Wharton County District Court, these three children – Bishop, Lourinda, and Nancy – claimed to be Clark's legitimate and closest heirs, and hence entitled to the vast proceeds of the estate. Perhaps even more surprising: the jury, concluding that Clark and Sobrina had been husband and wife, found in their favor.[6]

The story of John Clark and Sobrina defies easy categorization, but it is no doubt reflective of circumstances both typical and unusual. John Clark came to Texas in either 1821 or 1822 as part of Stephen F. Austin's Old Three Hundred, the name given to the original 300 colonists who ventured into the Texas territory soon after it fell from the hands of Spain to Mexico. The reason he left his native South Carolina is not known, but chances are that he came to Texas for the same reason that so many others came: opportunity and the prospect of a better life. At the time, land in Texas was practically for the taking. For the price of 12.5 cents an acre and the promise to put it to good use, colonists could acquire grants to land in the fertile region between the Brazos and Colorado Rivers, in the southeastern part of the territory. Austin himself was in charge of attracting the colonists and distributing the land. Each family engaged in farming was to receive one "labor" of land (or 177 acres), and each family who planned to raise stock was entitled to one "sitio" (or 4,428 acres).[7]

Clark, a single man at the time, called himself a stock-raiser and settled on a portion of the Colorado River near Peach Creek, about 50 miles north of the Gulf of Mexico and about 60 miles southwest of present-day Houston. Still a young man,

4 In the Estate of John C. Clark, dec'd, Probate Minutes Book "B," at 257, 257–64 (Tex. Cty. Ct. Wharton Cty. Feb. 1863) (collection of Wharton County Court Annex).

5 Fredrick Law Olmsted, THE COTTON KINGDOM: A TRAVELLER'S OBSERVATIONS ON COTTON AND SLAVERY IN THE AMERICAN SLAVE STATES 240 (Arthur M. Schlesinger ed., Alfred A. Knopf 1953) (1861).

6 Transcript of Trial to Supreme Court, Clark v. Honey, No. 789, at 1–2 (Tex. Dist. Ct. Wharton Cty. Dec. 1871) (collection of Texas State Library and Archives Commission) [hereinafter Transcript of Trial, Clark v. Honey] (plaintiff's petition), *aff'd* 37 Tex. 686 (1872).

7 Lester G. Bugbee, *The Old Three Hundred: A List of Settlers in Austin's First Colony*, I TEX. HIST. ASSOC. Q. 108, 108–09, 111 (1898).

in his mid-twenties, Clark no doubt possessed the adventurous spirit common to so many of the early settlers. In these first days, dressed in buckskin pants, Clark would have spent much of his time clearing enough land to plant his first crops as well as building a simple shelter. But like so many others who came with him, Clark did not seem much concerned with the fineries he left behind in the Old South. Even in later years, when the value of his estate reached into the hundreds of thousands of dollars, he proved content to live in a basic log cabin measuring about eighteen by twenty feet.[8]

When he arrived, Clark did not own any human chattels. In fact, he did not buy his first slaves until about 1830 or perhaps a year or two before, at a time when slavery in Austin's colony was still much in doubt. Yet, even before then, Clark no doubt hoped one day to count himself as a member of this privileged group. Indeed, by the time Clark arrived in Texas, many whites had begun to see slavery as more than just a tolerated evil; instead, it had become an essential part of the way they viewed themselves and the rest of the world. Blacks were better off in slavery, it was argued, both because of their supposed inferiority and because of the humane and uplifting aspects of the institution itself. "[T]he negro is indisputably adapted by nature, to the condition of servitude to the white man," ran one affirmative explanation of the institution, "enjoying a degree of health unequalled by any other servile class in any portion of the world." Others sought to tie slavery to democracy, insisting that that the latter could not survive without the former. As one contributor to the local paper mused, "The very existence of slavery keeps alive in the breast of every white citizen a jealous passion for liberty." In fact, so confident were Texans in the rightness of their institution, that one citizen had trouble fathoming anything different. "Hah!" he said, "You might as well talk about building a railroad to the moon as the making of a free State out of any portion of the Texas territory."[9]

In light of such testaments, it should come as little surprise that John Clark chose to invest some of his early capital in human property, even before Texas declared

---

[8] *See* Map of Wharton County (General Land Office 1880) (collection of The Center for American History, University of Texas) (showing Clark's land on the Colorado); Transcript of Trial, Clark v. Honey, *supra* note 6, at 81 (testimony of Stephen R. Herd) (stating that Clark's home was on Peach Creek); I H. Yoakum, HISTORY OF TEXAS: FROM ITS FIRST SETTLEMENT IN 1685 TO ITS ANNEXATION TO THE UNITED STATES IN 1846, at 229 (1855) (describing common dress and attitude of early settlers); I Louis J. Wortham, A HISTORY OF TEXAS: FROM WILDERNESS TO COMMONWEALTH 82, 129 (1924) (same). For the testimony about his cabin, see Transcript of Trial, Clark v. Honey, *supra* note 6, at 63 (testimony of Reason Byrne).

[9] A REPORT AND TREATISE ON SLAVERY AND THE SLAVERY AGITATION 4 (1857). William H. Parsons, *Negro Slavery*, TEXAS STATE GAZETTE, Apr. 14, 1860, at 1; *A Free State Out of Texas*, TEXAS STATE GAZETTE, Nov. 14, 1857 at 3. For a thorough discussion of slavery in Texas, including its status in the years before the War for Independence, see Randolph B. Campbell, AN EMPIRE FOR SLAVERY: THE PECULIAR INSTITUTION IN TEXAS, 1821–1865 (1989).

independence from Mexico and formalized the institution.[10] The first two persons he bought were an older woman named Clarisa and a young girl named Hannah, right around the time he sold half of his original land grant to a man named William Heard. Whether he sold the land specifically to acquire the money to buy slaves is not known, but, for the purchase price of 50 cents an acre, or approximately $1,100, it seems likely that it played at least a role, as the average price for slaves around this time was about $450. As for Clarisa and Hannah, we really know little about them. But it is likely that Clark purchased both to perform chores around the home. The move made sense. With two females to attend to the responsibilities of cooking, cleaning, and milking the cows, Clark could devote his attention to raising his stock and clearing even more land for the crops he planned to grow.[11]

Within a few years, Clark bought his third slave, a woman named Sobrina. This decision may have puzzled some of Clark's neighbors, as many may have thought the next logical purchase would have been a young man to help with the stock and in the fields. Indeed, if there is one thing that Clark's neighbors agreed on, it is that Clark rarely made foolish business decisions. Described by one witness as a "miserly man," perhaps a more apt description would have been a "shrewd man," for Clark in future years demonstrated a singular purpose and immense talent for acquiring property, both real and personal. In fact, the 139 slaves he owned when he died reflect an unprecedented rise in the slaveholding class – with this many, he would have owned more slaves than 99.8 percent of all slaveholders in Texas, a remarkable feat considering he started with so little.[12] To be sure, it may be that Clark saw something profitable in Sobrina. The records suggest that Hannah may have died by this point, and perhaps Clark wanted Sobrina to help out Clarisa, who was now close to sixty. It is also possible that Clark was intrigued by Sobrina's reproductive capacity. In her early thirties, Sobrina was already the mother of four children, and a good "breeder" was always a desirable asset. But whether these reasons played into Clark's decision or not, it seems clear enough that Clark bought Sobrina at least in part, if not primarily for, sexual reasons. As Clarisa remembered it, as soon as Clark

---

[10] *See* REPUB. OF TEX. CONST. of 1836, general provisions, § 9, *in* I THE LAWS OF TEXAS, 1822–1897, 1069, 1079 (H.P.N. Gammel ed., 1898).

[11] Transcript of Trial, Clark v. Honey, *supra* note 6, at 50, 55 (testimony of Aunt Clarisa Bird) (reporting that she "was the first negro [Clark] ever owned," and that "he bought me first & little girl named Hannah"); *see also id.* at 55 ("Capt. Herd bought his land from Master.").

[12] In 1860, there were 76,781 families in Texas. STATISTICS OF THE UNITED STATES (INCLUDING MORTALITY, PROPERTY, & C.) IN 1860; COMPILED FROM THE ORIGINAL RETURNS AND BEING THE FINAL EXHIBIT OF THE EIGHTH CENSUS 349 (1866). Of these, 21,878, or 28.5%, owned at least one slave. AGRICULTURE OF THE UNITED STATES IN 1860; COMPILED FROM THE ORIGINAL RETURNS OF THE EIGHTH CENSUS 242 (1864). Out of this relatively privileged group, moreover, only 54, or 0.2%, owned 100 or more slaves. *Id.*

came home, "he put Sobrina in the house and stated he wanted her for his own woman."[13]

By now, of course, Clark was in his mid-thirties. Still single, perhaps he also sensed that his prospects for finding a white wife were diminishing, as Wharton County during this period was still sparsely settled. There was some talk about how he once called on a white woman who lived nearby but whether the purpose was a romantic one is not known, and certainly nothing ever came of it. In all likelihood, then, Clark sought out Sobrina to fill a void in his life, left by the absence of a female companion. If he felt any pangs of guilt about his decision, or suffered through any moral qualms, it is not disclosed in the record. To the contrary, he probably looked upon his actions as nothing more than his right as a master and a man.[14]

It is well known, of course, that white men during slavery times regularly turned to black women to satisfy their sexual needs. As the escaped slave Harriet Jacobs once said in reflecting on the years of torment her master inflicted upon her, "Slavery is terrible for men; but it is far more terrible for women. Superadded to the burden common to all, *they* have wrongs, and sufferings, and mortifications peculiarly their own." There were laws on the books prohibiting the practice, but it seems clear enough that these were rarely, if ever, enforced against white men. This is not to say there were no limits. But the limits were most often the result of slave resistance or societal pressure, rather than the law. "It would not have done for any person to have introduced a black woman as his wife," reported I. M. Dennis, one of the white witnesses in the suit over Clark's estate, "Public sentiment was against it." Some slaveholders, of course, went to great lengths to downplay the amount of sexual contacts that took place in the slave South; others sought to blame slave women, crafting images of a sable race driven by passions and sexual desires. Yet the more thoughtful and observant among them knew better. One said that the practice "pervades the entire society," and another traveler was taken aback by the "boundless licentiousness" of the South. If these comments sound like exaggerations or abolitionist propaganda, surely the remarks of one Texas slave serve as a sobering reminder of how vulnerable black women in the end truly were: "I can tell you that a white man laid a nigger gal whenever he wanted her."[15]

---

[13] Transcript of Trial, Clark v. Honey, *supra* note 6, at 56 (testimony of Albert Horton) (identifying Sobrina's children before Clark). On the subject of the increased value of slave women as "breeders", see, e.g., Frederick Law Olmsted, A Journey in the Seaboard Slave States, with Remarks on Their Economy 49–50 (1856).

[14] Transcript of Trial, Clark v. Honey, *supra* note 6, at 52, 54, 56 (testimony of Aunt Clarisa Bird); *see also id.* at 63–64 (testimony of Reason Byrne) (noting that, at the time in question, "Wharton County was very sparsely settled – women were very scarce").

[15] Harriet A. Jacobs, Incidents in the Life of a Slave Girl: Written by Herself 77 (Jean Fagan Yellin ed., 1987); Transcript of Trial, Clark v. Honey, *supra* note 6, at 91 (testimony of I. M. Dennis).

Still, if the evidence is to be believed, it would be misleading to assume that relationships of a more substantial sort could not have emerged, even in the tortured
circumstances of the slave South. Some have proved reluctant to admit that this
was a possibility, arguing that in a system that denied black women the legal power
to refuse consent, all sex was essentially forced and, hence, rape. Yet, throughout
the South, records left behind reveal that such conclusions are no longer tenable,
and that sex between the races was much more intricate than these broad theories suggest. Court records seem especially important in this regard, because what
white Southerners refused to discuss in their diaries and personal letters inevitably
found its way into the everyday disputes over wills, divorces, and adulterous affairs.
In Texas, these cases appeared with some regularity.[16]

As we dig deeper into the records, moreover, some of the strongest voices for
deeper interracial relationships come from the former slaves themselves. Indeed,
although many spoke of sexual violence that happened regularly on the plantations,
others recalled instances of affectionate ties between the races. One former slave in
Arkansas, for example, recalled how his white father was a "fool" about his mother.
Another said: "Why, there was one white man in Texas had a cullud woman …
[and] when old Mistress died he wouldn't let this cullud woman leave, and he gave
her a swell home right there on the place." Later still, following the emancipation
of slaves, records from the Freedman's Bureau shed some light on the power of
black women to use the law to control and maintain relationships with white men.
Eliza Morgan, for example, had been living with a white man for two years, and,
after he "got her in a family way," she sought the help of the Bureau to force him
to pay child support. Emma Hartsfield, another black woman, proved particularly
resourceful. After the white man she had been living with for a year tried to leave
her, she finagled (with the help of the Bureau) a plot of land and house in Austin
out of the man. This is not to say that these relationships were ever approved or
condoned. Some, like John Smelser of Brazoria County, were prosecuted for violating the antimiscegenation laws, and others had to listen to the court refer to their

On efforts to downplay sex between white men and black women, see James Henry Hammond, *Letter
to an English Abolitionist*, in THE IDEOLOGY OF SLAVERY: PROSLAVERY THOUGHT IN THE ANTEBELLUM
SOUTH, 1830–1860, at 168, 182 (Drew Gilpin Faust ed., 1981). On efforts to blame her, see Thomas
R. R. Cobb, AN INQUIRY INTO THE LAW OF NEGRO SLAVERY § 107 (1858); William Harper, *Memoir
on Slavery*, in THE IDEOLOGY OF SLAVERY: PROSLAVERY THOUGHT IN THE ANTEBELLUM SOUTH, 1830–
1860, at 78, 104 (Drew Gilpin Faust ed., 1981); Mary Boykin Chesnut, MARY CHESNUT'S CIVIL WAR
29, 168 (C. Vann Woodward ed., 1981).
[16] Webster v. Heard, 32 Tex. 685, 707 (1870) (Webster left a large estate, consisting of land and personal
assets, to Betsy Webster, a woman of color and his slave, whom he also set free); Wilson v. Catchings,
41 Tex. 587, 588–89 (1874) ("she was the lawful wife of the deceased"); Oldham v. McIver, 49 Tex. 556,
557 (1878) (evidence that the master "lived with her as his wife").

longtime relationship as "illegal and immoral" and their conduct as "repulsive." But the more significant point is that the mere existence of these cases suggests that sweeping generalizations about the nature of interracial sex must give way to realities of individual circumstance.[17]

In John Clark's case, too, some of the most poignant testimony comes from the former slaves who lived on or near Clark's plantation. Collectively, the testimony reveals little doubt that the relationship evolved over time, from one based on exploitation to one based on something much more significant. All of them agreed that at the time of his death, Clark and Sobrina were living as husband and wife, and some of Clark's first slaves said the two had been living this way since the 1830s.[18] As evidence of the marriage, they spoke of how Sobrina and Clark lived together in the same cabin, and about how they ate together and drank together and slept in the same bed. Others spoke about how Sobrina was "the mistress of the plantation," and about how she "carried the keys and had management of everything."[19] Another remarked how Clark always treated her kindly, and more than one remembered

[17] Interview with Thomas Ruffin, *in* 10 THE AMERICAN SLAVE: A COMPOSITE AUTOBIOGRAPHY (sup.), pt. 6, at 97 [hereinafter THE AMERICAN SLAVE]; Interview with Francis Bridges, *in* 7 THE AMERICAN SLAVE, *supra* note 17, at 20, 23; Letter re: Eliza Morgan, RECORDS OF THE BUREAU OF REFUGE, FREEDMEN, AND ABANDONED LANDS, TEXAS, 1865–1872, v.49, at 210 (May 1867–Dec. 1868), *microfilmed on* M1912-Roll 12 (collection of National Archives Southwest Region in Fort Worth); Letter re: Emma Hartsfield, *id.*, v.52, at 5, (June 1867), *microfilmed on* M1912-Roll 12; Smelser v. State, 31 Tex. 95, 96 (1868); Clements v. Crawford, 42 Tex. 601, 604 (1874); Cartwright v. Cartwright, 18 Tex. 626, 642 (1857). For additional cases involving issues of interracial sex between white men and black women, see, e.g., Hagerty v. Harwell, 16 Tex. 663 (1856); Frasher v. State, 3 Tex. App. 263 (1877); *Ex parte* Francois, 9 Fed. Cas. 699 (1879); Francois v. State, 9 Tex. App. 144 (1880).

[18] On Clark and Sobrina as husband and wife, see Transcript of Trial, Clark v. Honey, *supra* note 6, at 52 (testimony of Aunt Clarisa Bird) ("Clark and Sobrina lived together as man and wife until their deaths."); *id.* at 56–57 (testimony of Albert Horton) ("J.C. Clark treated Sobrina as a wife and lived together as such all the time I knew them."); *id.* at 58 (testimony of James Montgomery) (stating that Clark treated Sobrina "exactly like a man does his wife"); *id.* at 71 (testimony of David Prophet) (testifying that Clark and Sobrina "continued to live together as husband and wife until Clark's death"); *id.* at 72 (testimony of Abraham Kincheloe) ("Sobrina had no other husband and Clark no other wife."); *id.* at 76 (testimony of Pleasant Ballard) (stating that Clark "regarded her as his wife and she was so considered").

[19] On evidence of the marriage, see Transcript of Trial, Clark v. Honey, *supra* note 6, at 51 (testimony of Aunt Clarisa Bird) ("Mr. Clark eat with her slept with her and drank with her" and stating that Sobrina was "the mistress of the plantation"); *id.* at 57 (testimony of Albert Horton) (stating that he saw "Clark take his meals with Sobrina and the children many times"); *id.* at 59 (testimony of James Montgomery) (stating that Clark ate "at table with Sobrina and children"); *id.* at 70 (testimony of David Prophet) (stating that there was only one bed in the room and that Clark and Sobrina slept in it) (stating that Sobrina "carried the keys and attended to household affairs"); *id.* at 72 (testimony of Abraham Kincheloe) ("There was only one bed in the room and they slept in it.") ("Sobrina had charge of his keys and money and everything pertaining to the place."); *id.* at 75 (testimony of Pleasant Ballard) (stressing that Sobrina "took all charge of everything as far as I could see").

how Clark referred affectionately to Sobrina as his "dear" and his "old woman" and about how she called him her "old man."[20]

Still others pointed to Clark's relationship with his children, and about how he always treated them with the type of affection expected of a father. When the children were little, for example, one former slave said he used to see Clark "nursing and petting" them, and another remembered that Clark often held Bishop in his lap. Others recalled that Bishop, Lourinda, and Nancy all called Clark "pappa," and that, as they got older, they were never compelled to work.[21] Two others also remembered how at some point, Clark took Sobrina and the children to the town of Washington. Evidently, they went in part because Clark wanted to get Sobrina out of the oppressive air of the river bottoms, and Washington's location on the bluffs above the Brazos River made it a desirable location. While there, he also enrolled his children in school. They stayed about a year, leaving after one of the girls "took sick."[22]

To be sure, we must be careful not to paint this relationship as something that it was not, a sort of romantic rupture in the Southern social order in which race and slavery somehow did not matter. In a world that subjected people of color to the most inhuman treatment, and looked upon them as "distinctively inferior intellectual being[s], incapable of self-elevation or moral improvement," it would be difficult, if not impossible, for either a white man or a black woman to love someone of a different race without some difficulty or confusion. Yet it would contradict neither the evidence nor what we know about human nature to say that this relationship evolved into something more. By the time Clark died in 1861, he had been living with Sobrina for close to thirty years. During that time, admittedly, Clark and Sobrina "fell out a little like all people." But there also seems no reason to doubt the insistence of those who arguably knew best – Clark's former slaves – that Clark always treated his family different from the others, and about how he once said that he would "forsake all others" for Sobrina. Summed up by two of the witnesses, in

---

[20]   On Clark's relationship with Sobrina, see *id.* at 57 (testimony of Albert Horton) ("dear"); *id.* at 59 (testimony of James Montgomery) ("my old man"); *id.* at 72 (testimony of Abraham Kincheloe) ("kindly"); *id.* at 73 (testimony of Pleasant Ballard) ("his old woman" and "her old man").

[21]   On Clark's relationship with his children, see *id.* at 57 (testimony of Albert Horton) (held on lap) ("pappa"); *id.* at 59 (testimony of James Montgomery) ("pappa"); *id.* at 69 (testimony of Sharp Jackson) ("nursing and petting"); *id.* at 71–72 (testimony of David Prophet) ("pappy") (explaining that Bishop only tended to the stock when needed); *id.* at 74, 76 (testimony of Pleasant Ballard) ("pappy") (stating that Bishop "worked when he pleased and [was] let alone when he chose").

[22]   On the trip to Washington, see *id.* at 54 (testimony of Aunt Clarisa Bird); *id.* at 70–71 (testimony of David Prophet); *see also* 6 THE NEW HANDBOOK OF TEXAS, *supra* note 11, at 833 (Washington-on-the-Brazos, Texas) (noting Washington's desirable location on the bluffs above the river). There were no schools in Wharton in 1850. See Table 1 Population by Counties – Classifications of Ages and Color – Aggregates, *in* THE SEVENTH CENSUS OF THE UNITED STATES: EMBRACING A STATISTICAL VIEW OF EACH OF THE STATES AND TERRITORIES, at 508–11 (1850).

words that resonate as strongly as any, Clark reportedly "cared for no other woman," and she "no other man."[23]

Notably, the twelve men assembled in the Wharton County Courthouse in December of 1871 agreed, and found that John Clark and Sobrina had been husband and wife. This decision, moreover, was upheld on appeal, with the Texas Supreme Court accepting as true that the couple had become common law husband and wife in the 1830s, while Texas was still under Mexican rule and at a time when interracial marriages were legal. As such, the court ordered the State of Texas to award Bishop and his two sisters the proceeds from the vast estate, sold in 1863 before anyone claimed the property, including some of the most productive land in the county. Sadly, however, the story does not end here, for some of Clark's distant white relatives, as well as a few unscrupulous lawyers, appear to have bilked the three children out of their property over the course of the next three decades. In fact, when Bishop passed away around the turn of the century (the last of the three children to die), he evidently was close to penniless. Despite this tragic – yet somehow expected – end, the story of John Clark and Sobrina stands for much more: that white men and black women sometimes could and did develop strong feelings for one another, despite the rigid racial lines that were designed to keep them apart.[24]

MATTIE HALLMARK AND BUBBER CALHOUN

More than 100 miles north of John Clark and Sobrina and several decades later, a different story was unfolding in Walker County, Texas. This one involved Mattie Hallmark, a poor white woman who had accused a black man, Bubber Calhoun, of raping her on a cool spring morning in 1918. This story has a different ending, however, than the usual one along such lines: Mattie was not believed, and the case against Bubber was dismissed.[25]

By now, every student of race relations is familiar with the terrible atrocities inflicted on countless black men who were – or at least who presumed to be – having

---

[23] SLAVERY AND THE SLAVERY AGITATION, *supra* note 9, at 3; Transcript of Trial, Clark v. Honey, *supra* note 6, at 51, 52, 55 (testimony of Aunt Clarisa Bird); *id.* at 60 (testimony of James Montgomery). *Accord* Eugene D. Genovese, ROLL, JORDAN, ROLL: THE WORLD THE SLAVES MADE 418–19 (1972) (arguing that, as a general matter, "blacks and whites were not free to love each other without considerable emotional confusion, marked in part by a self-contempt projected onto the other").

[24] Transcript of Trial, Clark v. Honey, *supra* note 6, at 111 (verdict and decree); Honey v. Clark, 37 Tex. 686, 708–09 (1872). For an in-depth coverage of the aftermath of the case, see Jason A. Gillmer, *Base Wretches and Black Wenches: A Story of Sex and Race, Violence and Compassion, during Slavery Times*, 59 ALA. L. REV. 1501, 1546–54 (2008).

[25] *See* Transcript of Trial to Court of Criminal Appeals, State v. Calhoun, No. 5163, at 1 (Tex. Dist. Ct. Walker Cty. Mar. 1918) (collection of the Texas State Archives) [hereinafter Transcript of Trial, State v. Calhoun] (indictment), *rev'd* 214 S.W. 335 (Tex. Crim. App. 1919). For the comment about the weather, see *id.* at 3 (testimony of Mattie Hallmark).

sexual relations with white women. One of the most heinous of all, in fact, comes from Paris, Texas, a town not too far from where Mattie Hallmark lived. In February of 1893, Henry Smith was tortured and burned in front of thousands of cheering onlookers for the alleged rape and murder of Myrtle Vance, the four-year-old daughter of a local police officer. The case against Smith, like in so many of these cases, was based on an explosive mix of allegations and exaggerations. Smith was mentally retarded, or at least "weak-minded," and whether he committed the crime of which he was accused is impossible to know. What is clear, however, is that Myrtle's father, Henry Vance, was known for his brutality, and he had recently arrested Smith for "being drunk and disorderly" and beaten him severely with a club. For this reason, when Myrtle was found dead, suspicion fell on Smith. Soon, the whole town starting looking for him, as the details of the killing expanded to include gruesome violations and efforts to tear her limbs from her body.

Smith was eventually captured in Hope, Arkansas, where he had fled after hearing he was wanted for the crime. Loaded onto a train, the authorities brought Smith back to Paris, where he was "met by a surging mass of humanity 10,000 strong." Upon his arrival in Paris, the mob immediately started tearing Smith's clothes off and scattering them in the crowd, with people catching the pieces and collecting them as mementoes. Smith, finally grasping the enormity of the situation, begged for protection. Instead, he was "placed on a carnival float, in mockery of a king upon his throne." Then, for the next fifty minutes, Henry Vance, his son, and two of his brothers, thrust hot irons into Smith's flesh, eventually burning out his eyes and forcing the rods down his throat. The crowd, meanwhile, was cheering every groan and contortion. Smith was then thrown into a fire, and, apparently still alive, managed to roll out briefly, only to have the people near him thrown him back in. Curiosity seekers, who had come from Dallas, Fort Worth, Texarkana, and elsewhere, celebrated by carrying away the charred remains.[26]

In the aftermath of the lynching, a number of whites of varying political stripes sought to defend the actions of the mob, trotting out the by now familiar myths of the black rapist and the pure white woman. Bishop Atticus Haygood, a local minister, was one such person. Acknowledging that a better course of action would have been to arrest Smith and have him punished according to law, Bishop Haygood nevertheless explained that he could hardly find fault with the mob's actions. "Sane men who are righteous will remember not only the brutish man who dies by the

[26] *See Another Negro Burned*, NY TIMES, Feb. 2, 1893. Ida B. Wells, one of the great leaders of the anti-lynching campaign, devoted considerable attention to the lynching of Henry Smith. Part of the narrative here is based on her description. *See* Ida B. Wells, *A Red Record: Tabulated Statistics and Alleged Causes of Lynchings in the United States, 1892–1893–1894, reprinted in* SOUTHERN HORRORS AND OTHER WRITINGS: THE ANTI-LYNCHING CAMPAIGN OF IDA B. WELLS, 1892–1900, at 91–98 (Jacqueline Jones Royster ed., 1997).

slow torture of fire; they will think also of the ruined woman, worse tortured than he." Others were not so reserved.[27]

Yet, not unlike the typical assumptions surrounding white men and black women, the traditional view that whites responded with a uniform voice when faced with knowledge of a relationship between a black man and a white woman must be approached with care. Indeed, upon closer examination, not only is there a growing recognition that relationships between white women and black men were far more common than previously imagined, but that these relationships – and the communities' response – were as intricate as those between white men and black women.[28]

Mattie Hallmark's story illustrates some of these complexities, for she clearly was not the idealized belle of Southern lore. Mattie, a twenty-nine-year-old woman, lived with her husband and her three children in a temporary logging town in Walker County, Texas, along a railroad track. They had been there about ten months; before that, they had lived in places like Fort Worth, Wichita Falls, and Oklahoma, moving around as jobs became available. Her husband, Rickerson, to whom she had been married for fourteen years and who was ten years her senior, supposedly was trained as a blacksmith, but there is little evidence to suggest that he was ever employed in this capacity. Instead, in this job, as in his others, Rickerson appears to have taken whatever was offered.[29]

Rickerson's current employer and owner of the logging camp was a man named W. F. Millwee. Like other men in his position, Millwee seemed to care more about turning a profit than about enforcing any rigid racial boundaries among his workers.

---

[27] Atticus G. Haygood, *The Black Shadow in the South*, 16 Forum 167 (1893–1894).

[28] For recent scholarship on black men and white women that challenges traditional assumptions, *see, e.g.*, Lisa Lindquist Door, White Women, Rape, & the Power of Race in Virginia 1900–1960 (2004); Martha Hodes, White Women, Black Men: Illicit Sex in the 19th-Century South (1997); Dianne Miller Sommerville, Rape & Race in the Nineteenth-Century South (2004). In my previous work, I have also urged a very careful analysis when faced with black-on-white rape, stressing complexity and contradiction rather than agreement and uniformity. *See* Jason A. Gillmer, *Poor Whites, Benevolent Masters, and the Ideologies of Slavery: The Local Trial of a Slave Accused of Rape*, 85 N.C. L. Rev. 489 (2007).

[29] Transcript of Trial, State v. Calhoun, *supra* note 25, at 2, 3, 5, 6 (testimony of Mattie Hallmark). The 1920 Census Records list "Vivian" Hallmark, wife of Rickerson Hallmark, as a 28-year-old woman, with three children, Claudia, Herman, and Kenneth. *See* Manuscript Census Returns, Trinity County, Tex., *in* Bureau of the Census, U.S. Dep't of Commerce, Population Schedules of the Fourteenth Census of the United States, at 69 (family #181) (1920) [hereinafter 1920 Census]. This is undoubtedly Mattie, as the same woman appears again in the 1930 Census Records, this time going by the name "Mattie." *See* Manuscript Census Returns, Trinity County, Tex., *in* Bureau of the Census, U.S. Dep't of Commerce, Population Schedules of the Fifteenth Census of the United States, at 74 (family #173) (1930) (listing a 42-year-old woman named Mattie with two children, Herman and Kenneth, and married to "Matthew R." Hallmark). In the trial, Mattie's husband is listed by his initials, "M.R.," and her daughter is listed as "Claudie." *See* Transcript of Trial, State v. Calhoun, *supra* note 25, at 6, 9 (testimony of Mattie Hallmark).

As such, he hired both blacks and whites – currently, there were three black families and two white ones – and they lived side by side. Each family, including the Hallmarks, made their home in one of the abandoned boxcars along the tracks. There is no description of the homes, but presumably they had been outfitted so that a family could live comfortably, if sparingly. Mattie's twelve-year-old daughter spoke of a kitchen, and no doubt there were a few crudely constructed pieces of furniture – a couple of beds, some chairs, and a table. Presumably, there was also a way to heat the home, as Texas during the winter, which Mattie and her family suffered through, can be quite cold.[30]

On the morning of the alleged attack, the accused, Bubber Calhoun, came to Hallmark's home and knocked on the door. That much is agreed on; the rest is in dispute. Mattie claimed that she had never seen him before, and that he asked to speak to her husband, whom she said was at the corral, about 100 yards away. Mattie's daughter, however, contradicted this testimony, stating that, when she answered the door, Bubber specifically asked to see her mother. From there, the evidence becomes even more tangled. Mattie claimed that, some time after Bubber's visit, she left the house to "attend to a call of nature." With no outhouse in the camp, Mattie ventured a short distance across an open area near the homes to the brush. On her way back, she claimed that Bubber, armed with a stick and a knife, grabbed her with one hand and put the other around her neck; however, she did not say how, or indeed why, he grabbed her with both hands if he was holding two potential weapons – a point of later contention. At that point, Mattie claimed that she called out for help "as loud as [she] could," and, although she thought the other families should have been able to hear her, no one did (again, a point of contention). Bubber then dragged her, she said, about a quarter of a mile back into the brush, where he "accomplished his purpose." Afterward, Bubber allegedly got up and left, and Mattie ran back to her home, calling out for her husband.[31]

Rickerson, Mattie's husband, said that he heard his wife's calls and that he ran back and met her in the yard, where he found her in an excited state. Mattie testified that she told her husband immediately what had happened, and he testified to the same, that a "negro had caught her and had outraged her." Yet, curiously, when the sheriff arrived several hours later, with his wife in the house, Rickerson made no mention of the rape and, when asked by the sheriff if one had occurred, he replied, "She says not." The sheriff subsequently conducted a preliminary investigation, including following some tracks to a place where the ground "was torn up

---

[30] Transcript of Trial, State v. Calhoun, *supra* note 25, at 13 (testimony of W. F. Millwee); *id.* at 2–3 (testimony of Mattie Hallmark); *id.* at 9 (testimony of Claudie Hallmark).

[31] Transcript of Trial, State v. Calhoun, *supra* note 25, 1–2, 4, 5 (testimony of Mattie Hallmark); *id.* at 9 (testimony of Claudie Hallmark). On the evidence being in contention, see Calhoun, 214 S.W. at 335, 337.

considerable" and where he found the print of a man's hand on the ground. It was only after he returned to the home and asked point blank why he was following the accused that Mattie said: "I hate to admit it, but he accomplished his purpose."[32]

The accused, Bubber Calhoun, presents even more of a puzzle. Thirty years old or so at the time of the alleged rape, he evidently lived near the logging camp, but not in it. Apparently, however, he was friends with Will Harmon, one of Mattie's African-American neighbors. In fact, after the investigation began, the sheriff's dogs tracked Bubber's scent to Harmon's house, and Harmon later accompanied Bubber when he turned himself in to local authorities. Perhaps it was through Harmon that Bubber got to know Mattie, or at least of her. For Mattie, it seems, spent much of her time with her black neighbors; much more than "decent white people," according to Lila Millwee, the daughter-in-law of the man who owned the logging camp. Mattie insisted she only went to the Harmon household to "get slop for the pigs" or to borrow something, but her white neighbors painted a very different picture. Dismissing her claims as outlandish because she did not even own pigs, these witnesses indicated that Mattie spent most of her time in the company of the other black families by choice and design. The owner of the logging camp, for example, observed that, "Every morning after her husband would got to work she would go to some of the negros [sic] and she would stay there all day." Others talked about how she would bum cigarettes from some of the men, and smoke and talk with them for hours, sometimes in the woods under "suspicious circumstances." She also evidently visited regularly with the black women in the camp, sharing conversations and meals in both their home and hers. Lila Millwee admitted that she also attended what she called the "negro festivals," but she was quick to add that she did so "in a proper way" – to "look on." Not so Mattie Hallmark. She "just associate[d] around with them generally," when no other whites were around.[33]

Yet, notwithstanding the disparaging tone of Mattie's white neighbors, the types of contacts described by them are the ones that have inevitably taken place whenever whites and blacks have intermingled on a daily basis. Indeed, Edmund Morgan has written about how, since the days when African slaves were first imported to work

[32] Transcript of Trial, State v. Calhoun, *supra* note 25, at 6, 7 (testimony of M. R. Hallmark); *id.* at 2 (testimony of Mattie Hallmark); *id.* at 10–12 (testimony of T. E. King).

[33] For details on Bubber's contact with the camp and his relationship with Harmon, see Transcript of Trial, State v. Calhoun, *supra* note 25, at 2–3, 4, 6 (testimony of Mattie Hallmark); *id.* at 10 (testimony of T. E. King). Bubber is listed in the 1920 Census Records as 32-year-old prisoner, held in the Walker County Jail. *See* 1920 CENSUS, *supra* note 29, Walker County, Tex., at 53 (family #145). It is unknown whether his detention was related to this case or another. He cannot be found in subsequent census records. On Mattie's relationship with her African-American neighbors, see Transcript of Trial, State v. Calhoun, *supra* note 25, at 5 (testimony of Mattie Hallmark); *id.* at 13 (testimony of W. F. Millwee); *id.* at 14 (testimony of Luther Millwee); *id.* at 15 (testimony of Lila Millwee); *see also* Brief for Appellant, Calhoun v. State, at 2.

alongside white indentured servants, the two groups have found things in common. Aligned in their shared circumstance, they developed friendships that transcended the color of their skin, getting drunk together, running away together, and making love with one another. This happened, moreover, as much with white women and black men as it did the reverse. Some of the early statutes indicate as much, lashing out, for example, at white women who, "to the Satisfaction of theire Lascivious & Lustfull desires," married black men. But the laws that were passed and the ideas they fostered never could stop the two groups from becoming intimate with each other. Just as there are abundant cases involving white men and black women, there are no shortage of records involving white women and black men. In Tennessee, Louisa Scott and Jesse Brady, "a mulatto man," lived together as "man and wife." In North Carolina, Elizabeth Walters left her husband and ran away with a black man, a slave, announcing in the process that "she loved him better than anybody in the world." And in Texas, Mary Moore caught the attention of local authorities because her husband Henry was black and she was white.[34]

Of course, relationships between white women and black men never would gain social approval in the South. But it seems beyond dispute that such unions occurred, and that they occurred with enough frequency that many communities accepted them as a part of their daily lives. To be sure, a few were prosecuted under the antimiscegenation laws and many more were brushed to the fringes of acceptable society. But in neighborhoods like Mattie Hallmark's, where rigid racial lines gave way to social and economic realities, many more likely continued on without much disruption from outside sources. There was the case from the city of Galveston, where Katie Bell, whose first husband was a white man and a Confederate soldier, married a black man. There was also Lititia Stewart of Jefferson County, who evidently found something in common with Henderson Ashworth, a free man of color, and tried to marry him. Samplings from census records from both before and after the Civil War also indicate that men of color like William Goyens, Edward and Alex Carter, W. G. Hudson, Louis Robinson, Edward Power, and other members of the Ashworth clan lived with white women as their wives.

The attorneys appointed to defend Bubber understood this common phenomenon; they understood that white women and black men could and did develop feelings for each other, even if they were frowned upon by the ruling elite. Thus, they drew out the testimony about Mattie's usual associations, from borrowing cigarettes from the men to dining with the women. In doing so, the defense made clear its

[34] Edmund S. Morgan, AMERICAN SLAVERY, AMERICAN FREEDOM: THE ORDEAL OF COLONIAL VIRGINIA 327 (1975); An Act of Aug./Sept. 1661, *in* 7 ARCHIVES OF MARYLAND: PROCEEDINGS AND ACTS OF THE GENERAL ASSEMBLY OF MARYLAND 203–04 (William Hand Browne ed., Baltimore, MD Hist. Soc'y 1889) ("An Act concerning Negroes & Slaves"); State v. Brady, 28 Tenn. (9 Hum.) 74, 74 (1848); Walters v. Jordan, 35 N.C. (13 Ired.) 361, 362 (1852); Moore v. State, 7 Tex. App. 608, 608 (1880).

theory of the case: that Mattie had not been raped at all, and "that, if there was any intercourse at all, it probably was by previous engagement between the parties."[35]

Throughout the day of the trial, the defense hammered away at its theory, questioning the witnesses about Mattie's reputation in the community. It was not good, all agreed, some implying that her associations with the men in her neighborhood may have been for sexual reasons. She was in the woods "a great deal," one insisted, and when her husband came home he would often "run all around there wanting to know where his wife was at." Even Mattie's trip to the woods to relieve herself was put in question, with the sheriff admitting that he found no evidence of Mattie having had a "call of nature" where she said. The implication surely was not lost on the jury. Bubber came to the house looking for her, and she used the excuse of answering nature's call to meet him in the woods.[36]

In the end, in this case as much as in the case of Henry Smith, it is impossible to know whether the accused committed the crime of which he was accused. Notably, the jury found the evidence sufficient to find Bubber guilty and imposed the death penalty. But Bubber appealed his conviction to the Texas Court of Criminal Appeals and had it reversed. The court thought that, in light of the "character of the prosecutrix, the peculiar circumstances of the case, [and] the severity of the penalty," it was "best to let another jury pass on the facts." On the state's motion for a rehearing, the court said the same, citing Mattie's inconsistent statements and her questionable associations. But even more to the point, at a time when traditional thinking tells us that the accusation of rape would have been met with a uniform voice, the story of Mattie Hallmark and Bubber Calhoun says something else: that a consensual relationship between a white woman and black man was not only possible but likely.[37]

---

[35] Bell v. State, 33 Tex. App. 163, 163 (1894); Ashworth v. State, 9 Tex. 490, 490 (1853); BUREAU OF THE CENSUS, U.S. DEP'T OF COMMERCE, POPULATION SCHEDULES OF THE SEVENTH CENSUS OF THE UNITED STATES; Jefferson County, Tex. at 246 (family #166) (Henderson Ashworth) (1850); *id.* at 234 (family #3) (Abner Ashworth); *id.* at 241 (family #107) (William Ashworth); *id.* Nacogdoches County, Tex., at 78 (family #344) (William Goyan); *id.* Ellis County, Tex., at 137 (family #2) (Edward and Alex Carter); Manuscript Census Returns, Schedule 1. – Free Inhabitants, McLennan County, Tex., *in* BUREAU OF THE CENSUS, U.S. DEP'T OF COMMERCE, POPULATION SCHEDULES OF THE EIGHTH CENSUS OF THE UNITED STATES, at 79 (family #515) (1860) (W.G. Hudson); Manuscript Census Returns, Schedule 1. – Inhabitants, Bexar County, Tex., *in* BUREAU OF THE CENSUS, U.S. DEP'T OF COMMERCE, POPULATION SCHEDULES OF THE TENTH CENSUS OF THE UNITED STATES, at 17 (family #157) (1880) (Louis Robinson); Manuscript Census Returns, Schedule 1. – Inhabitants, Harris County, Tex., *in* BUREAU OF THE CENSUS, U.S. DEP'T OF COMMERCE, POPULATION SCHEDULES OF THE TWELFTH CENSUS OF THE UNITED STATES, at 132 (family #115) (1900) (Edward Power); Brief of Appellant, Calhoun v. State, at 3.

[36] Transcript of Trial, State v. Calhoun, *supra* note 25, at 13 (testimony of W. F. Millwee); *id.* at 11 (testimony of T. E. King) ("I never saw any evidence there where any person had had a call of nature, or anything of that sort.").

[37] Transcript of Trial, State v. Calhoun, *supra* note 25, at 2–3 (verdict and judgment); Calhoun, 214 S.W. at 336, 339.

CONCLUSION

The stories retold here demonstrate the need to view interracial sex through a wide lens. In the decades before and after the Civil War, there is no doubt that sex between the races was used as a tool of violence, coercion, and patriarchal privilege. But searching out evidence from the margins – in the hot, humid air along the Colorado River, or in a logging camp north of Houston – reveals that interracial sex was also understood and tolerated as something more. These cases suggest that the rigid lines that white Southerners crafted to keep the races separate, physically and figuratively, sometimes broke down. When they did, members of local communities were forced to come together and refashion how they viewed themselves and the world in which they lived. Indeed, the Supreme Court's decision in *Loving v. Virginia* will be forever remembered as a bold step in rectifying racial relations. But of equal importance were the sentiments of Richard Loving, the man who married his childhood sweetheart, Mildred Jeter. "Mr. Cohen," he reportedly said to his lawyer, in words too often left out of most histories of interracial relations, "tell the Court I love my wife."

3

Loving in Indian Territory

Tribal Miscegenation Law in Historical Perspective

Carla D. Pratt

State antimiscegenation laws aimed to regulate white desire for black bodies in an effort to preserve white racial purity and ultimately white supremacy.[1] Facially, these laws did not regulate intimate relations when such relations involved only people of color. For example, state statutes typically did not preclude a Native-American person from marrying an African-American person. But a careful examination of the social and legal atmosphere that was created by state antimiscegenation laws reveals that these state laws did impact the desire of nonwhite people of color to marry black persons.

State miscegenation laws that ultimately permitted whites to marry Indians aided the assimilation of Indians into mainstream white America by operating as a form of racial rehabilitation. Indian assimilation, however, required more than Indians intermarrying with whites; it required the total indoctrination of Indians into the system of white supremacy. This meant that Indians needed to adopt white sexual mores, including the aversion to race mixing with blacks.

During the antebellum period, four of the tribes referred to by the federal government as the "Five Civilized Tribes" adopted miscegenation laws that attempted to preclude Indians from marrying or having sexual relations with blacks.[2] Through the regulation of Indian-black sexual relations, the tribes sought to avoid mixed-race offspring and thereby protect Indian identity from "corruption." Indians viewed themselves as a free and self-governing people, which was the basis for claiming tribal sovereignty. This view of self was in contradistinction to blacks who generally were not free, but bonded and without rights that the white man was bound to respect.

---

[1] *See generally*, Reginald Oh, *Regulating White Desire*, 2007 WISC. L. REV. 463 (2007).

[2] By the 1830s, the Choctaw, Cherokee, Chickasaw, and Creek tribes had codified slavery law. The Seminole tribe was governed by Creek law during this time, and remained subject to creek law until the two tribes entered a treaty in 1856 establishing the Seminole Nation as a separate and distinct Indian nation. Daniel F. Littlefield, Jr., AFRICANS AND SEMINOLES: FROM REMOVAL TO EMANCIPATION 174–75 (1977).

Tribal miscegenation laws regulating Indian-black relations sought to effectuate the racial preservation of "Indian" as a racial category separate and distinct from blacks for primarily two reasons: (1) to maintain the relatively privileged social and legal status of Indians as compared to blacks; and (2) to protect and maintain tribal sovereignty. Given the relatively privileged racial status of Indians, tribes established legal boundaries to ensure that Indian identity remained segregated from black identity. Through the adoption of such laws, the tribes gave yet another signal to whites that they were advancing toward civilization, and hence deserving of equality with whites.

NEGOTIATING RACIAL PRIVILEGE

During slavery, antiblack miscegenation laws protected the system of slavery by precluding a slave from escaping slavery through marriage. Moreover, "the ability of a slave to marry legally reinforced the humanity of individuals who were at once both property and human beings and fully neither."[3] Because slavery was race-based, it was necessary to determine who the law defined as "Negro" and therefore eligible to be enslaved. Race mixing frustrated the determination of racial identity, thereby complicating the law's ability to define and determine legal status.[4] Hence, laws designed to restrict race mixing served to strengthen the rigid boundaries between the races so that observers could readily determine an individual's status as "slave" or "free."

The Five Tribes ultimately became slaveholding nations, and it was in this context that they first enacted laws prohibiting miscegenation with blacks.[5] Miscegenation laws protected whites' and Indians' property interest in black bodies by helping ensure that slaves did not acquire the ability to escape slavery and "pass" undetected into American society.[6] The law prohibiting marriages between people of African descent and Indians also maintained the boundary between free Indians and bonded blacks, thereby maintaining the tribe's power to exercise sovereignty.

---

[3] Fay Yarbrough, *Legislating Women's Sexuality: Cherokee Marriage Laws in the Nineteenth Century*, 38 J. Soc. Hist. 385, 390 (2004).

[4] *See* Taunya Lovell Banks, *Unreconstructed* Mestizaje *and the Mexican Mestizo Self: No Hay Sangre Negra, So There Is No Blackness*, 15 S. Cal. Interdisc. L.J. 199, 211 (2006).

[5] The initial adoption of antiblack miscegenation laws by tribes was likely an act deemed necessary to preserve the institution of black slavery. Although the tribes' pre-removal form of slavery initially was different from slavery in the states, they gradually came more in line with their southern neighbors so that after removal, tribal laws institutionalizing slavery more closely resembled the slave codes of the southern states. Carla D. Pratt, *Tribes and Tribulations: Beyond Sovereign Immunity and Toward Reparation and Reconciliation for the Estelusti*, 11 Wash. & Lee Race & Ethnic Anc. L.J. 61, 75–96 (2005).

[6] *See* Randall Kennedy, Interracial Intimacies: Sex, Marriage, Identity, And Adoption 283–84 (2003) ("Passing is a deception that enables a person to adopt specific roles or identities from which

Tribal antiblack miscegenation laws served as evidence of the sexual assimilation of Indians. Both during and after the slavery era, the Five Tribes sought the privileges of whiteness by emulating whites or "acting white." They did this by modifying their form of government, their language, attire, religion, education, laws, and even who they married.[7] For example, Indians began to seek Euro-American education for their children. This was primarily achieved through Indian boarding schools established and operated by the federal government. These boarding schools "transformed" Indian children from their native culture to white American culture by teaching them a white Christian American curriculum in English, cutting their hair, and dressing them in white American attire.[8] This emulation of whiteness earned the Five Tribes the title of being "civilized," setting them apart from other "wild" Indians and making them even more acceptable as marriage partners for whites.

The extension of limited privilege to Indians is an example of what Professors Lani Guinier and Gerald Torres refer to as the "racial bribe."[9] Guinier and Torres describe the racial bribe as "a strategy that invites specific racial or ethnic groups to advance within the existing black-white racial hierarchy by becoming 'white.'"[10] By extending whiteness to those caught in the middle of the racial hierarchy of race, such as Latinos, the racial bribe seeks to accomplish four objectives: "(1) to defuse the previously marginalized group's oppositional agenda, (2) to offer incentives that discourage the group from affiliating with black people, (3) to secure high status for individual group members within existing hierarchies, and (4) to make the social position of 'whiteness' appear more racially or ethnically diverse."[11]

Essentially, whites offered to accept Indians into white American society and allow them to be semiautonomous, but only if Indians agreed to live how and where the dominant society wanted. According to this theory, whites offered the bribe, in part, to defuse the tribes' "oppositional agenda," which was to maintain an indigenous culture based on tribal customs that included communal land ownership in their homelands. The bribe not only required a significant level of assimilation by

he or she would otherwise be barred by prevailing social standards."); Angela Onwuachi-Willig, *Undercover Other*, 94 CAL. L.REV. 873 (2006); *see also*, Annette Gordon-Reed, THOMAS JEFFERSON AND SALLY HEMINGS: AN AMERICAN CONTROVERSY 53 (1997) (discussing Thomas Jefferson's emancipation of four slaves who were white enough in appearance to pass as white persons).

7 Theda Purdue, MIXED BLOOD INDIANS: RACIAL CONSTRUCTION IN THE EARLY SOUTH 53–56, 73, 87 (2005).

8 *See* Hayes Peter Mauro, MADE IN THE U.S.A.: AMERICANIZING AESTHETICS AT CARLISLE 190–213 (PhD dissertation, 2006) discussing the Carlisle Industrial Indian School in Carlisle, Pennsylvania. *See also*, Francis Paul Prucha, THE GREAT FATHER 687–700 (1995) (discussing Indian education by white Americans as the ultimate effort to reform and "civilize" the Indians).

9 Lani Guinier & Gerald Torres, THE MINER'S CANARY: ENLISTING RACE, RESISTING POWER, TRANSFORMING DEMOCRACY 224–25 (2002).

10 *Id.* at 225.

11 *Id.*

the Indians, but also their cooperation in maintaining the existing racial hierarchy. The bribe also enabled individual Indians to secure higher social and economic status through the opportunity to marry whites. In addition, these interracial marriages permitted Indians to impart the benefits of whiteness to their children[12] who could be received into white society as white but with Indian ethnicity. Individual Indians were also offered the opportunity to attend schools with curricula aimed at assimilating the Indian into white culture and preparing them for self-sustaining work in the white-dominated economic world[13] and the opportunity to participate in the growing plantation economy by exchanging their labor for compensation or by owning black slaves.

Intermarriage secured a higher status for some Indians within the existing racial hierarchy.[14] Moreover, Indian intermarriage with whites promoted America as a multiracial democracy. With some affluent Indians owning slaves and operating plantations, whites no longer appeared to be imposing a "racial dictatorship,"[15] but rather seemed willing to share social and economic status with other racial groups.

If the tribes had permitted individual Indians to marry blacks, the offspring from those unions would have been deemed "Negro" in the eyes of the states and the federal government. Hence such intermarriage with blacks could have erased the Indianness of the tribe, ultimately resulting in a loss of tribal sovereignty. Facing this choice, each of the tribes accepted the racial bribe and began emulating whites

[12] Cheryl I. Harris, *Whiteness as Property*, 106 HARV. L. REV. 1707, 1718 (1993) (describing some of the benefits associated with being white); *see also*, Stephanie M. Wildman, *The Persistence of White Privilege*, 18 WASH. U. J.L. & POL'Y 245 (2005); Peggy McIntosh, *White Privilege and Male Privilege: A Personal Account of Coming to See Correspondences Through Work in Women's Studies* (1988), *in* POWER PRIVILEGE AND LAW: A CIVIL RIGHTS READER 22–33 (Leslie Bender & Daan Braveman, eds. 1995) (chronicling the privileges of whiteness).

[13] *See* David Wallace Adams, EDUCATION FOR EXTINCTION: AMERICAN INDIANS AND THE BOARDING SCHOOL EXPERIENCE, 1875–1928, at 51–53 (1995).

[14] Claudio Saunt has opined that intermarriage with whites gave Indians the means and the will to become active participants in a slave economy. "Their [white] fathers gave them the skills – the ability to speak English, to read and write – and the desire to pursue wealth through slavery." Claudio Saunt, *A Conversation with Dr. Claudio Saunt*, 1 VOICES OF INDIAN TERRITORY 58, 60 (2005). Orlando Patterson has called this exchange of culture in interracial marriages "cultural dowries." *See* Orlando Patterson, *The Nexus Between Race and Policy: Interview with Orlando Patterson, Professor of Sociology at Harvard University* 4 GEO. PUBLIC POL'Y PEV. 107, 112 (1999).

[15] *See* Michael Omi & Howard Winant, RACIAL FORMATION IN THE UNITED STATES: FROM THE 1960S TO THE 1990S 65–66 (2d ed. 1994). Professors Michael Omi and Howard Winant describe the United States as a "racial dictatorship" from 1607 to 1865, because nonwhites were excluded from the political sphere. They list some consequences of this racial dictatorship, including defining American identity as white; organizing the color line as the fundamental division in American society; and creating an oppositional racial consciousness and organization, in which the identity of nonwhites was measured against the identity of whites, and nonwhites were lumped into overly broad categories that ignored cultural difference. For example, whites would see all Indians as one category, instead of differentiating between the Creek, Cherokee, or Choctaw.

in virtually every way they could. This necessarily meant adopting an antiblack bias and disassociating with blacks. This disassociation placed significant social distance between blacks and Indians and left the existing racial hierarchy in America unchallenged.

ADOPTING MISCEGENATION LAWS

Choctaw Law

As one might expect, the substance of tribal miscegenation law varied from tribe to tribe. Two common themes emerge, however. First, the tribes' internalization of the racialization of Indian identity is evident from the fact that these laws did not seek to regulate intertribal relations. Each tribe's miscegenation laws allowed Indian members of the tribe to marry an Indian from another tribe. This suggests that the tribes were more concerned with preserving Indianness in racial terms than they were with preserving their members' individual ethnic identity as, for example, Creek or Choctaw. Second, the tribes did not seek to ban Indian marriage to whites. The Choctaw Nation's miscegenation laws not only addressed intermarriage between Indians and blacks, but also attempted to prevent extramarital interracial sex with blacks. The 1838 Choctaw miscegenation law was entitled *An Act Prohibiting Any Choctaw Citizen From Cohabiting With a Slave* and provided

> that from and after the passage of this act, that if any person or persons, citizens of this Nation shall take up with a negro slave, he or she so offending shall be liable to pay a fine not less than ten dollars nor exceeding twenty-five dollars, and shall be separated. And for the second offence of a similar nature the party shall receive not exceeding thirty-nine lashes, nor less than five on the bare back, as the court may determine, and be separated.[16]

One might surmise from the language of the Choctaw Act that the law permitted cohabitation between a Choctaw citizen and a free "Negro," given that a literal interpretation would preclude only cohabitation between a Choctaw citizen and a "Negro slave." This assumption, however, may not be warranted. The Choctaw had adopted the dominant culture's view of blacks as an inferior people.

Another way to interpret the statute is to find that the tribes precluded any Choctaw citizen from cohabitating with a "Negro." For example, the Virginia statute that made slave status inheritable through the maternal ancestral line used the terms "Negro" and "slave" synonymously when stating that it was aimed at resolving doubts regarding "whether children got by any Englishman upon a Negro woman

---

[16] THE CONSTITUTION AND LAWS OF THE CHOCTAW NATION 27 (MISSION PRESS 1847).

should be slave or free." The Choctaw statute probably used the term "Negro slave" instead of "Negro" because there were likely no free Negroes living in the Choctaw Nation at that time. Even prior to the law mandating eviction of all free blacks, a freed black slave would likely migrate to Mexico, because slave catchers patrolled Indian country, kidnapped blacks, and sold them back into slavery.[17]

In theory, not all blacks were slaves. In practice, however, tribal law operated to virtually ensure that blacks living in the Choctaw Nation would be slaves by precluding their emancipation unless the slave's owner demonstrated that he was completely debt-free.[18] Even if the slave-owning Choctaw citizen did so, emancipation was not possible until the General Council of the Choctaw Nation passed an act setting the slave free. Moreover, once such an act was passed, Choctaw law required the freed slave to leave the Choctaw Nation within thirty days. If the freed slave failed to leave the Nation, or returned after leaving, the former slave would be subject to arrest by the Choctaw police and exposed to public sale for a five-year term of enslavement. By requiring all freed slaves to leave the Nation, the Choctaws demonstrated their intent to not have black citizens.[19]

Tribal banishment of free blacks restricted Indian access to black bodies, thereby reducing the chances that Indians would become sexual partners with blacks. This banishment may have informally occurred prior to codification into law, which may explain why tribal miscegenation law banned only cohabitation with a slave, instead of banning cohabitation with "Negroes." Because Choctaw law made it very difficult for a slave to become free – and ultimately precluded free blacks from residing in the Nation – the tribe's law prohibiting cohabitation only needed to ban cohabitation with a slave to effectuate an imperfect ban on sex between Choctaws and blacks.

Creek Law

The Creek Nation regulated interracial marriage between Indians and blacks in a peculiarly indirect manner. The Creek Nation first reduced its laws to writing in English in 1825. Prior to 1818, the leadership apparently retained all Creek law orally within the tribe, as was the custom with many indigenous American nations. The first English codification of the Creek miscegenation law is quite direct, perhaps

---

[17] Theda Purdue, Mixed Blood Indians: Racial Construction in the Early South 6 (2005).

[18] *See* Constitution and Laws of the Choctaw Nation § 5.

[19] Such laws restricted the potential for Indian-black interracial sex and romance, regardless of their intended purpose. Banishment laws for free blacks were not an indigenous invention; Virginia enacted a banishment law in 1806. *See* A. Leon Higginbotham, Jr. & F. Michael Higginbotham, *"Yearning to Breathe Free": Legal Barriers Against and Options in Favor of Liberty in Antebellum Virginia*, 68 N.Y.U. L. Rev. 1213, 1266 (1993). The Choctaw may have taken the idea for banishment of blacks from their neighboring slaveholding states.

owing to the simplicity an oral legal tradition required. Furthermore, it was silent with respect to Creek marriage to whites, and did not bar marriage between Indians and blacks. Instead, it acted as a strong deterrent by disinheriting offending Indians or divesting them of the possessions that their families had bestowed on them. The law provided that "if any of our people have children and either of the children should take a Negro as a husband or wife – and should Said child have a property given to it by his or her parent the property shall be taken from them and divided among the rest of the children as it is a disgrace to our Nation for our people to marry a Negro."[20]

The Creek's adoption of whites' belief that Indians occupied an elevated status over blacks on the racial hierarchy is evident from the concluding clause of the law. Also evident in this clause is the tribal leaders' concern that, because the human body stood for the national body in miscegenation discourse, the actions of an individual within the tribe could be imputed to the entire Nation. The imputation might also have been a result of the tribal leaders' awareness of the tendency of whites to attribute the conduct of individual Indians within the tribe to the entire race or the whole tribe.

The Creek's decision to disinherit those who married blacks indicates some respect for Creek free will. By refusing to criminalize interracial marriage, the law did not technically preclude Creeks from choosing who they married, but rather created a strong disincentive to marrying black.

The Nation's choice of disinheritance as punishment may have been rooted in a sophisticated understanding of the relationship between miscegenation and property. Indian marriage to blacks threatened the existing definitions and distributions of property. Black miscegenation was therefore an act against property, and given that most property was held communally by the tribe, an act against property was an act against the tribe. Moreover, the role of marriage was, in part, to keep land and material goods in the family, which necessarily meant keeping them in the tribe. Consequently, a property-based penalty for miscegenation protected Creek property interests. If permitted to lay claim to Creek possessions, an Indian-black couple would be able to convey their property interest to their offspring who, under state law (and possibly tribal law), would be defined as "Negro," not Indian. This would result in the potential transfer of Creek property out of the tribe and into the black community – a consequence that the Creek sought to avoid.

Despite the tribes' adoption of laws designed to prevent Indians from marrying blacks, interracial sexual relationships did occur. Missionaries and government agents who interacted with the tribes in the nineteenth century documented the presence of people with mixed Indian and African ancestry. Many of the Five Tribes'

---

[20] Antonio J. Waring, *Introduction*, in LAWS OF THE CREEK NATION 21 (Antonio J. Waring, ed., 1960).

former slaves recounted their experiences to government workers during the Great Depression. Many of these ex-slaves referenced their Indian ancestry when giving their accounts of life as a slave.[21] Historian Tiya Miles has also explored Indian-black sexual relations and mixed-race Indian-black identity in the Cherokee Nation through her study of the relationship between noted Cherokee war hero Shoe Boots and his African slave, Doll.[22] These contemporary examinations of Indian and black relations reveal that tribal antiblack miscegenation laws were not able to prevent the existence of mixed-race persons of Indian and black ancestry.

THE ROLE OF TRIBAL MISCEGENATION LAWS IN PROTECTING TRIBAL SOVEREIGNTY

The fact that the tribes permitted their members to marry whites reveals that the tribes did not desire to maintain the identity of "Indian" as a pure racial category void of all other racial categories. This is probably because whiteness had socially elevating effects on Indians without any corrupting effect on Indian identity. In other words, Indians could marry with whites for generations and become white in appearance, thereby attaining all of the privileges of whiteness, yet still not lose the capacity to claim an Indian identity. Tribal miscegenation laws were exclusively anti-black in nature because they only sought to protect Indian identity from the racial category that possessed the power to strip Indians of their Indianness and therefore their sovereignty. The only racial category with that level of corruptibility was, of course, the black or "Negro" category. Accordingly, tribal miscegenation laws only needed to proscribe Indian-black marriage and sex in order to ensure the continued existence of Indian identity.

Tribal leaders, however, likely understood that whites perceived individual Indians not merely as members of an autonomous political community, but also in racialized terms. Federal Indian law – with which tribal leaders were undoubtedly familiar – reflected whites' racialized perception of individual Indian identity. The U.S. government had jurisdiction over a person charged with a crime committed in Indian territory, unless that person fell within the "Indian exception,"

---

[21] *See, e.g.,* BLACK INDIAN SLAVE NARRATIVES (Patrick Minges ed., 2004); Celia E. Naylor-Ojurongbe, *"Born and Raised Among These People, I Don't Want to Know Any Other": Slaves' Acculturation in Nineteenth-Century Indian Territory, in* CONFOUNDING THE COLOR LINE: THE INDIAN-BLACK EXPERIENCE IN NORTH AMERICA 161 (James F. Brooks ed., 2002) (examining the black Indian slave narratives from a historical perspective); THE WPA OKLAHOMA SLAVE NARRATIVES 440 (T. Lindsay Baker & Julie P. Baker eds., 1996); *see also* Fay A. Yarbrough, *Power, Perception, and Interracial Sex: Former Slaves Recall a Multiracial South,* 71 H. S. HIST. 559 (2005).

[22] Tiya Miles, TIES THAT BIND: THE STORY OF AN AFRO-CHEROKEE FAMILY IN SLAVERY AND FREEDOM, at xiii (2005).

which excluded "crimes committed by one Indian against the person or property of another Indian."[23]

One of the first cases to define individual Indian identity in racialized terms was *United States v. Rogers*.[24] William Rogers, a white man, was indicted for the murder of another white man; the crime allegedly occurred in the Cherokee Nation. Rogers claimed that both he and his victim were Indian and, therefore, the circuit court lacked personal jurisdiction. Rogers based this claim on the fact that he had lived among the Cherokee Indians within the geographic boundaries of the tribe for many years, had married a Cherokee woman, and had children with her. Furthermore, Rogers had renounced his U.S. citizenship and the Cherokee tribe adopted him as a full member, granting him all the rights and privileges of a natural-born Cherokee.

In interpreting the statute, the Court had to give meaning to Congress's use of "Indian." In doing so, the Court revealed its conception of Indian identity as a race, and not merely a political community. The Court interpreted the Indian exception as "confined to those who by the usages and customs of the Indians are regarded as belonging to their race. It does not speak of members of a tribe, but of the race generally."[25] Without referencing the legislative history of the Act, or the meaning of the term "Indian" in other statutes, the Court held that Rogers was not "Indian" as that term was used in the statute. The Court stated that it was "very clear, that a white man who at mature age is adopted in an Indian tribe does not thereby become an Indian, and was not intended to be embraced in the exception."[26] Thus, as early as 1846, the Supreme Court articulated a conception of "Indian" as a racial identity rather than a political identity grounded in tribal membership.

This racialization of Indian people further destabilized tribal sovereignty by imposing an identity on indigenous people that they may not have chosen for themselves. In fact, the *Rogers* opinion suggests that the tribe had not chosen a racialized conception of "Indian" because it had adopted Rogers as a member of the "Indian family" despite the fact that he was racially "white."

Federal law also defined "Indian" in racial terms by requiring a sufficient quantum of "Indian blood." Paul Spruhan, an expert in federal Indian law, found that the earliest use of blood quantum arose in the context of colonial law seeking to define the status of mixed-race individuals.[27] In 1866, Virginia extended blood quantum to define Indian as "every person, not a colored person, having one-fourth or more

---

[23] Act of June 30, 1834, ch. 161, 4 Stat. 729 (1834) (titled "An Act to Regulate Trade and Intercourse with the Indian Tribes, and to Preserve the Peace of the Frontiers").

[24] United States v. Rogers, 45 U.S. (4 How.) 567, 571 (1846).

[25] *Id.* at 573.

[26] *Id.* at 572–73.

[27] *See* Paul Spruhan, *A Legal History of Blood Quantum in Federal Indian Law to 1935*, 51 S.D. L. Rev. 5 (2006).

of Indian blood."[28] This definition confirms that having African ancestry, or being deemed "colored," negated one's ability to claim an Indian identity. In an effort to ascertain the rights of mixed-blood Indians of European and Indian ancestry, blood quantum was used in treaties between the federal government and various Indian tribes between 1817 and 1871. By the early twentieth century, Indians were beginning to think of themselves in racialized terms. This is evident from the discourse of some tribal leaders who "themselves used the language of blood and descent to debate how to define [tribal] membership."[29]

The leadership of the Five Tribes understood the dominant society's racial ideology – that an individual's appearance as black heavily influenced whites' willingness to perceive and accept an individual as Indian. They may also have understood that the surrounding states constructed black racial identity in terms of hypodescent, which meant that any known African ancestry could relegate an individual to the status of "Negro." Thus, Indians understood that mixing with blacks could have a corrupting effect on Indian identity and potentially destroy it.

Hence, Indians sought to protect Indian identity from the corrupting effects of blackness. One way to do this was through laws prohibiting race mixing between Indians and blacks. Indian leaders likely predicted that whites would apply the eugenic notion of racial identity to mixed-race Indians. In the nineteenth century, the dominant social understanding of mixed-race children was that they inherited the status of the racially inferior parent.

The Five Tribes understood that the southern states surrounding them would classify an individual with mixed Indian and Negro "blood" in accordance with state race classification laws. This meant that the physical appearance of individual Indians could subject them to being classified as "Negro." For example, slave catchers mistook many dark-skinned Narragansett Indians for escaped slaves. In response, the Narragansett tribe issued membership certificates so that individuals could easily prove that they were Indian. Even in a post-slavery environment, Indians had an incentive to maintain racial distance between themselves and blacks to protect themselves from the indignities of Jim Crow.

MISCEGENISTIC EXCEPTIONALISM

The racial integrity law at issue in *Loving* was an example of "miscegenistic exceptionalism"[30] because it excepted certain "white Indians." Thus, the offer of acceptance

---

[28] *Id.* (citing Act of Feb. 27, 1866, ch. 17, § 1, 1866 Va. Acts 84, 84).

[29] *Id.* at 11 n.75.

[30] Kevin Noble Maillard, *The Pocahontas Exception: American Indians and Exceptionalism in Antimiscegenation Law*, 12 MICH. J. RACE & L. 107 (2007).

into white society was extended only to Indians who had no African ancestry. To maintain the status of acceptable marriage partners for whites, Indians had to maintain their "racial virginity" by preserving their status as chaste, African-less beings. The demand for racial virginity by Indians is evident in Virginia's racial integrity law, which not only regulated marriage, but also regulated racial classification by giving the Secretary of Vital Statistics the power to "classify all Virginia Indians as 'Negroes.'"[31] The Secretary, Walter Plecker, had famously denied the existence of Indians in the state and argued that all Virginia Indians had intermarried with blacks for generations and therefore had become black or "Negro." Plecker felt the need to protect whites from the black blood carried by Virginia Indians. Thus, he reviewed generations of "vital records, identifying all surnames listed as anything other than 'White' ... and then directed all county clerks to make sure that any citizens bearing these surnames were classified as 'Negro.'"[32] Plecker particularly targeted the Monacan tribe, altering their birth records to reflect a racial designation of "Negro." Plecker's campaign of racial reclassification had a severe effect not only on the Monacans, who neither the state nor federal government recognized as a sovereign Indian tribe, but on all Indians residing in Virginia. Because Plecker and others viewed Virginian Indians as racial degenerates, contaminated by black blood, Virginia's segregation laws were enforced to preclude Indian children from attending schools with white children and white churches began to exclude Indians from worship services.[33]

THE LEGACY OF TRIBAL MISCEGENATION LAWS

Today, the Five Tribes no longer have laws proscribing intermarriage with blacks, but the legacy of tribal antiblack miscegenation laws still lingers. Ideologies regarding reverence for lighter skin and aversion to African skin continue to inform contemporary marriage choices for Indians. Indeed, as one scholar aptly noted, "the number of Indian-black marriages remains low ... indicat[ing] a potential racial boundary between blacks and Indians as deep as that between whites and blacks."[34]

Despite tribal efforts to socially distance Indians and blacks, intermarriage and sexual relations nevertheless occurred. The result of this defiance of miscegenation

[31] Samuel R. Cook, *The Monacan Indian Nation: Asserting Tribal Sovereignty in the Absence of Federal Recognition*, 17 WICAZO SA REV. 91, 97 (2002).

[32] *Id.* at 98.

[33] Laura L. Lovett, *"African and Cherokee by Choice": Race and Resistance Under Legalized Segregation*, 22 AM. INDIAN Q. 203, 220 (1998).

[34] Ann McMullen, *Blood and Culture: Negotiating Race in Twentieth Century Native England*, in CONFOUNDING THE COLOR LINE: THE INDIAN-BLACK EXPERIENCE IN NORTH AMERICA 268 (James F. Brooks ed., 2002).

law was that the tribes and federal government constructed the social and legal identity of many mixed-raced Indians as black. In doing so, the tribes, in partnership with the federal government, tried to erase the memory of what law could not successfully prevent: black Indians.

In recent years, some descendants of slaves owned by Indians (freedmen) have sued their tribe or the federal government attempting to claim their Indian heritage and obtain tribal membership. Many of these recent challenges, however, have been based on the freedmen's right to tribal citizenship provided under post–Civil War treaties between the tribes and the U.S. government, not on claims of having Indian blood. The freedmen's non-blood approach to tribal inclusion is necessitated by the fact that most freedmen descendants are unable to prove a blood connection to the tribe within the established legal structure. This is because the Dawes Commission, an agency of the federal government, operated within the parameters of then-existing race law when it created the official list of "real Indians" and therefore failed to record many freedmen's Indian ancestry during the process of compiling the rolls, instead logging them as "just black."

The tribes, as the dominant parties in these disputes, are perpetuating the political myth that, prior to *Loving*, Indian identity was African-less. This myth manifests itself in the disputes' focus on the freedmen's blackness and past slave status, thus operating to ignore many freedmen descendants' Native-American ancestry and obfuscating the racial inconsistencies of the Dawes Rolls. By focusing the public consciousness on the freedmen's blackness and their ancestral slave status, the tribes construct the freedmen descendants as identity opportunists seeking to shed the stigma of blackness and capitalize on the extant economic gains of Indian nations.

The freedmen descendants who assert that they have Indian ancestry or "blood" are challenging the racial ideology that dictates that the right to claim a multiracial identity is reserved to those people born of legally endorsed post-*Loving* unions, and not from some more remotely contributed Indian ancestry. These freedmen reject the notion that contributions of multiracial ancestry must be interpreted in accordance with the rules of race that governed at the time their ancestors engaged in race mixing. Instead, they are embracing a conception of Indian identity grounded in notions of actuality rather than what was legally possible at the time. The freedmen descendants who claim Indian ancestry boldly remind their tribes that in a world that professes racial equality, a post-*Loving* adjudication of whether a black person is Indian should not be based on a pre-*Loving* conception of racial identity.

CONCLUSION

An examination of tribal miscegenation laws yields a deeper understanding of both the laws at issue in *Loving* and racial identity in America. Despite the fact that state miscegenation statutes did not technically apply to Indian tribes, they had a powerful influence on tribal law. As "domestic dependent sovereigns" with limited power, the tribes had little choice but to conform their laws to the dominant legal paradigm. In doing so, they played a crucial role in the dominant society's efforts to maintain the boundaries of racial categories, thereby maintaining the established racial hierarchy. Whites allowed Indians to maintain tribal sovereignty, but only if Indians became participants in the efforts to maintain a racial hierarchy with blacks on the bottom. In the process, Indians managed to protect themselves from the stigma of blackness, and perhaps from extinction, but at significant costs to blacks. In short, tribal miscegenation laws were an important component of the effort to define Indian identity as African-less.

   The tribes' alignment with whites continues to impact the thousands of people of African ancestry who, but for racially discriminatory laws of racial assignment that existed in the past, would have their racial and political identity as Indians recognized by law. These people are presently excluded by the tribes' rigid adherence to the validity of unconstitutional miscegenation laws. The legacy of sexual assimilation of Native Americans contributes to the contemporary disconnect between the Five Tribes and their freedmen descendants. Through the project of sexual assimilation, whites imparted to indigenous people not only whiteness, but also the dominant society's attitudes toward blackness. It remains to be seen whether the tribes will continue to hold on to the notions of self that were generated through the project of sexual assimilation, or whether they will exercise their sovereignty to challenge racial hierarchy and forge new meanings of Indian identity independent of pre-*Loving* conceptions of indigenous people.

4

American Mestizo

Filipinos and Antimiscegenation Laws in California

Leti Volpp

In 1933, the California Court of Appeals was faced with the following question: Should a Filipino be considered a "Mongolian"?[1] Salvador Roldan, a Filipino man, and Marjorie Rogers, a white woman, had applied for a license to marry. Was this marriage acceptable under the state's antimiscegenation laws, which prohibited marriages between "whites" and "Mongolians"?[2] This chapter explores the legal history of prohibition of marriages of whites to Filipinos in the state of California and, in so doing, seeks to reshape the terrain of antimiscegenation laws. The exploration of this history is important given the paucity of legal writing about the Filipina/o-American community and about miscegenation laws targeting Asian Americans in general.[3]

I am particularly interested in complicating how we understand antimiscegenation efforts as they relate to race, gender, class, and sexuality. I also aim to underscore how colonialism and immigration law have shaped our understanding of identity and interracial relationships. By examining the history of antagonism directed against Filipinos in California in the 1920s and 1930s, this chapter illuminates how antagonism against Asians, while economic in its roots, reached

---

[1] Roldan v. Los Angeles County, 129 Cal. App. 267, 268, 18 P.2d 706, 707 (1933). While Roldan's first name was spelled "Solvador" in the legal proceedings, his signature in the case file spells his name "Salvador."

[2] See CAL. CIV. CODE § 69 (1906) (amended 1937, 1959) (prohibiting issuance of license authorizing marriage of "a white person with a negro, mulatto, or mongolian"); CAL. CIV. CODE § 60 (1906) (amended 1937, repealed 1959) (making marriages of "white persons with negroes, Mongolians, or mulattoes ... illegal and void"); Roldan, 129 Cal. App. at 268, 18 P.2d at 707.

[3] Whether to use the term "Asian American" or "Asian Pacific American" is a question fraught with political significance. See J. Kehaulani Kauanui & Ju Hui "Judy" Han, "Asian Pacific Islander": Issues of Representation and Responsibility, in THE VERY INSIDE: AN ANTHOLOGY OF WRITING BY ASIAN & PACIFIC ISLANDER LESBIAN AND BISEXUAL WOMEN 37 (Sharon Lim-Hing ed., 1994) (cautioning against irresponsible uses of "Asian Pacific" or "Asian Pacific Islander" that engulf concerns of Pacific Islanders within those of Asian Americans).

its most fevered pitch concerning Filipino relations with white women. This anxiety led to various efforts to classify Filipinos under the state's antimiscegenation statute as "Mongolian," so they would be prohibited from marrying whites.
As this chapter argues, we can understand these efforts as attempts to shift the
legal entitlements bundled with the marriage contract away from Filipino men,
symbolizing the desire to deny Filipinos membership in the national political
community.

CALIFORNIA: ASIAN INVASIONS

Although the focus of this chapter is the experience of Filipinos in California, it is
important to briefly note what occurred nationally. By the time the Supreme Court
finally declared antimiscegenation laws unconstitutional in *Loving v. Virginia*, thirty-
nine states had enacted antimiscegenation laws; in sixteen of these states, such laws
were still in force at the time of the decision.[4] While the original focus of these laws
was primarily on relationships between blacks and whites, also prohibited were marriages between whites and "Indians" (meaning Native Americans), "Hindus" (South
Asians), "Mongolians" (into which were generally lumped Chinese, Japanese, and
Koreans), and "Malays" (Filipinos). Nine states – Arizona, California, Georgia,
Maryland, Nevada, South Dakota, Utah, Virginia, and Wyoming – passed laws that
prohibited whites from marrying Malays.[5]

In 1850, California enacted a law prohibiting marriages between "white persons" and "negroes or mulattoes."[6] Twenty-eight years later, a referendum was
proposed at the California Constitutional Convention to amend the statute to
prohibit marriages between Chinese and whites.[7] While the so-called Chinese
problem was initially conceptualized as one of economic competition, created
by the importation of exploitable laborers without political rights, the issue of
sexual relationships between whites and Chinese also functioned as a prime site
of hysteria.[8]

---

[4] *See Loving v. Virginia*, 388 U.S. 1, 6–7 n.5 (1967).
[5] For citations to specific code sections, see Leti Volpp, *American Mestizo: Filipinos and Antimiscegenation
     Law*, 33 UC DAVIS L. REV. 795, 799 n.18–19 (2000).
[6] *See* Act Regulating Marriages, ch. 140, 1850 Cal. Stat. 494 (codified as CAL. CODE § 35 [1853]) ("All
     marriages of white persons with negroes or mulattoes are declared to be illegal and void.").
[7] *See* Megumi Dick Osumi, *Asians and California's Anti-Miscegenation Laws*, in ASIAN AND PACIFIC
     AMERICAN EXPERIENCE: WOMEN'S PERSPECTIVES 1, at 5–6 (Nobuya Tsuchida ed., 1982) (examining
     referendum proposed at the California Constitutional Convention to proscribe marriages between
     whites and Chinese).
[8] *See* Ronald Takaki, IRON CAGES: RACE AND CULTURE IN 19TH CENTURY AMERICA 215–49 (1990 ed.,
     1979) (describing the role of industrialists in creating a "permanently degraded caste labor force" and
     the response by the labor movement in California that fostered the anti-Chinese movement).

Invoked were fears of hybridity. John Miller, a state delegate, speculated that the "lowest most vile and degraded" of the white race were most likely to amalgamate with the Chinese, resulting in a "hybrid of the most despicable, a mongrel of the most detestable that has ever afflicted the earth."[9] Some argued that American institutions and culture would be overwhelmed by the habits of people thought to be sexually promiscuous, perverse, lascivious, and immoral.[10] For example, in 1876, various newspapers stated that Chinese men attended Sunday school in order to debauch their white, female teachers. In response to the articulation of these fears, in 1880, the legislature prohibited the licensing of marriages between "Mongolians" and "white persons."[11]

The next large group of Asian immigrants – those from Japan – was also the subject of antagonism, leading to further amendment of the antimiscegenation laws. While the impetus for tension was, again, economic, two prime sites of expressed anxiety were school segregation and intermarriage. Those who sought school segregation depicted the Japanese as an immoral and sexually aggressive group of people, and disseminated propaganda that warned that Japanese students would defile their white classmates.[12] The *Fresno Republican* described miscegenation between whites and the Japanese as a form of "international adultery," in a conflation of race, gender, and nation.[13] In 1905, at the height of the anti-Japanese movement, the state legislature sealed the breach between the license and marriage laws and invalidated all marriages between "Mongolian" and white spouses.[14]

"LITTLE BROWN MEN"

Tension over the presence of Chinese and Japanese had led to immigration exclusion of Chinese and Japanese laborers through a succession of acts dating between 1882 and 1924. Because industrialists and growers faced a resulting labor shortage, they began to import Filipinos to Hawaii and the mainland United States.[15] Classified as

[9] Osumi, *supra* note 7, at 6 (citing I DEBATES AND PROCEEDINGS OF THE CONSTITUTIONAL CONVENTION OF CALIFORNIA, 1878–79, at 632 [Sacramento State Office, 1880]).

[10] Robert S. Chang, *Dreaming in Black and White: Racial-Sexual Policing in the Birth of a Nation, the Cheat, and Who Killed Vincent Chin?*, 5 ASIAN L.J. 41, 57–58 (1998).

[11] *See* 1880 Cal Stat. Ch. 41, Sec. 1, p. 3; Osumi, *supra* note 7, at 8.

[12] *See* Osumi, *supra* note 7, at 13. Osumi has written that anti-Japanese spokesmen warned that Japanese students knew "no morals but vice, who sit beside our sons and daughters in our public schools that they may help to debauch, demoralize and teach them the vices which are the customs of the country whence they come." *Id.*

[13] *Id.* For theorizing on the relation between race, gender, and the nation state see ROBERT S. CHANG, DISORIENTED: ASIAN AMERICANS, LAW AND THE NATION STATE 123–35 (1999).

[14] *See* CAL. CIV. CODE § 60 (1906) ("All marriages of white persons with negroes, Mongolians, or mulattoes are illegal and void.")

[15] For further exploration of the history of migration of Filipinos/as, see Luciano Mangiafico, CONTEMPORARY AMERICAN IMMIGRANTS: PATTERNS OF FILIPINO, KOREAN, AND CHINESE SETTLEMENT

"American nationals," because the United States had annexed the Philippines follow-ing the Filipino-American War, Filipinos were allowed entry into the country. On the mainland, a majority of Filipinos resided in California, with sizable numbers also in Washington and Alaska.[16] By 1930, the number of Filipinos on the mainland reached more than 45,000. During the winter, they stayed in the cities – working as domestics and gardeners, washing dishes in restaurants, and doing menial tasks others refused. In the summer, they moved back to the fields and harvested potatoes, strawberries, lettuce, sugar beets, and fruits. Filipinos were kept segregated from other immigrant groups in an attempt to prevent the formation of multiethnic labor unions,[17] but ended up spearheading labor organizing in Hawaii and on the mainland.[18] Subsequently, the same economic antagonism that was at the base of the anti-Chinese and anti-Japanese movements was turned against Filipinos. But the primary source of antago-nism appeared to be linked, even more dramatically, to sex. This became particularly evident in violence and riots that centered on dance halls where Filipinos could pay ten cents to dance one minute with hired dancers, usually white women.[19]

Anti-Filipino spokesmen also raged about the evils of intermarriage. The Northern Monterey Chamber of Commerce charged, "[i]f the present state of affairs continues there will be 40,000 half-breed[s] in California before ten years have passed."[20] Two representatives from the Commonwealth Club and the President of the Immigration Study Commission warned of "race mingling" that would create a "new type of mulatto," an "American Mestizo."[21]

IN THE UNITED STATES 31 (1988); Renato Constantino, *The Miseducation of the Filipino, in* THE FILIPINOS IN THE PHILIPPINES AND OTHER ESSAYS 39 (1966), excerpted *in* THE PHILIPPINES READER: A HISTORY OF COLONIALISM, NEOCOLONIALISM, DICTATORSHIP, AND RESISTANCE 45, 47 (Daniel B. Schirmer & Stephen Rosskamm Shalom, eds. 1987) [hereinafter THE PHILIPPINES READER]. During the 1920s, more than 65,000 men, 5,000 women, and 3,000 children came to Hawaii under contract. By the mid-1920s, Filipinos comprised half of all plantation workers in Hawaii and 75% by 1930. With the Great Depression, many of these workers were repatriated to the Philippines. *See* Mangiafico, *supra* note 15, at 34.

[16] *See* Takaki, *supra* note 8, at 315–24 (discussing the annexation of the Philippines and explaining that between 1910 and 1930, the Filipino population in California jumped from 5 to 30,470).

[17] *See* Mangiafico, *supra* note 15, at 35–36 (explaining the various jobs Filipinos held in the 1930s).

[18] *See* Takaki, *supra* note 8, at 321–24.

[19] *See* Rhacel Salazar Parreñas, *"White Trash" Meets the "Little Brown Monkeys": The Taxi Dance Hall as a Site of Interracial and Gender Alliances Between White Working Class Women and Filipino Immigrant Men in the 1920s and 30s,* 24 AMERASIA J. 115 (1998); *Ministers Protest Filipino Dance Hall,* S.F. CHRON., Oct. 5, 1934, at 21 (reporting protest in San Jose of dance hall allegedly threatening mor-als of neighborhood); *see also, Dancing Partners May Be Had at One Dime per Dance,* L.A. TIMES, May 10, 1925 (describing dance halls where women dance from eight until midnight and engage in from sixty to one hundred dances each night; out of the 10-cent ticket purchased for each short whirl around the floor, "the girl receives five cents").

[20] *See* THE PHILIPPINES READER, *supra* note 15, at 59–60.

[21] *See* Osumi, *supra* note 7, at 18 (citing COMMONWEALTH CLUB, TRANSACTIONS 24, at 341 (1929); C. M. Goethe, *Filipino Immigration Viewed as Peril,* CURRENT HISTORY 353–56 [1931]).

There appears to have been a greater level of tension felt about Filipino male sexuality than about that of Chinese and Japanese men. While Chinese and Japanese were also considered sexually depraved – and, perhaps, more sexually perverse – Filipinos appeared to be specifically characterized as having an enormous sexual appetite, as more savage, as more primitive, as "one jump from the jungle."[22] Their sexual desires were thought to focus on white women.[23]

A possible reason for any sexual differentiation of Filipino men from Chinese or Japanese men was the link to Spanish colonialism. Some contemporary writers suggested that there was greater focus on Filipino male sexuality than that of the Chinese and Japanese populations because of the skewed sex ratio in who immigrated: with few Filipinas around, Filipino men turned to dance halls and dance girls for company. And whereas more Japanese women were able to immigrate to the United States, the Chinese population was, like the Filipino one, heavily male.[24] What may have been different between the Chinese and Filipino male immigrant populations was their behavior: Chinese men did not set up dance halls with white taxi dancers, perhaps reflecting a change in what hovered at the limits of tolerable behavior between 1880 and 1920, both for Asian men and for white women.[25] Filipinos may also have spurred controversy because of a stronger sense of entitlement to their rights and a greater willingness to engage in confrontation, stemming from their identity as colonial subjects, schooled in the idea that they were "nationals" of the United States.[26] This history suggests there were and are qualitative differences in racial sexualization among Asian Americans. What is clear is that generalizing across diverse experiences is too limited.

LEGAL CHALLENGES

The right of Filipinos to intermarry was not seriously challenged in California until the early 1920s. As Filipino immigration increased, county clerks were faced with the question of deciding whether to issue marriage licenses to Filipinos, in essence choosing whether or not to classify Filipinos as "Mongolians." The County Counsel of Los Angeles advised in 1921 that Filipinos were not "Mongolians." The opinion reasoned that at the time of enactment of antimiscegenation legislation in 1905, there was a "Chinese problem," and that the statutory inclusion of "Mongolian"

---

[22] H. Brett Melendy, ASIANS IN AMERICA: FILIPINOS, KOREANS AND EAST INDIANS 59 (1977).
[23] *See, Free Blames Sex in Filipino Row*, S.F. CHRON., Sept. 16, 1930, at 3.
[24] *See* Sucheng Chan, ASIAN AMERICANS: AN INTERPRETIVE HISTORY, at 103–09 (1991).
[25] Ronald Takaki asserts that men from the Philippines seemed to seek out white female companionship and to be attractive to white women to a greater degree than men from China, Japan, Korea, and India. *See* Takaki, *supra* note 8, at 328.
[26] I am indebted to Rachel Moran for this suggestion.

was intended to refer only to the "yellow" and not the "brown" people. The opinion further noted that choosing not to classify Filipinos as Mongolians rested on the assumption that the problem under consideration involved a Filipino who belonged to one of the Malay tribes, and who was not "a Negrito or in part Chinaman."[27] This opinion letter appears to have been followed by the Los Angeles County Clerk, L. E. Lampton, in granting marriage licenses, until 1930.

In the meantime, tension over relationships between Filipinos and white women was heightened in the wake of the *California v. Yatko* case, which took place in 1925 in Los Angeles.[28] Timothy Yatko, a Filipino waiter, had married Lola Butler, a white woman, in San Diego. The couple had met at a dance hall in Los Angeles and lived together after their marriage until Butler left Yatko. She worked as a singer and a dancer in a girl show where Harry Kidder, who was white, also worked as a substitute piano player. Yatko spotted the two together and when he saw Kidder kissing his wife in Kidder's apartment, he stabbed Kidder, who died.[29] In the murder trial, the state collaterally attacked the legality of the marriage in order to permit Lola Butler to testify against Yatko. Counsel for the state contended that the marriage was void because Yatko was Filipino, and therefore "Mongolian." The court was asked to rule on the racial classification of Filipinos because there was no earlier decision on the subject. Contemporary accounts referred to the antimiscegenation statute as what was, at that point in time, "an old and almost forgotten State law."[30]

In arguing the point of whether or not Yatko should be considered a "Mongolian," counsel cited ethnologists, the encyclopedia, and various federal decisions in naturalization cases. Counsel for the state discussed the evil effects of miscegenation generally, and pointed to Mexico as a specific example of the effects of race mixture. "We see the result that the Mexican nation had not had the standing, had not the citizens as it would otherwise if it had remained pure." This reference to purity, not surprisingly, was intended to describe the Spanish colonizers, not indigenous people, for counsel went on to state that "when the white people, or the Caucasians, came to the United States they did not intermarry with the Indians, they kept themselves pure."

---

[27] Nellie Foster, *Legal Status of Filipino Intermarriage in California*, 16 SOC. & SOC. RES. 447–48 (1932), reprinted in ASIAN INDIANS, FILIPINOS, OTHER ASIAN COMMUNITIES AND THE LAW 5 (Charles McClain ed., 1994).

[28] *See id.* at 444–45 (citing California v. Yatko, No. 24795, Superior Court of Los Angeles County, May 11, 1925); *Filipino Pleads Unwritten Law in Murder Case*, L.A. TIMES, May 4, 1925, at 18 [hereinafter *Unwritten Law*]. Foster's article contains significant material not contained in the Los Angeles County records of the case.

[29] *See Unwritten Law, supra* note 28, at 2.

[30] *See Old Law Invoked on Yatko*, L.A. TIMES, May 6, 1925, at 5; *Unwritten Law, supra* note 28, at 2.

The judge agreed. He stated:

[T]he dominant race of the country has a perfect right to exclude all other races from equal rights with its own people and to prescribe such rights as they may possess. ... Our government is in control of a large body of people of the insular possessions, for whom it is acting as a sort of guardian and it has extended certain rights and privileges to them. ... Here we see a large body of young men, ever-increasing, working amongst us, associating with our citizens, all of whom are under the guardianship and to some extent the tutelage of our national government, and for whom we feel the deepest interest, of course, naturally ... the question ought to be determined whether or not they can come into this country and intermarry with our American girls or bring their Filipino girls here to intermarry with our American men, if that situation should arise.

The judge alluded several times to his long residence in the South, and shared his "full conviction" that:

[The] Negro race will become highly civilized and become one of the great races only if it proceeds within its own lines marked out by Nature and keeps its blood pure. And I have the same feeling with respect to other races. ... I am quite satisfied in my own mind ... that the Filipino is a Malay and that the Malay is a Mongolian, just as much as the white American is of the Teutonic race, the Teutonic family, or of the Nordic family, carrying it back to the Aryan family. Hence, it is my view that under the code of California as it now exists, intermarriage between a Filipino and a Caucasian would be void.[31]

Accordingly, the court allowed Lola Butler to testify. She represented Yatko "as the aggressor and Kidder as her chivalric defender."[32] Yatko was convicted and sentenced to serve a life sentence in San Quentin.[33]

LOS ANGELES CIVIL CASES AND LEGISLATIVE RESPONSE

The opinion of the judge in the *Yatko* case, that Filipinos, or Malays, were Mongolian, was shared by the Attorney General of the State of California, U. S. Webb.[34] In 1926, Webb authored an opinion letter stating that "Malays belong to the

---

[31] Foster, *supra* note 27, at 445–46. While mention was made of the fact that Yatko's paternal grandfather was half Chinese – in other words, that Yatko was one-eighth Chinese – this did not lead the judge to rule on that basis that Yatko was "Mongolian." *See id.* at 445–46.

[32] *Unwritten Law, supra* note 28, at 2.

[33] *See* Foster, *supra* note 27, at 444; *Life Sentence to Be Imposed on Yatko Today*, L.A. TIMES, May 11, 1925, at 17; *Life Term for Filipino Slayer*, L.A. TIMES, May 9, 1925, at 2. Yatko appealed his conviction, principally on the grounds of the decision to allow Lola Butler to testify. The appeal was denied. *See Deny Filipino New Trial in Kidder Murder*, L.A. TIMES, May 12, 1925, at 5.

[34] Webb subsequently testified for Filipino exclusion in 1929 Commonwealth Club forums and the 1930 Congressional hearings. *See* Osumi, *supra* note 7, at 18.

Mongoloid race." The letter was in response to an inquiry from the District Attorney of San Diego County, who wondered whether the San Diego County Clerk should issue marriage licenses to "Hindus and white persons and to Filipinos and white persons." Webb called this "more a question of fact than one of law," noted that he was unable to find any judicial determination of these questions, and proceeded to share the prevailing ethnology of the day. While "the Hindu," reported Webb, generally did not appear ethnologically to be a member of the Mongolian race, "Malays" were indeed so classified. While the first "great ethnologist," Blumenbach, had divided the human race into five classes (white, black, yellow, brown, and red), the "most recent and best recognized variation" reduced the classification to three divisions by combining brown and red with the Mongolian in a division generally referred to as "Mongolian-Malay or yellow-brown."[35] While Webb's letter was written to influence the action of counties, it was not binding, and the reaction of county clerks appears to have been mixed.[36]

The analysis in Webb's letter was embraced by a Los Angeles superior court judge, who issued the first of five decisions on this question. These five cases appear to be the only litigation – other than as collaterally raised in *Yatko* – on the question of whether Filipinos were Mongolian for purposes of the state's antimiscegenation law.[37] In this first case, a white woman, Ruby F. Robinson, sought to wed a Filipino named Tony V. Moreno. Robinson's mother filed a suit against Los Angeles County and secured first a temporary, and later a permanent, injunction against L.A. County Clerk Lampton to restrain him from issuing a marriage license.[38] Evidence as to Moreno's race adduced by the county's counsel and by the attorneys representing the mother "ranged over the whole of anthropological literature, from Linnaeus and Cuvier in the eighteenth century down to recognized textbook writers of today." The county argued that, according to the best authorities, Filipinos are Malays, and that Malays are not Mongolians. The mother's counsel, assisted by expert testimony, argued that all the brown races are Mongolian. Judge Smith ruled in favor of Robinson's mother, holding that Filipinos were Mongolians.[39] The decision was followed by protest in the Filipino community.[40]

[35] Letter from Attorney General U. S. Webb to the Honorable C. C. Kempley, District Attorney of San Diego County 6 (June 8, 1926) (on file with author).
[36] Confusion among county clerks on this issue was the norm. See Bruno Lasker, Filipino Immigration to Continental United States and to Hawaii 118 (1931).
[37] See Foster, *supra* note 27, at 448–52; *Racial Divorce Plea Rejected: Judge Rules Law Needed to Bar Filipino Weddings; White Girl Denied Freedom on Skin Color Basis*, L.A. Times, Oct. 11, 1931, at 5 [hereinafter *Racial Divorce Plea Rejected*].
[38] See Foster, *supra* note 27, at 448 (describing Petition for Writ of Prohibition, Robinson v. Lampton, No. 2496504, Superior Court of Los Angeles County).
[39] Lasker, *supra* note 36, at 118–119.
[40] See, *S.F. Filipinos Oppose Ruling*, S.F. Chron., Feb. 27, 1930, at 6.

Following the Robinson case, L.A. County Clerk Lampton appeared to begin to deny marriage licenses to Filipinos seeking to marry white women. In 1931, Gavino C. Visco petitioned to marry Ruth M. Salas. Lampton denied this petition on the grounds that Visco was a Mongolian and Salas was white. The couple appealed, and Superior Court Judge Guerin ordered Lampton to issue a license. The case did not turn on Visco's Filipino identity, but rather on the identity of Salas. The court held that Salas was "not a person of the Caucasian race." Salas, born in Mexico, had a mother born in Los Angeles and a father born in Mexico. As a nonwhite, Salas was not barred from marrying a Filipino, no matter whether Visco was classified as Mongolian, or otherwise nonwhite.[41]

The third and fourth cases in which this issue surfaced involved attempts at annulments of marriage. Estanislao P. Laddaran sought an annulment of his marriage to Emma F. Laddaran, on the basis that the marriage had been in violation of the law, because he was "of the Filipino race" and his wife was "of the Caucasian, or white race." The court refused.[42] Shortly thereafter, in the *Murillo* case, Judge Gould also refused to annul a marriage, this time on the wife's petition that her Filipino husband was a member of the Mongolian race. In *Murillo*, Judge Gould noted that, while it was true that modern ethnologists had limited the number of racial groups to the white, the black, and the yellow, "these writers warn us that there is no fixed line of demarcation, that these classifications are simply loose fitting generalizations, that the races are still differentiating, and that the race divisions are simply convenient terms as an aid in classification." The judge rejected the modern-day scientific definition of Mongolian in favor of what the state legislature had in mind when it enacted the law. He asserted that if the legislators had anticipated modern scientific classifications, not only would whites be prohibited from marrying "Chinese, Japanese and Koreans (who are popularly regarded as Mongolians)," and "not only with Filipinos and Malays," but also "Laplanders, Hawaiians, Esthonians, Huns, Finns, Turks, Eskimos, American Indians, native Peruvians, native Mexicans and many other peoples, all of whom are included within the present day scientist's classification of 'Mongolian.'"[43]

The fifth case before the Superior Court was *Roldan v. Los Angeles County*.[44] Roldan, "in whose blood was co-mingled a strain of Spanish," sought to marry

---

[41] See Visco v. Lampton, No. C319408, Petition for Order of Alternative Mandamus (June 3, 1931, Superior Court of Los Angeles County, Judge Walter Guerin); *see also* Foster, *supra* note 27, at 449–50. On the racial classification of Mexican Americans, see generally Laura E. Gómez, Manifest Destinies: The Making of the Mexican American Race (2007).

[42] See Foster, *supra* note 27, at 450 (discussing Petition for Annulment of Marriage, Laddaran v. Laddaran, No. D95459 [Los Angeles Super. Ct. 1931]).

[43] See *id.* at 451–452 (discussing Murillo v. Murillo, No. D97715 [October 10, 1931], Superior Court of Los Angeles County, Judge Thomas C. Gould).

[44] See Roldan, *supra* note 1 at 268.

Marjorie Rogers, a "Caucasian" from England. Los Angeles County Clerk Lampton refused. Ruling that neither Rogers nor Roldan were Mongolians, Judge Gates approved the marriage petition. The state appealed the case to the California Appellate Court, which upheld the superior court's decision, holding that there was no legislative intent to apply the name Mongolian to Malays when the statute had been enacted and amended. As in the *Murillo* case, the opinion, written by Judge Archbald, expressly followed, not the scientific, but the common understanding of what Mongolian meant at the enactment of the antimiscegenation statute. The opinion noted that the classification of races into the five grand subdivisions of white, black, yellow, red, and brown was commonly used in 1880 and 1905, the dates when the statute was amended to cover "Mongolians."[45] Because Salvador Roldan was Malay, and not a Mongolian, the L.A. County Clerk was forced to issue him a marriage license.[46]

In most of these opinions, the judges were careful to note that they were not addressing the "social question" of these marriages, and suggested that if the "common thought" of today required, the legislature should address the issue.[47] The legislature complied. Nine days before the *Roldan* decision was issued, State Senator Herbert Jones, an exclusionist, introduced senate bills to amend the antimiscegenation statute to include "Malays."[48] On the same day, the Secretary of the California Joint Immigration Committee requested its sponsoring organizations, the American Legion, the Native Sons and Daughters of the Golden West, and the California State Federation of Labor, to ask members to urge adoption of the bills. Two months later, both bills passed the Senate unanimously.[49] The only dissenting voice in the Assembly was a Los Angeles County representative whose district included a large Filipino community. In April, Governor James Rolph, a prominent member of the Native Sons, signed the bills into law, retroactively voiding and making illegitimate all previous Filipino/white marriages by defining any marriage of Caucasians with "negroes, Mongolians, members of the Malay race, or mulattoes to be illegal and void."[50]

---

[45] *See id.* at 268–69.
[46] *See id.* at 273. In concluding that a Malay is not a Mongolian, the judge relied heavily on the definition of a "Mongolian" from the encyclopedia and on the original legislative intent of enacting laws restricting marriages between whites and Mongolians.
[47] *See, e.g., Roldan,* 129 Cal. App. at 273, 18 P.2d at 709 (deferring to legislature).
[48] *See* Osumi, *supra* note 7, at 20.
[49] *See* 1905 Cal. Stat. 104 (amending section 60 of Civil Code to read: "All marriages of white persons with negroes, Mongolians, members of the Malay race, or mulattoes are illegal and void"); 1905 Cal. Stat. 105 (amending section 69 of Civil Code to read: "no license must be issued authorizing the marriage of a white person with a negro, mulatto, Mongolian or member of the Malay race").
[50] *See* CAL. CIV. CODE § 69 (1937) (amended 1959 to exclude race as a criterion for legal marriage); CAL. CIV. CODE § 60 (Deering 1937) (repealed 1959).

The 1934 passage of the Tydings-McDuffie Act,[51] promising eventual independence to the Philippines, effectively halted Filipino immigration – and indeed was
successfully enacted because of the efforts of those seeking to exclude Filipinos
from the United States.[52] Exclusion led to the dissipation of obsessive anxiety over
Filipino sexuality.[53] While California subsequently became the first and only state
after Reconstruction to rule that its state's antimiscegenation laws were unconstitutional in the 1948 case *Perez v. Sharp*,[54] the legislature did not expunge the invalidated laws from the California Civil Code until 1959.

HISTORY LESSONS

This history reveals nuanced dimensions of antimiscegenation laws and complicated
stories about the relationship of these laws to race, gender, class, and sexuality. In
particular, it suggests that antimiscegenation efforts targeting Filipinos demonstrate
a differing history of racialization.[55] Robert Chang has suggested that miscegenation laws functioned as racial-sexual policing to discipline the transgressive sexuality
of whites and people of color in order to preserve the proper racial, national, and
familial order. He has argued that, with regard to laws restricting Asian miscegenation, racial preservation and economic preservation were linked, so that we can see
the accompanying of antimiscegenation statutes by immigration and naturalization
restrictions and alien land laws.[56]

We can glimpse the trace of differing racializations relating to antimiscegenation efforts that could be described as connected to slavery, foreignness, or colonization. Miscegenation laws directed against excludable "racial aliens" – whether
Chinese, Japanese, or Filipino – were sharply linked to both sex-specific patterns
of migration and calls for expulsion. Where racialization of Chinese and Japanese
may have diverged from Filipinos is in the history of U.S. colonization. The colonization of Filipinos, accompanied by Americanization projects, may have facilitated
a racialization that differentiated Filipinos from Chinese and Japanese through the
perception of Filipinos as less foreign.[57] While there was enormous uproar over

51 Tydings-McDuffie Act, Pub. L. No. 73–127, 48 Stat. 456 (1934).
52 *See* Bill Ong Hing, MAKING AND REMAKING ASIAN AMERICA THROUGH IMMIGRATION POLICY, 1850–
    1990, at 35 (1993).
53 E. San Juan has suggested that this obsessive anxiety only temporarily lived an underground existence,
    but metamorphized into anxiety over G.I. brides at the end of World War II, and now has manifested
    in anxiety over the so-called mail-order bride syndrome. *See* E. San Juan, Jr., *Configuring the Filipino
    Diaspora in the United States*, 3 DIASPORA 117, 120 (1994).
54 32 Cal. 2d 711, 198 P.2d 17 (1948).
55 *See* Eva Saks, *Representing Miscegenation Law*, 8 RARITAN 39, 40–42, 64 (1988).
56 *See* Chang, *supra* note 10, at 59–60.
57 Kevin J. Mumford, INTERZONES: BLACK/WHITE SEX DISTRICTS IN CHICAGO AND NEW YORK IN THE
    EARLY TWENTIETH CENTURY 67 (1997).

miscegenous interactions between Filipinos and white women, the uproar was nonetheless ambiguous. For example, certain commentators seem to have understood why some white women would see Filipino men as desirable objects of affection, which contrasts with a seemingly greater repugnance directed against Chinese and Japanese men.

Second, it is important to examine what this history of antimicegenation laws tells us about gender. Peggy Pascoe did significant research analyzing the manner in which the campaign to prohibit interracial marriage reflects U.S. gender, as well as racial, hierarchies. She examined miscegenation laws that were sex-specific in their enumeration of prohibited arrangements, and has also examined gender hierarchies structured by miscegenation laws that were formally gender-neutral. Pascoe found that, in the western United States, laws were applied more stringently to groups whose men were thought likely to marry white women, and less stringently to groups whose women were thought likely to marry white men. Gender also inflected why individuals chose to cross racial boundary lines and get married, as well as shaped when cases would be brought.[58]

The history of Filipinos in California makes vivid the gendered relationship between racial identity and the marriage contract. It reveals a complicated desire to protect white women from "brown men." This desire must be understood as being shaped by class. White women who associated with Filipino men appear to have been largely working-class women – not women considered deserving of greater protection because of middle-class status. The research of Rhacel Salazar Parreñas indicates that there were actually several distinct opinions among whites concerning these relationships: upper-class white women that formed commissions to control "promiscuity" in the dance halls, white working-class men that initiated anti-Filipino race riots to protect white women's purity from Filipino men, and upper-class white men that enacted legislation to protect white purity. But, significantly, Parreñas has added that there were some upper-class white men who saw the working-class women that would associate with Filipinos as so "cheap" and "inferior" that they tainted innocent Filipino men.[59] The concern to protect "women" was of course also racialized. While young Mexican women were also thought to be the target of Filipino male affection, interactions among Mexican women and Filipino men did not appear to incite any uproar beyond occasional rhetorical inclusion as subjects in need of protection. In fact, in the *Visco* case, Ruth Salas, as Mexican, was quite literally thrust out of the category "white" that the state sought to protect from marriage to Filipinos.

---

[58] *See* Peggy Pascoe, *Race, Gender, and Intercultural Relations: The Case of Interracial Marriage*, 12 FRONTIERS 5, 7–8 (1991); *see also* Peggy Pascoe, WHAT COMES NATURALLY: MISCEGENATION LAW AND THE MAKING OF RACE IN AMERICAN (2009).

[59] *See* Parreñas, *supra* note 19, at 116, 124–28.

While scholars writing about miscegenation law have recognized the bundle of legal entitlements associated with the marital contract that women in miscegenous relationships lost if their marriages were declared void, what has not been examined by these scholars is the relationship of interracial marriages to immigration consequences.[60] As of 1790, only whites – and after 1870, only whites and those of African descent or nativity – were allowed to naturalize to become U.S. citizens, until the middle of the twentieth century.[61] Thus, anyone not considered to fall within one of those two categories was considered ineligible to naturalize as a U.S. citizen. Filipinos were considered racially ineligible to naturalize,[62] and, as "nationals" of the United States, were not citizens.

In 1907, Congress passed the Expatriation Act, which provided that any American woman who married a foreigner was automatically denaturalized.[63] Congress partially repealed the law in 1922, but continued to require that any woman who married a man ineligible to naturalize – in other words, one racially barred from doing so – would lose her citizenship. This provision remained law until 1931.[64] Thus, a white U.S. female citizen who married a Filipino faced a Catch-22. If her marriage was seen as violating an antimiscegenation statute, the marriage would be void. However, if it were upheld as a legitimate marriage, that marriage could subject her to expatriation.[65]

Considering the relationship of gender to miscegenation law requires a recognition of the manner in which the control of women and their sexuality is understood as necessary to maintaining and reproducing the identity of communities and nations.[66] Women are thought to guard the purity and honor of communities.

---

[60] For a discussion of these consequences, see generally Candice Lewis Bredbenner, A NATIONALITY OF HER OWN: WOMEN, MARRIAGE, AND THE LAW OF CITIZENSHIP (1998); Martha Gardner, THE QUALITIES OF A CITIZEN: WOMEN, IMMIGRATION, AND CITIZENSHIP, 1870–1965 (2009); Leti Volpp, *Divesting Citizenship: On Asian American History and the Loss of Citizenship Through Marriage*, 53 UCLA L. REV. 405 (2005) [hereinafter Volpp, *Divesting Citizenship*].

[61] Act of March 26, 1790, ch. 3, 1 Stat. 103; Act of July 14, 1870, ch. 255, section 7, 16 Stat. 254.

[62] *See, e.g.*, Morrison v. California, 291 U.S. 82, 85–86 (1934) ("'White persons' within the meaning of the [Naturalization Law of 1790] are members of the Caucasian race, as Caucasian is defined in the understanding of the mass of men. The term excludes the Chinese, the Japanese, the Hindus, the American Indians and the Filipinos"); *see also* Toyota v. United States, 268 U.S. 402, 410–12 (1925).

[63] Act of March 2, 1907, Pub. L. 193, ch. 2534, section 3. This provision was upheld as constitutional in Mackenzie v. Hare, 239 U.S. 299, 311–12 (1915), in which the Supreme Court upheld the power of Congress to expatriate a female U.S. citizen who obtained foreign nationality by marriage to a foreign national during the period of coverture, because such action was a "necessary and proper" implementation of the inherent power of sovereignty in foreign relations.

[64] *See* Act of Sept. 22, 1922, ch. 411, section 3; 42 Stat. 1022; Act of March 3, 1931, ch. 442, secs 4(a),(b), 46 Stat. 1511.

[65] For a discussion of the case of Mary Ann Montoya, an Austrian immigrant married to a Filipino man, informed that so long as she remained married that she was precluded from naturalization, see Volpp, *Divesting Citizenship, supra* note 60 at 440–41.

[66] On the relationship of nationalism, gender, race, and sexuality, see generally Leti Volpp, *Blaming Culture for Bad Behavior*, 12 YALE J.L. & HUMAN. 89 (2000). We should also examine how scholarship

Nationalism entwines with race so that women are subjected to control in order to achieve the aim of a national racial purity. This is visible in the history described here. Filipino male sexual engagement with white women was considered a national threat, requiring the literal expulsion of Filipino men from the body politic, accomplished through the simultaneous granting of independence to the Philippines and the revocation of "national" status that had formerly allowed Filipinos to freely travel to the United States.

CONCLUSION

This chapter focused on a community whose legal history has been sorely neglected. In interpreting the history of antimiscegenation efforts prohibiting Filipinos from marrying whites in the state of California, I have sought to complicate our narration of miscegenation laws. Generalizations about miscegenation laws or about the impetus for them do not do justice to the specific histories that have impacted particular communities.

The history presented in this chapter suggests that greater attention should be paid to the role of U.S. colonialism in shaping racialization and connections we might make between different communities. There is nothing natural or preordained about the classification of Filipinos as "Malay" or as "Mongolian" – or as any other identity. Racial identity is shaped in relation to other forces. Here, such forces include assumptions about racialized sexuality, colonial relations between the United States and the Philippines, the importation of exploitable laborers without political rights, and the intertwining of gender and nationalism. The legal history of the shifts in racial classification of Filipinos in California, between "Mongolian" and "Malay," underlines the manner in which race is made.

on miscegenation law has shaped our understanding of male and female sexuality and, specifically, shaped these understandings through the lens of presumptive heterosexuality. For examples of scholarship that are exceptional in this regard, see Nayan Shah, CONTAGIOUS DIVIDES: EPIDEMICS AND RACE IN SAN FRANCISCO'S CHINATOWN (2001), and Mumford, *supra* note 57.

5

Perez v. Sharp and the Limits of *Loving*

Robin A. Lenhardt

At the center of *In re Marriage Cases*, the 2008 California Supreme Court decision that attracted national attention for temporarily extending marriage rights to same-sex couples, was a little-known 1948 case called *Perez v. Sharp*.[1] The first post-Reconstruction case to invalidate an antimiscegenation law, *Perez* involved plaintiffs who were as courageous as any involved in landmark civil rights cases. Andrea Perez, the daughter of Mexican immigrants, and Sylvester Davis, the product of African-American migrants from the deep South, met while working on an assembly line in World War II, Los Angeles. They fell in love and decided to marry. But when the couple went to get a marriage license, the county clerk informed them that Andrea could not legally marry a black man. California's antimiscegenation law technically did not constrain the marriage choices of Mexican Americans. In fact, it made no mention of them at all. But, in California, Mexicans had long been regarded as white and thus prohibited from marrying African Americans, among other groups.

With the aid of a civil rights attorney, Dan Marshall, Andrea and Sylvester decided to fight the clerk's refusal to issue them a marriage license, putting together a legal case that would shake the foundations of California's carefully constructed racial hierarchy and ultimately pave the way for the U.S. Supreme Court's decision in *Loving v. Virginia* nearly twenty years later. Outside the small

---

[1] Perez v. Sharp, 198 P.2d 17, 25 (Cal. 1948) [hereinafter "PEREZ"]; *see also* Peggy Pascoe, *Miscegenation Law, Court Cases, and Ideologies of "Race" in Twentieth-Century America*, 83 J. AM. HIST. 44, 61 n.42 (1996) (explaining that, because of leadership changes at the L.A. County Clerk's office, *Perez* is sometime referred to as *Perez v. Moroney* or *Perez v. Lippold*). The November 4, 2008 passage of Proposition 8, a ballot initiative recently upheld by the California Supreme Court, meant that the rights of gay and lesbian couples to marry in California acknowledged in *In re Marriage Cases* were only temporary. *See* Strauss v. Horton, 207 P. 3d 48 (Cal. 2009). Proposition 8 amended the state constitution to provide that "[o]nly marriage between a man and a woman is valid or recognized in California." California Const., Art. I, sec. 7.5 (2008). Its adoption does not affect the 18,000 marriages that took place prior to November 5, 2008, but does mean that any occurring after that time will not have the force of law. A federal challenge to Proposition 8's constitutionality has been filed in federal court.

community of lawyers and activists who, in recent years, have relied on *Perez* in litigating cases seeking to secure equal marriage rights for gay and lesbian couples, few people have even heard of Andrea and Sylvester or the important legal decision their case produced. For the most part, *Perez*'s greatest claim to fame has been a footnote mention in Chief Justice Warren's much-celebrated majority opinion in *Loving*. To the extent it has been considered at all, it has primarily been treated as a stepping-stone to the *Loving* decision, as a case that merely underscores *Loving*'s core holding, not one capable of communicating important lessons in its own right.[2]

Perez is more than just a prelude to *Loving*. In ignoring *Perez*, legal scholars have missed out on lessons that are critical to understanding race, the current debate about equal marriage rights, and the meaning of citizenship in the twenty-first century. Moreover, they have forgone an opportunity to comprehend more fully the meaning and effect of the Supreme Court's decision in *Loving*. For, in expanding on issues pertaining to race, marriage, and membership in American society, former Justice Traynor's majority opinion in *Perez* exposes the problems inherent in the approach taken by the Court in *Loving*. As I explain in more detail in the pages that follow, *Perez* arguably offers better insight into the limitations of racial categories and a more fulsome account of the place of marriage in modern society than *Loving* ever could.

THE *PEREZ* DECISION

The county clerk's denial of Andrea and Sylvester's application for a marriage license had its roots in antimiscegenation provisions as old as California's founding. Section 69 of the California Code provided that "no license may be issued authorizing the marriage of a white person with a Negro, mulatto, Mongolian or member of the Malay race." Section 60 further explained that "[a]ll marriages of white persons with negroes, Mongolians, members of the Malay race, or mulattoes are illegal and void."[3]

These provisions, with their complex racial styling, evinced California's attempt to corral what, for this time period, was the unique diversity of her denizens. They also reflected the broad consensus then supporting antimiscegenation laws. In 1947, California was one of thirty states that proscribed interracial marriages. This reality, coupled with the fact that no post-Reconstruction state or federal court had ever

---

[2] *See* Orenstein, *supra* n. 2, at 388–90; R. A. Lenhardt, *Beyond Analogy: Perez v. Sharp, Antimiscegenation Law, and the Fight for Same-Sex Marriage*, 96 CAL. L. REV. 839, 854–55 (2008).

[3] CAL. CIV. CODE § 69 (West 1941), *invalidated by* Perez v. Sharp *supra* n.1; CAL. CIV. CODE § 60 (West 1941), *invalidated by* Perez v. Sharp, *supra* n.1.

overturned an antimiscegenation law, meant that Andrea and Sylvester faced a truly uphill battle.[4]

The U.S. Supreme Court's 1883 decision in *Pace v. Alabama* presented a significant barrier to success. *Pace* held that an Alabama law penalizing interracial adultery more severely than same-race adultery was not inconsistent with the Fourteenth Amendment's equal protection guarantees. Given the *Pace* Court's conclusion that race-based distinctions in law were permissible insofar as they treated individuals within specific racial categories the same, it seemed unlikely that any court would divert from past practice and strike down such a distinction.[5] But, as detailed herein, that is exactly what happened. Led by then-Justice Roger Traynor, who wrote the majority opinion in *Perez*, the California Supreme Court made history on October 1, 1948, by ruling in Andrea and Sylvester's favor. With a 4–3 vote, the Court invalidated California's interracial marriage ban and granted a writ of mandamus permitting Andrea and Sylvester to begin their married life together.

JUSTICE ROGER TRAYNOR'S MAJORITY OPINION

In 1947, the unfortunate decisions in U.S. Supreme Court cases such as *Hirabayashi v. United States* and *Korematsu v. United States* were only a few years old. Courts were actively engaged in determining how best to understand the idea that "[o]nly the most exceptional circumstances can excuse discrimination on th[e] basis [of race] in the face of the equal protection clause."[6] Within this context, Justice Traynor – a pragmatist committed to the "eliminat[ion] of legal rules that ... no longer served their purpose" – concluded that his task as a jurist was to determine whether the race-based impairment of marriage rights effected by California law could be justified given relevant social science research.[7] This focus made all the difference.

---

[4] *See* R. A. Lenhardt, *The Story of* Perez v. Sharp: *Forgotten Lessons on Race, Law, and Marriage*, in Race Law Stories 341–77 (Devon Carbado & Rachel Moran, eds., 2007) [hereinafter "Lenhardt, *Forgotten Lessons*"]; Peter Wallenstein, Tell the Court I Love My Wife: Race, Marriage and Law 199 (2002); Rachel Moran, Interracial Intimacy: The Regulation of Race and Romance 84 (2001).

[5] The Alabama statute imposed a prison term of two to seven years for interracial adultery, but imposed only a fine and up to six months imprisonment for same-race adultery. *See* Cheryl I. Harris, *In the Shadow of* Plessy, 7 U. Pa. J. Const. L. 867, 881 (2005). In concluding that this was not constitutionally problematic, *Pace* arguably paved the way for the separate-but-equal system of racial segregation specifically endorsed by *Plessy v. Ferguson*, 163 U.S. 537 (1896). *See* Peggy Cooper Davis, Neglected Stories: The Constitution and Family Values 67 (1997).

[6] Oyama v. California, 332 U.S. 633, 646 (1948).

[7] Ben Field, Activism in the Pursuit of the Public Interest: The Jurisprudence of Chief Justice Roger Traynor 7 (2003); Lenhardt, *Forgotten Lessons, supra n.* at 4 at 358.

Not surprisingly, California relied heavily on the work of eugenicists in defending its antimiscegenation policy. The state argued that interracial marriages – "especially with respect to the 'Negro race,' which was described as 'biologically inferior to the white' – not only produced 'undesirable biological results,'" but also created social problems, such as the "birth of interracial children who, as the offspring of parents 'lost to shame,' would be 'social outcasts.'"[8]

But, as he had been since oral argument in the case, Justice Traynor was most intrigued by new research completed by social scientists, such as Gunnar Myrdal, Franz Boas, and Otto Kleinberg, that discredited eugenicists. As a result, Justice Traynor found utterly unpersuasive the notion that California's law was justified because it avoided social tensions or "prevented the Caucasian race from being contaminated." Likewise, he dismissed out of hand the notion that whites were superior to blacks and other minorities. Justice Traynor thus concluded, using the language of the new strict scrutiny analysis, that the state's asserted purposes could not be deemed "compelling."

As if to underscore this, he emphasized that, in light of more recent social science research, the racial categories employed by the state were "illogical and discriminatory," and arguably rendered the state's statutes "void for vagueness." Among other things, he criticized the state for not explicitly stating which officials had responsibility for making determinations about racial identity or clarifying how such determinations should be made – for example, by "physical appearance," "genealogical research," or some other mechanism. He also bemoaned the legislature's inattention to the perplexing issue of how persons of mixed ancestry should be regarded under the statute. Justice Traynor found absurd the notion under California's statute that a "Mulatto can marry a Negro" or, for example, that "[a] person having five-eighths Mongolian blood and three-eighths white blood could properly marry another [sic] person of preponderantly Mongolian blood" under the statute, but white and black persons could not marry one another.[9]

These ruminations on the fallacy of white supremacy and the illogic of racial categories help make *Perez* a veritable treasure trove. But it is in Justice Traynor's eloquence in addressing the questions about the importance of marriage that the judicial acumen that earned Traynor the reputation for being one of the "ablest judge[s] of his generation" becomes most apparent. In a move that advocates of marriage rights for gay men and lesbians now celebrate, Justice Traynor refused to treat

[8] Petitioners' Reply Brief at 24, *Perez*, 198 P.2d 17 (No. L.A. 20305); Lenhardt, *Forgotten Lessons, supra* n. at 355 (quoting Petitioners' Reply Brief at 110, *Perez*, 198 P.2d 17 [No. L.A. 20305]); Respondent's Supplemental Brief in Opposition to Writ of Mandate at 78, 97–119, *Perez*, 198 P.2d 17 (No. L.A. 20305).
[9] *Perez, supra* n.1, at 23, 26–28.

Perez as a case about race alone, insisting that it also concerned the right to marry "the person of one's choice."

Importantly, no direct precedent existed for this formulation of the issues. The Supreme Court did not recognize marriage as a fundamental right until 1967 in *Loving*, when it invalidated the antimiscegenation statutes then in effect on Fourteenth Amendment grounds.[10] Traynor's approach was both novel and strategically astute. By framing the issues in this way, Justice Traynor managed to avoid the unfavorable precedent established by the Court's decision in *Pace*. Asserting that "human beings ... [were not] as interchangeable as trains," Traynor dismissed the separate-but-equal understandings reflected in *Pace* as applicable primarily to cases involving access to goods – such as trains and education – that, prior to the 1954 decision in *Brown v. Board of Education*, were still thought capable of being equalized even where racially segregated by law. Such cases, he explained, were "inapplicable." In Traynor's view, "the essence of the right to marry" is not the freedom to marry a partner that the state identifies as acceptable. Rather, it "is the freedom to join in marriage with the person of one's choice," an individual who, while possibly undesirable in the state's eyes, "may be irreplaceable." This civil entitlement, Traynor explained, is one that "a segregation statute for marriage necessarily impairs."[11]

THE CONCURRING AND DISSENTING OPINIONS

Perez fractured the California Supreme Court. The justices in concurrence embraced the core of Justice Traynor's majority opinion, but offered differing rationales for its judgment. Justice Edmonds, a Christian Scientist, argued – as Andrea and Sylvester had in their initial briefs – that the First Amendment's Free Exercise Clause required a ruling for the plaintiffs. In contrast, Justices Jesse W. Carter and Phil Gibson – citing normative principles of equality set forth in the Fourteenth Amendment, the Declaration of Independence, and the recently enacted Charter of the United Nations – wrote separately to argue that California's law "violate[d] the very premise on which [the United States] and its Constitution were built." Sections 60 and 69, in their view, were flawed from the outset and would have raised constitutional problems, even without the new social science research on which Justice Traynor relied so heavily.[12]

---

[10] Because *Loving* rested on dual constitutional grounds – pertaining to race and marriage – some scholars argue that the first clear articulation of the fundamental nature of the right to marry did not come until the Court's 1978 decision in *Zablocki v. Redhail*, 434 U.S. 374 (1978). *See, e.g.*, Joseph A. Pull, *Questioning the Fundamental Right to Marry*, 90 MARQ. L. REV. 21, 21 (2006).

[11] *Perez, supra* n.1, at 20–21, 25.

[12] *Perez, supra* n.1, at 29, 34. For more on the separate opinions, see Orenstein, *supra* n. 2, at 390.

Three justices – John W. Schenk, B. Rey Schauer, and Homer R. Spence – dissented, lamenting the majority's willingness to ignore nearly 100 years of California law and the favorable treatment interracial marriage bans had consistently received in other jurisdictions. In the dissenters' view, the majority opinion could not be reconciled with *Pace* and its holding that the Fourteenth Amendment did not prohibit bans on interracial intimacy. The freedom to marry, they maintained, simply did not encompass some broader right to marry "the person of one's choice," irrespective of race. Under *Pace*, Justice Schenk wrote at one point in his dissent, it is enough that "each petitioner has the right and the privilege of marrying within his or her own group."[13]

LEGISLATIVE AND JUDICIAL REACTIONS TO THE *PEREZ* DECISION

Within California, the impact of the decision in *Perez* was plain. For the first time in the state's history, the choice of individuals to marry outside of their racial group was not constrained. Andrea and Sylvester were finally able to marry in their home church, which had been a primary motivation in launching the lawsuit. Outside of California, however, *Perez*, at least initially, had almost no decipherable effect. It did not prompt the immediate repeal of antimiscegenation laws in other states, and few courts felt compelled even to cite it, let alone follow its holding. Those that did were not complimentary. For example, the Virginia Supreme Court acknowledged *Perez* in *Naim v. Naim* – an antimiscegenation case concerning the legality of a marriage between a white woman and Chinese man – but then quickly dismissed it as "contrary to the otherwise uninterrupted course of judicial decision."[14]

It would take until 1967, when the U.S. Supreme Court decided *Loving*, for *Perez* to get any favorable notice outside of California. Chief Justice Warren, the author of the majority opinion in *Loving*, had been Governor of California at the time that *Perez* was decided. He was not only aware of the *Perez* decision but, quite possibly, was influenced by it as he wrote the *Loving* opinion. Although shorter and, as discussed later, in some ways more limited in scope, *Loving* picks up on many of the core themes Justice Traynor addressed in *Perez*. It, too, takes pains to challenge the myth of white superiority, derisively dismissing "the racial classifications" embedded in Virginia's antimiscegenation statute "as measures designed to maintain White Supremacy." Also similar to *Perez*, the *Loving* opinion emphasizes the fundamental nature of marriage in American society. Although the "person of one's

---

[13] *Perez, supra* n.1, at 46.
[14] Orenstein, *supra* n.2, at 38. Indeed, California, like many other states, itself took some time to repeal its antimiscegenation law provisions. *See* Wallenstein, *supra* n.5, at 199, 253–54.

choice" language now so often linked to *Perez* does not appear in the *Loving* decision, Warren made clear that, under the Fourteenth Amendment, the right to marry entails a choice that "resides with the individual," one that cannot be "restricted by invidious racial discriminations." Interestingly, despite all of this, Chief Justice Warren barely acknowledges his arguable debt to Justice Traynor and his years in California, managing only to cite *Perez* in a footnote to the *Loving* decision.[15]

Perez *as a Lens on* Loving *and Its Limitations*

Over the last two decades, the notion, implicit in Chief Justice Warren's majority opinion, that *Perez* is best understood as footnote to *Loving*, has persisted. In the area of race and intimacy, *Loving* and its very aptly named plaintiffs occupy the field. We know the story of Richard and Mildred Loving's forced exile from their home state and their courageous legal battle to challenge Virginia's ban on interracial marriage. But we hear comparatively little about Andrea Perez and Sylvester Davis. Indeed, were it not for attorneys who have placed *Perez* and its characterization of marriage as the freedom to select the "person of one's choice" center stage in recent litigation to secure marriage rights for gay and lesbian couples, few people would know anything at all about their story. Legal scholars have overlooked *Perez* for years, wrongly presuming that it has no special insights to offer in this area.[16]

Without questioning in any way the special position that *Loving* holds in our constitutional law canon, I want to suggest that legal scholars interested in questions pertaining to race and intimacy should also be "loving" *Perez*. As a case decided in 1948, *Perez* provides us with a unique window onto the early development of the concept of color-blindness in American race law and the evolution of substantive due process principles pertaining to marriage. In drafting his majority opinion in *Perez*, Justice Traynor necessarily grappled with the meaning of the Court's decisions in race cases such as *Hirabayashi v. United States* and *Korematsu v. United States*, and substantive due process cases such as *Meyer v. Nebraska* and *Pierce v. Society of Sisters*.[17] His opinion thus stands as an important artifact of that period, a window onto how lower courts and perhaps even the U.S. Supreme Court thought of principles that, although now well established, were very much in flux at the time.

[15] 388 U.S. 1, 11 (1967).
[16] *Perez* has been deployed by advocates in almost every case challenging gender-based restrictions on marriage in recent years. See Lenhardt, *Beyond Analogy, supra* n.3 at 839, 854–55, fn.101 (citing cases). Only a handful of legal scholars have considered *Perez* in detail. See, e.g., Moran, *supra* n. 5, at 85–88; Randall Kennedy, *Interracial Intimacies: Sex, Marriage, Identity, and Adoption* 259–66, 269 (2003); Kevin R. Johnson & Kristina L. Burrows, *Struck by Lightning? Interracial Intimacy and Racial Justice*, 25 HUM. RTS. Q. 528 (2003) (reviewing Moran, *supra* n. 5).
[17] 323 U.S. 214 (1944); 262 U.S. 390 (1923); 268 U.S. 510 (1925).

At the same time, Traynor's opinion also provides a map of the road not taken by the Court in making determinations about questions of race and family. *Perez* contains the threads to a jurisprudence of race and family that, had they been followed in *Loving* and other cases, might very well have led us to a doctrinal place very different from the one in which we now find ourselves where questions of racial discrimination and marriage are concerned. It is in this sense, then, that *Perez* also helps expose the limitations of the Court's decision in *Loving*. Invariably, those who object to the use of *Perez* in recent same-sex marriage cases argue that the problem lies in the efforts of advocates, who, the argument goes, cling to phrases such as the "person of one's choice" in an effort to mask the illegitimacy of their claim on marriage rights for gay and lesbian couples. Cases such as *Perez* and *Loving*, critics imply, are, first and foremost, precedents about race, not marriage, and certainly not about anything but the most traditional understanding of that institution. Upon closer examination, however, it seems more likely that the fault may rest, at least in part, with *Loving* itself. For, as important a decision as it is, *Loving* offers limited opportunities with questions of race and marriage that now lie at the heart of what it means to "belong" to American society in the twenty-first century.

Racial Vagueness and the Problem of Race-Based Categories

Significantly, the attention *Perez* now garners in marriage cases has very little to do with those aspects of Justice Traynor's majority opinion concerning race. The focus, as discussed in more detail in the section that follows, is typically placed on those portions of the opinion addressing marriage. But it may be in the area of race that the difference in the contributions made by *Perez* and *Loving* can best be seen.

In *Loving*, one finds the seeds of the modern Supreme Court's race jurisprudence. Indeed, *Loving* crystallized the strict scrutiny analysis now so much a part of Equal Protection cases. The almost obligatory incantation of the principle of color-blindness – the notion that the Constitution does not see race, and that judges, as a consequence, should regard all uses of race, whether intended to be harmful or beneficial, with deep skepticism – so common in the Court's more recent race cases, significantly, does not appear in Chief Justice Warren's opinion for the Court. In 1967, the affirmative action policies that prompted the excavation of the color-blindness concept from former Justice Harlan's dissent in *Plessy* had not yet come into being. But the moral rebuke of race-based categories underlying the embrace of color-blindness is, nonetheless, palpable in *Loving*.[18] No doubt, this is because it served to highlight so compellingly the normative problems inherent in the identity-based restrictions Virginia placed on marriage and biological accounts of race more generally.

---

[18] 388 U.S. 1, 11 (1967); Cass R. Sunstein, *Homosexuality and the Constitution*, 70 IND. L.J. 1, 17 (1994)).

Perez also signals strong moral disapproval of California's antimiscegenation law. But, in attempting to apply the Court's World War II race precedents, Justice Traynor goes beyond mere moral commentary, offering a critical discussion of the biological irrelevancy of race. His inclination, it seems, was to use social science research to question the very existence of race and to reveal the illogic of the mechanisms deployed by the state in trying to define it. The first evidence of this came in Traynor's colloquy with the state's attorney, Charles C. Stanley, during the oral argument in *Perez*:

> MR. JUSTICE TRAYNOR: What is a negro?
>
> MR. STANLEY: We have not the benefit of any judicial interpretation. The statute states that a negro [sic] cannot marry a negro, which can be construed to me a full-blooded negro, since the statute says mulatto, Mongolian, or Malay.
>
> MR. JUSTICE TRAYNOR: What is a mulatto? One-sixteenth blood?
>
> MR. STANLEY: Certainly certain states have seen fit to state what a mulatto is.
>
> MR. JUSTICE TRAYNOR: If there is 1/8 blood, can they marry? If you can marry with 1/8, why not 1/16, 1/32, 1/64? And then don't you get in the ridiculous position where a negro cannot marry anybody? If he is white, he cannot marry black, or if he is black, he cannot marry white.
>
> MR. STANLEY: I agree that it would be better for the legislature to lay down an exact amount of blood, but I do not think that the statute should be declared unconstitutional as indefinite on this ground.
>
> MR. JUSTICE TRAYNOR: That is something anthropologists have not been able to furnish, although they say ... there is no such thing as race.[19]

Justice Traynor's earlier-mentioned vagueness holding reflects a similar commitment. That California's antimiscegenation provisions might be void for vagueness was not an issue the court needed to reach to resolve Andrea and Sylvester's lawsuit. It seems likely that Andrea's attenuated connection to whiteness motivated Traynor to consider the problem of racial definition. The discussion of "persons of mixed ancestry" in the majority opinion, along with the references to Mexican Americans that appear throughout the opinion, reveals his discomfort with Andrea's classification as white, a status whose benefits she arguably never enjoyed:

> If the statute is to be applied generally to persons of mixed ancestry the question arises whether it is to be applied on the basis of the physical appearance of the individual or on the basis of genealogical research as to his ancestry. If the physical appearance of the individual is to be the test, the statute would have to be applied on the basis of subjective impressions of various persons. Persons having

---

[19] Transcript of Oral Argument at 3–4, *Perez*, 198 P.2d 17 (No. L.A. 20305).

the same parents and consequently the same hereditary background could be classified differently. On the other hand, if the application of the statute to persons
of mixed ancestry is to be based on genealogical research, the question immediately arises what proportions of Caucasian, Mongolian, or Malayan ancestry, or is it
some unspecified proportion of such ancestry that makes a person a Mongolian or
Malayan within the meaning of section 60?[20]

Justice Traynor's statements on racial vagueness open the door to a conversation
about race in America, one at which *Loving*, despite its indictment of white supremacy, never even hints. *Perez* invites not just expressions of moral outrage, but an
exploration and deeper understanding of the race-related rules enlisted by states
such as California, and the role that they played in erecting the "American pig-
mentoracy."[21] As I have noted elsewhere, states deployed wildly divergent and sometimes conflicting mechanisms in this area, focusing on "physical characteristics"
like hair texture or even foot size to denote an individual's racial classification in
some instances, and resorting to inquiries about racial reputation or tests focusing
on blood quantum or ancestry in others. The arbitrariness of such measures leads
one to question, as Justice Traynor implicitly did, whether race means anything if it
means so many different and contradictory things to so many different people.

Even more, *Perez* underscores the critical role that law has played in affecting
the social construction of race in America. Critical Race Theory (CRT) has long
embraced the central insight reflected in Justice Traynor's opinion – that the state
is intimately involved in the formation of race and racial structures in our society.[22]
But a close reading of *Perez* suggests new inquiries into the particular mechanisms
through which race is defined and understood today, when interracial marriage is
more common than it has ever been and multiculturalism has become prevalent.
To what extent do determinations about racial identity still turn on hair texture or
social reputation? How has the rise in transracial adoptions complicated racial defi-
nition? Questions about whether U.S. Supreme Court Justice nominee Judge Sonia
Sotomayor is truly the first Latino member of the Court and whether President Barack
Obama, the product of a white mother and black father, can properly be regarded as
African American underscore the continued salience of these and other matters.

---

[20] *Perez, supra* n.1 at 28. As was common at this time, California treated Mexican Americans as white
for purposes of marriage, but not necessarily where access to other public goods or institutions was
concerned. *See* Orenstein, *supra* n. 2, at 348; *see also* Ian F. Haney López, RACISM ON TRIAL: THE
CHICANO FIGHT FOR JUSTICE (2003).

[21] *See* Randall Kennedy, *Lecture, Race Relations Law in the Canon of Legal Academia*, 68 FORDHAM L.
REV. 1985, 1990 (2000).

[22] Lenhardt, *Forgotten Lessons, supra* n. 5, at 378–79; Michael Omi & Howard Winant, RACIAL
FORMATION IN THE UNITED STATES 82 (2d ed. 1994); *see also, e.g.,* Ian Haney López, WHITE BY LAW
(10th ANNIV. ED. 2006).

Finally, *Perez* compels us to pay greater attention to the lives and intimate associations of Latinos in the United States, especially Mexican Americans. We have yet to explore in any serious way the questions about race and culture presented by California's treatment of Mexican Americans as white for purposes of marriage. By what processes did Andrea become white for purposes of marriage but nonwhite for others? Likewise, we can do more to understand the kinds of intimate choices that Latinos make. While interracial marriages still remain relatively uncommon, those involving Latinos and African Americans are even more rare. What accounts for this? *Loving*, on its own, provides us with little insight into such questions.[23]

MARRIAGE AND THE RIGHT TO CHOOSE
THE "PERSON OF ONE'S CHOICE"

As the reemergence of *Perez* in recent cases on same-sex marriage arguably suggests, the explanatory shortcomings of the *Loving* decision are not confined to those that pertain directly to race. They extend to issues pertaining to marriage and its significance in modern society as well. Litigants in lawsuits such as *In re Marriage Cases* and *Goodridge v. Dep't of Pub. Health* obviously deployed *Loving* in making their case for gay and lesbian marriage rights. As a U.S. Supreme Court case, *Loving* carries precedential value that a state court decision like *Perez* simply does not. But litigants nevertheless draw heavily on *Perez* as well, sometimes resting the bulk of their claim for relief on its back.

Such reliance exposes how anemic *Loving's* language is compared to *Perez's* wonderfully expressive statement about "the person of one's choice." It also reveals the ways in which *Loving's* articulation of the fundamental right to marry falls short, the extent to which it fails to capture the true meaning of modern marriage. When Sylvester Davis and Andrea Pérez decided to challenge the refusal of the county clerk to grant them a marriage license, they had in mind very particular ideas about what it would mean to marry. They were not, for example, merely looking for sexual intimacy. Neither of them wanted simply to cohabitate, an option that was available to them given that California's antimiscegenation law proscribed only interracial marriage, not sex. They wanted marriage on their own terms, in a way that honored not just their religious beliefs as Catholics, but also their aspirations as members of the community. A religious ceremony without state sanction would have been unappealing. Receiving the sacrament of marriage in their home church and in their home state was the goal.

---

[23]　For a discussion of the racialization of Mexican Americans and the role of the Treaty of Guadalupe in it, *see* Laura Gomez, Manifest Destinies: The Making of the Mexican American Race (2007); *see also* Lenhardt, *Forgotten Lessons, supra* n.4, at 378–79.

Significantly, conceptions about the institution of marriage have changed a great deal since 1948. As Rachel Moran reminds us in an article commemorating the fortieth anniversary of *Loving*, marriage itself has changed dramatically over the years. Whereas marriage, as the U.S. Supreme Court's decision in *Zablocki v. Redhail* intimates, used to be the primary site for sexual intimacy, procreation, parenting, and economic well-being, it no longer holds this exalted position in our society. Premarital sex and out-of-wedlock births no longer carry the stigma they did when Sylvester and Andrea were dating. Indeed, more and more parents, particularly women, are raising children outside of the structure of a marital relationship. Likewise, more people than ever before are choosing to divorce or never to marry at all. "[M]arriage accounted for 84 percent of households" in 1930, but just "49.7 percent of American households" in 2006.[24]

It cannot be said that the justices in *Loving* or *Perez* thought for a moment that their judgments would be used to support claims for same-sex couples to marry. In both instances, it was enough that a majority could be found to hold race-based restrictions within different-sex marriage unconstitutional. That either court could have anticipated the changes in society and its attitudes about marriage discussed earlier seems far-fetched at best. And yet, current cases on same-sex marriage nonetheless require us to consider the staying power of their respective decisions.

Certainly, *Loving* says something about the role of marriage in society. Chief Justice Warren set down an important marker by acknowledging that "[m]arriage is one of the 'basic civil rights of man.'" This served both to signal the unique status of the right of which Virginia endeavored to strip Richard and Mildred Loving, and to make clear that the Due Process Clause would stand, alongside the Equal Protection Clause, as one of the legs on which *Loving* rested. At the same time, however, the *Loving* Court's specific thoughts on marriage cannot be easily discerned from its opinion. Even as he talked about "the freedom of choice to marry," Chief Justice Warren omitted more expansive discussions of substantive due process rights that had appeared in early drafts of his decision. All that can be said for certain is that the Court, at a minimum, endorsed a fairly traditional understanding of marriage and meant to reject race-based obstacles to its enjoyment.

Perez, in contrast, offers a textured account of marriage and the problems inherent in identity-based restrictions on it that resonates strongly, even though it was obviously drafted to respond to the concerns of a different era. In *Perez*, both the equal protection and due process prongs of the court's analysis are fairly well developed. Traynor's discussion of social science research on race and contention that

[24] Rachel F. Moran, *Loving and the Legacy of Unintended Consequences*, 2007 WIS. L. REV. 239, 268–69, 274–76 (2007; *See* Cass. R. Sunstein, *Liberty After Lawrence*, 65 OHIO ST. L. J. 1059, 1071 (2004); Jane Mauldon, *Family Change and Welfare Reform*, 36 SANTA CLARA L. REV. 325, 332 (1996).

"[h]uman beings are bereft of worth and dignity by a doctrine that would make them as interchangeable as trains" goes directly to matters of equality and caste, rejecting the easy formalism of *Pace*. But it also speaks clearly to marriage and the meaning of decisions to enter into it. In many ways, *Perez* helps give additional content to the freedom to marry. It sheds light on the public and private dimensions of modern marriage and the citizenship or public standing that marriage confers – issues *Loving* never fully tackles.[25]

Traynor recognized that marriage is a mechanism for cementing an intimate, human association. His opinion acknowledges the fundamental dignity and humanity of Andrea and Sylvester, as well as the expressive content inherent in selecting – through a state-sponsored system – the "person of one's choice" as a life partner. In this sense, *Perez* is very much in line with more recent Supreme Court marriage decisions, such as *Turner v. Safely*, which invalidated a prison regulation prohibiting inmate marriage. It is also arguably in line with the Court's 2003 decision in *Lawrence v. Texas*. While *Lawrence* concerned criminal prohibitions on gay sex that reached into the private sphere, not marriage per se, many scholars have read it to be more about human "dignity and equal respect for people involved in intimate relationships," whether they be private or public.[26]

BELONGING AND THE MEANING OF IDENTITY-BASED RESTRICTIONS ON THE RIGHT TO MARRY

Finally, *Perez* and the story of Andrea and Sylvester's court battle tells us something about "belonging" and the citizenship effects of identity-based restrictions on marriage that *Loving* does not communicate.[27] Chief Justice Warren's opinion, of course, makes it plain that depriving an individual of one of the "basic civil rights of man" on the basis of race presents a serious constitutional problem: a denial of the guarantee of equal treatment under the law that the Fourteenth Amendment affords. From this alone, however, we can discern little about what this means in concrete terms, how exclusion of this sort operates at a human level.

[25] *See* Moran, *Loving and the Legacy, supra* n. 24, at 269. *See* Cass R. Sunstein, *The Right to Marry*, 26 Cardozo L. Rev. 2081, 2096 (2005). Laurence H. Tribe, Lawrence v. Texas: *The Fundamental Right That Dare Not Speak Its Name*, 117 Harv. L. Rev. 1893, 1948 (2004); Judith N. Shklar, American Citizenship: The Quest for Inclusion 2 (1991).

[26] *See* Griswold v. Connecticut, 381 U.S. 479, 479 (1965); Turner v. Safely, 482 U.S. 78, 96, 98 (1987); Lawrence v. Texas, 539 U.S. 558 (2003). *See also*, Suzanne J. Lenon, *Marrying Citizens! Raced Subjects? Re-thinking the Terrain of Equal Marriage Discourse*, 17 Canadian J. Women & L. / Revue Femme et Droit 405, 412 (2005); David B. Cruz, *"Just Don't Call It Marriage": The First Amendment and Marriage as an Expressive Resource*, 74 S. Cal. L. Rev. 925 (2001).

[27] Kenneth Karst introduced the term "belonging" in discussing the concept of equal citizenship. *See, e.g.*, Kenneth L. Karst, Belonging to America: Equal Citizenship and the Constitution 3 (1989).

In conceptualizing marriage as not simply the right to marry someone, but the freedom to select "the person of one's choice," however, *Perez* speaks directly to this issue, making plain the extent to which California's race-based restrictions on marriage deprived those they affected of "belonging." Andrea and Sylvester sought more than a paper license when they consulted the Los Angeles county clerk. For them, marriage served, at least in part, as a vehicle for gaining civic membership. Civil marriage affirmed the legitimacy of their union in the eyes of the law, but – to the extent that marriage functions as "the authentic marker of a serious and committed love relationship, a symbolic rite of passage into adulthood" – it also arguably gained them entrance into the broader community.[28]

Opponents of same-sex marriage have tried to limit *Perez* to its facts, suggesting that only the stigma that flows from race-based restrictions raises constitutional concerns. It is not at all clear, however, that *Perez* can be so compartmentalized. Based on Justice Traynor's capacious formulation of the issues, it is hard to see how "the person of one's choice" would be any less "irreplaceable" because they were put out of reach, as a formal matter, by laws addressing matters of gender or sexual orientation rather than race. Indeed, the California Supreme Court said as much in its decision in *In re Marriage Cases*. Ultimately, identity-based restrictions on marriage tell us something about where someone stands in the community – how they should be legally, socially, and politically regarded.

That choosing to marry no longer has the social or cultural significance it carried sixty years ago does not, I think, change this calculus. Marriage, as Moran notes, "remains far and away the single most important way in which the government recognizes and supports intimate relationships." Whatever one thinks of marriage as an institution or the state's role in it, the choice to marry still means something, perhaps even more today than it did sixty years ago, when Andrea and Sylvester won the right to wed, because people – given the many options for organizing one's intimate life now available – no longer *have* to marry to lead fulfilling, economically stable lives. Indeed, as *Perez* underscores, it may well be in the choosing – whether it occurs for love, as in Andrea or Sylvester's case, or for more practical reasons – that an individual asserts his or her individual autonomy, needs, hopes, and desires.

Perez suggests that state-imposed limits on one's ability to choose from amid the full panoply of alternatives for ordering one's intimate associations imposes a stigma that violates notions of human dignity and fairness that are not resolved by the availability of alternatives such as civil unions or the notion that the prohibition on marrying a person of the same sex affects all citizens equally. As the Massachusetts

---

[28] Marriage served a similar role for freedmen and women in the wake of the Civil War. *See* Katherine M. Franke, *Becoming a Citizen: Reconstruction Era Regulation of African American Marriages*, 11 Yale J.L. & Human. 251, 252 (1999).

Supreme Judicial Court explained in *Goodridge*, "[w]ithout the right to marry – or more properly – the right to choose to marry – one is excluded from the full range of human experience and denied full protection of the laws for one's 'avowed commitment to an intimate and lasting human relationship.'"[29]

CONCLUSION

This chapter has tried to dispel the misconception that the story of *Perez* and its courageous plaintiffs, Andrea Perez and Sylvester Davis, has little to offer scholars and advocates concerned about questions of race and intimacy. Despite its title, this chapter is not intended to be an effort to somehow dethrone *Loving* from its place in the American legal canon or our hearts. I do not mean to diminish the significance of that important precedent. Instead, I want only to establish the unique place *Perez* holds in our legal history. My sense is that, by "loving" *Perez*, with its unusually nuanced account of race and expansive understanding of marriage, as well as the Supreme Court's decision in *Loving*, we will better comprehend the contributions of both cases and develop new ways of addressing the issues of race, intimacy, and citizenship that confront us today.

[29] Goodridge, 798 N.E.2d at 947 (Mass. 2003) (quoting Baker v. State, 744 A.2d 864 [Vt. 1999]).

PART THREE

Loving and Interracial Relationships: Contemporary Challenges

6

The Multiracial Epiphany, or How to Erase an Interracial Past

Kevin Noble Maillard

In the collective memory of the United States, mixed race did not exist until 1967. By giving legal recognition to interracial marriage, *Loving v. Virginia* established a new context for racial possibilities in the United States. In addition to allowing marriage across the color line, *Loving* required states to give legal credence to the existence of interracial sex and romance. In theory, *Loving*, as a juridical approval of race mixing, heralds the development of a racially nuanced and complex America. This decriminalization shifted the legal discourse of miscegenation from illicit to legitimate, beginning with the status of the mixed-race offspring. For the children of *Loving*, legal obstacles to interracial kinship became a thing of the past.

Praise of *Loving* as a transformative decision limits itself to a post-1967 epiphanic moment that heralds the arrival of a new, multiracial United States. Professor Jim Chen notes that "[i]ntermarriage and its handmaiden, interbreeding, are running riot in America."[1] From another angle, Deborah Ramirez declares that "the number of biracial babies is increasing at a faster rate than the number of monoracial babies."[2] Mass media express wonder at the "biracial baby boom,"[3] and open declarations of mixed parentage are common, perhaps even fashionable.[4] Novelist Danzy

[1] *See* Jim Chen, *Unloving*, 80 Iowa L. Rev. 145, 153 (1994).

[2] Maria P. P. Root, The Multiracial Experience: Racial Borders as a Significant Frontier in Race Relations *reprinted in* The Multiracial Experience: Racial Borders as the New Frontier, at xiv (Maria P. P. Root ed., 1996).

[3] *See* Maria P. P. Root, The Multiracial Contribution to the Psychological Browning of America, *in* American Mixed Race: The Culture of Microdiversity 231, 231 (Naomi Zack ed., 1995) ("The biracial baby boom has significant implications for ... discussing the physical and psychological 'browning of America.'"); Vincent J. Schodolski, *Mixed-Race Americans Feel Boxed in by Forms*, Chi. Trib., Feb. 14, 1996, at 8 ("[T]he number of mixed-race Americans has grown quickly."); *see also*, *Interracial Marriages Increase*, Wall St. J., May 9, 1994, at B1; *For the First Time, More Americans Approve of Interracial Marriage Than Disapprove*, Gallup Poll Monthly 311, Aug. 1991, at 60–62.

[4] Many popular articles trace the growing popularity of interracialism in America. *See* Ellis Cose, *Our New Look: The Colors of Race*, Newsweek, Jan. 1, 2000, at 29 ("The rise of the mixed-race – or *café au lait* – society"); *see also* Rob Walker, *Whassup, Barbie? Marketers Are Embracing the Idea of a*

Senna (who is black, white, and Jewish) proclaims that "America loves us in all our half-caste glory."[5] In a combination of popular and scholarly work, Gary Nash gloriously portends:

> The invisible Berlin Wall, the racial wall, is being dismantled stone by stone. ...
> Today, in Hawaii, 60 percent of babies born each year are of mixed race. In Los
> Angeles County, the rise in the percentage of Japanese American women who
> marry out of their ethnic group has risen from one of every ten in the 1950s to
> two of three today. Similar trends pertain to other Asian American groups. Seventy
> percent of American Indians tie bonds with mates who are not Indian. Even the
> most enduring nightmare of Euroamerica – racial intermarriage between Black
> and white partners – is no longer extraordinary. Outside the South, more than 10
> percent of all African American males today marry non-Black women, and Black-
> white marriages nationwide have tripled since 1970. Mestizo America is a happen-
> ing thing. A multiracial baby boom is occurring in America today.[6]

Such statistics trace their origins back to the initial legal moment of *Loving*. The growth of interracial marriage and multiracial children occurred after the dismantling of the antimiscegenation regime that came to an end in 1967. Along with the end of legally mandated segregation, the gates to previously prohibited choices had been opened. A recent Gallup poll showed that white approval of interracial marriage increased from 17 percent in 1968 to 84 percent in 2011.[7] Without a doubt, the total number of interracial marriages increased as a result of *Loving*, from 2.4% of newly married couples in 1960 to 14.6% of the same grouping in 2010.[8]

This increase is undeniably laudable, and at the same time mistakenly limited. *Loving* has claimed a place in the legal imagination as the landmark event for legitimating the existence and condoning the formation of multiracial families in America. The scholarly and popular banter celebrating the new "Brown America"[9] treats 1967 as the collective genesis for the legitimation of mixed race in America. Such a level of recognition routinely assigns and grants this single case the special status of the Multiracial Epiphany: both courts and critics routinely cite *Loving* as

---

Post-Racial America: Goodbye Niche Marketing, BOSTON GLOBE, Jan. 12, 2003, at D1; Muhammad Lawrence, *Hip to Be Hybrid*, COURIER-JOURNAL (Louisville, Ky.), Aug. 8, 1999 at H1. Danzy Senna, author of the novel *Caucasia*, has written a satirical piece on fetishistic treatments of miscegenation.

[5] Danzy Senna, Mulatto Millenium, in HALF AND HALF: WRITES ON GROWING UP BIRACIAL AND BICULTURAL at 12 (Claudine O'Hearn, ed., 1998)

[6] Gary B. Nash, *The Hidden History of Mestizo America*, 82 J. AM. HIST. 941, 959 (1995).

[7] Jeffrey Jones, *Record-High 86 Approve of Black-White Marriages*, http://www.gallup.com/poll/149390/record-high-approve-black-white-marriages.aspx (last visited October 26, 2011).

[8] Pew Research Center, *Marrying Out*, June 4, 2010.

[9] Richard Rodriguez popularized "the browning of America," the idea of an intermixture of ethnicities and race in the new millennium. *See generally* Richard Rodriguez, BROWN: THE LAST DISCOVERY OF AMERICA (2002).

the watershed moment in the legal regulation of intimacy and marriage. It cannot be argued that *Loving* did not have a monumental impact on the fundamental right to marriage, but crediting *Loving* as the defining legal moment for mixed race in America undergirds the idea that racial hybridity and relationships did not exist before 1967.

THE PRE-*LOVING* ERA AND ITS LEGACY

Loving is generally praised for opening new doors, not closing old ones. *Loving* is overemphasized as the enabler for mixed race in the United States, and concomitantly, so is its effect on legitimating a varied interracial past. Gary Nash's thesis demonstrates a notable irony: If our just, democratic system openly permits and justifies the "happening thing" of mixed race, why is this same valorization and recognition not extended to the pre-*Loving* era? Turning to a single court case to celebrate a social phenomenon that has existed at the margins of American culture mistakenly erases the past of racial amalgamation that preexisted the legality that *Loving* provided. In the system of the racial binary that has been established in the United States, mixtures that disrupt the notion of racial purity, particularly those that originate in the time period before *Loving*, are presumed to be deviant and abnormal. The collective racial memory in the United States, unlike that of Mexico[10] or Brazil,[11] operates from an assumption of racial purity and sexual avoidance of miscegenation. This national culture of disbelief in racial intermixture has permeated our look at history and law.

Looking to *Loving* as the birthplace of interracialism reinforces the legal authority and resultant legacy of the antimiscegenation regime that it replaced. In addition to outlawing interracial marriage, these restrictive laws created a lasting presumption of illegitimacy for historical claims of racial intermixture. Defenders of racial purity could depend on these laws to render interracial relationships, whether married or unmarried, improbable and illegitimate.[12] Not all states had antimiscegenation

---

[10] *See* Leslie Espinoza & Angela P. Harris, *Afterword: Embracing the Tar-Baby – LatCrit Theory and the Sticky Mess of Race*, 85 CAL L. REV. 1585, 1608 n.69 (explaining that "mixed race is almost part of the official culture in Mexico"). *See generally,* Colin M. MacLachlan & Jaime E. Rodríguez, THE FORGING OF THE COSMIC RACE: A REINTERPRETATION OF COLONIAL MEXICO (1980)

[11] *See* Gilberto Freyre, THE MASTERS AND THE SLAVES: A STUDY IN THE DEVELOPMENT OF BRAZILIAN CIVILIZATION (2d ed. 1986). *But c.f.,* Carl N. Degler, NEITHER BLACK NOR WHITE: SLAVERY AND RACE RELATIONS IN BRAZIL AND THE UNITED STATES (1971).

[12] Jesse H. Choper, *Consequences of Supreme Court Decisions Upholding Individual Constitutional Rights*, 83 MICH. L. REV. 1, 135–38 (1984) (describing the effect of antimiscegenation law on the status of children); Josephine Ross, *The Sexualization of Difference: A Comparison of Mixed-Race and Same-Gender Marriage*, 37 HARV. C.R.-C.L. L. Rev. 255, 268 n.59 (2002) (noting the children born to interracial couples were disinherited and considered illegitimate).

laws,[13] but the sting of restriction extended to other states to forge a collective for-getting and denial of the existence of mixed race. The absence of a national, judicial acceptance of mixed race facilitated a collective belief in racial purity. Because it was illegal and immoral, then it could not have occurred. With states withholding the marital right from biracial couples, they attempted to deny and erase the inti-mate reality of persons, like the Lovings, who would have sought alternatives to the prohibitive law. It is this dominant imagination of the past that present assertions must face and overcome.

ANTIMISCEGENIST RHETORIC

The collective memory of race relations in the United States overlooks and omits the reality of mixed race. There has existed a squeamishness, a disgust, a denouncement of "race mixing" that has sparked riots,[14] instituted legal prohibitions,[15] and con-structed categories,[16] each of which insist on the genealogical separation of black, white, and red. Accepting the alternative entails a violation of the law, social mores, and perhaps morality – each is a considerable factor in assessing historical possibil-ities in the interpretation of the past. At the same time, recognizing the validity of a mixed-race past in defiance of a prohibitive law challenges the antimiscegenation regime that insists on racial polarity, even in the practical face of contradiction.

Conceptions of a monoracial, pre-*Loving* past perpetuate a static approach to mixed race that definitively precludes the legitimization of its existence. These con-ceptions, however, are accumulations of historical contingencies; memory itself is an anachronism. An examination of the past of mixed race reveals a historical context where this existence was ignored and suppressed. This entails two primary misapplications of contemporary standards for past situations. First, this presents a

---

[13] For a thorough chronological list of state laws prohibiting interracial marriage, including specific inter-mixtures, see Phyl Newbeck, Virginia Hasn't Always Been for Lovers: Interracial Marriage Bans and the Case of Richard and Mildred Loving 227–31 app. C (2004).

[14] The Tulsa Race Riots of 1921 were said to have been sparked by an incident involving a black man, Dick Rowland, and a white woman, Sarah Page, in a downtown elevator. Walter F. White, *The Eruption of Tulsa*, The Nation, June 29, 1921, at 909–10.

[15] In Virginia, the Racial Integrity Act of 1924 prohibited most marriages between whites and nonwhites, with an exception for American Indians of limited blood degree. See Kevin Noble Maillard, *The Pocahontas Exception: The Exemption of American Indian Ancestry from Racial Purity Law*, 12 Mich. J. Race & L. 351, 357 (2007).

[16] Virginia's Racial Integrity Act required citizens to register their race with the state Bureau of Vital Statistics. See id. at 369. Louisiana had a similar agency for racial registration and approval, with Naomi Drake wielding cruel power over those persons she suspected of hiding nonwhite ancestry. Drake was described as "an autocrat [who] was for fifteen years the arbiter of who was black and who was white." See Randall Kennedy, Interracial Intimacies: Sex, Marriage, Identity, and Adoption 5–6 (2003).

skewed view of past events according to dominant and desired conceptions of what the past could or should have been, rather than the actual past itself. Thus, reliance on this past (that never "existed") to justify present manifestations of interracialism (that do "exist") makes for a Sisyphean task. Second, present imaginations of the past are largely based on unquestioned representations that stack rhetorical possibilities against personal narrative. Such assumptions stem from a dominant historical belief in the rarity of amalgamation and the repugnance of race mixing. It is within this temporal misplacement that the memory of racial purity gains political legitimacy, resulting in exasperation for the mixed-race subjects who seek legitimacy.

Against a collective memory and legal framework where races are forbidden to intermingle, both asserters and deniers of a mixed racial past measure the probability of its occurrence. On both sides, narrators conflate fact and fiction, or history and memory, to retell the past to their best advantage. These individual renditions show the political motivations and legal justifications within different allegations of the "truth." Deniers of mixed race quickly rely on legal and social privilege to create an alternative memory that rejects the possibility of such liaisons. They are aided by antimiscegenist rhetoric and practice, which not only delegitimates interracial intimacies, but insists on their legal impossibility. At the same time, the claimant/asserter must confront the collective memory and legal prohibition that forgets and refuses his or her cross-racial connection. Such claims rooted in the past face a roadblock of denial anchored by 1967's *Loving* decision, which outlawed the last institutionalized vestiges of racial difference and inequality. *Loving* did not instantly change American attitudes about sex, marriage, and family, but it opened up new possibilities for intimacy. As Rachel Moran states, "*Loving* aspired to change the law, but the human heart lay beyond its realm."[17]

Even today, in the midst of the *Loving* era, mixed race remains a threat to political stability and social respectability.[18] "Great efforts are made today to deny that this or that great man had illicit relations with Negro women," wrote J. A. Rogers in 1942.[19] Decades later, in the post-*Loving* era, the same statement rings true. As recently as 1999, U.S. Senator Robert Bennett created a controversy that framed interracial sex as the penultimate destroyer of political careers. Commenting on George W. Bush's security as a Republican nominee for President, Bennett predicted no problems unless Bush "step[ped] in front of a bus" or "some black woman [came] forward

---

[17] Moran, INTERRACIAL INTIMACY at 99.

[18] This disapproval of interracialism is most fervent in the discomfiture accompanying black male–white female pairings. *See generally*, Elise Lemire, "MISCEGENATION": MAKING RACE IN AMERICA (2002); Martha Hodes, WHITE WOMEN, BLACK MEN: ILLICIT SEX IN THE NINETEENTH CENTURY SOUTH (1997).

[19] J. A. Rogers, SEX AND RACE: A HISTORY OF WHITE, NEGRO, AND INDIAN MISCEGENATION IN THE TWO AMERICAS: VOL. 2: THE NEW WORLD 221 (1970).

with an illegitimate child."[20] Recent events further illustrate the endurance of interracial controversy. A commercial during the 2005 Super Bowl sparked a flood of
complaints to the Federal Communications Commission (FCC) when it featured
a blonde white woman disrobing in the locker room in front of a clothed black
football player.[21] Many of the complaints focused on the suggested nudity, with an
unannounced statement that the interracial content of the commercial was "inappropriate."[22] In October 2006, opponents of Tennessee Senate candidate Harold Ford,
Jr. aired commercials that drew attention to his interracial dating patterns.[23] Both the
Super Bowl and the Ford commercials capitalize on the insecurities of a viewing
populace accustomed to suppressing overt racial antipathy. Modern progressiveness
and interracial tolerance fail to overcome deep-seated insecurities about conduct
that is no longer prohibited by law but still discouraged in practice.

PUBLIC SECRETS

Examining the instability of the color line in the most public examples shifts the
collective awareness of interracialism from margin to center. Public debates reveal
an underlying notion of fear and disbelief: fear of the erosion of racial boundaries
and also of venerable cultural memories. Disbelievers and protectors of the fiction
of racial purity rely on legal impossibility to refute the legitimacy of interracial relations between blacks and whites. Even in virtually irrefutable contexts, old notions
of racial boundaries insist on reappearing – ridiculously so.

On December 13, 2003, Essie Mae Washington-Williams, a seventy-eight-year-
old woman of color, stepped forward and revealed herself as the unacknowledged
daughter of the late Senator and segregationist, Strom Thurmond.[24] At first glance,
the dichotomy is unlikely: staunch segregationist and interracial sex.[25] Strom
Thurmond's impassioned speeches for states' rights demonstrate an unwavering
stance for enforcement of racial boundaries. Speaking at a 1948 presidential campaign rally, the Dixiecrat candidate held forth that: "There's not enough troops in

---

[20] *N.A.A.C.P. Infuriated by Remark about Bush*, N.Y. TIMES, Aug. 17, 1999, at A12.
[21] Judy Battista, *ABC Puts N.F.L. in "Desperate" Situation*, N.Y. TIMES, Nov. 17, 2004, at D1.
[22] Clay Calvert, *The First Amendment, the Media and the Culture Wars: Eight Important Lessons from
      2004 about Speech, Censorship, Science and Public Policy*, 41 CAL. W. L. REV. 325, 355 (2005).
[23] Ford, an African-American bachelor, had attended a fundraiser sponsored by *Playboy* magazine. The
      ad featured a young blonde woman staring coquettishly at the camera, seductively beckoning Ford to
      "call me." Robin Toner, *In Tight Senate Race, Attack Ad on Black Candidate Stirs Furor*, N.Y. TIMES,
      Oct. 26, 2006, at A1 (describing the controversial Republican campaign commercial).
[24] Michael Janofsky, *Woman, 78, Says She Is a Daughter of Thurmond*, N.Y. TIMES, Dec. 14, 2003,
      at 41.
[25] Thurmond once espoused that segregation laws "are essential to the protection of the racial integrity
      and purity of the white and Negro races alike." Kari Frederickson, THE DIXIECRAT REVOLT AND THE
      END OF THE SOLID SOUTH 106 (2001).

the Army ... to force the Southern people to break down segregation and admit the Negro race into our theaters, into our swimming pools, into our schools and into our homes."[26] Nine years later, he staged a twenty-eight-hour filibuster in the U.S. Senate to protest a federal housing scheme that he characterized as "race mixing." Despite Thurmond's later record of race-friendly policies and programs,[27] these persistent memories define him as the historical frontman for a politically sanctioned racial hierarchy.

Three months after the Senator's death, the "walnut complexioned"[28] woman confirmed long-standing rumors by announcing to the media that she was the product of an affair between a twenty-two-year-old Thurmond and a sixteen-year-old black maid, Carrie Butler, in 1925.[29] Essie Mae's relationship with Thurmond provides an optimal study for denial, because the chain of evidence still exists. Essie's physicality is her proof, and circumstantial evidence corroborated by others makes her claim unassailable. "I feel as though a tremendous weight has been lifted," revealed Essie Mae in reference to going public with her story.[30] This weight refers to a comprehensive, unspoken agreement of silence, which remained intact until Thurmond's death.[31] Thurmond similarly stayed silent about Essie Mae, his firstborn child, and he quietly communicated to her that this treatment would not change during his lifetime. The totality of this silence extended beyond the immediate family, with the convenient compliance of South Carolina news sources and citizens facilitating the nonrecognition of the obvious. During Essie Mae's years as a student at South Carolina State College, Thurmond, then-governor of the state, regularly visited

---

[26] Bob Herbert, Op-Ed., *Racism and the G.O.P.*, N.Y. TIMES, Dec. 12, 2002, at A39.

[27] In a Senate Memorial Address celebrating the memory of Strom Thurmond, Senator Joe Biden recalled,

> The *New York Times*, the liberal *New York Times*, in the late forties – it must have been 1947 – wrote about this guy, Strom Thurmond, a public official in South Carolina, who got himself in trouble and lost a primary because he was too empathetic to African Americans. When he was a presiding judge, he started an effort statewide in South Carolina to get better textbooks and materials into black schools, and he tutored young blacks and set up an organization to tutor and teach young blacks how to read. I think it was in 1946 or 1947. The essence of the editorial was that this is "the hope of the South." In the meantime, he got beat by a sitting Senator for being "weak on race."

R. J. Duke Short and Bob Dole, THE CENTENNIAL SENATOR: TRUE STORIES OF STROM THURMOND FROM THE PEOPLE WHO KNEW HIM BEST 368 (2008).

[28] Darryl Fears, *'At Last I Feel Completely Free', Mixed Race Daughter of the Late Strom Thurmond Steps into Spotlight*, WASH. POST, Dec. 18, 2003, at A2.

[29] Essie Mae Washington Williams, *A 62-Year Old Secret: 'Strom Thurmond Was My Father'*, L.A. TIMES, Dec. 17, 2003, at B13.

[30] *Thurmond's Daughter Days Disclosure Set Her Free*, N.Y. TIMES, Dec. 17, 2003.

[31] Her children urged her to come forward, although they previously kept quiet because "it was the best overall for everybody." Valerie Bauerine and Lauren Markoe, *She's a Quiet Person, a Very Thoughtful Person*, THE STATE (Columbia, SC), Dec. 17, 2003

her, with little attempt to hide his intentions or identity on campus.[32] Students did not question his visibility on campus, and they did not publicly insinuate a father-daughter relationship. They just assumed without acknowledgment.

Making sense of racial boundaries necessitates the compartmentalization of fact and fiction in order to render once-incontrovertible facts questionable.[33] This creative construction of alternative reality dismisses the incongruous so that the illogical becomes rational. With Essie Mae, her children, and her friends each possessing knowledge of her famous father, they observed a tacit agreement to de-register the relationship as a speakable fact. This repression of not only the past but also the very real present registers as a function of Southern etiquette that turns a polite eye to the taboo of interracial relations. As the mores and laws of the South made such liaisons illegitimate by law and nonexistent in speech, race mixing became an erasable element of one's past. Sexual intimacy between blacks and whites was not a subversive act provided it was not formally acknowledged.[34] Voluntary distinctions of this type singularly define a regional culture reluctant to come to terms with its historical schizophrenia. To have these two conflicting terms coexist (racial proximity and racial separation) requires regulation of plausibility. Thus, selective memory and willful amnesia expunge contradictory and problematic elements, creating a prevailing memory of past and present that, for practical purposes, has never existed.

Divulging the previously hushed information clearly defies a cultural code that turns a blind eye toward miscegenation. In this regulation of race and memory, the task of bringing interracialism to a discursive forefront continues to agitate detractors who wish to suppress interracial deviance and uphold traditional boundaries. U.S. Representative Joe Wilson[35] criticized Essie Mae's revelation as a "smear on the image that [Thurmond] has as a person of high integrity," placing doubt on

---

[32] Students and faculty would clear out of the designated building where Thurmond and Essie Mae were to meet. He would arrive on campus in a "big, black Cadillac limousine" and park in a conspicuous location on campus. Other students had no confusions that the then-governor visited a student at the all-black college. Ken Cummins, *Strom's Secret*, THE BLACK COMMENTATOR, *available at* http://www.blackcommentator.com/21_re_print.html (last visited Feb. 25, 2008).

[33] Even if circumstances dictate a probable connection between black and white, such as between Thurmond and Essie Mae, the fiction of racial separation allows deniers and silencers to reasonably portray it as unlikely. This refashioning of fact to align it with fiction quietly imposes convention on truth, shaping reality in a way that transforms incontrovertible truths into frivolous impossibilities.

[34] Antimiscegenation law's focus on delegitimizing interracial unions secured the sexual freedom of white men by providing a legal loophole that outlawed marriage only. Written law remained silent on unrecorded relationships, thus creating a legal fiction that did not countenance interracial sexuality despite its obvious and repeated occurrence. *See generally*, Charles Frank Robinson II, DANGEROUS LIAISONS: SEX AND LOVE IN THE SEGREGATED SOUTH (2003); Winthrop D. Jordan, WHITE OVER BLACK: AMERICAN ATTITUDES TOWARD THE NEGRO, 1550–1812 (1977).

[35] The same Joe Wilson infamously called President Obama a "liar" during a speech to a joint session of Congress in September 2009.

the biracial woman's claims that Thurmond was her father.[36] Wilson also perceived an attack on the dead as a "tawdry" stain on the image of those "unable to defend themselves."[37] Joining the camp of resistance, State Senator John Courson criticized the story for being "ludicrous" and "absolutely bizarre." But most intriguingly, he objected to Essie Mae's claim because he had "never heard of any of this from the [S]enator or anyone."

Living witnesses in the position of a narrative minority must overcome presumptions of illegitimacy, with the majority retaining the final judgment on truth. Essie Mae's self-affirmation did not rest as the lone authoritative source. The deniers mentioned earlier, Wilson and Courson, changed their stances, apologizing and calling her a "class act" once the Thurmond family came forward to confirm the connection. Two days after the public revelation, the family swiftly issued a press release stating that they "acknowledge[d] Ms. Essie Mae Washington-Williams' claim to her heritage."[38] Little resistance came from Strom Thurmond, Jr., who announced "We have no reason to believe that Mrs. Williams was not telling the truth." These statements revealed a sly concession to her claims, but they do not invite the possibility of establishing a relationship, and they refuse to relax the conventions that had previously maintained the silence and separation. This eloquent and removed ombudsmanship provided the final voice in the Essie Mae-Thurmond controversy. Even though Essie Mae, as a living witness and article of evidence, could prove herself as the black daughter of Strom Thurmond, she still did not possess the final, authoritative voice that conclusively ruled her story as true. Her challenge to the racial binary only finds resolution in the adjudicating voice of the protected white family.

TOWARD INTERRACIAL LEGITIMACY

Traditional historians embrace a common trope of denial: genetic evidence does not represent conclusive proof, subjective accounts of kinship do not become truth unless mutually verified, and recorded oral history potentially memorializes historical exaggerations. Each of these methods of questioning the legitimacy of historic interracial intimacy operate from a legal standpoint that presumes the impossibility of verifying such claims. Because each of these stories originated during a period where open and legitimate race crossing was viewed as subversive, the act of defying the prevailing historical silence imposes a legal anachronism. How does one legitimate a bloodline form a prevailing paradigm that declares it illegitimate? In the antimiscegenation regime that permitted interracial sex but refused interracial

[36] Jennifer Talheim, *Reactions to Claim of Kinship Mixed*, SUN NEWS, Dec. 14, 2003, at A1.
[37] Joe Wilson, Letter to the Editor, THE STATE (Columbia, SC), Dec. 16, 2003.
[38] Michael Janofsky, *Thurmond Kin Acknowledge Black Daughter*, N.Y. Times, Dec. 16, 2003, at A28.

marriage, a telling distinction arises. If marriage symbolically solidifies the union of two persons, and this liaison is ratified by the church and/or state, what becomes of the human outcomes of inevitable sexual contact outside of this realm of official approval? The prevailing legal system that separated blacks and whites in the Jim Crow South had ripple effects across the United States. Non-Southern jurisdictions may not have prohibited state- or church-sanctioned relationships between men and women of different races, but this absence of prohibition fails to create a political atmosphere of racial equality and unbridled interracial association. The sting of miscegenation, whether illegal or not, did not depend on the vote of a state legislature.

Geography does not indicate an open acceptance of interracialism, and neither does time. *Loving* may have established a legal precedent for state-sanctioned marital freedom, but it still does not eviscerate the lingering taboo of miscegenation that affects contemporary interactions between people of different races. The antimiscegenation laws that once existed to prevent the soiling of the white race reify the property value concomitant with white racial identity. This "power of exclusion" maintains the elevated value of whiteness, not only environmentally, as with neighborhoods and schools, but also transhistorically. Contemporary assertions of multiracial identity rooted in the past, when examined by the majority, remain illegitimate and improbable until accepted by the white ratifying authority. These stories of interracial affiliation seem implausible, and the narratives appear as romanticized fabrications of a marginalized people asserting their voice. When such assertions link to a collective political struggle of validating marginalized voices, this plea for acceptance calls for a progressive reinterpretation of racial possibilities.

The enforcement of anachronism must be reversed. By pairing the racial restrictions imposed by the pre-*Loving* regime with contemporary debates over a multiracial past, we may clearly understand the continuing influence of antimiscegenation law. The weight of the felonious past erects a monumental barrier to developing a collective memory of a racially mixed nation. When the law exists as a Holmesian repository of all things that a society deems important, changes in the legal system demonstrate a significant shift in the attitudes, beliefs, and desires of that society's members. Whether society follows law or law follows society goes beyond the scope of inquiry for this paper. Yet *Loving* stands as a dramatic shifting point that demonstrates the absence of barriers to achieving the nightmare that segregationists feared. The potential to legitimate all possibilities of race crossings – past, present, and future – should be realized as a result of this case. Compartmentalizing a racially varied nation only to events beginning after 1967 reaffirms the legitimacy of antimiscegenation laws that tautologically question the legitimacy of historically based, pre-1967 interracial roots. Looking back to *Loving* as the multiracial epiphany reinforces the prevailing memory of racial separatism while further underscoring the illegitimacy of miscegenations past.

7

Love at the Margins

The Racialization of Sex and the Sexualization of Race

Camille A. Nelson

The U.S. Supreme Court holds steadfast to the theory of a color-blind America.[1] While this may be a worthy aspiration, those of us involved in black-white interracial relationships know that color-blindness is but a legal fiction. As a black woman in a long-term relationship with a white man in America, I will analyze some of the sociopolitically and socioculturally imposed challenges faced by black-white interracial couples. While such disparate scrutiny oscillates between curiosity, fascination, and hostility, there remains a racial fixation that reveals the Supreme Court's theory of color-blindness as wishful thinking. In this respect, interracial couples might be the proverbial canaries in the coal mine, revealing suffocating racial dynamics at work just beneath the surface.

Critical Race Theory's narrative style exposes the ways in which the personal is political. Put another way, the intimate is deeply sociopolitically enmeshed. By exploring the ways in which my interracial relationship has been scrutinized and hypersexualized, I posit that much of the way we comprehend race in America is sexualized, and that much of the way we understand sex is racialized. As such, racism is also often sexualized. This chapter connects such racialized sexualization to its historical roots. Thus, while we have progressed a great deal since the landmark decision of the Supreme Court in *Loving v. Virginia*,[2] there exists a troubling racial

---

[1] Justice Harlan's dissent in *Plessy v. Ferguson* famously stated, "There is no caste here. *Our constitution is color-blind, and neither knows nor tolerates classes among citizens.* ... The law regards man as man, and takes no account of his surroundings or of his color when his civil rights as guaranteed by the supreme law of the land are involved." *Plessy v. Ferguson*, 163 U.S. 537, 559 (1896) (Harlan, J., dissenting) (emphasis added). Recently Chief Justice Roberts, writing for the plurality in *Parents Involved in Community Schools v. Seattle School Dist. No. 1*, reinforced this constitutional norm of color-blindness in prohibiting school districts from using race to determine student school placements. He candidly stated, "The way to stop discrimination on the basis of race is to stop discriminating on the basis of race." 127 S.Ct. 2738 at 2768 (2007). To support this vision, Justice Roberts relied on a long line of constitutional jurisprudence.

[2] 388 U.S. 1 (1967).

fixation in America that is revealed when one gazes through the lens of encounters faced by black-white interracial couples.

RACIALIZED SEX, SEXUALIZED RACE

External curiosity and assessments are central to the life of many interracial couples – someone is always trying to figure us out. The relationship is at times interpreted as an exercise in fetishization, adventure, deviance, self-hatred, payback, or exploration.[3] A culture of racialized sexual preoccupation continues to have contemporary resonance, affecting both partners in a black-white interracial relationship – we are deemed "kinky" because of our historically forbidden racialized relationship.[4]

For our tenth wedding anniversary, my husband and I traveled to an all-inclusive resort in the Caribbean. We were thoroughly enjoying our time alone, it being our first trip without our children. Enjoying drinks in the piano lounge, the query of an American man sitting nearby shocked us: "Are you two porn stars?" he asked.[5] I nearly fell off the barstool. After regaining my composure, I explained to him that we were vacationing in celebration of our tenth anniversary, that we had three children, that I was a law professor, and that my husband worked in film (but not *that* way). We had no time to summon the full force of our annoyance, as we were both so shocked.

Interestingly, noted legal scholar Patricia Williams recognizes that "[l]iving life as the pornographic target of another's fantasies is always a nightmare, even when the fantasy is one of idealized desire – never mind when the fantasy is one of disdainful vilification. Life as a bull's-eye has nothing to do with who you really are, or the statistical realities of the group you represent."[6] There, in the lounge, an external assessor and his lascivious questioning eclipsed our romantic musings. Our critical consciousness demanded that we both simultaneously "claim the normal."[7] We both

---

[3]   *See* Anita Kathy Foeman & Teresa Nance, *From Miscegenation to Multiculturalism: Perceptions and Stages of Interracial Relationship Development*, 29 J. BLACK STUDIES 540, 545 (1999); Maria P. P. Root, LOVE'S REVOLUTION: INTERRACIAL MARRIAGE 49–70 (2001).

[4]   Randall Kennedy, INTERRACIAL INTIMACIES: SEX, MARRIAGE, IDENTITY, AND ADOPTION 14 (2003) ("Race has – and has long had – a massive presence in the sexual imaginations of Americans."); Rachel Moran, INTERRACIAL INTIMACY: THE REGULATION OF RACE AND ROMANCE 115–16 (noting the sexual titillation and exoticism of interracial relationships); *see also* Jared Sexton, *The Consequence of Race Mixture: Racialized Barriers and the Politics of Desire*, 9 SOC. IDENTITIES 241, 242 (2003) (exploring "the domain of sexuality," which is intrinsic to the construction of race as sexual predilection).

[5]   I feel compelled to mention that we were dressed inconspicuously, if not conservatively. Indeed this particular resort mandated that men wear jackets in restaurants and lounges. I was dressed in a simple, but formal, dress that I had worn to dinner. There was certainly nothing salacious or provocative about our attire.

[6]   Patricia J. Williams, THE ROOSTER'S EGG 170 (1995).

[7]   *See* Dustin R. Alcala, *Physical Boundaries of Color/Cultural Boundaries of Place*, 9 BERKELEY MCNAIR RES. J. 93, 97 (2001) ("Claiming ordinariness may also be a way of claiming achievement over racism.

resorted to the tried-and-true strategy used by many interracial couples – we essentialized ourselves as just another regular married couple. No, we were not porn stars; we wanted, in that moment, to blend in and not be seen – nothing unusual here, no racialized spectacle to be observed, just plain, ordinary, and racially average. Our celebratory mood was dampened by the ruminations of this white American stranger who felt compelled to interrupt our private discussion with a most inappropriate question.

If it were possible, we would have gladly embraced color-blindness in that moment. In this man's mind, our relationship was sexualized because of our respective races – what else could we have been but porn stars? The thought that we were celebrating a decade together as a married couple never crossed his mind, nor his lips. Indeed, he could have asked, "Are you two celebrating a special occasion?" Instead, he quickly betrayed an essential truism about American culture, the deep-seated preoccupation with the racialization of sex and the sexualization of race. Indeed, I wonder if such preoccupations are more prevalent in the white cultural imagination? Specifically, black people have never asked us such intrusive questions.

Instead, the chasm between black and white is vast. Any relationship that seemingly bridges this gulf invites an inquisition, especially where the black-white binary is compromised to the point of allowing for intimacy and sex. The callous nature of these observations is symptomatic of a jarring reality for many interracial couples. Amorous intentions are interrupted by the cruel reality of a piercing, often hostile, world. To be an interracial couple is to be laid bare to the most probing of gazes. It is telling that this man felt perfectly comfortable making these assessments of our relationship. It is one thing to *think*, "they must be porn stars" to yourself and to leave it there, in the confines of one's own mind; it is quite another to approach strangers, interrupt a conversation, and ask them about the most intimate of subjects. But we were the only interracial couple, possibly at the entire resort, and therefore we stood out like a sore thumb. Such conspicuousness is part of what attracts unwanted attention. Blending into the surrounding "coupledom" is not usually an option.

These external assessments also pertain to my partner, who is often given what I will call a "black pass" – he is accorded temporary black privileges, as oxymoronic as that seems, because of his interracial relationship. Unlike mine, his "street cred" is not just intact, but is actually enhanced. He must not be one of those white men who oozes patriarchal white heterosexual privilege; essentially he must not be "da man" if his intimate partner is black. While I concede that my partner is a progressive white man, his race, gender, and heterosexuality nevertheless privilege him

Couples in this research seek to enjoy the ordinariness of married life as well as the uniqueness of their multicultural relationship. Their challenges, argument content, and conflict resolution strategies are common to most couples" [citation omitted]).

in many ways too complicated to fully unpack in this short space. The cumulative privilege that his majority identities generate is so deeply ingrained in the fabric of our lives that to exist otherwise would require wholesale deconstruction of socio-political and sociocultural systems. In short, dismantling heterosexual white male privilege would require a cultural revolution.

Interestingly, in keeping with the hypersexualization of interracial relationships, my partner's "black pass" also attaches to his sexual construction. He is accorded sexual deference, and constructed as sexually black, by those who assume I would not be in a relationship with a white man unless he could fulfill me as a black man could.[8] Over the last fifteen years of our marriage, various people – friends, colleagues and strangers, gay and straight alike – have curiously felt comfortable either making statements, joking, or asking questions about my partner's sexual prowess. These assessments are not benign as they fixate on supposed hallmarks of race, particularly blackness.

Same-race heterosexual sex is less politicized than the sex lives of interracial couples. That people feel comfortable commenting on such things reveals the normative construction of black-white interracial relationships as inherently sexual. It is unlikely that same-race heterosexual couples have to deal with inquiries into the sufficiency of their respective sexual gratification. They match and somehow their relationship makes sense. Their sex lives are their own, unless they choose to make a spectacle of themselves. We, on the other hand, are constructed as sexualized spectacle.

These moments of sociopolitical puncture provide insight into assumed societal access to and understanding of black-white interracial relationships. It never ceases to amaze me that people have little compunction about probing into our sexual relationship. To my mind this indicates that black-white interracial couples have decreased access to true privacy. As a legal scholar, I am left to wonder whether such racialized sexualization means that we face diminished reasonable expectations of privacy. It is unfortunate that now, whenever strangers approach us, I am a little nervous about what might come out of their mouths. In essence, society seeks to peer inside, if not puncture, the interracial relationship – it is this piercing gaze that disrupts and disturbs our private sanctuary. Again, the relationship cannot be about love; there must be sexual motivations propelling it.

---

[8]   *See* Kennedy, *supra* note 4, at 14–18 (discussing the sexual stereotypes surrounding black manhood). *See generally* Sander L. Gilman, DIFFERENCE AND PATHOLOGY: STEREOTYPES OF SEXUALITY, RACE, AND MADNESS 109–28 (1985) (examining black sexuality in modern consciousness); Jan Nederveen Pieterse, WHITE ON BLACK: IMAGES OF AFRICA AND BLACKS IN WESTERN POPULAR CULTURE (1992) (examining stereotypical images of blacks as entertainers, servants, athletes, and in the sexual arena).

Interestingly, in commenting on the fact that she was just "an ordinary black woman who fell in love with an ordinary white man,"[9] Mildred Loving made the following comments almost twenty years after her beloved Richard tragically died in an automobile accident: "We weren't bothering anyone. And if we hurt some people's feelings, that was just too bad. All we ever wanted was to get married, because we loved each other. Some people will never change, but that's their problem, not mine. I married the only man I had ever loved, and I'm happy for the time we had together. For me, that was enough."[10]

Despite the centrality of the love my partner and I share, the reality is that the rhetoric of sexuality is a powerful component of the cultural script that is imposed on us. Sex and sexuality are used as shorthand in attempts to comprehend race and racialization. It would appear that the black-white couple has such sociocultural, and thus sociolegal, force in America precisely because sex and sexuality are a significant part of how we experience race as a concept. Accordingly, interracial unions have been subjected to myriad forms of regulation, both historically and in contemporary society, as a means of policing not just interracial mingling, but even the prospect of interracial sex.

The Cambria List provides an interesting framework for analyzing this point. This list was developed by an attorney representing a number of pornographers who wanted to prevent obscenity charges being brought by the Justice Department under George W. Bush. Fearing a crackdown spurred on by the religious Right, the guidelines offer suggestions for restrictions for pornography shown in America.[11] The list seeks to restrict the depiction of certain sexual activities or sexual activities in certain settings. There are, however, three identity restrictions: no bisexual sex, no transsexuals, and no sex between a black man and a white woman. The list reveals that America remains fixated with the intersection of race, gender, and sex. One of the curiosities of this list is that while depictions of interracial sex between white men and black women are not proscribed, depictions of interracial sex between

---

9   *See* Robert A. Pratt, *Crossing the Color Line: A Historical Assessment and Personal Narrative of Loving v. Virginia*, 41 HOWARD L.J. 229, 244 (1998).

10   *Id.* at 244 (quoting Interview with Mildred Loving in Milford, Va. [Oct. 12, 1994]).

11   *See* Frontline, PBS, American Porn, http://www.pbs.org/wgbh/pages/ frontline/shows/porn/prosecuting/cambria.html (last visited May 22, 2009) ("Do not include any of the following: No shots with appearance of pain or degradation; No facials (bodyshots are OK if shot is not nasty); No bukakke; No spitting or saliva mouth to mouth; No food used as sex object; No peeing unless in a natural setting, e.g., field, roadside; No coffins; No blindfolds; No wax dripping; No two dicks in/near one mouth; No shot of stretching pussy; No fisting; No squirting; No bondage-type toys or gear unless very light; No girls sharing same dildo (in mouth or pussy); Toys are OK if shot is not nasty; No hands from 2 different people fingering same girl; No male/male penetration; No transsexuals; No bi-sex; No degrading dialogue, e.g., "Suck this cock, bitch" while slapping her face with a penis; No menstruation topics; No incest topics; No forced sex, rape themes, etc.; No black men-white women themes.")

black men and white women are discouraged as taboo. In this way the pornography industry replicates and reinforces the historic American approach to black-white interracial sex – black women were constructed as sexually available to white men, whereas black men who became intimate with white women often risked their lives. Clearly the intersection of race, gender, and sex produces contemporary disparities firmly anchored in American sociolegal history.

Interestingly, sex also preoccupies the minds of those assessing same-sex relationships. In attempting to dismantle this sexual default for gay male relationships in particular, queer activists also seek to claim the normal.[12] In advocating for the articulation of a gay male masculinity, Professor G. W. Dowsett states that "[t]he greatest challenge facing masculinity research and men's studies lies in dealing with the actuality of homoeroticism and gay sex."[13] As with black-white interracial relationships, eroticism, not love, is centered. Like black-white relationships to external assessors, assumptions about sex and sexuality define gay male relationships. In making this point, Joseph Bristow states that "[w]e are – to the heterosexual world – walking definitions of sex. We mean sex. Our lifestyle is defined as a sexual lifestyle that says 'fuck.'... Gay men provide a convenient target for the displacement and projection of widespread social confusion about heterosexuality on to a small 'perverse' group."[14] Similarly, black-white interracial couples are a target for the displacement and projection of widespread social condemnation or preoccupation with the intersection of race and sexuality. We are constructed as "perverse" and non-normative in our sexuality because of our racialization.

Thus, as with many same-sex couples, interracial couples are often essentialized in a way that centers sex and marginalizes love. It seems society remains unable to appreciate that such relationships could not endure without the existence of committed love; there is simply too much societal interference – racialized static – to survive as an interracial couple in the absence of genuine love.

As society intrudes on such relationships in constant and disruptive ways, interracial relationships are inherently political. This is the level at which the personal becomes political. Interracial relationships and mixed-race families cannot escape societal assessments and impositions based on external value judgments. Race, despite being a construct, is real and tangible. Thus race is not only noticed, but it is acted on.

---

[12] *See, e.g.,* G. W. Dowsett, *I'll Show You Mine, if You'll Show Me Yours: Gay Men, Masculinity Research, Men's Studies, and Sex,* 22 THEORY & SOC'Y 697 (1993).
[13] *Id.* at 705.
[14] *Id.* at 706 (quoting Joseph Bristow, *Homophobia/Misogyny: Sexual Fears, Sexual Definitions, in* COMING ON STRONG: GAY POLITICS AND CULTURE 54, 74 [Simon Shepherd & Mich Wallis eds., 1989]) (emphasis omitted).

CONSCIOUSLY RECLAIMING LOVE

Loving v. Virginia explicitly recognized the racialized foundation for antimiscegenation laws. Delivering the majority opinion in *Loving*, Chief Justice Earl Warren exposed antimiscegenation laws as rules designed to preserve white supremacy when he noted: "The fact that Virginia prohibits only interracial marriages involving white persons demonstrates that the racial classifications must stand on their own justification, as measures designed to maintain White Supremacy."[15] Despite the magnitude of this decision, however, there is a glaring omission.

While laudable, the *Loving* decision failed to explicitly recognize the right to love whom one chooses despite – or, more appropriately, beyond – race. The decision marginalized the love at issue. In finding a violation of the Fourteenth Amendment, the Court recognized that "Marriage is one of the 'basic civil rights of man,' fundamental to our very existence and survival,"[16] but nowhere did the Court situate marriage in love or love in marriage. Instead, the Court focused on marriage as the proper venue for procreation and emphasized the guaranteed continuation of humanity. Undoubtedly a more expansive approach to the case would have rankled many, especially in 1967.

Pronouncements in support of unrestricted love, beyond the realm of marriage, would have alarmed constituencies disinclined to be supportive of interracial mixing more generally and might have opened a Pandora's box implicating same-sex marriage, polygamy, consanguinity prohibitions, and age-of-consent issues. Indeed, even in 2009 we heard similar concerns being voiced from some constituencies, as the topic of marriage equality for gays and lesbians became an important sociopolitical issue.[17] So instead of centering love, while carving out appropriate age and consanguinity restrictions, the Court took the safe route and held that:

> To deny this fundamental freedom on so unsupportable a basis as the racial classifications embodied in these statutes, classifications so directly subversive of the principle of equality at the heart of the Fourteenth Amendment, is surely to deprive all the State's citizens of liberty without due process of law. The Fourteenth Amendment requires that the freedom of choice to marry not be restricted by invidious racial discriminations. Under our Constitution, the freedom to marry or not marry, a person of another race resides with the individual and cannot be infringed by the State.[18]

[15] *Loving v. Virginia*, 388 U.S. 1, 11–12 (majority opinion).
[16] *Id.* at 12 (majority opinions).
[17] *See* American Family Association, *Gay Marriage: Why Would It Affect Me? Ten Arguments Against Same Sex Marriage*, http://civilliberty.about.com/gi/dynamic/offsite.htm?zi=1/XJ&sdn=civilliberty& cdn=newsissues&tm=51&f=10&tt=3&bt=1&bts=1&zu=http%3A//www.nogaymarriage.com/tenarguments.asp (last visited May 24, 2009).
[18] *Loving*, 388 U.S. at 12 (majority opinion).

Excellent legal reasoning, but where is the love? Even the Declaration of Independence enshrined an entitlement to the pursuit of happiness as an inalienable right. Perhaps there is no room in abstract legal reasoning to recognize what should be at the heart of intimate relationships. Perhaps, however, recognition of actual love across and beyond race is so at odds with our perception of such relationships as to be unfathomable and hence unmentionable. As a socioculturally constituted and permeated institution, the Supreme Court Justices were also limited in their ability to appreciate the love in *Loving* and, indeed, in interracial unions more generally.

Richard Loving eloquently invoked the forgotten love at the heart of the *Loving* case. American Civil Liberties Union attorney Bernard Cohen remarked in his oral arguments before the U.S. Supreme Court that Richard had asked him to relay the following message: "Tell the Court I love my wife, and it is just unfair that I can't live with her in Virginia."[19] This simple message highlights what the Court marginalized: the unfairness and injustice of denying the possibility of love beyond race. The denial of interracial love has a long and deep history in America. For the Lovings, the denial of interracial love meant criminalization and banishment from Virginia.

Theirs is a love story, pure and simple – a love that is often lost when external assessors judge interracial relationships. It would seem that a hallmark of interracial relationships is the external gaze and the corresponding marginalization of the love that fuels any lasting relationship. The public evaluation seldom settles on the private answer of love. Wherever an interracial couple venture, they risk being faced with intrusive comments and questions, attempted separation, and stares or glares. For interracial couples, public spaces can be precarious.

Thus navigation of public venues, versus the private sanctuary,[20] is an issue requiring some deliberation and consensus on the part of many interracial couples. Like other racialized[21] couples, my partner and I do not have the privilege of simply

---

[19] Robert A. Pratt, *Crossing the Color Line: A Historical Assessment and Personal Narrative of Loving v. Virginia*, 41 Howard L.J. 229, 239 (1998) (quoting 64 Landmark Briefs and Arguments of the Supreme Court of the United States: Constitutional Law 741, 959 [Philip B. Kurland & Gerhard Casper eds., 1975]). *See generally* Peter Wallenstein, Tell the Court I Love My Wife: Race, Marriage, and Law – An American History (2002).

[20] This Article uses "private sanctuary" to refer to the personal space, often a home, created by interracial couples as a "raceless" refuge. While race continues to exist, the private sanctuary allows for freedom from the baggage the external world foists on one as racialized other. In the private sanctuary, most of the time, there is no such baggage; the negative social constructs attached to skin color do not operate, or at least not quite so obviously.

[21] Racialization is the process through which ascriptions are made about race and skin color. Racialization reveals that race is a social, rather than a biological, construct, as people racialized as other are marginalized by virtue of societal perspectives rather than biological determinants. *See* Ian F. Haney López, White by Law: The Legal Construction of Race at 111 (stating "Races are social products. It follows that legal institutions and practices, as essential components of our highly legalized society, have had a hand in the construction of race.")

venturing uncritically and without aforethought where we might.[22] Our reality is that we reflect on whether certain venues will be welcoming, comfortable, or safe. These discussions are now part of our routine – they are our sociopolitical commonplace.

While it would be ideal if people in public spaces were merely indifferent to our interracial relationship, thereby recognizing our union as legitimate, this aspiration is seldom achieved. We are not generally "normalized" in the world external to our home. Instead, those around us in public spaces are highly attuned to our mismatched races. We are not typically recognized or treated as a couple or a family at restaurants, hotels, airports, stores, or other public spaces. Rather than recognize our relationship given our interactions, spatial proximity, and contextual behavior, customer service representatives assume that we are with any nearby person of the matching race and opposite sex – my partner must be in a relationship with the nearest white woman and I must be coupled with a black man, if there is one nearby. These racially motivated societal intrusions include hostility or rudeness, sexual probing, attempted separation, or assumptions that the relationship does not exist. Such default assumptions of race matching always amaze me, especially when we are with our children who are clearly mixed-race – the attendants still fail to recognize us a family unit, asking stupid questions about who is with whom and splitting our party. Contrary to the pronouncements of the Supreme Court, American society is not blind to race or color.

Accordingly, those of us in interracial relationships occasionally struggle to find a way through this public race maze. Richard and Mildred Loving must have explored these public-private distinctions together in deciding whether to challenge the Virginia statute. Undoubtedly, they did not make this decision lightly. Honest communication in any interracial relationship must include recognition of raced societal assumptions and impositions. I call this necessity the requirement of critical consciousness.

---

[22] Couples of color and interracial couples often think about the places they will visit together. Part of the lack of freedom stemmed from segregation; there were simply some places in which people of color were not welcome. Even today, there are some occasions on which hostile sentiments surface through words, deeds, or looks, such as the belief that "blacks are genetically inferior and race mixing is the nearest thing to the end of the world this side of Armageddon." Elinor Langer, THE AMERICAN NEO-NAZI MOVEMENT TODAY: SPECIAL REPORT, *reprinted in* Juan F. Perea et al., RACE AND RACES, CASES AND RESOURCES FOR A DIVERSE AMERICA 481 (2000). Such sentiments hearken back to the days when lynching was commonplace, and the "quintessential lynching offence was social contact with a white woman by a black man, whether or not the contact had been mutually arranged." Emma Coleman Jordan, *Crossing the River of Blood Between Us: Lynching, Violence, Beauty, and the Paradox of Feminist History*, 3 J. GENDER RACE & JUST. 545, 558 (2000). *See generally* Rachel Moran, *supra* note 4 (exploring the ways in which the law was used to enforce the separation of the races). As Professor Randall Kennedy noted, "There are ... powerful forces arrayed against increased rates of black-white intermarriage. ... Through stares, catcalls and even ... violence, they put a pall over interracial intimacy." Randall Kennedy, *How Are We Doing with Loving? Race, Law, and Intermarriage*, 77 B.U. L. REV. 815, 820 (1997).

This enhanced interracial consciousness further demands that partners in such relationships recognize that societal pressures might disparately impact internal relationship dynamics. This, in turn, might hamper effective communication, seamless interaction, and prospects for harmony and longevity. Obviously, such external puncture is to be guarded against and strategically avoided. But this, in turn, requires mutual recognition that enhanced societal pressures are a relationship issue. In short, critical consciousness is a must.

LEGACY AND HISTORY

The vital sociohistorical place of interracial relationships in the American cultural imagination is revealed by a perennial political debate about the supposed dangers of interracial sex, love, and reproduction.[23] Historically, interracial sexual liaisons, consensual or otherwise, were closely regulated given their ability to produce offspring who were racially ambiguous.[24] The policing of the American color line required clear racial distinctions. Interracial unions were problematic as they held within them the specter of racial transcendence and seepage.

This theory of racial contamination is evident from the words of those who "warned that American democracy would be in jeopardy if the color line were compromised," thereby creating a Nation of mongrels.[25] In seeking to construct a racially pure space, these men feared that a burgeoning mixed-race population would convert America into a nation made up of a racially indeterminate populace.

Indeed, courts too relied on the presumed logic of a racialized order of existence. It was simply unnatural, in the minds of many an esteemed jurist, for the races to intimately mingle – to do so would produce devastating results. For instance, in *Scott v. Georgia*, the court stated as follows: "The amalgamation of the races is not only unnatural, but is always productive of deplorable results. ... [T]he offspring of these unnatural connections are generally sickly and effeminate, and ... they are inferior in physical development and strength, to the full-blood of either race. ...

---

[23] *See, e.g.*, Scott v. Georgia, 39 Ga. 321, 324 (1869) (analogizing interracial marriage to marriage between "idiots," as regulating both are "necessary and proper regulations"); State v. Gibson, 36 Ind. 389, 403–04 (1871) (extolling marriage as an "institution established by God" and warning of the dangers of corruption of blood posed by racial amalgamation); State v. Jackson, 80 Mo. 175, 176 (1883) (commenting that interracial relationships were akin to incest and thus were within the lawful ambit of state regulation).

[24] *See* Moran, *supra* note 4, at 20–27 (discussing the issue of "the mulatto" and the ways in which laws were enacted and altered to ensure that the racial boundaries between whiteness and blackness remained firm).

[25] Moran, *supra* note 4, at 57; *see* Kennedy, *supra* note 4, at 13–14 ("[T]he country's population is already what racial purists have long feared it might become: a people characterized by a large measure of admixture, or what many have referred to distastefully as 'mongrelization.'").

They are productive of evil, and evil only, without any corresponding good."[26] The stability of such disdain for mixed-race people is revealed in the consistency of the judicial commentary and legislative unease. Note the striking similarity of the language used in *Eggers v. Olson* – an action to quiet title addressing the question of whether a black man was legally married to "a restricted Choctaw Indian":[27] "The purity of the public morals, the moral and physical development of both races, and the highest advancement of civilization ... all require that they should be kept distinctly separate, and that connections and alliances so unnatural should be prohibited by positive law and subject to no evasion."[28]

Even a cursory review of American political discourse and jurisprudence reveals this deep-seated historical fascination with and repulsion by the thought of intimate interracial mingling. For instance, Benjamin Franklin, in *Observations Concerning the Increase of Mankind*, was preoccupied with racial segregation to maintain white racial purity, culture, language, and even complexion: "[W]hy increase the Sons of Africa, by Planting them in America, where we have so fair an Opportunity, by excluding all Blacks and Tawneys, of increasing the lovely White and Red? But perhaps I am partial to the Complexion of my Country, for such kind of Partiality is natural to Mankind."[29]

Similarly, the desire to protect white racial purity is echoed in comments of founding father Thomas Jefferson, that blacks' "amalgamation with the other color produces a degradation to which no lover of his country, no lover of excellence in the human character can innocently consent."[30] It would seem, therefore, that much contemporary thought on sex, race, and color is informed by our history – a deeply racialized history. There is an ascertainable sociopolitical continuity of thought in our encounters with interracial couples. The challenges faced by black-white interracial couples are part of a robust legacy dating back to the founding of this nation.

CONCLUSION

Even in the twenty-first century, private relationship choices are subject to racialized assessments and societal disapproval. In contrast to these persistent pressures, I cherish the only semblance of racial relaxation that I have ever truly experienced.

---

[26]   39 Ga. 321, 323 (1869).
[27]   *See* 231 P. 483, 483 (Okla. 1924).
[28]   *Id.* at 484 (quoting 18 RULING CASE LAW *Marriage* § 31 [1917]).
[29]   Benjamin Franklin, *Observations Concerning the Increase of Mankind, in* THE PAPERS OF BENJAMIN FRANKLIN 229–31, 233–34 (Yale Univ. Press, 1961).
[30]   Thomas Jefferson, THE PORTABLE THOMAS JEFFERSON 546 (Merrill D. Peterson ed., 1975); Thomas Jefferson, *Jefferson to Edward Coles, August 25, 1814, Thomas Jefferson, Writings* (New York: The Library of America, 1984) *in* RACE AND RACES, *supra* note 22 at 102.

Specifically, in our private and intimate lives, we are just who we are, with no excessive comparing and contrasting along racial lines. But when we exit our private sanctuary and proceed into the external world, we often face intrusive public assessments of our interracial relationship and the racialization of our children. Undoubtedly, such navigation of sociopolitical assessments resonates for many couples – fitting is not easy or necessarily attainable. Most same-race heterosexual couples, however, do not stand out quite so starkly – their races match, and therefore their union is sensible, cognizable, and expected, even if they are unwelcome for other reasons.

This dichotomized racialization is a function of American demographics, revealing persistent segregation in our daily lives.[31] This point is particularly important with respect to black-white interracial relationships as blacks and whites still maintain the greatest social distance in America.[32] Our reality is that part of our critical

---

[31] The Metropolitan Racial and Ethnic Change, which computes racial segregation or disparity using the 2000 Census, has found that, in the metropolitan St. Louis area, whites and blacks score an 82.8 out of 100 on the dissimilarity index. METRO. RACIAL & ETHNIC CHANGE – CENSUS 2000, ST. LOUIS, MO-IL MSA, http://mumford1.dyndns.org/cen2000/WholePop/WPSegdata/7040msa.htm (last visited Aug. 14, 2007). A high value indicates that these two groups tend to live in different areas. *Id.* Other compared groups include blacks with hispanics (70.1), blacks with Asians (79.5), whites with hispanics (29.4), and whites with Asians (41.3). *Id.* According to isolation indices, 93.2% of whites live in an area heavily populated by whites and 74.7% of blacks live in an area heavily populated with blacks. *See id.* Hispanics with Hispanics and Asians with Asians are 1.7% and 1.5%, respectively. *See id.; see also* Jomills Henry Braddock II & James M. McPartland, *Social-Psychological Processes that Perpetuate Racial Segregation: The Relationship Between School and Employment Desegregation*, 19 J. BLACK STUD. 267, 285–86 (1989).

[32] Studies prove that blacks and whites maintain the greatest social distance of any pairing or racial groups. Erica Chito Childs, *Looking Behind the Stereotypes of the "Angry Black Woman": An Exploration of Black Women's Responses to Interracial Relationships*, 19 GENDER & SOC'Y 544, 544 (2005) ("Blacks and whites continue to be the two groups with the greatest social distance, the most spatial separation, and the strongest taboos against interracial marriage."); see comments of the first African-American Attorney General, Eric Holder, Remarks as Prepared for Delivery by Attorney General Eric Holder at the Department of Justice African American History Month Program (Feb. 18, 2009) *available at* http://www.justice.gov/ag/speeches/2009/ag-speech-090218.html (last visited June 3, 2011):

As a nation we have done a pretty good job in melding the races in the workplace. We work with one another, lunch together and, when the event is at the workplace during work hours or shortly thereafter, we socialize with one another fairly well, irrespective of race. ... On Saturdays and Sundays America in the year 2009 does not, in some ways, differ significantly from the country that existed some fifty years ago. This is truly sad. Given all that we as a nation went through during the civil rights struggle it is hard for me to accept that the result of those efforts was to create an America that is more prosperous, more positively race conscious and yet is voluntarily socially segregated. ... By creating what will admittedly be, at first, artificial opportunities to engage one another we can hasten the day when the dream of individual, character based, acceptance can actually be realized. To respect one another we must have a basic understanding of one another. And so we should use events such as this to not only learn more about the facts of black history but also to learn more about each other. This will be, at first, a process that is both awkward and painful but the rewards are potentially great. The alternative is to allow to continue the polite, restrained mixing that now passes as meaningful interaction but that accomplishes little.

consciousness demands that we accept this racialization of our individual and coupled lives. It is our norm. Such incongruence is possibly one of the defining characteristics of interracial relationships. Like all couples, we seek to achieve a peaceful solace in our private life together. Nonetheless, we experience periodic racialized disruptions from the sociopolitical hyperscrutiny to which we, and our family, are subjected in the public realm. Mixed couples must be weary of such interracial fatigue and must actively work to protect their union both from the typical race-neutral challenges that are the stuff of all relationships, as well as the external pressures specifically directed at interracial relationships.

It is imperative that both partners in an interracial relationship be critically conscious of race, racism, and identity constructs. Rejecting legalized notions of color-blindness is often essential for the maintenance and protection of the relationship – one cannot preserve the relationship if one is unable to assess and counter the sociopolitical intrusions. Societal pressures force couples to adopt a supportive criticality and conscious fortitude. Although such relationships are not to be regarded as definitively alien or "other," some preparation for dealing with racialized treatment is in order.

As such, interracial relationships are simultaneously vulnerable to common and sociopolitically founded relationship threats. Of course we experience the run-of-the mill nonracialized relationship concerns, but we are also subjected to external pressures that are largely a function of long-standing American cultural unease with race mixing and miscegenation. Thus when societal attitudes are examined through the lens of black-white interracial relationships, the surfacing of by-products of our racialized and sexualized history reveals that we have much work to do when it comes to achieving color-blindness. Couples involved in interracial relationships are the proverbial canaries in the coal mine – we encounter racialized assessments and behaviors based on our private lives, thereby indicating ongoing racism. Our private lives become public sites on which deep racial and sexual unease is projected. Abstract pronouncements of the Supreme Court regarding race cannot change the reality that color-blindness remains a theoretical fiction rather than an everyday reality.

8

The Crime of Loving: *Loving, Lawrence*, and Beyond

I. Bennett Capers

The past is never dead. It's not even past.

– William Faulkner[1]

The Charleston of my youth had only one interracial couple. In South Carolina, nobody paid them much attention, but everybody noticed and knew of them. It was like they were ignored and scrutinized at the same time. I never saw anyone talk to them, even to say, "How d'you do?" But as far as I know, no one ever yelled at them, or threw anything at them, or was outright mean to them. They were students at the College of Charleston, and I think most folks thought of them as transients/hippies/not-from-around-here, so that probably helped. And at least the white person in the couple was the guy, and homely looking at that. That probably helped too.

This occurred post–*Loving v. Virginia*, but back then, I had never heard of the case. I'm sure my elders had, or at least knew that interracial marriage was no longer prohibited as a matter of law. They certainly knew it was possible – popular culture showed the possibilities of intermingling. There was Tom and Helen Willis on *The Jeffersons*, for one. And everybody knew that Diana Ross had married a white man. But being possible someplace in New York or in Hollywood wasn't the same thing as being possible in Charleston, South Carolina. Besides, my elders still remembered how, just a dozen or so years before *Loving* was decided, a black boy in Mississippi named Emmett Till had been lynched for just whistling at a white woman. They remembered, going even further back, that their idol Jack Johnson, the first black heavyweight champion of the world, had been prosecuted under the White-Slave Traffic Act for just taking his white girlfriend across state lines.[2] Nobody in my

---

[1]   William Faulkner, Requiem for a Nun 92 (1951).
[2]   For more on Jack Johnson generally, see Denise C. Morgan, *Jack Johnson: Reluctant Hero of the Black Community*, 32 Akron L. Rev. 529 (1999) and Geoffrey C. Ward, Unforgivable Blackness: The Rise and Fall of Jack Johnson (2004).

hometown, or my entire state, as far as I could tell, took *Loving* as carte blanche to rush to the altar or jump any brooms. Even that one college couple, as far as I know, only dated. But they only stayed four years, long enough to graduate, and I don't know what they did after.

That was the one interracial couple in town, but that does not mean no one else engaged in interracial sex. Interracial sex, however, was kept on the down-low. I personally can attest to this. There was a white girl at the integrated high school where I was transferred to during my senior year when my family moved from Charleston proper to the suburbs. She liked black boys, which is how I met her, but she was dirt-poor, and the white students had turned her name into a rhyme that was melodious and sweet, until you paid attention to the words.

Perhaps it is odd that I'm thinking about this couple at the college and about this girl. This is, after all, supposed to be my reflection on *Loving* as someone who teaches and writes about the intersections of criminal law, race, gender, and culture. But I want to talk about *Loving*, not as a landmark equal protection or due process case, but as a criminal case. A case that began with an anonymous tip and an arrest.[3] Eventually, I know, I want to suggest that *Loving* exemplifies the existence of another law that can, at times, have even more force than black-letter law. Because this other law is, so often, invisible, but in existence nonetheless, much like white-letters on a white page, I refer to it as white-letter law. Eventually, I want to talk about *Loving's* "kissing cousin": another case that also began with a tip and an arrest, a case that also involved the policing of intimacy, and that coincidentally also involved an interracial couple: *Lawrence v. Texas*.[4] But first, for this to make sense – or rather for me to get across what I'm hoping to get across – I need to say a little bit more about myself and the town that I grew up in. To borrow from Patricia Williams, the subject position is everything in my analysis of the law.[5]

Why were there so few black-white couples in a town of more than 100,000, and in a town that was about half-black and half-white, no less? Residential segregation probably had a bit to do with it. In Charleston proper, there was, and still is, a white side of town – the part tourists visit and reminisce about when they talk of beautiful Charleston – and a black side of town, even though the dividing line was, and still is, just a street. The fact that the schools were, and still are, for the most part segregated probably had something to do with it too. Rather than risk integration after *Brown v. Board of Education*, most whites pulled their children out of public schools and put them into private ones. Even today, the public high school in Charleston proper is all-black. That my state flew the confederate flag atop the state capitol – it has since

3   Robert A. Pratt, *Crossing the Color Line: A Historical Assessment and Personal Narrative of Loving v. Virginia*, 41 How. L.J. 229, 236 (1998).
4   539 U.S. 558 (2003).
5   Patricia J. Williams, ALCHEMY OF RACE AND RIGHTS 3 (1991).

been moved to the front of the capitol[6] – and is the home of Bob Jones University, which, to this day, still bans interracial dating,[7] didn't help either. But, mostly, there were so few black-white couples because, *Brown* or no *Brown*, *Loving* or no *Loving*, people knew their place. And one's social place was related to one's geographic *place*. Which is perhaps why my brother, who married a white woman, moved to another state to do so. And maybe why I, who met a white man twenty-odd years ago, who's been my partner ever since, moved away; or fled, to be more truthful. And because truth is everything, let me amend what I said when I said that people knew their place. What's more truthful is that there were a whole host of mechanisms, both legal and extralegal, both black-letter and white-letter, that reminded people of their place and reminds them still.

Sixteen states had antimiscegenation statutes at the time that the Supreme Court decided *Loving*.[8] *Loving*, of course, invalidated them all. Finding that "[t]here can be no question but that Virginia's miscegenation statutes rest solely upon distinctions drawn according to race,"[9] the Supreme Court held that Virginia's statutes – part of its Racial Integrity Act – violated the Equal Protection Clause. As a racial classification, it required strict scrutiny, and there was "no legitimate overriding purpose independent of invidious racial discrimination" to justify the classification. The Court added, "The fact that Virginia prohibits only interracial marriages involving white persons demonstrates that the racial classifications must stand on their own justifications, as measures designed to maintain White Supremacy."[10] The Court also found that the statute violated the Due Process Clause. The right to marry, the Court held, was a fundamental right that could not "be infringed by the State."[11]

  This was in 1967, and I can only imagine that the Supreme Court thought that it was now time, as compared to the way that it hadn't been time, a century earlier in *Pace v. Alabama*,[12] when the Court upheld Alabama's law punishing interracial fornication and adultery more severely than intraracial fornication and adultery. Or the way that it hadn't been time in 1956 with *Naim v. Naim*,[13] in which the

---

[6] For a discussion of the confederate flag in South Carolina, see I. Bennett Capers, *Flags*, 48 How. L.J. 121 (2004) (exploring the confederate flag as a signifier of protection, allegiance, and stasis).

[7] Bob Jones University prohibited interracial dating outright until 2000. Since then, it allows interracial dating, but only if each student first obtains written permission from his or her parents. *See Parents' Note Needed for Interracial Dates*, N.Y. TIMES, Mar. 8, 2000, at A20.

[8] As many as thirty states at one time banned interracial marriage; *see* Rachel F. Moran, INTERRACIAL INTIMACY: THE REGULATION OF RACE AND ROMANCE 17 (2001); *see also* Edward Stein, *Past and Present Proposed Constitutional Amendments*, 82 WASH. U. L.Q. 611, 627–28 (2004).

[9] *Loving v. Virginia*, 388 U.S. 1, 11 (1967)

[10] *Id.*

[11] *Id.* at 12.

[12] 106 U.S. 583 (1882).

[13] 350 U.S. 891 (1955), *appeal reconsidered*, 350 U.S. 985 (1956).

Supreme Court sidestepped an earlier challenge to the antimiscegenation provisions of Virginia's Racial Integrity Act.[14]

By 1967, it was time, and the Chief Justice and author of the *Loving* opinion was, after all, Earl Warren. Not only had Chief Justice Warren written *Brown*; he had presided over a sea change in our understanding of the criminal rights of suspects and defendants in such decisions as *Mapp v. Ohio*,[15] *Gideon v. Wainwright*,[16] *Massiah v. United States*,[17] and *Miranda v. Arizona*;[18] and, one year later, would write perhaps the most important Fourth Amendment decision of all, *Terry v. Ohio*.[19] Chief Justice Warren also had some familiarity with what it meant to invalidate an antimiscegenation law; he was governor of California at the time when the highest court there had invalidated California's antimiscegenation statute in *Perez v. Sharp*.[20]

Even more significant, the Court had built up to *Loving* by deciding, three years earlier, *McLaughlin v. Florida*.[21] In *McLaughlin*, which also started off with a tip and an arrest, a black man and a white woman that considered themselves married, even if Florida did not, challenged their conviction for adultery and lewd cohabitation, arguing, inter alia, that because the statute imposed harsher punishment on interracial couples than intraracial couples, the statute violated their equal protection rights. Overruling its decision in *Pace*, the Court agreed and threw out their convictions. This paved the way for *Loving*.

Loving also presented the right facts. By "the right facts," I'm referring not so much to the fact that, based on an anonymous tip, the sheriff and two officers raided Richard and Mildred Loving's home early one morning and confronted the couple in bed, or that Mildred asserted her right to be there by proclaiming that she was Richard's wife. Nor am I referring to the fact that the couple, upon being convicted, received a one-year suspended sentence conditioned on their leaving Virginia and

---

[14]   The challenge in *Naim* was not a direct one. Naim, a Chinese seaman, had circumvented Virginia's antimiscegenation statute by marrying his white wife in North Carolina. Later, his wife filed for annulment in Virginia on the ground that the marriage was invalid in Virginia. The trial court granted the annulment, and Naim appealed arguing, inter alia, that Virginia's antimiscegenation law violated his due process and equal protection rights. The Virginia Supreme Court disagreed, finding that the regulation of marriage as Virginia saw fit was safeguarded from attack by the Tenth Amendment, and that Virginia's antimiscegenation law was in any event appropriate "to preserve the racial integrity of its citizens" and to prevent "the corruption of blood," "a mongrel breed of citizens," and "the obliteration of racial ride." Naim v. Naim, 87 S.E.2d 749 (Va. 1955). After some internal wrangling, the Supreme Court declined to hear the case for failure to present a question of federal law. Naim v. Naim, 350 U.S. 985 (1956). For more on *Naim*, see Moran, *supra* note 8, at 89–90.

[15]   367 U.S. 643 (1961).

[16]   372 U.S. 335 (1963).

[17]   377 U.S. 201 (1964).

[18]   384 U.S. 436 (1966).

[19]   392 U.S. 1 (1968).

[20]   198 P.2d 17 (Cal. 1948).

[21]   379 U.S. 184 (1964).

not returning for twenty-five years, although maybe someone on the Court noticed the perverse irony of it all: banishment, it turns out, was the statutory punishment under Virginia's original antimiscegenation statute back in 1691.[22] Lastly, I am not referring to Richard Loving's heartfelt instruction as his lawyer prepared to argue before the Supreme Court, "Tell the Court I love my wife, and it is just unfair that I can't live with her in Virginia." By "the right facts" I mean the fact that Richard, the man in the relationship, was white, and Mildred was black, and not the other way around. As the Court must have realized when it thought of its audience, this configuration – which the South was used to, after all, however unsaid, however secret, however Strom Thurmond-ish[23] – would at least have made the decision bearable to Southern whites.

Read literally, *Loving* was an incredibly potent decision. It ended, in one fell swoop, the nearly 300-year history of prohibiting interracial marriage in various states. In another way, however, the decision was oddly impotent. Rates of cross-racial marriages are still low, especially between whites and blacks. This is especially true in the sixteen states that had antimiscegenation statutes at the time of the *Loving* decision. When I visit Charleston now, which is still about half-black and half-white, there are still no interracial couples.

Which brings me back to *Loving* and its relation, or lack thereof, to Charleston. That Richard and Mildred had the opportunity to fall in love had much to do with the rural community of Central Point, Caroline County, Virginia, where they lived. Their families lived just up the road from one another, and Central Point was more integrated, in many ways, than the rest of the South. As historian Robert Pratt has observed, Central Point had developed "an interesting history of black-white sexual relationships over the years," resulting in a community where a number of blacks were mixed-race, and where many blacks were able to, and often did, "pass." Because of these dynamics, "when white Richard Loving, age seventeen, began courting 'colored' Mildred Jeter, age eleven, their budding romance drew little attention from either the white or the black communities."[24]

---

[22] In 1691, Virginia passed a statute that provided, in relevant part: "[W]hatsoever English or other white man or woman, bond or free, shall intermarry with a Negro, mulatto, or Indian man or woman, bond or free, he shall within three months be banished from this dominion forever." STATUTES AT LARGE OF VIRGINIA, VOL. 3, at 86–88 (William W. Hening ed., 1819–20).

[23] In 2003, America learned that Senator Strom Thurmond, who built his career on a segregationist platform, had in fact had an affair with a black sixteen-year-old and fathered a child. *See* Jeffrey Gettleman, *Final Word: 'My Father's Name Was James Strom Thurmond*, N.Y. TIMES, Dec. 18, 2003, at A1; *see also* Osagie K. Obasogie, *Anything but a Hypocrite: Interactional Musings on Race, Colorblindness, and the Redemption of Strom Thurmond*, 18 YALE J.L. & FEMINISM 451 (2006).

[24] Robert A. Pratt, *Crossing the Color Line: A Historical Assessment and Personal Narrative of Loving v. Virginia*, 41 How. L.J. 229, 234–35 (1997–98).

The community of Central Point, Virginia, also assumed a pivotal role in the couple's eventual marriage and Supreme Court case. It was a community in which they knew they could live as husband and wife. Indeed, after they married in Washington, DC, they returned to Central Point to live, staying with Mildred's parents. The community of Central Point did not mind their presence; it was the county sheriff who did. It was only when the Lovings were convicted and sentenced to one year in prison, suspended on the condition that they leave the state of Virginia for a period of twenty-five years, that the Lovings moved to Washington, DC, where they lived for five years and began raising a family. But it was Central Point that they yearned for. It was Central Point that prompted Mildred Loving, in 1963, to write a letter to Robert Kennedy, the U.S. Attorney General, about returning to Virginia. That letter in turn prompted the American Civil Liberties Union (ACLU) to take up her case.[24a] In short, *Loving* happened because the Lovings saw Central Point as a place to which they could return. As a place where they would be welcomed. As a place they could call home.

It is possible, of course, to imagine *Loving* happening someplace else – New Orleans, comes to mind – but not most places down South. And not Charleston. Even now, it is hard for me to imagine a black person and a white person falling in love there, or even having the opportunity to do so. There is little evidence of "race mixing" there. The blacks in Charleston, unlike the blacks in Central Point, tend to be very dark – "pure black," outsiders sometimes say – so much so that the few light-skinned blacks that are there are still viewed with a mixture of envy and suspicion. And it is all but impossible for me to imagine a black person and a white person, as a married couple, wanting to stay there, or being welcomed there.

Race is still everything in Charleston. It prides itself, not only on its antebellum homes and Southern charm, but also on its connection to Fort Sumter, where Southern secessionists fired the shots that triggered the Civil War; on its "slave market," which is still the center of downtown; on the Citadel, the military college that was founded in response to the slave uprising of Denmark Vesey; on its surrounding plantations – indeed, even many of the housing subdivisions are wistfully named after plantations. In other words, it prides itself on its past, the fact that it was largely untouched by the civil rights movement, and the hermeticism of its own world.

And race is still everything for South Carolina, as the controversies over the Confederate flag and interracial dating at Bob Jones University attest to. It is a place where miscegenation was so unthinkable that for the longest time, no black-letter prohibition was necessary; it was only after the South lost the war that the state rushed to enact an antimiscegenation statute. Later, for good measure, the prohibition against interracial marriage was actually written into the state Constitution.[25] It

[24a] See id. at 235–238.
[25] S.C. Const. Art. III, § 33.

is a place where, even after *Loving*, South Carolina kept its antimiscegenation statute on the books, repealing it by referendum only in 1998, and even then, 38 percent
of the voters opposed its repeal.[26] In Montgomery County, Georgia, the schools hold
racially segregated proms.[27] Nothing so official is needed in South Carolina. Kids
know their place.

When I was in law school, one task was to master the black-letter law. It was only
after law school, when I gained some distance, that I realized that there was also
another type of law that I think of now as white-letter law.[28] Unlike black-letter law –
which brings to mind statutory law, written law, the easily discernible law set forth
as black letters on a white page – white-letter law suggests societal and normative
laws that stand side by side and often undergird black-letter law but, as if inscribed
in white ink on white paper, remain invisible to the naked eye. I also began to think
about "trespass," which suggests a line crossed, and which has particular salience
given this country's history of cultural, social, and geographic segregation along race
lines. Still later, I realized that part of what I was bringing to the law was a different type of reading, a reading that was both counterhegemonic and attuned to the
frequencies and registers of race, a reading practice I described in an essay titled
Reading Back, Reading Black.[29]

Some of these ruminations seem useful here. The reason I can read *Loving* as not
changing anything, even as groundbreaking as the decision may be, is because it did
little to disrupt the white-letter law of racial trespass. Think about it. Even before
Virginia enacted its antimiscegenation law, first in 1662,[30] but really in 1691, a type of
unwritten, white-letter law was already in place that imposed harsh punishment on
black-white fraternization. We know from court records, for example, that in 1630,
a white man named Hugh Davis, presumably an indentured servant, was "whipt ...
[for] defiling his body in lying with a negro."[31] We know that in 1640, a black woman

---

[26] Randall Kennedy, INTERRACIAL INTIMACIES: SEX, MARRIAGE, IDENTITY, AND ADOPTION 279–80 (2003)
       (setting forth the dates of various repeals; Alabama repealed its statute in 2000, making it the last state
       to do so).
[27] Sarah Corbett, *A Prom Divided*, N.Y. TIMES, May 21, 2009, at A1, *available at* http://www.nytimes.
       com/2009/05/24/magazine/24prom-t.html?pagewanted=1 (last visited June 14, 2011).
[28] *See* I. Bennett Capers, *The Trial of Bigger Thomas: Race, Gender, and Trespass*, 31 N.Y.U. REV. L. &
       SOC. CHANGE 1, 4–5 (2006).
[29] I. Bennett Capers, *Reading Back, Reading Black*, 35 HOFSTRA L. REV. 9 (2006).
[30] In 1662, the Virginia legislature addressed interracial intimacy by doubling the punishment. Act XII
       provided: "Children got by an Englishman upon a Negro woman shall be bond of free according
       to the condition of the mother, and if any Christian shall commit fornication with a Negro man or
       woman, he shall pay double the fines of a former act." STATUTES AT LARGE OF VIRGINIA, VOL. 1, at 170
       (William W. Hening ed., 1823).
[31] MINUTES OF THE COUNCIL AND GENERAL COURT OF COLONIAL VIRGINIA, 1622–1632, 1670–1676, at
       479 (H.R. McIlwaine ed., 1924).

who bore a child by Robert Sweat, a white man, was ordered "whipt at the whipping post," and that Sweat was ordered to "do public penance for his offense at James City church." While it is possible that it was the act of fornication that rankled Virginia, and not the race of the actors, it seems likely that race did matter.[32]

Still later, when as many as half of the states had laws prohibiting interracial intimacy, another type of white-letter law held sway. It was primarily interracial intimacy between black men and white women that was policed. Intimacies between white men and black women, as long as kept on the down-low, enjoyed a white-letter exemption.

And it is this white-letter law that best explains our history of lynching to police interracial intimacy, to protect "white Southern womanhood." Yet, even after lynchings fell out of favor and were no longer events during which white crowds brought picnic baskets and white children played, the white-letter law still stood strong.

Consider *Story v. State*,[33] a rape case involving a black defendant. Alabama's highest court held that it was reversible error not to permit the defense to introduce evidence showing that the prosecutrix had a reputation of "having practiced her lewdness with negroes." The court's reasoning is revealing:

> Deeply depraved as are those white women who practice prostitution among members of their own race, those few white women (if such there be) who may practice their lewdness among negroes are yet lower in the scale of depravity – are yet beneath those who entirely forfeit respect by the barter of their very character. Reclamation may be made of one; but, for the other, there is little, if any, hope. . . . [A] white woman prostitute is yet, though lost of virtue, above the even greater sacrifice of the voluntary submission of her person to the embraces of the other race.

Or consider the Scottsboro Boys case, in which nine black youths were prosecuted for the capital crime of raping two white women, even after one of the women recanted her story and testified for the defense.[34] Or consider *McQuirter v. State*,[35] in which a black man was charged with "an attempt to commit an assault with intent to rape." McQuirter's crime: saying something "unintelligible" and opening his truck door as Mrs. Ted Allen, a white woman, passed his truck, and then later failing to step aside when she wanted to pass. The court's view of proper considerations: "In determining the question of intention the jury may consider social conditions and

---

[32] Leon Higginbotham reached a similar conclusion. *See* A. Leon Higginbotham, Jr., IN THE MATTER OF COLOR: RACE AND THE AMERICAN LEGAL PROCESS: THE COLONIAL PERIOD 24 (1978).
[33] 59 So. 480 (1912).
[34] For more on this case, see Dan T. Carter, SCOTTSBORO: A TRAGEDY OF THE AMERICAN SOUTH (1969).
[35] 36 Ala. App. 707, 63 So.2d 388 (Ala. App. 1986).

customs founded upon racial differences, such as that the prosecutrix was a white woman and the defendant was a Negro man."[36] The verdict: guilty.

Indeed, the way rape law evolved in this country speaks volumes about both black-letter law and white-letter law. It was not only that different punishments were authorized under black-letter law – early Pennsylvania and New Jersey laws, for example, prescribed castration for blacks convicted of raping, or attempting to rape, white women; the Virginia Code, after initially authorizing castration, authorized the death penalty for a black convicted of rape, but set the maximum punishment for a white convicted of rape at twenty years' imprisonment.[37] It was also the fact that whether and how these cases were resolved depended, to a large extent, on an unwritten white-letter law of trespass, of crossing a racial line.

Traditionally, rape was defined as sexual intercourse with a woman by force and against her will. The key was non-consent, and initially, whether the victim had manifested non-consent depended on whether she had resisted to the utmost. As one court put it, "Not only must there be entire absence of mental consent or assent, but there must be the most vehement exercise of every physical means or faculty within the woman's power to resist the penetration of her person, and this must be shown to persist until the offense is consummated."[38] Or, as another court put it in explaining the utmost resistance requirement, "[I]f a woman, aware that it will be done unless she does resist, does not resist to the extent of her ability on the occasion, must it not be that she is not entirely reluctant?"[39]

The "utmost resistance" requirement was clear, but what it meant in practice – in terms of which victims were believed, which men were prosecuted, and which defendants found guilty – turned on what was often unsaid – in other words, the white-letter law. Two cases illustrate this point. In *Brown v. State*, a sixteen-year-old girl was forced to the ground as she walked across the fields to her grandmother's house and screamed as hard as she could, repeatedly tried to get up, clawed at the grass, and kept screaming until her attacker almost strangled her.[40] Nonetheless, the court concluded that her attacker (white) was *not* guilty of rape *because she didn't resist enough*. By contrast, *Hart v. Commonwealth* involved a seventeen-year-old girl who was attacked by "a full-grown negro man," but did not cry for help when two white men were in earshot; instead, she freed herself and "walked to the nearest house" to call for help.[41] That she could have done more to resist, and therefore

---

[36] *Id.* at 709.
[37] For more on these early laws, see Winthrop D. Jordan, THE WHITE MAN'S BURDEN 81–82 (1974); D. H. Partington, *The Incidence of the Death Penalty for Rape in Virginia*, 22 WASH. & LEE L. REV. 43 (1965).
[38] Brown v. State, 106 N.W. 536 (Wisc. 1906).
[39] People v. Dohring, 59 N.Y. 374, (1874).
[40] *See* supra n. 38.
[41] 109 S.E. 582 (Va. 1921).

did not resist to the utmost, was beside the point. The white-letter law of trespass dictated that there was more than enough evidence to overlook the "utmost resistance" requirement and find her attacker guilty of attempted rape. After all, he was a "full-grown negro man." The white-letter law also dictated that there was more than enough to sentence him to death.

By the 1950s and 1960s, of course, the requirement that women resist to the utmost had given way to the requirement that they resist when it is reasonable to do so. But again, this black-letter requirement had a white-letter emendation. Whether or not the victim's decision to resist was reasonable – that is, whether she was reasonably in fear of her attacker – could now turn simply on the race of the defendant. In other words, the presence of a black man was often enough to raise a *presumption* of reasonable fear. As the court put it in *People v. Harris*, a rape case involving a "young, white woman returning home" and encountering a "strange, male person of the Negro race" on a quiet street, "it would border upon the stupid to find that she freely acquiesced in his acts as he ravished her body. While she made some resistance, it may be safely presumed that she would have rebelled with a vengeance but for her fear of bodily harm."[42] After all, the defendant was a "strange, male person of the Negro race."

In addition, long after the black-letter law ceased to mete punishment for rape along lines of race, the white-letter still did. Between 1930 and 1967 (the year that *Loving* was decided), 89 percent of all of the men *officially* executed for rape in the United States were black.[43] A separate study concluded that the overwhelming majority – 85 percent – of legal executions for rape involved a particular dyad, black male defendants and white female victims, and that a black man found guilty of raping a white woman was eighteen times more likely to receive a death sentence than an offender in any other offender-victim dyad. Perhaps most revealing: no one, white or black, has been executed for raping a black woman.[44] It was racial disparity resulting from this white-letter law that finally prompted the Court, ten years after it decided *Loving*, to remove the death penalty as a possible punishment for rape in *Coker v. Georgia*.[45] Of course, this removed the racial disparity in the use of the death penalty for rape. It did nothing to remove the racial disparity in terms of imprisonment for rape.

[42] 238 P.2d 158 (Cal. Dist. Ct. App. 1951).
[43] *See* Marvin Wolfgang, *Racial Discrimination in the Death Sentence for Rape, in* EXECUTIONS IN AMERICA 110–20 (William J. Bowers ed., 1974).
[44] *See* Coramae Richey Mann & Lance H. Selva, *The Sexualization of Racism: The Black as Rapist and White Justice*, 3 W. J. BLACK STUDIES 168 (1979).
[45] 433 U.S. 584 (1977) (holding that the imposition of death for the crime of rape of an adult woman was grossly disproportionate in violation of the Eighth Amendment.)

Loving, then, may have changed the black-letter law, so to speak, but it did little to disturb the white-letter law that polices interracial intimacy. Thus, years after *Loving*, black men and white women keeping company with one another could still be deemed suspect and charged with vagrancy, as was the case in *Papachristou v. Jacksonville*.[46] This white-letter law is why, long after *Loving*, there is still a prurient frenzy that accompanies any crime involving a white female victim and a black male defendant – *see* O. J. Simpson; *see also* Kobe Bryant; *compare* Mike Tyson.[47] It is why an eighteen-year-old in Georgia can be prosecuted for statutory rape for sleeping with his just-shy-of-fifteen white girlfriend.[48] It is why, in Spike Lee's film *Jungle Fever*, when Wesley Snipes and his white girlfriend begin horsing around one night on a quiet New York street and a resident sees and misreads them, the prospect of the police showing up seems so real. It is why, in Paul Haggis's film *Crash*, the perception that Terrence Howard's character has an expensive car and a light-skinned girlfriend is enough to prompt a police stop, which leads to a real assault. It is why, even in the liberal enclave of Cape Cod, Massachusetts, discussions about the race of the defendant – "a big black guy," which was apparently reason alone to induce "fear" in at least one of the jurors – could make its way into jury deliberations in a rape-and-murder trial involving a white victim.[49] It is why, in Tennessee, a single television ad showing a white woman seductively murmuring, "Harold, call me" could derail the campaign of a promising black candidate for U.S. senator.[50]

The overlap between the states that prohibited sodomy in 2003 with those states that prohibited interracial marriage in 1967 is striking. At the time the Court decided *Lawrence* in 2003, thirteen states criminalized sodomy, with four of those states enforcing the prohibition only in cases involving same-sex sodomy. Before 1961, all fifty states had sodomy laws in effect.

---

[46] 405 U.S. 156 (1972). The facts, as stipulated, were that two black men were in a vehicle with two white women when they were arrested for vagrancy on the theory that they were "prowling by auto." The arresting officer denied race was a factor. The Supreme Court overturned their convictions, holding the vagrancy ordinance void for vagueness.

[47] For a discussion of the role of race in the media frenzy accompanying the O. J. Simpson and Kobe Bryant cases, see *The Color of Scandal* (Aug. 8, 2003) *at* http://www.onthemedia.org/transcripts/transcripts_080803_media.html. The media devoted relatively less coverage to the prosecution of Mike Tyson for raping Desiree Washington, a black woman.

[48] *See* Ariel Hart, *Child Molesting Conviction Overturned in Georgia Classmate Case*, N.Y. TIMES, May 4, 2004, at A20; Courtland Milloy, *Marcus Dixon Doesn't Belong in Ga. Prison*, WASH. POST, Jan. 25, 2004, at C01; Andrew Jacobs, *Student Sex Case in George Stirs Claims of Old South Justice*, N.Y. TIMES, Jan. 22, 2004, at 14.

[49] *See* Abby Goodnough, *Jurors in Cape Cod Case Testify About Racial Remarks*, N.Y. TIMES, Jan. 11, 2008, at A1.

[50] *See* Robin Toner, *In Tight Senate Race, Attack Ad on Black Candidate Stirs Furor*, N.Y. TIMES, Oct. 26, 2006, at A1; Peter Wallstein, *GOP Attack Ad Draws Heat for Racial Overtones*, L.A. TIMES, Oct. 24, 2006, A14.

Loving and *Lawrence* both serve as cautionary reminders of the long leash we have given to criminal law. The state's "police power" has been described as "the most essential, the most insistent, and always one of the least limitable of the powers of the government."[51] It allows states to criminalize whatever conduct it reasonably deems harmful, so long as it does not prohibit a constitutionally protected individual right, and the criminalized conduct is rationally related to the harm sought to be avoided. But this gives states a long leash. States have used this "police power" to criminalize adultery, premarital sex, assisted suicide, illicit cohabitation, homosexuality, pornography, gambling, and a whole host of victimless crimes. In *Loving* and *Lawrence*, this "police power" initially gave the states the authority to regulate love.

Lawrence, after all, began when the police responded to a 9-1-1 call that a "black man was going crazy in [an] apartment" and was armed with a gun.[52] What the police found, of course, when they entered Lawrence's apartment was, not a black man with a gun, but a black man, Tyron Garner, and a white man, Lawrence, engaging in sex.

Although invalidating their convictions, the Court adhered to a broad interpretation of the police power. *Lawrence* may have protected liberty and privacy, but failed to prevent states from enacting criminal laws to impose its morality on individuals or otherwise criminalize individual behavior that causes no harm. It seems to me that this should be the next battle.

But mostly what interests me is the interracial aspect of both *Lawrence* and *Loving*. Both cases involved interracial couples interrupted in bed, although *Lawrence* elided this fact. Of course, it was the very fact that the Lovings were interracial that was the crux of the case. By contrast, the race of the men in *Lawrence* was, arguably, immaterial.

But it is also possible that the sexual sameness of the defendants in *Lawrence* trumped their racial difference. After all, our response to interracial intimacy has always been tied to gender, to who was putting what where and in whom. At the same time that states policed intimacy between black men and white women, states mostly turned a blind eye to intimacies between white men and black women. At the same time that states authorized castration and death for black men convicted of raping, or attempting to rape, white women, states refused to recognize the rape of black women by white men as even a crime.

To put it differently, it is not simply interracial intimacy that was policed and continues to be policed now through white-letter law; rather, the extent of the policing is very much dependent on race and gender, and this, I think, adds another layer

---

[51] 16A Am. Jur. 2d *Constitutional Law* § 317.
[52] Dale Carpenter, *The Unknown Past of* Lawrence v. Texas, 102 MICH. L. REV. 1464, 1479 (2004) (quoting from the probable cause affidavit).

to *Lawrence*. The absence of gender difference made it easy for the Court to erase racial difference, to treat the petitioners as raceless. In other words, the gay black man in *Lawrence* was treated as white.

It is hard for me to think of the interracial aspect of *Lawrence* without looking inward and thinking about my own life. About how, prior to *Lawrence*, my partner and I would have been deemed criminals in the state where I'm from. About what it means to be in a same-sex, interracial relationship post-*Loving*, post-*Lawrence*. And maybe because distance fails me, objectivity fails me, this is the most difficult part.

The last time I was in the town I'm from, several years ago now, it was to bury my mother. I stayed several days, and as far as I could tell, there were still no interracial couples, or rather none but for the interracial couples who had come back for the funeral: my brother and his wife; me and my partner. Whenever my partner and I went out, we received confused looks. Not because anyone was thinking the gay thing. It was just seeing a black man and a white man together socially, eating dinner, having drinks, that stood out. I could imagine the stares that my brother and his wife got. Maybe the town that I grew up in, *Loving* or no *Loving*, just isn't used to change. Charleston, after all, recently elected its mayor, Joseph P. Riley, to serve his ninth term, which is another way of saying that the mayor when I was in elementary school is still the mayor today.[53]

The town I live in now is New York City, although my partner and I recently bought a weekend/summer house in Northwest Connecticut. And here's the difficult part: when my brother and his wife come to visit me in New York, they are still suspect, subject to the look, an "interracial tax."[54] With Seth and me, it's different, both in New York and Connecticut. Any suspicion that attaches to me as a black male – as criminal, as threatening, as "bestial"[55] – is neutralized by Seth. When I walk around or drive through a predominantly white neighborhood by myself, I risk suspicion. When I walk around or drive through a predominantly white neighborhood with Seth, his presence explains mine.

In my more positive moods, I tell myself that it is because black-white same-sex relationships have so little history. The "negro" that Hugh Davis lay with in 1630 may have been male. We don't know. The one antebellum story that I do know dates

---

[53] Mayor Riley reflected on his thirty years as mayor during an interview on National Public Radio. The interview is available at http://www.npr.org/templates/story/story.php?storyId=18259135

[54] Camille A. Nelson, *Lovin' the Man: Examining the Legal Nexus of Irony, Hypocrisy, and Curiosity*, 2007 Wis. L. Rev. 543, 573.

[55] N. Jeremi Duru has explored the myth of the bestial black man, and describes the myth as predicated on three assumptions: (1) black men are animalistic; (2) black men are inherently criminal; (3) black men are hypersexual. *See* N. Jeremi Duru, *The Central Park Five, the Scottsboro Boys, and the Myth of the Bestial Black Man*, 25 Cardozo L. Rev. 1315, 1320 (2004).

back to 1647, in New Amsterdam, when Harmen van den Bogaert, one of the pillars of the colony, was caught in *flagrante delicto* with his black servant, Tobias. Van den Bogaert fled, was captured, and fled again. To make his escape, he ran across the frozen expanse of a river. Ice, of course, can be deceptive, and deceived Van den Bogaert, who fell through and drowned.[56] In terms of interracial same-sex history, or at least my knowledge of it, that is it.

In my darker moods, I tell myself that, partnered with a white man, I am marked as safe, I'm allowed to pass through. Sometimes, when my mood is darker still, I use the words "assimilated" and "domesticated." Me, marked as assimilated and domesticated, allowed to pass, I become not black. Black no more. Or, at least, a good black.

And when my mood is darkest, I wonder if all of this is calculated. I sometimes joke with my friends that the reason I chose Seth is so that he can hail us cabs. But there is more I don't say. I am well aware, for example, that heterosexual black males, to advance in corporate America, often deploy strategies to desexualize themselves in order to make whites more comfortable. Was that my strategy, to do that, and one better? Is that why, when I meet new people, especially other academics, I am quick to bring up that my partner is white? Kenji Yoshino has talked about the pressure that gays often feel to cover and to downplay their gay identity. In my own career, I have found the opposite. It is telling people I have a white partner that has served me well, that has made me acceptable. Palatable. So, has it all been calculated on my part? Part of my careerist agenda?

But then I look at Seth, now my husband thanks to a Massachusetts court decision, and think/hope that history and non-history have nothing to do with us. I tell myself that we are *sui generis*.

Which I suppose is a way of bringing me back to *Loving*. And rethinking *Loving*, a case that could not be more appropriately named. I said before that *Loving*, like *McLaughlin* before it and *Lawrence* after it, began with a tip and an arrest. But I was wrong.

> *Loving*, I'm sure, began with a look.
> With a kiss.
> With love.
> I'm sure.

[56] *See* Russell Shorto, THE ISLAND AT THE CENTER OF THE WORLD 187–88 (2004).

9

What's *Loving* Got to Do with It?

Law Shaping Experience and Experience Shaping Law

Renée M. Landers

In 1955, I was born to a white mother and an African-American father in Springfield, Illinois. Except for the three years that my family lived in Germany, we lived in a transitional neighborhood near where Abraham Lincoln lived when he was elected president. Railroad tracks at 10th Street separated the neighborhood from the center of town determined by the Old State Capitol Building where Lincoln delivered the "House Divided" speech. During my youth, the neighborhood was an integrated neighborhood of middle-class white and African-American residents, but eventually became an African-American neighborhood comprised of families of more fragile economic status. When I was about ten, an African-American playmate, whose family was relatively new to Springfield, asked whether it was illegal for my parents to be married.[1] I was surprised to discover that I would be expected to defend my parent's marriage even as I was developing my own sense of racial identity and coming to terms with the racial identities assigned me by others.

That first childhood encounter with other people's views of the racial identity of my family illustrates both the liberating and limiting impacts of law in shaping the lived experience of families formed through interracial marriages. Today, as an adult and a lawyer, I have the tools to reflect on the transformative impact of the Supreme Court's decision in *Loving v. Virginia* – and other civil rights cases of the 1950s and 1960s – in enabling me to make certain life choices, such as where to go

---

[1] Phyl Newbeck, VIRGINIA HASN'T ALWAYS BEEN FOR LOVERS: INTERRACIAL MARRIAGE BANS AND THE CASE OF RICHARD AND MILDRED LOVING 228 (2004). Illinois enacted an antimiscegenation law in 1829. The ban was repealed in 1874. *Id.* at 40, 45–46, 49, 51, 228. In 1874, Illinois omitted the law from its statutes, an action that may have been accidental. *Id.* at 45–46. Public reaction to the marriage of black boxing champion Jack Johnson to a white woman, Lucille Cameron, in 1913 spawned the introduction of antimiscegenation bills in Illinois as well as other states where interracial marriage was not prohibited. Five bills were filed in Illinois where the marriage took place. Only one of these bills was reported favorably from committee and none made any further progress. *Id.* at 49. Another bill died in committee in 1915. *Id.* at 51.

to school, where to live, where to eat and shop, and who to marry, on the same basis that white Americans had long taken for granted. While *Loving* gave the imprimatur of the legal establishment to the concept of interracial marriage, my conversation with a childhood neighbor and other personal experiences illustrate that legal recognition is not sufficient to alter settled societal expectations and practices. Race still matters in the choices most individuals make regarding marriage and in their reactions to the marriages of others. *Loving* did not settle these matters for all time and for all Americans. A parallel[2] history is evolving as the legal system and society react to demands of same-sex couples for full equality with respect to legal recognition of their relationships and all the rights and responsibilities such recognition entails.[3] Whether law will lead public opinion, or social acceptance will ultimately transform the law, remains to be seen in this contemporary struggle. The experience since *Loving* makes clear that, however valuable societal approval may be, it cannot substitute for the concrete entitlements that only law can convey.

PERSONAL EXPERIENCES

My mother dealt with racial discrimination by giving us extensive instructions about how to conduct ourselves, especially before we ventured into any new setting or venue. On official forms at school or elsewhere, she instructed us to respond "other" when asked to identify our race. In retrospect, she reasoned that her children's achievement would not be subject to any criticism that their shortcomings were owing to being "colored," "mulatto," or "black." She instructed us to refuse to respond to questions about our race, on the theory that anyone who asked was motivated by bad intentions. Both of our parents were clear that a person's race was hardly ever relevant information and it was wrong, therefore, to ask such questions. On this point she reasoned that our mixed-race heritage would make any other category – such as white or black – inaccurate and incomplete. "Other," our mother

---

2   *See* Catherine Smith, *Queer as Black Folk*, 2007 WIS. L.REV. 379, 386–7 (criticizing the comparison of racism to prejudice against gay, lesbian, bisexual, and transgender person because it obscures the different experiences and ignores the white and heterosexual privileges members of majority enjoy). I use the word "parallel" in the sense used in geometry to describe straight lines, "lying in the same plane but never meeting no matter how far extended," to indicate that while it is useful to compare the issue of interracial marriage with issues surrounding same-sex marriage to identify analogies or similarities, the two situations can never entirely overlap or be the "same" or "equal" in the other sense of the word. THE AMERICAN HERITAGE DICTIONARY OF THE ENGLISH LANGUAGE (4th ed. 2006) *available at* http://dictionary.reference.com/browse/parallel

3   *See* William N. Eskridge, Jr., EQUALITY PRACTICE: CIVIL UNIONS AND THE FUTURE OF GAY RIGHTS 129–31, 140–41 (2002); *see also* Evan Gerstmann, SAME-SEX MARRIAGE AND THE CONSTITUTION 46–51 (2004) (describing "problems" with analogy to *Loving* that prohibitions on same-sex marriage constitute sex discrimination in violation of the equal protection clause) [hereinafter Gerstmann].

concluded, was more accurate. In this way, her thinking anticipated some of the movement toward allowing people to check multiple categories or to identify themselves by the "multiracial" category.[4] On the one hand, our mother recognized that the world would see us as African-American, black, or as "other," but she was trying not to have our view of our opportunities, our confidence in situations outside the home, limited by how others might see us.

Imagine my surprise and dismay during my first year as an undergraduate at Harvard-Radcliffe at being asked, almost daily by people I was meeting, what my ethnic background was. Many of the questions, in retrospect, I know, were motivated by mere curiosity. For some reason the social constraints that operate to prevent us from asking other personal questions out of curiosity, such as asking a woman whether she is pregnant, or inquiring about the identity of the biological father of the children of a same-sex couple, do not seem to constrain people in questions of race. Other people think they have a right to know because so much social interaction is mediated by real and perceived racial identities. For example, in September 2009, the "Miss Conduct" etiquette column in *The Boston Globe Magazine* published a question from a reader, who self-identified as "of mixed race," asking for advice on how to respond to the random "What are you?" question.[5]

When I worked in Washington, DC, from 1993 to 1997, I rarely enjoyed a taxi ride without the driver – usually African-American – asking where I was from or what my ethnic background was. I was on a crowded elevator in the Department of Justice with my two-week-old son when another department employee gestured to my son and asked, "Is this your adopted baby?" My husband is white, and my son was born with red hair and hazel eyes. In the uncomfortable silence after the question, I finally was able to respond, "No, he just looks a lot like his father right now." Recognizing her faux pas, the woman looked at the floor for several seconds and then tried to recover with "You didn't look as if you could have just had a baby."

Where race is concerned, people think they are entitled to detailed information about the lives of strangers. When my husband, son, and I were in London

---

4   *See, e.g.,* Deborah Ramirez, *Multicultural Empowerment: It's Not Just Black and White Anymore, in* MIXED RACE AMERICA AND THE LAW 198 (Kevin R. Johnson ed., 2003); Susan R. Graham, *The Real World, in* MIXED RACE AMERICA AND THE LAW 203 (Kevin R. Johnson ed., 2003) ("the multiracial category enables multiracial people to have the choice of an accurate designation. It is an important option for any person with parents of different races. ... Some multiracial people choose to identify with one race only. They have every right and every opportunity to do so in our society").

5   Robin Abrahams, *Miss Conduct, A Question of Race: How to Respond to "What Are You?",* THE BOSTON GLOBE MAGAZINE, Sept. 27, 2009, at 8. The advice from Miss Conduct was to respond by advising the person in a conversational tone that the question is not appropriate to ask and to change the subject. "You state your boundaries, pirouette, and give the other person a graceful escape route." The columnist also advised to "Accept any apologies casually and with the awareness that you've probably asked your share of uncool questions, too."

in 2000, the taxi driver who transported us to the airport for our flight home to Boston began a round of questioning about where we were from. My husband, who is white, responded "Boston." Eventually, the driver got around to asking the question to which he really wanted to know the answer – what were all of our racial backgrounds. The questions have not abated. Our son, now fifteen, takes music lessons – pennywhistle and piano – at a suburban music school. A few years ago, we were enjoying cake and punch after our son had played in a recital. A man came up to us and remarked, "Wow, your family is certainly a walking United Nations, isn't it?" We were all rendered nearly speechless by this comment.

RESISTANCE TO INTERRACIALISM

These experiences demonstrate a collective resistance to the erosion of racial boundaries. Rachel Moran notes that some have trumpeted interracial marriage as the melting pot that will naturally heal America's racial divide[6]: "In their view, formal legal distinctions are secondary to the power of informal relationships to transform race. Despite this optimism, changes in marital choice have been modest at best. ... So far, then, race has not readily dissolved through intermarriage, and here as elsewhere, blacks remain separate to a significant degree."[7] Most marriages still take place between people of the same race.[8] "The normative ideal of colorblindness in the regulation of marriage is well established [but] interracial marriages, particularly between blacks and whites, remain an anomaly."[9] In 1960, for example, marriages involving blacks and whites numbered 51,000 out of more than 1.5 million total marriages, or less than 4 percent of all marriages. By 2006, marriages involving blacks and whites numbered 403,000 out of 2,193,000, or about 18 percent of the total.[10] The statistics also reveal marriages involving black women and white men are less frequent than marriages involving black men and white women.[11]

Moran makes three arguments concerning black-white intermarriage: that this gender disparity is surprising given that, historically, most race mixing occurred

---

[6] *See generally* Rachel Moran, INTERRACIAL INTIMACY (2001) [hereinafter Moran]. *See also,* Jim Chen, *Unloving,* 80 IOWA L.REV. 145 (1994).

[7] Moran, *supra* note 6 at 192.

[8] *Id.* at 191 (noting that 95% of all marriages in America take place between people of the same race and that "[t]he proportion of marriages that are interracial remains quite small, but in the ... decades since *Loving* these unions have grown increasingly respectable").

[9] *Id.* at 101.

[10] U.S. Dept. of Health and Human Services, National Center for Health Statistics, *available at* www.cdc.gov/nchs/; *see also,* Marion Kilson & Florence Ladd, IS THAT YOUR CHILD?, 119 (2008) (showing gender breakdown of black/white marriages).

[11] Moran, *supra* note 6, at 104–05. Also, black women are less able to transmit privileges of white identity to their children. Moran analyzes the complex historical and contemporary attitudes toward gender that influence attitudes toward marriage and who makes suitable marriage partners. *Id.* at 102–105.

between white men and black women; that there are substantially fewer mar-
riageable black men than black women in the population; and that black women
should be able to use their superior levels of educational and occupational attain-
ment as compared to black men to attract white husbands. She hypothesizes that
success in those realms does not translate into greater cross-racial appeal for black
women as it does for men.[12]

THE PERSONAL IS POLITICAL

Marriage has long been a flashpoint for engendering opposition to equality for
African Americans.[13] The speeches during the Illinois Senatorial campaign in 1858,
including speeches the candidates made during the Lincoln-Douglas debates, routinely addressed this asserted link between eliminating slavery and policies relating to miscegenation.[14] In an 1857 speech on the *Dred Scott* decision, for example,
Abraham Lincoln noted that Stephen Douglas argued that all who contended that
the Declaration of Independence includes "ALL men, black as well as white," "do
so only because they want to vote, and eat, and sleep, and marry with negroes!"[15]
Lincoln protested "against that counterfeit logic which concludes that, because I do
not want a black woman for a *slave* I must necessarily want her for a *wife*."[16] In the
same speech, Lincoln noted that he "agreed for once – a thousand times agreed"
with Douglas on the horror "at the thought of the mixing blood by the white and
black races."[17] Lincoln then proceeded to analyze census statistics showing that the
"mulatto" population in the United States in 1850 consisted predominantly of offspring of black slaves and white masters to show that "slavery is the greatest source
of amalgamation."[18]

---

[12] *Id.* at 104–5.
[13] Moran, *supra* note 6, at 4 ("antimiscegenation laws treated sex and marriage across racial boundaries
     as antisocial, dangerous acts" to keep distinctions between black and white, slave and free).
[14] Abraham Lincoln, SPEECHES AND WRITINGS 1832–1858, 455 (Library of America 1989) (July 10, 1858
     speech at Chicago, Illinois, where Stephen Douglas was not present) [hereinafter Lincoln]; *id.* at 517
     (August 21, 1858, First Debate at Ottawa, Illinois, Lincoln's Reply); *id.* at 636–37 (September 15, 1858,
     Fourth Debate at Charleston, Illinois, Lincoln's Speech); *id.* at 694–95 (October 7, 1858, Fifth Debate
     at Galesburg, Illinois, Douglas's Speech); *id.* at 703 (October 7, 1858, Fifth Debate at Galesburg,
     Illinois, Lincoln's Reply); *id.* at 732 (October 13, 1858, Sixth Debate at Quincy, Illinois, Lincoln's
     Speech); *id.* at 751 (October 13, 1858, Sixth Debate at Quincy, Illinois, Douglas's Reply).
[15] Lincoln, *supra* note 14, at 397.
[16] *Id.* at 398 (emphasis in the original).
[17] *Id.* at 400.
[18] *Id.* at 400–01. The continued existence of racially segregated proms in some parts of the South is evi-
     dence that while the law no longer prohibits interracial marriages, the fear of intermarriage still perme-
     ates some parts of the culture. Gene Owens, *Alabama Voters To Decide Fate of Miscegenation Ban*,
     Stateline.org, (October 23, 2000), *at* http://www.stateline.org/live/viewPage.action?siteNodeId=136&la
     nguageID (last visited February 7, 2010) (quoting a journalist writing about desegregation in the 1950s as

While *Loving* has legitimized love across the color line, disapproval remains. At the time *Loving* was decided, most states no longer banned interracial marriage, but in 1968, 72 percent of Americans did not approve of interracial marriage and only 20 percent supported it.[19] At the beginning of the twenty-first century, Alabama was the last state to repeal a provision contained in its constitution prohibiting the legislature from authorizing interracial marriage. Supporters of the constitutional amendment wanted to remove the provision to demonstrate the state's contemporary stand on the issue and viewed the vote optimistically as a reflection that many whites wanted to turn the page on a segregationist past.[20] According to press reports, public opposition to the amendment came from a coalition of chapters of the Southern Party arguing that the amendment was vaguely worded and was not needed because interracial couples could marry. In November 2000, 40 percent of Alabama's voters voted to keep the constitutional provision. Even though it had been nearly four decades since the *Loving* decision invalidated bans on interracial marriage, the vote indicated that the level of social acceptance, while more favorable than at the time *Loving* was decided, remains far from universal.

INTERSECTING RACE AND SEXUALITY

The personal experiences recounted here and the Alabama episode, among other recent examples,[21] indicate that the law cannot eradicate individual racial bias or

stating that the real fear in that era was not integration; it was intermarriage). The same article noted that in 2000, when the Alabama constitutional provision banning interracial marriage was repealed, only 31% of the whites sampled approved of interracial marriage, but most favored removing the provision from the constitution. While schools have been integrated, the segregated proms are organized outside of the schools by committees of students and parents. Even though whites and blacks report that friendships regularly cross racial lines and students of different races engage in myriad activities together, whites justify the continued existence of separate proms on the basis of "tradition" and "how [it's] always been." Sara Corbett, *A Prom Divided*, N.Y. TIMES MAGAZINE, May 24, 2009, 24. A black parent who attended a segregated prom when she graduated from Montgomery County High School in Alabama in 1978 expressed distress that more than thirty years later in 2009, her daughter was attending the high school's racially segregated prom, lamenting whether "things will ever change around here." *Id.* at 29.

[19] Gerstmann, *supra* note 3 at 201 & n.26 (citing NEW YORK TIMES, *Information Bank Abstracts*, August 30, 1978).

[20] *Alabama Removes Ban on Interracial Marriage*, USA TODAY, November 7, 2000, *available at* http://www.usatoday.com/news/vote2000/al/main03.htm. African Americans represented only about 26% of the Alabama population at the time of the vote, so a great many whites had to vote to repeal the ban. At the time the ban was repealed, there were at least 1,600 mixed-race couples in Alabama.

[21] E.g., Associated Press, *Governor Calls for Firing of Justice in Interracial Marriage Case*, October 16, 2009, *available at* http://articles.cnn.com/2009–10–16/us/louisiana.interracial.marriage_1_interracial-marriages-keith-bardwell-marriage-license?_s=PM:US (last visited Sept. 14, 2011). In October 2009, a Louisiana justice of the peace, Keith Bardwell, made headlines when he refused to issue a marriage license to an interracial couple. *See id.* Bardwell stated that because white and blacks do not readily accept the children from such marriages, he did not want to be part of any suffering these children

command integration in the purely personal or family relationship; it merely has the ability to affect discriminatory actions only in civil societal interactions. As stated in *Palmore v. Sidoti,* while such "private biases may be outside the reach of the law ... the law cannot directly or indirectly, give them effect."[22]

In walking the tightrope to balance liberty with equality, courts have achieved mixed results. In the school desegregation cases, for example, the road followed by the Courts has not been met with success if measured by the level of segregation in the nation's public schools. The reasons that the *Brown v. Board of Education's* statement of formal legal equality in the educational sphere[23] has failed to achieve actual integration in educational experience have been well documented. First, implementation of the *Brown* doctrine met with resistance in school districts throughout the nation.[24] Professor Erwin Chemerinsky has explained well how the federal courts, and particularly the Supreme Court, have undermined the goal of integrated education promised in *Brown* by not vigorously enforcing its principles and by acquiescing to resistance to implementing school desegregation orders.[25]

---

might experience. *See id.* Bardwell stated, also, that in his experience, most interracial marriages do not last long. *See id.*

[22] 466 U.S. 429, 433 (1984). In *Palmore v. Sidoti,* the Supreme Court unanimously overturned a state court decision denying a white mother custody of a child because the mother had married a man of a different race. The state court had reasoned that living in a biracial household might subject the child to stigma and discriminatory experiences, so the child's best interests would be served by awarding custody to the father.

[23] 347 U.S. 483, 494 (1954).

[24] *See, e.g.,* Charles Ogletree, ALL DELIBERATE SPEED: REFLECTIONS ON THE FIRST HALF CENTURY OF *Brown v. Board of Education* 124–134 (2004); Gerald N. Rosenberg, THE HOLLOW HOPE: CAN COURTS BRING ABOUT SOCIAL CHANGE? (1993); Robert J. Cottrol et al., *Brown v. Board of Education:* CASTE, CULTURE, AND THE CONSTITUTION (2003); Erwin Chemerinsky, *Lost Opportunity: The Burger Court and the Failure to Achieve Equal Educational Opportunity,* 45 MERCER L. REV. 999 (1994) [hereinafter Chemerinsky, *Lost Opportunity*]; Erwin Chemerinsky, *The Segregation and Resegregation of American Public Education: The Courts' Role,* 81 N.C. L. REV. 1597 (2003) [hereinafter, Chemerinsky, *The Courts' Role*].

[25] Chemerinsky argues that federal courts failed: (1) to establish rigorous timetables for achieving desegregation, Chemerinsky, *Lost Opportunity, supra* note 24 at 1003–04; Chemerinsky, *The Courts' Role, supra* note 22 at 1604; (2) did not permit interdistrict remedies to promote desegregation, Chemerinsky, *Lost Opportunity,* at 1005, 1009–11 (referring the Court's decision in *Milliken v. Bradley,* 418 U.S. 717, 741–45, restricting the ability to use interdistrict remedies); Chemerinsky, *The Courts' Role, supra* note 24, at 1607; (3) declined to identify education as a fundamental right or to mandate reform for school financing systems, Chemerinsky, *Lost Opportunity, supra* note 24 at 1008–09 (discussing the impact of the Court's decision in *San Antonio Independent School District v. Rodriguez,* 411 U.S. 1, 28–29, 33 (1973), holding that school funding disparities did not constitute an equal protection violation and refusing to declare that education was a fundamental right); Chemerinsky, *The Court's Role, supra* note 24 at 1611–13; and (4) ended desegregation orders prematurely before desegregation could be firmly institutionalized in communities, Chemerinsky, *Lost Opportunity, supra* note 24 at 1013–15 (discussing *Board of Education v. Dowell,* 498 U.S. 237 (1991); *Freeman v. Pitts,* 503 U.S. 467 (1992), both limiting the time a court desegregation order can be enforced); Chemerinsky, *The Courts' Role, supra* note 24 at 1615.

The Roberts Court majority appears to be unconcerned with the realities of continued segregation and inequality in public education.[26] In *Parents Involved in Community Schools v. Seattle School District No. 1*, the five justices in the majority rejected the notion that school desegregation plans can be used to address the consequences of societal discrimination, such as racially identifiable housing patterns or resistance to court desegregation orders.[27] In a concurrence in the *Parents Involved* case, Justice Kennedy wrote separately to chide the plurality for "an all-too-unyielding insistence that race cannot be a factor" in addressing "the problem of *de facto* resegregation in schooling" expressed in the Chief Justice's opinion. Justice Kennedy termed Justice Harlan's dissenting statement in *Plessy v. Ferguson* that the Constitution is "color-blind" as aspirational, and argued that, "In the real world, it is regrettable to say, it cannot be a universal constitutional principle."[28] Unlike the majority in *Parents Involved*, Justice Kennedy perceives that, at some point, the Court's color-blind approach means that the law is giving effect to societal discrimination.

Experience in enforcing *Brown*'s ambition reinforces Justice Kennedy's perception that the goal of a color-blind Constitution has not yet been attained. *Brown* has not led to fully integrated schools, nor has it been the catalyst for a satisfactory level of integration or equality in all other aspects of political and social life.[29] Similarly, the removal of prohibitions on interracial marriage has not produced a mixed-race society where race has become irrelevant. Although *Brown* and *Loving* have fallen short of expectations, both decisions had a transformative effect on the lives of individuals directly affected by the decisions – people like me – and have served as catalysts for the evolution of public opinion about race over time.

Legal recognition of same-sex marriage has the same potential for personal and social impact. Information regarding public attitudes toward interracial marriage

---

[26] *Parents Involved in Community Schools v. Seattle School District* No. 1, 551 U.S. 701 (2007). For a discussion of *Parents Involved*, see Renée M. Landers, *Massachusetts Health Insurance Reform Legislation: An Effective Tool for Addressing Racial and Ethnic Disparities in Health Care?*, 28 HAMLINE J. OF PUB. L. & POL'Y 1 (2007).

[27] *Parents Involved*, 551 U.S. at 748.

[28] *Id.*, at 787–88. (Kennedy, J., concurring).

[29] Associated Press, *U.S. Report: Racial Disparities Continue, Differences in Income, Education, Home Ownership Continue, Data Finds*, November 14, 2006, *available at* http://www.msnbc.msn.com/id/15704759 (last visited September 14, 2011) (reporting that "Decades after the civil rights movement, racial disparities in income, education and home ownership persist and, by some measurements, are growing"). Findings of the report issued by the Census Bureau indicated that the median income for white households in 2005 was $50,622, $30,939 for black households (60% of the figure for white households), $36,278 for Hispanic households (72%) and $60,367 for Asian households (119%). In other words, median income for black households has stayed at 60% of the income for white households since 1980. Poverty rates in 2005 tell a similar story: 24.9% for blacks, 21.8% for Hispanics, 11.1% for Asian Americans, and 8.3% for whites.

at the time of the *Loving* decision and today indicate that opposition to interracial marriage was at least as strong as current opposition to same-sex marriage.[30] Today, children are still asked why they have two parents of the same sex and whether their family structures are legitimate. Families have to bear the economic and social disadvantages of the inability to marry.[31] As a person who has had to answer these questions about my race, and the races of my parents, my spouse, and my child for my entire life, I see a role for the law to play in removing the legal distinctions that give rise to similarly intrusive questions for families formed by same-sex couples.

SAME-SEX MARRIAGE: WHAT'S LOVING GOT TO DO WITH IT?

In *Goodridge v. Department of Public Health*,[32] the Massachusetts Supreme Judicial Court was the first state supreme court to hold unconstitutional a state ban on same-sex marriage.[33] The *Goodridge* court drew analogies to the role of courts in invalidating laws prohibiting interracial marriage.[34] First, the Massachusetts court observed that the long history of prohibiting interracial marriage "availed not when the Supreme Court of California held in 1948 that a legislative prohibition against interracial marriage violated the due process and equality guarantees of the Fourteenth Amendment."[35] While noting the situation had improved somewhat by the time the

[30] Gerstmann, *supra* note 3 at 202. Gerstmann reports that in 1968, the year after the *Loving* decision, "72% of the American public disapproved of interracial marriage, while only 20% supported it." *Id.* at 201 & n.26 (citing New York Times, Information Bank Abstracts, August 30, 1978). The *Loving* decision met with little public resistance, and there were no serious moves to amend the Constitution.

[31] *See, e.g.,* Tara Siegel Bernard, *To Cover Tax, Google to Add To Gays' Pay*, N.Y. Times, July 1, 2010, at B1, B5 (reporting that the Internet search firm Google will increase the pay of gay and lesbian employees whose partners receive domestic partner health benefits to compensate them for an extra tax they must pay because federal tax law does not consider domestic partners to be dependents, and noting that several other companies also provide such enhanced compensation).

[32] Goodridge v. Dep't of Pub. Health, 798 N.E. 2d 941, 948 (Mass. 2003).

[33] In the first case in which the U.S. Supreme Court was asked to decide the rights of homosexual persons, *Bowers v. Hardwick*, 478 U.S. 186 (1986), the Court declined to extend the level of respect to relationships involving persons of the same sex that previous decisions had accorded heterosexual relationships in cases such as *Griswold v. Connecticut*, 381 U.S. 479(1965) and *Eisenstadt v. Baird*, 405 U.S. 438 (1972).

[34] *See Goodridge*, 798 N.E. 2d at 957. Interestingly, the two dissenters in *Bowers* also had noted similarities to *Loving*. Justice Blackmun, in his dissent, wrote "the parallel between *Loving* and this case is almost uncanny." *Bowers*, at 210, n.5. Justice Stevens's dissent noted that at the time *Loving* was decided, sixteen of the states still outlawed interracial marriage, and at the time of the *Bowers* decision, twenty-four states and the District of Columbia had sodomy statutes. Still, the *Loving* court ruled that the prohibition on interracial marriage at issue in *Loving* violated the Equal Protection Clause and the Due Process Clause. *Id.* at 216 & n.9. Seventeen years later, the Court overruled *Bowers* in *Lawrence v. Texas.* 539 U.S. 558, 577–78 (2003).

[35] *Goodridge*, 798 N.E. 2d at 327 (citing Perez v. Sharp, 198 P.2d 17 [1948]). In a footnote, the *Goodridge* Court noted that at the time *Perez* was decided, "racial inequality was rampant and normative, segregation in public and private institutions was commonplace, the civil rights movement had not yet

Supreme Court decided *Loving*, the *Goodridge* court remarked that the "lack of pop-ular consensus favoring integration (including interracial marriage)" did not deter the *Loving* court from a remedy that did not reflect a broad social consensus.[36]

Even though *Brown* has not succeeded in creating truly integrated public schools, the decision and its progeny have made formal legal equality, if not actual equality, a bedrock assumption of national life. *Loving* has succeeded in protecting the ability of interracial couples to marry and form families, even if social and isolated pockets of official disapproval remain. Because only five of the states have recognized same-sex marriages, same-sex couples do not experience even the basic formal equality now enjoyed by interracial couples because of the *Loving* decision.

While predicting public reaction to legal developments is an art, not a science, and understanding what public opinion polls mean is also difficult, information regarding public attitudes toward interracial marriage at the time of the *Loving* decision indicates that opposition to interracial marriage was at least as strong as current opposition to same-sex marriage.[37] Since same-sex marriage became legal in Massachusetts in May 2004,[38] more than 11,000 same-sex couples have married in Massachusetts.[39] At the time the Massachusetts legislature rejected a proposed constitutional amendment to define marriage as a union involving a man and a woman, polling showed that 56 percent of Massachusetts residents surveyed opposed the amendment.[40] In contrast, a May 2006 Gallup poll found that 58 percent of Americans opposed same-sex marriage and 39 percent favored it.[41] One year after

---

been launched, and the 'separate but equal' doctrine of *Plessy* was still good law." *Goodridge*, 798 N.E. 2d at 327 n.16.

[36] *Id.*

[37] *See* note 30 *supra.*

[38] Pursuant to the Massachusetts Supreme Judicial Court's decision in *Goodridge v. Department of Public Health*, 798 N.E. 2d 941, 969 (Mass. 2003), same-sex marriage became legal in Massachusetts on May 17, 2004, the fiftieth anniversary of the U.S. Supreme Court decision in *Brown v. Board of Education.*

[39] Pam Belluck, *Massachusetts Gay Marriage to Remain Legal*, N.Y. TIMES, June 15, 2007, at A16 (report-ing approximately 8,500 marriages at that time); David Fillipov, *5 Years Later, Views Shift Subtly on Gay Marriage*, BOSTON GLOBE, November 17, 2008.

[40] Pam Belluck, *Massachusetts Gay Marriage to Remain Legal*, at A16. The rejected amendment pro-vided as follows:

When recognizing marriages entered into after the adoption of this amendment by the people, the Commonwealth and its political subdivisions shall define marriage only as the union of one man and one woman.

Proposal for an Initiative Amendment to the Constitution to Define Marriage, Senate No. 2220 of 2007, *available at* http://www.mass.gov/legis/bills/senate/185/st02/st02220.htm (last visited September 14, 2011); *see also*, House No. 4617 of 2006.

[41] See the summary of various poll result on the website of Religious Tolerance available at http://www. religioustolerance.org/hom_marp.htm (last visited September 14, 2011) (citing May 2005 *Boston Globe* poll). Opposition dropped to 56% when survey respondents were asked about marriage for "same-sex couples" rather than "homosexuals".

Massachusetts legalized same-sex marriage, a national poll showed that 79 percent think that gays and lesbians should be able to serve in the military, whereas in 2000, only 57 percent were in favor.[42] The same poll found that only 41 percent believed that same-sex sexual behavior is always wrong. In an article examining public views five years after same-sex marriage became legal in Massachusetts, *The Boston Globe* reported that, "Gay and lesbian couples ... said they are attracting fewer startled looks when they rent cars, less consternation when they hold hands, fewer awkward questions when they visit spouses in hospital rooms."[43] Gay marriages have comprised about 4 percent of all marriages in Massachusetts in recent years, and Massachusetts remains the state with the lowest divorce rate in the country. In July 2008, the Massachusetts legislature repealed a 1913 law banning out-of-state couples from marrying in Massachusetts, which has made it possible for same-sex couples from other states to marry in Massachusetts.[44]

Whether courts in ruling on contentious issues should lead public opinion or conform decisions to majoritarian societal consensus depends on whether courts are viewed as protecting vulnerable minorities from the "tyranny of the majority" or as mere enforcers of existing orthodoxies. This question of the appropriate role for the courts informed public responses to decisions such as *Brown* and *Loving*, and lies at the heart of public debate about the role of courts in determining what rights gays and lesbians are entitled to enjoy. While the immediate reaction to *Loving*, for example, was not positive, it did not provoke sustained and serious efforts to overrule it. Nor did *Loving* engender the sustained resistance that the *Brown* decision spawned, perhaps because the choice of a marriage partner still devolved to the individual, with limited state regulation. *Brown*, on the other hand, required social engagement by nearly every family with a child in public schools. Forty years later, a majority of Americans do not oppose interracial marriage, although most people of all races still marry persons of the same race as their own.

The same claim cannot be made for the public reaction following the *Goodridge* decision. *Goodridge* accelerated a movement that began when the Supreme Court of Hawaii held in *Baehr v. Lewin* that a state statute outlawing same-sex marriage

---

[42] *Id* (citing Scott S. Greenberger, *One Year Later, Nation Divided on Gay Marriage: Split Seen by Region, Age, Globe Poll Finds*, BOSTON GLOBE, May 15, 2005); *see also*, Gerstmann, *supra* note 3 at 201–02 (discussing results of polls on same-sex marriage). The recent recommendation by the Chairman of the Joint Chiefs of Staff and the Secretary of Defense that Congress repeal the statute imposing a "don't ask, don't tell" rule for gays and lesbians serving in the military is further evidence of greater tolerance for homosexuality. *Top Defense Officials Seek to End 'Don't Ask, Don't Tell,'* N.Y. TIMES, Feb. 2, 2010.

[43] David Fillipov, *5 Years Later, Views Shift Subtly on Gay Marriage*, BOSTON GLOBE, Nov. 17, 2008, available at http://www.massequality.org/content/5-years-later-views-shift-subtly-gay-marriage (last visited September 14, 2011).

[44] The 1913 statute was enacted at a time when states were erecting barriers to prevent interracial couples from marrying in states where interracial marriages were permitted.

created a sex-based classification subject to strict-scrutiny review.[45] The *Baehr* decision sparked the passage of the Federal Defense of Marriage Act (DOMA) in 1996
that bars federal recognition of same-sex marriages and permits states to refuse to
recognize same-sex marriages performed in other jurisdictions.[46] Subsequently, the
Hawaii legislature overturned the decision in *Baehr* and banned same-sex marriage
in 1997.[47] Although efforts to amend the U.S. Constitution to incorporate a definition of marriage have not been successful, numerous states have adopted constitutional amendments defining marriage as a relationship involving one man and one
woman, and others have adopted statutes similarly defining marriage. Even though
six states, the District of Columbia, and one Indian tribe now permit same-sex marriage, most court decisions and ballot referenda have declined to follow the lead of
Massachusetts in recognizing a right to same-sex marriage when given the opportunity.[48] On the one hand, this legislative and ballot activity can be viewed as cause for
courts – including the U.S. Supreme Court – to be cautious about extending recognition of marriage to same-sex couples because the majoritarian consensus seems
to be moving in another direction. Conversely, all this activity could be viewed by
courts as evidence of animus against homosexual persons.[49] Courts have been more
open to find rights for gays and lesbians short of marriage in areas such as access to
civil unions and domestic partnerships, ability to adopt children, access to partner
health care benefits, and to protection from other forms of discrimination.[50]

Opposition to the *Brown* decision and resistance to subsequent court decisions
implementing the *Brown* mandate have had the effect of limiting the jurisprudence
following *Brown* and, consequently, the impact of *Brown*. The hysteria surrounding
the marriage question seems reminiscent of the ways in which opposition to school
integration and interracial marriage has been used as a shield to resist other forms

---

[45] Baehr v. Lewin, 852 P.2d 44, 64–67 (1993).
[46] 1 U.S.C. § 7 (1996); 28 U.S.C. § 1738C (1996).
[47] HAW. REV. STAT. § 572.
[48] In addition to Massachusetts, New Hampshire, Connecticut, Iowa, New York, Vermont, the District
      of Columbia, and the Coquille Indian Tribe in Oregon now permit marriages between same-sex
      couples. Voters in California have overturned a California Supreme Court decision making same-sex
      marriage lawful, but that action is now the subject of a court challenge. Similarly, voters in Maine
      reversed a law enacted by the Maine legislature authorizing same-sex marriage.
[49] For example, in *Lawrence v. Texas*, the Court took the proposition that laws "born of animosity toward
      the class of persons affected" were invalid. *Lawrence*, 539 U.S. at 574 (quoting *Romer v. Evans*, 517 U.S.
      620, 634 (1996)). In *Romer*, the Court had invalidated an amendment to Colorado's Constitution that
      prohibited homosexuals, lesbians, or bisexuals from the protection of the state's antidiscrimination
      laws. *Romer*, 517 U.S. at 624.
[50] Even civil unions or domestic partnerships fail to confer all the rights marriage confers. *See, e.g.*,
      Alison Leigh Cowan, *Gay Couples Argue Civil Unions Aren't Enough*, N.Y. TIMES, March 17, 2008,
      at A19 (documenting the myriad contexts in which civil unions require "haggling, litigation and
      explanation.").

of racial equality. Perhaps the *Goodridge* decision will play a leadership role that *Perez* did in the movement to invalidate bans on interracial marriage. It took the U.S. Supreme Court nineteen years to follow the California Supreme Court's decision in *Perez*. Seventeen years have elapsed between *Bowers* and *Lawrence*.[51] In the meantime, the growing social and political acceptance of gays and lesbians stands in contrast to the outraged responses to efforts to establish formal legal recognition for same-sex marriage. Perhaps in the case of same-sex marriage, formal legal equality will follow this change in public attitudes instead of serving as a catalyst for such change as the Supreme Court decisions in *Brown* and *Loving* have provided. Until that time, families formed by same-sex couples will continue to bear the legal and other burdens that formal equality could remove.

The prospect of movement – expansion – of rights, and of more accepting public opinions and political attitudes, is "like the fuel which keeps you going."[52] As Patricia Williams has written:

> In my own lifetime, segregation and antimiscegenation laws were still on the books in many states. During the lifetimes of my parents and grandparents and for several hundred years before them, laws were used to prevent blacks form learning to read, write, own property, or vote, blacks were, by constitutional mandate, outlawed from the hopeful, loving expectations that come from being treated as a whole rather than three-fifths of a person.[53]

Professor Williams concludes by noting that, "When every resource of a wealthy nation is put to such destructive ends, it will take more than a few generations to mop up the mess."[54] Like the experiences of Professor Williams, my life illustrates that changes in the law and the decisions of courts are essential, but not sufficient, to the task of engendering universal acceptance of interracial marriage. Gay and lesbian couples, while achieving some limited public rights and privately negotiated benefits, await the recognition that only federal law is able to convey to form the basis for building sustained acceptance.

[51] *See supra* notes 29 and 30 for discussion of the *Bowers* and *Lawrence* cases.
[52] Mamphela Ramphele, A LIFE 222 (1995) (writing about the effect of "The small changes you are able to bring to the institutions in which you work.").
[53] Patricia Williams, THE ALCHEMY OF RACE AND RIGHTS: DIARY OF A LAW PROFESSOR 60 (1991).
[54] *Id.* at 61.

10

Fear of a "Brown" Planet

Jacquelyn L. Bridgeman

Although mulattos were living symbols of the violation of the caste system, unions between blacks and whites in Natchez [Mississippi] still existed. [Some talk] about the commonality of common law marriages, or "permanent alliances," in 1930s Natchez. Charlotte Mackel Harrison's husband, Robert, grew up knowing a white Jewish grandfather, Charles Moritz. Harrison's grandmother Dorcas Walker had two daughters[, Julie and Lucille,] with Moritz, who took an active role in raising the girls. ... Under Mississippi state law[,] Moritz could not marry Harrison's grandmother. If the two had chosen to cohabit, which they did not, the social mores of Natchez society would have tolerated such an arrangement, even though many residents – black and white – would have objected. ... Walker and Moritz never married anyone else, and fittingly[,] they died in the same year.[1]

I wonder if Dorcas Walker and Charles Moritz ever contemplated, or dreamed, of the world that now exists in the aftermath of *Loving*. This is a world where their grandson, who was considered black, would be allowed to marry, and would marry, not one, but two white women prior to his death; where three of their six great-grandchildren are currently in interracial marriages, as is one of their four great-great-grandchildren. Would they approve and cheer, be happy that their descendents are now able to marry people of any race? Or would they, despite their own actions, deride and decry the miscegenation that runs rampant in their family? Did they have conversations about how to raise their mixed-race children in the increasingly segregated South? Or was that a non-issue because their children resided with their mother and were considered culturally, socially, and legally to be black and identified as such? As their great-great-granddaughter, who self-identifies – and is phenotypically, culturally, and socially identified – as black, but is in an interracial relationship, raising a multiracial daughter, I wish I could ask them these questions.

---

[1] Jack E. Davis, Race against Time: Culture and Separation in Natchez since 1930, 94 (2001).

In the fall of 2006, I found out I was pregnant with my daughter. I first began to suspect that I might be pregnant during a road trip that my husband, stepfather, and I took, during which we visited my husband's family who live close to Yellowstone and Grand Teton national parks. This was a beautiful, yet very rural, area of northern Wyoming, the state that my husband and I are from and currently call home. We decided to take this trip, in part, so that my husband and his family could show my stepfather areas of the state that he had not seen before, but with which they were intimately familiar, having resided in the area for generations. On this particular day, my husband's grandfather, who had hunted and fished the area since childhood, agreed to take us fishing. He showed us all of the best spots unknown to – and thus, untainted by – tourists. At one point during our expedition, my husband's grandfather began to reminisce and, in doing so, explained how he and his brothers used to "nigger fish" off the side of the bridges as kids. This meant, as I later found out, that they would tie a string to the end of a stick and drop it into the water, rather than use a regular fishing pole, which they could not afford.

Had any other white man said that particular word in my presence, we would likely have come to blows, or, at the very least, it would have been a "teachable moment." Yet, as initially taken aback as I was, I did not say anything. This man had welcomed me into his family with open arms and had never been anything but nice to me. I had grown very fond of him, and I never contemplated that what he said might have been offensive to me. That never crossed his mind.

So, I did not say anything; but neither did I quite let it go. A week later, I received confirmation that I was in fact expecting my first child and, shortly thereafter, the realization hit that, not only would this child be black like me, but also white like my husband. While Dorcas Walker, Charlie Moritz, and their daughter Lucille might be my child's ancestors, so, too, would be the man who "nigger fished" as a child. At this point, the aftermath of *Loving* hit home. For, in that moment, I realized that my daughter was not going to be black in the same way that I am black. She would not phenotypically look like me in the way that I look like my mother, and while there would be similarities, she and I would likely not share the same culture either. Whereas Walker and Moritz's mixed-race daughters identified as, grew up as, and were always considered to be black, that is not likely to be the case for my daughter. For her to identify as I identify, and for her to know and adopt my culture as I know and adopt it, would require her to deny half of herself. Yet, neither will she look like my husband, identify as he does, or completely share his culture. In much the same way that, although she has my eyes and nose and my husband's cheeks and mouth, her hair texture, eye color, and skin color will be uniquely her own, I suspect that the identity that she will form and the culture that she will adopt will be unique unto themselves as well. At least I hope that they will be, for I think that may be the only way that my daughter can embrace all parts of herself and be comfortable with them. That may be the only way that she does not have to choose between black and white; the only way she can be both.

I hope this for my daughter, but I feel a profound sense of loss at the prospect. I feel a sense of loss because I am so strongly black-identified and because I take pride and comfort in what I consider to be my black racial heritage, identity, and culture. It is the most salient characteristic of who I am. Yet, it likely will not be as defining a characteristic for my daughter. At the same time, I am also scared. I hope that she will find a middle path and that my husband and I will help her do so, but she may not. She may choose to be white; she may be able to pass for white. Given the predominantly white area in Wyoming where we live, she may have a strong incentive to make this choice. She may also choose to be black, or even take a third route, similar to that taken by one of my friends who predominantly identifies as Latina, although that is not the culture or race that my friend inherited.

In contemplation of my daughter's birth, I came face to face with what this really meant: I had to reconcile my own interests in racial justice with my assumption that my daughter would share in my identity as a black woman. Helping her form a racial identity would incorporate both me my and my husband's ancestries. She would not be black, like me, and she would not be white, like him.

On a larger scale, much of the aftermath of *Loving* forces this type of reconciliation. To reach the ideal of true equality, we have to let go of our race-based identities. We have to begin to contemplate a society where our identities are based on something other than race. American racial identity is primarily informed by the black-white binary construction of race where black and white identities historically have been defined in opposition to each other. We must find a way to define ourselves beyond this binary defined in relationship to whiteness. We must do this, not only for ourselves, but also for the children in our post-*Loving* world.

AMERICA'S CHANGING DEMOGRAPHICS

On November 4, 2008, the United States elected its first "black" president, quashing months of speculation by professional and lay critics whether white voters would vote for a black president. Throughout the 2008 presidential campaign, I found myself absurdly wondering if whites would vote for a "black" man with equal amounts of black and white genes. Obama embodies the extremely diverse landscape that is the United States of America, a landscape that continues to change.[2] According to the

2   John A. Powell, *A Minority-Majority Nation: Racing the Population in the Twenty-First Century*, 29 FORDHAM URB. L.J. 1395, 1395–96 (2002); Bureau of the Census, CURRENT POPULATION REPORTS: POPULATION PROJECTIONS OF THE UNITED STATES BY AGE, SEX, RACE, AND HISPANIC ORIGIN: 1995 TO 2050, 1–2 (1996) *available at* http://www.census.gov/prod/1/pop/p25–1130.pdf (last visited September 25, 2011).

2010 U.S. Census, whites were a clear majority.[3] Although blacks were the largest minority group in 1990,[4] by 2010, they fell behind Hispanics, who now constitute the largest minority group in the United States.[5] The Asian population has grown significantly over the last several years as well.[6] Both of these rapidly growing groups do not fit neatly into the black/white binary. It is also not clear on which side of the black/white divide these heterogeneous groups might ultimately fall.[7] By 2060, there will be no clear racial majority in the United States,[8] which invokes a shifting of white majority rule and social dominance.[9]

One possible outcome of this change is a backlash. As Derrick Bell explained, minority advancement occurs when it is in the interest of whites, and such periods of advancement have been followed by a reassertion of the status quo where whites remain on top and everyone else occupies a space somewhere below.[10] Others imagine that whites will remain at the top, but, in order to do so, the definition of who is white – or, more accurately, who is considered part of the powerful majority – will expand and change. Michael Lind states,

> There is not going to be a non-white majority in the 21st century. Rather, there is going to be a mostly white mixed-race majority ... [which is not] likely to be split two ways between whites and nonwhites. Rather, we are most likely to see

[3] Press Release, U.S. Census Bureau, *2010 Census Shows America's Diversity, Hispanic and Asian Populations Grew Fastest During the Decade* (Mar. 24, 2011), http://www.census.gov/newsroom/releases/archives/2010_census/cb11-cn125.html (stating that whites account for 72% of the U.S. population) (last visited September 25, 2011).

[4] Powell, *supra* note 2 at 1396 (noting that, as of the 1990 Census, whites were 74% of the U.S. population); Claudette Bennett, Census Bureau, Current Population Reports: The Black Population in the United States: March 1996 (Update) (1997) (indicating that as of 1996, the black population constituted 12.8% of the total American population).

[5] *See* Press Release, *supra* note 3 (stating that Hispanics accounted for 16% of the U.S. population and blacks accounted for 13% of the population).

[6] *See id.* (reporting that Asian population comprised 5% of the population).

[7] Rachel F. Moran, Interracial Intimacy 30, 106 (2001) (indicating that up until 1923, at least a portion of the heterogeneous group we now denote as Asian – those that were Indian by origin – were considered Caucasian, if not white, and that some speculate that with the ability of Asians to assimilate through intermarriage, coupled with high rates of outmarriage, that some among that population, such as the Japanese, will soon be fully absorbed into the white community).

[8] Frank Pellegrini, *The Coming of the Minority Majority*, Time, Aug. 31, 2000, *available at* http://www.time.com/time/search/article/0,8599,53774,00.html (last visited June 6, 2011).

[9] *Id.* (noting that despite the changing racial demographics, a small proportion of the American population controls the wealth and that small portion is overwhelming white, as is the racial makeup of the people who control Congress, the Supreme Court, corporations, and the vast majority of positions of power in the United States); Ian Haney López, White by Law: The Legal Construction of Race 145 (2006) [hereinafter López].

[10] Derrick Bell, Silent Covenants 49–58 (2004); Kimberlé Williams Crenshaw, *Race, Reform, and Retrenchment: Transformation and Legitimation in Antidiscrimination Law*, in Critical Race Theory: The Key Writings That Formed the Movement 103–22 (Kimberlé Crenshaw, et. al. eds. 1995).

something more complicated: a white-Asian-Hispanic melting pot majority – a hard to differentiate group of beige Americans – offset by a minority consisting of blacks who have been left out of the melting pot once again.[11]

Although a white/nonwhite dichotomy may not result, some speculate that, if such shifting of racial lines does in fact happen, there will likely be a black/nonblack dichotomy. This view posits that as time goes on, Asians and Hispanics will become more integrated and less differentiated from whites, but blacks will not.[12]

In this shift of the color line, African Americans may remain the racialized other, against whom everyone else's white, privileged identity is formed. To further support this notion, commentators point to the history of southern and eastern European groups who, over time, became incorporated into the white racial mainstream.[13] They point out as well that while interracial marriage may be up, blacks as a group marry outside of their race far less frequently than their minority counterparts, suggesting that blacks are less likely to be seen as equal and viable marriage partners.[14] This, many assert, is an indication that they are far from being fully subsumed into mainstream, American society.

Another perspective projects a "Latinization" of the United States, where the racial hierarchy allows for more gradations, with whites and blacks occupying the two extremes of a continuum and everyone else located somewhere in between. While each of these three hypotheses imagines an alternate racial dynamic in the near future, they contemplate race as an enduring and defining force in American identity and culture. More importantly, each assumes that whiteness, however it may be constructed, will continue to be the norm against which all others are defined. Privileges are still doled out on the basis of skin color, with those occupying places closer to the white end of the spectrum enjoying more privileges than those who do not. Thus, even though the effects of race may be less, they continue to play a significant role in the formation of the social hierarchy and of an individual's identity.

THE BLACK-WHITE BINARY AND IDENTITY CONSTRUCTION

In *The Black/White Binary Paradigm of Race*, Juan F. Perea describes the way in which American racial dynamics and discourse have centered on a black-white binary.[15] He argues that "race in America consists, either exclusively or primarily, of only two

---

[11] Michael Lind, *The Beige and the Black*, N.Y. TIMES MAG., Aug. 16, 1998, at 38–39.

[12] Lopez, *supra* note 9, at 145–46

[13] *Id.* at 149.

[14] Moran, *supra* note 7, at 103–05; Randall Kennedy, *How Are We Doing with Loving?: Race, Law, and Intermarriage*, 77 B.U. L. REV. 815, 817–19 (1997).

[15] Juan F. Perea, *The Black/White Binary Paradigm of Race: The "Normal Science" of American Racial Thought*, 85 CAL. L. REV. 1213 (1997).

constituent racial groups, the Black and the White."[16] As a result, Perea argues that those who are not considered black or white are largely left out of the equality and civil rights discourse. Using Thomas Khun's theory of scientific paradigms, Perea explains how the racial binary limits our ability to see viable alternatives of racialized identities. Looking to Chicano civil rights as an example, he cites a leading constitutional law textbook's exclusive use of the black-white binary when talking about racial issues. As he describes, the authors tell a "linear, paradigmatic version of the story of civil rights and equality [as] a story of an exclusively Black struggle for equality and a gradual, progressive White concession to Black demands."[17] As a result, the important stories of the struggles of others, such as segregation of Latino/as in public schools and the political coalitions of black and brown, are rendered nonexistent.

However, even if one were to include these stories, it would not serve to challenge the present hierarchy. Instead, under that vision, rather than a black-white binary, the discussion of race would look more like a multi-spoked wheel where the various nonwhite races make up the spokes, yet whiteness remains preeminent and at the center. Until whiteness no longer holds this position of dominance, we cannot approach an ideal of race equality.

A BRIEF HISTORY OF RACIAL FORMATION IN THE UNITED STATES

While records indicate that the first Africans landed in what was to become the United States in 1619, the harbingers of the system of chattel slavery and its concomitant race-based ideology do not appear with any clarity and frequency until several decades later.[18] While certainly the physical differences between Europeans and Africans was remarkable, the distinction between black and white and the status ascribed to a particular race did not initially exist as we know it today. As scholars have explained, the rise of race consciousness, or at least consciousness of blacks as a distinct race group, went hand in hand with the entrenchment of chattel slavery.[19] Leon Higginbotham has argued that there was no clear distinction between white indentured servants and African laborers, at least with respect to race.[20] However, as chattel slavery became entrenched, dark skin became the symbol of slave status.

---

[16] *Id.* at 1219.
[17] *Id.* at 1242.
[18] A. Leon Higginbotham, Jr., IN THE MATTER OF COLOR: RACE AND THE AMERICAN LEGAL PROCESS 19–40 (1978); Bruce Baum, THE RISE AND FALL OF THE CAUCASIAN RACE: A POLITICAL HISTORY OF RACIAL IDENTITY 46–47 (2006).
[19] BAUM, *supra* note 18, at 34–36, 40–49; *see generally* Higginbotham, *supra* note 18; Theodore W. Allen, THE INVENTION OF THE WHITE RACE, Vol. 2 (1994).
[20] Baum, *supra* note 18, at 34–36, 40–49; *see generally* Higginbotham, *supra* note 18; Theodore W. Allen, THE INVENTION OF THE WHITE RACE, Vol. 2 (1994).

As the comingling of slaves and others increased and the hues became blended, it became increasingly more difficult to differentiate between slave and free. Fear increased that those held in bondage together would rebel together as well.[21] Thus, more and more rigid rules were put in place to prevent insurrection. Breaking from previous law, which accorded familial rights based on patrilineage, new laws required a child to follow the racial and political condition of the mother.[22] These laws were an obvious attempt to keep a higher proportion of mixed-race, or mulatto, children in a condition of bondage.[23] As the comingling continued, it became harder to classify people. Eventually, the social and legal distinctions made on the basis of skin color grew into a complete and entrenched racial hierarchy with whites, particularly wealthy white men, at the top and blacks at the bottom.[24]

THE DEVELOPMENT OF RACE

Two points are germane to the present discussion. First, the black-white binary was developed as a tool to separate the people of what would become the United States into slave and free, black and white, oppressed and oppressor. Second, a racist ideology developed, centered on that binary, as a way to justify chattel slavery and the subordination of nonwhites.[25]

While scholars have correctly pointed out that race is a social construction,[26] they fail to question how a particular race may be in constant flux. In American history,

---

[21] Moran, *supra* n.7, at 18–21 (describing the way antimiscegenation laws arose to help demark the boundary between slave and free and white and black); Allen, *supra* note 19, at 244–49 (describing the way distinctions between white and black were made by ruling-class whites as a way to quell rebellions and stabilize a highly class-stratified system).

[22] A. Leon Higginbotham, Jr. & Barbara K. Kopytoff, *Racial Purity and Interracial Sex in the Law of Colonial and Antebellum Virginia*, 77 GEO. L.J. 1967, 1970–73 (1989).

[23] The reason for this, as Randall Kennedy, among others, has vividly explained, is that, prior to the Civil War, a large proportion of interracial sex was between white men and black women. Thus, without such a law, there would be an increasingly large number of children born to slave women who would ultimately be free and eligible to inherit from their slave-owning fathers. Randall Kennedy, INTERRACIAL INTIMACIES: SEX, MARRIAGE, IDENTITY AND ADOPTION 41–69, 162–77 (2003).

[24] Audrey G. McFarlane, *Operatively White? Exploring the Significance of Race and Class Through the Paradox of Black Middle-Classness*, 72 LAW & CONTEMP. PROBS. 163, 195–196 (2009).

[25] For a discussions of how race has been used to quell class divisions throughout American history, *see* Allen, *supra* note 19, at 244–53; C. Vann Woodward, THE STRANGE CAREER OF JIM CROW 77–93 (1974). For a discussion regarding the way in which racism and sexism have gone hand in hand, particularly because white supremacy is in part about defining masculinity, *see generally*, Abby l. Ferber, WHITE MAN FALLING: RACE, GENDER, AND WHITE SUPREMACY (1999).

[26] Ian F. Haney López, *The Social Construction of Race: Some Observations on Illusions, Fabrication, and Choice*, 29 HARV. C.R.-C.L. L. REV. 1 (1994).

however, what it means to be white has been fairly stable, largely being equated with a range of privileges denied to those considered nonwhite.[27]

Thus far in our national history, no other racial group has achieved the same level and status as whites. Equality of status has only been achieved when members of a group have been redefined in such a way that they are included in the white classification. This suggests that if we are going to move to the point where race no longer matters, then one of two things must occur: (1) the institution of widespread assimilation, where virtually all are considered to be white; or (2) the destabilization of the concept of white so that it no longer exists as a recognizable racial concept. As long as the contemporary concept of white remains in place, it will always be the norm. It is the restrictive standard against which everyone else is defined and judged. Whiteness encapsulates positive traits and confers race-based privileges to those designated as "standard."

Large-scale assimilation into whiteness on the part of all Americans is not likely, nor is it necessarily desirable. At the same time, I do not believe that calls to be more inclusive, or to renounce white privilege, will be effective because such approaches fail to disturb the enduring concept of whiteness. Instead, I believe there has to be a reformation of American identity that is not centered on whiteness. I imagine that such an identity would look like that which I hope for my daughter – an identity that is both black and white, yet neither.

However, I am not sure that we will ever get to this new identity because it will mean getting past some seemingly insurmountable fears and letting go of certain aspects of ourselves that we hold dear. What is important, however, is not the entrenched racial hierarchy that has become part of the American cultural fabric, but the way in which this hierarchy has led to a sense of identity and self-definition based on race.

THE CENTRALITY OF RACE TO IDENTITY

The centuries of racial dictatorship have had three very large consequences: first, they defined "American" identity as white, as the negation of racialized "otherness".... Second, racial dictatorship organized (albeit sometimes in an incoherent and contradictory fashion) the "color line" rendering it the fundamental division in U.S. Society. ... Third, racial dictatorship consolidated the oppositional racial consciousness and organization originally framed by marronage and slave revolts, by indigenous resistance, and by nationalism of various sorts. Just as the conquest

---

[27] George Lipsitz, The Possessive Investment in Whiteness: How White People Profit from Identity Politics 2–3 (2006); Peggy McIntosh, *White Privilege and Male Privilege: A Personal Account of Coming to See Correspondences through Work in Women's Studies*, in Power, Privilege and Law: A Civil Rights Reader 22–33 (Bender & Bravemaan, eds. 1994).

created the "native" where once there had been Pequot, Iroquois, or Tutelo, so too it created the "black" where once there had been Asante or Ovimbundu, Yoruba, or Bakongo.[28]

As discussed, the black-white binary developed out of the need to differentiate slave from free and as a way to justify the harsh and inhumane system of chattel slavery; over time, these classifications took on a life of their own. Such designations are now extremely significant components of American identity. As Toni Morrison explains, it was through the black-white binary that whites formed an identity that would eventually encompass the meaning of American identity as a whole.

> I want to suggest that these concerns – autonomy, authority, newness and diffe-
> rence, absolute power … that each one is made possible by, shaped by, activated
> by a complex awareness and employment of a constituted Africanism. It was this
> Africanism, deployed as rawness and savagery, that provided the staging ground
> and arena for the elaboration of the quintessential American identity. … Race in
> fact, now functions as a metaphor so necessary to the construction of Americanness
> that it rivals the old pseudo-scientific and class-informed racisms whose dynamics
> we are more used to deciphering. As a metaphor for transacting the whole process
> of Americanization, while burying its particular racial ingredients, this Africanist
> presence may be something the United States cannot do without. Deep within the
> word "American" is its association with race. To identify someone as South African
> is to say very little; we need the adjective "white" or "black" or "colored" to make
> our meaning clear. In this country it is quite the reverse. American means white.[29]

As Barbara Flagg has explained, the markers of white identity have become so con-flated with American identity that the connection has become transparent. Many whites do not realize what they identify as "normal" is in fact part and parcel of, and flow directly from, them being white.[30] Yet, the centrality of race to one's identity, whether a person is aware of it or not, applies to many groups. While there may be whites who would not give up being white for all the money in the world, there are also nonwhites who feel the same about their racially constructed identities. Accordingly, while such race-dependent identities have supported systems of sub-ordination and discrimination, such identities have also influenced how we make sense of the world. As a result, many want to preserve these racial categories, despite the fact that doing so may prolong the salience of race in American society.

I believe that as long as race, particularly whiteness, continues to exist as a con-cept in its present form, we will always fall short of the ideal of equality. White is

---

[28] Michael Omi & Howard Winant, RACIAL FORMATION IN THE UNITED STATES, 66 (1994).

[29] Toni Morrison, PLAYING IN THE DARK: WHITENESS AND THE LITERARY IMAGINATION 44–47 (1992).

[30] Barbara Flagg, *"Was Blind, But Now I See": White Race Consciousness and the Requirement of Discriminatory Intent*, 91 MICH. L. REV. 953, 957, 970–73 (1993).

defined as the norm in opposition to others. Thus, anything that is not white is definitively less because it does not fit the norm. For us to get past race, we must get past whiteness, and we must get past the fear and anxiety that comes from an identity constructed on something other than race.

FACING OUR FEARS: EMBRACING THE "BROWN" PLANET

In 1967, the U.S. Supreme Court put an end to legally sanctioned antimiscegenation laws – laws that, for hundreds of years, have played an integral part in constructing the black-white binary and ensuring that the United States became, and remained, a racially stratified, white hegemonic state. In the aftermath of *Loving*, we now are all, at least legally, free to marry across racial lines, yet many of us do not. While the legal prohibitions regarding interracial marriage may have been lifted, the vestiges of hundreds of years of racial subordination, built on those laws, still remains. The black-white binary that helped form and entrench them endures. The racial identities that these laws helped form, as socially constructed and ever-shifting as they may be, remain intact. The fear of losing those identities helps prevent us from moving past them to a less racially stratified and more equal state.

Yet, perhaps the white supremacists who pushed for laws prohibiting interracial intimacy, and even those who are in favor of them now, are on to something. I have learned through my own personal experience that miscegenation produces mixed-race people whose outward appearances may be ambiguous and thus disruptive to clear racial dividing lines. At the same time, interracial intimacy and multiracial children force us to confront our fears and rethink our notions of race, its meaning, and its place. Traditionally, we have resolved this disruption and ambiguity by requiring people to choose a race or by choosing one for them. I am arguing here that instead we should encourage and create space for those who would claim all parts of their multiracial identities and who are working to define themselves in terms beyond race.

Throughout his long presidential campaign, Barack Obama spoke of Americans struggling against their fears, doubts, and cynicism. Invoking change as his campaign theme, he spoke of a battle in our hearts and minds about what kind of country we want and how change will require great struggle and sacrifice from everyone. On the night he won the election, he informed us that change had, in fact, come to America. I do not know if any of us has a clear picture of what that change will look like; however, as I watched Obama make his speech the night that he won the presidential election, and I thought of the world that my daughter will inherit, I found myself hoping that part of the changed world would include a United States where our identities are no longer centered on race. A changed world where we imagine ourselves as a newly defined collective; a collective whose identity is not an assimilated whiteness, but instead is a new, non-race-based, American identity. An identity that incorporates and syncretizes the best that all of us have to offer. A post-*Loving* world where my daughter, unlike President Obama, does not have to choose to be black or white or have a race chosen for her.

As I continue to wrestle with my own fears and the fact that bringing about this world that I hope for will require sacrifice, I find myself questioning whether such sacrifice and eventual transcendence is possible. Yet, despite my skepticism, I still find myself having, to use President Obama's words, the "audacity to hope."[31] For I know that as long as race remains as it is, whiteness, hegemony, and subordination will remain. I do not believe that we can overcome this hegemony, or this subordination, and keep intact our race-based identities. Having said this, I do not mean that we give up all of who we are, or refuse to acknowledge where we come from. Like I hope for my daughter, I hope for an America where we can take all that we have to offer and meld it into something new; something that contains the best part of all of us, yet is something altogether different.

[31]   Barack Obama, THE AUDACITY OF HOPE (2006).

PART FOUR

Considering the Limits of *Loving*

11

Black Pluralism in Post-*Loving* America

Taunya Lovell Banks

"There is something called *black* in America and there is something called *white* in America and I know them when I see them, but I will forever be unable to explain the meaning of them."[1]

Since 1967, the number of multiracial individuals with some African ancestry living in the United States has increased dramatically as a result of increased out-marriage by black Americans and the immigration of large numbers of multiracial individuals from Mexico, the Caribbean, as well as Central and Latin America. With the removal of national origin quotas in the 1965 immigration reform law,[2] more people with some African ancestry have entered this country over the past forty years than at any other time in our history.[3] Consequently, the face of late-twentieth and early-twenty-first-century America has changed, as have attitudes about race, especially about persons with some African ancestry.

Much of the conventional public, political, and judicial rhetoric, however, does not reflect the heterogeneity of African Americans. The ongoing rhetoric of mono-racialism may be the by-product of at least two factors. Legally, the law played a dominant role in constructing and reifying a "single" black race. Throughout the twentieth century, blackness in America was "seen as so self-evident" that one was considered black if one's African ancestry was visible or known.[4] Politically, scholars have long contended that diversity within the black community was suppressed for strategic purposes, so that monoracialism could become a unifying and primary

---

1 Carl Hancock Rux, *Eminem: The New White Negro, in* EVERYTHING BUT THE BURDEN: WHAT WHITE PEOPLE ARE TAKING FROM BLACK CULTURE 15, 36 (Greg Tate ed., 2003).
2 Pub. L. No. 89–236, 79 Stat. 911 (codified as amended in scattered sections of 8 U.S.C.).
3 Sam Roberts, *More Africans Enter U.S. Than in Days of Slavery*, N.Y. TIMES, Feb. 21, 2005, at A1.
4 Neil Gotanda, *A Critique of 'Our Constitution is Colorblind*,' 44 STAN. L. REV. 1, 25 (1991). Yet as Neil Gotanda posits in this article, race – particularly the racial category "black" – while a consistent and constant "social divider," is not a "stable, coherent legal and social concept." *Id.* at 23. He identified four racial categories – historical race, status race, formal race, and cultural race – used by the U.S. Supreme Court, which reflect distinct ideas about race. *Id.* at 4–5.

organizing principle in the fight against race discrimination.[5] These legal and political accounts of blackness continue to this day.

Contemporary rhetoric still assumes that black Americans are a homogenous group with a shared common identity and history.[6] Nevertheless, "[i]mportant shifts in the composition of the U.S. population and contemporary constructions and representations of biological and cultural mixture, problematize the very nature of [b]lack identity and the [b]lack experience in [twenty-first century] America."[7] As legal scholar Kenneth Karst predicted more than a decade ago, the static and monolithic racial legal category "black" has changed "[a]s perceptions of race meld further into perceptions of culture."[8]

Recently the Pew Research Center found that "nearly four-in-ten African Americans (37%) say that blacks can no longer be thought of as a single race" because of increasing diversity within that community.[9] Unsurprisingly, perceptions about the disaggregation of blackness are stronger among younger black Americans, particularly the post-*Loving* generation, those who were born after *Loving v. Virginia*, and are more likely than their older counterparts to report that blacks are no longer a single race. More importantly, the Pew study merely quantifies what many black Americans already know: class- and generation-based differences in values and experiences transcend racial differences, even for black Americans. Some even argue that we are living in a post-black era.[10]

Many members of the post-*Loving* generation came of age in the 1990s without memories of de jure racial segregation laws or the need for the 1960s civil rights legislation to combat overt racial discrimination. Accordingly, they see race, racism, and identity through a different lens. In other words, we are witnessing a significant generational shift in thinking, which is beginning to be reflected in popular culture

---

[5] Religious scholar Zipporah G. Glass argues that "mestizaje has always been a part of Blackness in the United States, but it was … [suppressed] to make Blackness the primary organizing principle" to fight de jure segregation. Zipporah G. Glass, *The Language of Mestizaje in a Renewed Rhetoric of Black Theology*, in Racial Thinking in the United States: Uncompleted Independence 3 (Paul Spickard & G. Reginal Daniels, ed., 2004).

[6] Kenneth L. Karst, *Myths of Identity: Individual and Group Portraits of Race and Sexual Orientation*, 43 UCLA L. Rev. 263, 344 (1995).

[7] *Id.* at 341.

[8] *Id.* at 344.

[9] Pew Research Center, Blacks See Growing Values Gap Between Poor and Middle Class: Optimism About Black Progress Declines 4, 24 (2007), *available at* http://pewsocialtrends.org/assets/pdf/Race.pdf (this survey was conducted in association with National Public Radio). The survey included "a nationally representative sample of 3,086 adults … [and] included an oversample that brought the total number of non-Hispanic black respondents to 1,007." *Id.* at i. Only 53% of non-Hispanic black Americans polled thought that "blacks can still be thought of as a single race." *Id.* at 24.

[10] Linda Nicholson, *The Politics of Identity after Identity Politics*, 33 Wash. U. J.L. & Pol'y 43, 43 n.2 (2010) (noting suggestions by others that that we are currently living in a post-black world).

and scholarly literature about race and identity, but not in the courts. American judges and policy makers, composed primarily of the children of *Brown v. Board of Education*,[11] remain stuck in a racial jurisprudence and rhetoric of the late twentieth century that focuses on intentional and overt monoracial discrimination. There is little recognition by courts of the multiple levels of race-related discrimination, or that persons with some African ancestry may experience discrimination differently.

This chapter illustrates the changing perceptions of identity for individuals with partial African ancestry – those born shortly before and post-*Loving* – and the implication of black pluralism on contemporary antidiscrimination law. Specifically, this chapter analyzes the experiences of, and public dialogues about, children of interracial parentage, and how their differential treatment by nonblacks, as well as blacks, raises legal issues that courts are not prepared to address. The first *Loving*-era child discussed here is President Barack Hussein Obama, born six years before the *Loving* decision to a black Kenyan father and a white Kansan mother, and raised in Hawaii. The Harvard Law School graduate's skin tone and other physical features identify him as someone with African ancestry. He also self-identifies culturally as a black American; nevertheless, because of his interracial parentage, controversy arose during his successful runs for the U.S. Senate and presidency about whether he is "authentically" black.

The blackness of the second *Loving*-era child, Maria O'Brien Hylton, born to an Afro-Cuban mother and white Australian father of Irish ancestry, seven years before the Supreme Court case, was also publicly questioned. Unlike President Obama, Hylton's physical appearance is more racially ambiguous, and her identity is further complicated by her Latin ancestry. Hylton made national headlines when black members of the Northwestern University Law School community objected to her being hired as a minority faculty member, arguing that Hylton was not black enough because of her light skin tone and alleged lack of cultural identity.[12]

The public controversies surrounding the racial identities of President Obama and Professor Hylton reflect contemporary public discourses on race, and suggest the potential legal implications of being "black" in "post-black" America. These discussions signal how the generational shift in race discourse impacts Americans with interracial parentage and some African ancestry. This transition raises interesting questions about the continued viability of late-twentieth-century antidiscrimination race jurisprudence, especially as applied to people traditionally "raced," or identified as black or African American. Discussions about their racial identity provide an opportunity to examine the struggle occurring within the community of

---

[11]   347 U.S. 483 (1954).
[12]   Leonard Baynes, *Who Is Black Enough for You?: An Analysis of Northwestern University Law School's Struggle over Minority Faculty Hiring*, 2 MICH. J. RACE & L. 205, 210 (1997).

Afro-descendants, and larger American community, about the meaning and mea-surement of blackness and "racial authenticity" in twenty-first-century America.

As the following discussion suggests, the notion of "racial authenticity" is illusive. It operates slightly differently for individuals whose physical appearance comports with conventional notions of blackness than for more racially ambiguous indi-viduals. The focus of discussion for racially distinctive individuals, like President Obama, is whether their interracial parentage makes them less black socially, less representative of perceived black political interests, and less likely to experience traditional forms of race-based discrimination. More specifically, one emerging question is whether mixed-race individuals are more likely to experience situational blackness[13] – whether one can be black for some but not for other purposes, and if so, when is one black for antidiscrimination purposes.

This question is even more sharply drawn when questions about racial authen-ticity arise for individuals whose African ancestry is less apparent. As this chapter explains, the overriding question in both cases is whether interracial parentage affects Afro-descendant children differently than individuals whose formal racial classification is black, and if so, whether antidiscrimination law should take these differences into account.

LOVING'S CHILDREN IN POST-BLACK AMERICA: BARACK OBAMA AND RACIAL AUTHENTICITY

Historically, the law discouraged interracial parentage and penalized their offspring by consigning children to the "lower" of the two racial categories, but in post-black America, many of these children refuse to be defined primarily under one racial cat-egory.[14] Nevertheless, the public remains fixated on assigning a single racial group to mixed-race children rather than accepting how they characterize themselves. The public discussions about President Obama's race illustrate this problem.

Although the media initially characterized Barak Obama as black or African American, others were not so sure. During his 2004 senatorial campaign, his Republican opponent, Alan Keyes, an African American, suggested that, because Obama is not descended from enslaved West Africans, he really is not an African American. Obama's African ancestry, physical features – brown skin tone, hair tex-ture, and broad nose – and self-identification as a black or African American is

---

[13] *See* Lu-in Wang, *Race as Proxy: Situational Racism and Self-Fulfilling Stereotypes*, 53 DePaul L. Rev. 1013, 1020 (2004). Professor Wang argues that "racially biased conduct is situation sensitive." *Id.*

[14] Haya El Nasser, *Multiracial No Longer Boxed in by the Census*, USA Today, Mar. 2, 2010, *available at* http://www.usatoday.com/news/nation/census/2010-03-02-census-multi-race_N.htm (last update Mar. 15, 2010) (providing examples of mixed-race children who chose to self-identify as multiracial in the 2010 Census).

insufficient, in Keyes's mind, to make him an "authentic" African American. Thus, for Keyes, authentic blackness is based on a direct connection or link to the slave experiences of West Africans in the Americas and the segregation that followed into the mid-twentieth century, before *Loving* and the 1965 immigration reform. Thus, persons with any African ancestry who lack this background are racially suspect.

Indeed, some have intimated that a black individual's lack of ancestral ties to slavery constituted a positive attribute. During the 2008 presidential race, political scientist Ron Walters, an African American, built on Keyes' distinction, suggesting that the absence of a direct ancestral link to enslaved West Africans benefitted Obama in his run for the presidency. According to Walters, Obama was a more acceptable presidential candidate to white Americans than earlier black candidates, like Jesse Jackson and Al Sharpton. Unlike Obama, Jackson and Sharpton, the descendants of slaves, embodied "the traditional African-American identity [which] is more threatening [to whites], because it raises … the culpability of whites in slavery."[15]

Linking authentic blackness to American slavery is problematic. The Keyes/Walters definition of African American overemphasizes the connection between slavery and anti-black bias, rather than dominance of a white supremacy ideology in America. Neil Gotanda calls this approach "historical race," a concept that "embodies past and continuing racial subordination … [that represents] the meaning of race … [which] the [Supreme] Court contemplates when it applies 'strict scrutiny' to racially disadvantaging government conduct."[16] This definition framed in the American slave experience seems to exclude someone like President Obama, even though he has the physical attributes of blackness, self-identifies as black, and may experience race-based discrimination.

Questions about President Obama's racial authenticity also tend to conflate self-identified (cultural) race with historic race. When the readers of nationally syndicated columnist Clarence Page, an African American, wrote to Page, asking him to stop calling Obama "black" because of his interracial parentage, Page reminded his readers that Obama self-identifies as black. Page asserts Obama's cultural race as proof of his blackness, whereas his readers seem to reflect Ron Walters's belief that Obama's perceived identity status is different from conventionally black Americans because of his interracial parentage.

Historically, the offspring of "interracial reproduction" were classified as *mulatto*, or some fractional label. In most instances, this label had no legal significance in the United States; one was still black. This traditional ascription of race, however, was not applied to President Obama. Even though he looks like many black American

---

15 Jean Marbella, *Who's Right When Race Lies Below the Surface*, Balt. Sun, Feb. 6, 2007 at 1B, 9B, *available at* http://articles.baltimoresun.com/2007–02–06/news/0702060097_1_african-american-obama-joe-biden

16 Gotanda, *supra* note 4, at 4.

products of slave-era miscegenation, his racial authenticity is suspect. The public saw him as different from black Americans because his mother is white and his father is a Kenyan not descended from enslaved West Africans. Further, his Kenyan father lived briefly in United States in the 1960s and never experienced the hardships and deprivations caused by Jim Crow laws of the late nineteenth and the first half of the twentieth century. Thus, Walters and Keyes suggest that President Obama's interracial parentage translates into a different identity status.

While the Supreme Court's antidiscrimination jurisprudence is grounded in the American experiences of West African slaves and their descendants, it has never limited relief for race-based discrimination to this group of black Americans. If a court were to consider President Obama's racial status, it would likely conclude that he is black. In 1995, a Massachusetts court was called upon to determine the legal racial status of twin brothers, Philip and Paul Malone, who, after identifying themselves as black, obtained positions as firefighters with the Boston Fire Department as a result of an affirmative action program.[17] Subsequently, the Malone brothers, who looked and lived white, were fired for filing falsified applications after a hearing officer determined that they were not black. The brothers appealed, saying that there was no criteria for determining racial identification and that thus the Department only required self-identification.

In an unreported decision, the Supreme Judicial Court of Suffolk County upheld the firing, saying that the brothers failed to establish their claimed racial identity using any of three types of evidence: (1) phenotypical – a visual observation of their features; (2) genealogical – using documentary evidence to establish black ancestry; and (3) cultural – providing evidence that the family held itself out as black and were considered black by their community.[18] Whereas the Malone brothers failed to satisfy any of these tests, President Obama easily meets all three tests including the genealogical test because legal blackness in America is defined as *any* known *African* ancestry.[19]

---

[17] Malone v. Haley, No. 88–339 (Sup. Jud. Ct. Suffolk County, Mass. July 25, 1989).

[18] *Id.* at 16. Two years earlier they applied for the same position, identifying themselves as white, but failed to get hired after scoring poorly on the competitive civil service examination. Their racial identity became a problem when they applied for a promotion to lieutenant ten years later and the Fire Commissioner noticed they were identified as black. The hearing officer "found that they have fair skin, fair hair coloring, and Caucasian facial features." *Id.* at 17. The brothers' documentary evidence, their parents' birth certificates, which identified the race of their grandparents, showed that both sides of the family had been identified as white for three generations. *Id.* at 18. "[T]he only indication of [b]lack ancestry offered by the Malone brothers was the questionable and inconclusive photograph of a woman they claimed to be Sarah Carroll, their maternal great-grandmother," whose existence the brothers "discovered" in 1976. *Id.* at 19. There also was no evidence that the brothers were considered black by their community. *Id.*

[19] Angelique Davis, Political Blackness: A Sociopolitical Construction of Blackness Post-*Loving v. Virginia*, chapter 12 (explaining that the Census defines any person with a trace of African ancestry as Black).

The questioning of President Obama's racial authenticity confuses "[t]ranscendent community interests ... with a simplistic belief that the African-American community is a monolithic entity in which all people of color live identical lives in every respect[,] agree with one another, or even like one another."[20] But black Americans, like other individuals, are more than their chosen or assigned racial identity; they have multiple identities that intersect or overlap in ways not anticipated by law's conventional unitary approach to race-based discrimination. Increasingly these cultural and imposed identities influence both how we see ourselves and how others see us in America. The political and cultural divisions between black ethnics is an example of multiplicity *within* a racialized legal identity – black multiplicity.

Black multiplicity is a subset of racialized identity, not another category of identity like class, gender, or sexuality. For example, ethnicity within a racialized group may influence how racial bias is experienced. Recently arrived Afro-Caribbean immigrants may be preferred over native-born black Americans because the former often are perceived as hardworking individuals who hold multiple jobs as compared to the more negative stereotypes advanced about conventional black Americans as lazy. Similarly, Afro-Latinas/os might be treated or perceived as being different from black descendants of American slaves because of their Latin ethnicity. In other words, they may not be seen or see themselves as black. Thus, the racialized portion of one's identity does not operate in a unitary fashion.

The problem of different racialization among black Americans is not limited to children of interracial parentage. Skin tone privilege – colorism – is widely believed to confer privileges on light-skinned black Americans without regard to parentage. But courts have difficulty recognizing and accepting that black Americans can experience discrimination differently based on parentage, phenotype, and ethnicity.

The public discourse about President Obama's racial authenticity suggests the emergence of a different type of intra-racial privilege among black Americans. Having one white parent may confer an actual or perceived racial privilege even on a self-identified African American. For example, one writer asks:

> What makes [Obama] 'black' rather than 'white'? ... Socially, he is as white as he is black .... he had to learn how to be black in the social world ... and even had to be mentored by a friend at school to learn how to 'act black'. ... He seems to see himself as a human bridge. ... His blackness is largely a figment of white imaginings.[21]

[20] Lisa A. Kelly, *Race and Place: Geographic and Transcendent Community in the Post-*Shaw *Era*, 49 VAND. L. REV. 227, 235 (1996).
[21] Gabe Heilig, *Red, White and Blue*, BALT. SUN, May 23, 2008, at 21A, *available at* http://articles. baltimoresun.com/2008–05–23/news/0805220224_1_pink-black-and-white-black-candidate (last visited June 7, 2011).

Further, this different racial status attaches without regard to the individual's racial performance. In other words, whether one racially identifies as white, black, or mixed-race, where interracial parentage is known, one is considered by the public, but not the courts, as less conventionally black.

There are a few employment cases where claimants alleged discrimination because of their mixed-race status.[22] The courts in these cases refuse to treat discrimination based on interracial parentage as a basis for a race discrimination claim. Instead, they tend to adopt a monoracial approach, looking for discrimination based on the race of one parent rather than on interracial parentage itself.

If interracial parentage confers a perceived different racialized identity on individuals who appear phenotypically black, then the perception of privilege may be even stronger for individuals whose physical appearance is more racially ambiguous. These individuals may be seen and treated as inauthentic black Americans because of their appearance *and* parentage. This perception, commonly held both intraracially and interracially, is even more problematic when the result is discriminatory decision making. Courts are even less prepared to handle these cases using conventional race antidiscrimination law.

LOVING'S RACIALLY AMBIGUOUS CHILDREN: MARIA O'BRIEN HYLTON

The controversy surrounding consideration of Maria O'Brien Hylton for a tenure-track position at Northwestern Law School illustrates, at least for antidiscrimination law purposes, another aspect of the issue about post-*Loving*, post-black blackness. Unlike President Obama, whose physical appearance comports more with conventional notions about who "looks black" and who openly identifies as black, Professor Hylton, the sister of CNN commentator Soledad O'Brien and wife of a black law professor, looks more racially ambiguous. Her racial ambiguity might free her from everyday racism like racial profiling while shopping or driving a car; nevertheless, she may experience race-based discrimination in situations where her remote African ancestry is known and used as a factor in making adverse employment decisions.

When Professor Hylton applied for a faculty position at Northwestern Law School, a senior black faculty member called her black identity into question, in essence asking her "How black are you?"[23] Applying the factors considered by the court in the Malone Brothers case, Professor Hylton clearly satisfies the genealogical test

[22] Nancy Leong, *Judicial Erasure of Mixed-Race Discrimination*, 59 AM. U. L. REV. 469, 501–04 (2010) (discussing cases where courts reflected "animus" against claims of race discrimination by multiracial plaintiffs).
[23] Baynes, *supra* note 12, at 210.

for blackness. Her mother's Afro-Cuban ancestry would satisfy the genealogical test establishing her partial black ancestry. So she would be considered black for antidiscrimination purposes, even though her physical appearance does not clearly signal her black ancestry. The court in the Malone Brothers case suggested that any of the three tests – phenotypical, genealogical, or cultural – could be used to establish racial identity, but genealogy was not enough for some nonwhite members of the Northwestern Law School community. They complained that not only did Professor Hylton not look black, but some doubted whether she culturally identified as a black American.

There were conflicting accounts about whether she self-identified as black, at least in conventional U.S. terms. To further complicate matters, a Latino law student group said Hylton was not Latino because they felt she identified more with being *black* than being Latino – suggesting that these are mutually exclusive categories. Professor Hylton initially refused to be drawn into what seemed like a discussion of identity politics, telling "the *New York Times* that she did not define herself in 'racial terms'. ... However, in a *Boston Globe* interview, [she] reported that she identified herself as 'Black' on a form she completed as a clerk for a federal judge ... had been a member of Black organizations in college, in law school, and while practicing ... [saying] 'I have always thought of myself as black.'"[24] The controversy ended when she and her husband accepted a job at Boston University. Professor Hylton has gone on to have a successful academic career.

Professor Hylton was targeted because of her physical appearance and perceived cultural identification. Without question, "phenotype goes a long way in facilitating racial identity because it is the foundation for the social interaction with others by which one largely comes to identify one's self."[25] Some social scientists speculate that "profit-maximizing firms and utility-maximizing individuals have a preference for blacks with light skin hues."[26] Thus, individual members of the same race, even those like President Obama who appear visibly black, may be treated differently based on phenotypical characteristics, including skin tone. These preferences are most obvious in employment settings.

Indeed, racially ambiguous children of interracial parentage with some black ancestry may have even more difficulty navigating mixed-race ancestry. They are

[24] *Id.* at 211.
[25] Maurice R. Dyson, *Multiracial Identity, Monoracial Authenticity & Racial Privacy: Towards an Adequate Theory of Multiracial Resistance*, 9 MICH. J. RACE & L. 387, 408 (2004).
[26] Kwabena Gyimah-Brempong & Gregory N. Price, *Crime and Punishment: And Skin Hue Too?*, AM. ECON. REV., May 2006, at 246, 246 (citing Arthur H. Goldsmith et al., *From Dark to Light: Skin Color and Wages Among African-Americans* (unpublished paper, 2005); *see also* Arthur H. Goldsmith et al., *From Dark to Light: Skin Color and Wages Among African-Americans*, 42 J. HUM. RESOURCES 701 (2007)).

disproportionally the beneficiaries of various forms of skin tone and/or appearance privilege. Skin tone discrimination, or colorism, is related to, but different from, racial passing, a second form of skin tone privilege where self-identified or racially classified black Americans with light skin tones are either misclassified as white, or are seen as racially ambiguous, as opposed to black.

The preference for light skin tones may be a result of unconscious bias, what Jerry Kang calls "racial mechanics – the ways in which race alters intrapersonal, interpersonal, and inter-group interactions."[27] There are explicit and implicit racial meanings assigned to the racial categories created by law and cultural practices; and the racial meanings associated with these categories are triggered when we interact with others. As a result, implicit racial biases – negative stereotypes and prejudices – influence our interactions. These reactions are automatic in the sense that they are unintentional and outside the actor's awareness.

A few empirical studies found that unconscious or automatic negative stereotype biases influence decision making.[28] Further, there is evidence that skin tone affects wages, employment opportunities, access to health care, and even the accumulation of intergenerational wealth. Individuals with features most commonly attributed to black Africans are likely to be judged more harshly than members of the same formal racial group with less "Afrocentric" features as a result of automatic or implicit racial attitudes.[29] It should be noted, however, that lighter-skinned African Americans also experience discrimination, albeit in a different manner from their "darker" counterparts. The perceived and actual benefits racially ambiguous individuals with some African ancestry gain in securing employment triggers resentment among more racially identifiable black Americans. As Professor Hylton's case demonstrates, such "benefits" may even result in adverse employment decisions.

Several factors distinguish Professor Hylton's case from a conventional colorism case. First, unlike most colorism claims, her light skin did not confer an economic advantage, but rather resulted in a disadvantage. Second, both blacks and Latina/

---

[27] Jerry Kang, *Trojan Horses of Race*, 118 HARV. L. REV. 1489, 1493 (2005) (citing Jerry Kang, *Cyber-race*, 113 HARV. L. REV. 1131, 1138–46 (2000)).

[28] *See, e.g.*, Natsha T. Martin, *Pretext in Peril*, 75 MO. L. REV. 313, 317 n.11 (2010) (citing studies of how unconscious racism has affected plaintiffs' claims in employment discrimination cases); Andrew E. Taslitz, *Judging Jena's D.A.: The Prosecutor and Racial Esteem*, 44 Harv. C.R.-C.L. L. Rev. 393, 448 n. 417 (2009) (citing empirical data showing how unconcious bias influenced judges and juries in criminal trials).

[29] Irene V. Blair et al., *The Automaticity of Race and Afrocentric Facial Features in Social Judgments*, 87 J. PERSONALITY & SOC. PSYCH. 763 (2004); Irene V. Blair, *The Malleability of Automatic Stereotypes and Prejudice*, 6 PERSONALITY & SOC. PSYCH. REV. 242 (2002); Keith B. Maddox & Stephanie A. Gray, *Cognitive Representations of Black Americans: Reexploring the Role of Skin Tone*, 28 PERSONALITY & SOC. PSYCH. BULL. 250, 254 (2002) (measuring how "perceivers can use skin tone as organizing principles in social perception, apart from the presence of other facial features").

os at the law school questioned her racial "authenticity." Unlike President Obama, her mixed-raced parentage had both a racial and ethnic component. Latina/os questioned her ethnic authenticity suggesting that she must choose between being black and being Latina, leaving no room to embrace all aspects of her parentage, her mother's *Afro*-Cuban background, and her father's Australian-Irish ancestry. Her choice was to identify as either black or a deracialized Latina.

Racially ambiguous individuals of interracial parentage like Professor Hylton are more likely to experience situational race, "racially biased conduct [that] is situation sensitive,"[30] because they cannot blend in with more visibly black Americans. Thus their "racial authenticity" is constantly being questioned. In contrast, President Obama's visible appearance minimizes or erases his white ancestry unless he or someone else invokes it.

Scholars use the term "situational race" to denote several different, but related, phenomena. Situational race may refer to what happens to racially ambiguous mixed-race individuals who look nonwhite but not identifiably black. Thus, a person who self-identifies as black and who has some African ancestry may be "misidentified" as belonging to some other racialized group and treated accordingly.

Maria O'Brien Hylton's experience at Northwestern, however, does not neatly fit within the racial misclassification category. Her opponents knew about her remote African ancestry, but her racially ambiguous appearance and interracial parentage caused nonwhites to conclude that the genealogical connection was insufficient for minority representational purposes. They demanded information about her cultural identity. In the end, their criteria for rejecting her as a minority faculty representation was based on subjective criteria that was "racially biased" and "situation sensitive" – situational blackness.

Situational blackness, unlike situational race, is not limited to racial misclassification (appearance) or cultural identity. Situational blackness also incorporates aspects of performative race, focusing on factors like parentage, education, socioeconomic status, and the circumstances triggering the racial identification of the individual. Thus, media discussions of President Obama's race are instances of situational blackness when they mention his white mother, his Harvard education, and relatively affluent adult lifestyle.

What is operating in these situations is a complex formula of racialization that results in an unstable definition of blackness. In the twenty-first century, blackness is no longer determined solely by ancestry, but is shaded by factors such as parentage, education, appearance, cultural identification, and socioeconomic factors.

Courts are unprepared for the more complex race cases presented by children of interracial parentage. Antidiscrimination jurisprudence is based on notions of racial

---

[30] Wang, *supra* note 13, at 1020.

immutability – racial status as static, unchanging.[31] The Northwestern Law School Community used a monoracial, monoethnic approach to define Professor Hylton's racial identity. Similarly, courts traditionally resolve discrimination claims by mixed-raced individuals using a monoracial approach that fails to capture the essence of the claims. This point is discussed briefly in the next section.

THE NEED FOR NEW THEORIES TO ADDRESS EMPLOYMENT DISCRIMINATION

As mentioned previously, race discrimination based on appearance is more likely to be automatic or unconscious, whereas discrimination based on known ancestry is more likely intentional but less common. Falling somewhere in between is racial decision making based on stereotypic notions about differences between blacks based on ethnic group membership or, in the case of *Loving's* children, interracial parentage. This latter form of race-related discrimination, whether intentional or unintentional, results in employment preferences based on multiple aspects of an individual's identity that the law fails to recognize.

The unitary way that law treats race-based discrimination as affecting all black Americans equally is insufficient to handle the increasingly complex forms of race-*related* discrimination. To illustrate this point, let us reconsider what might have happened had Maria O'Brien Hylton filed an employment discrimination claim against Northwestern Law School for racial discrimination in hiring. Title VII of the 1964 Civil Rights Act prohibits discrimination in employment based on race, color, religion, sex, or national origin. Under this provision, Professor Hylton's chances of success might depend on the law school's subsequent actions.

If the law school subsequently hired a "black" law professor for the position for which Professor Hylton was considered, some courts might conclude there was no race-based discrimination because the law school simply preferred one qualified black candidate over another. If the law school hired a "Latino" law professor for the position, a few courts might inquire more closely to determine, where possible, whether Professor Hylton and the successful candidate were of the same race. Very few courts seem more willing to recognize intra-ethnic discrimination among Latina/os because of their mixed ancestry then intra-racial discrimination claims.[32] But these cases usually involve Latina/o plaintiffs with phenotypical characteristics closely associated with black Americans. Where the parties are racially ambiguous,

---

[31] Ken Nakasu Davison, Note and Comment: *The Mixed-Race Experience: Treatment of Racially Miscategorized Individuals Under Title VII*, 12 Asian L. J. 161 (2005).
[32] *See* Taunya Lovell Banks, *Colorism: A Darker Shade of Pale*, 47 UCLA L. Rev. 1705, 1732–36 (2000).

courts assume no racial bias. Courts literally tend to see race in black and white terms – racial absolutes.

When the claim is interethnic, courts tend to treat all racially ambiguous Latina/os alike. These courts fail to appreciate the racial overtones and anti-black bias in inter-ethnic employment discrimination claims by Latina/os, because of the myth that racism, particularly anti-black bias, does not exist in racially mixed Latin America.[33] So, if the Latina/o candidate selected was not Cuban, then these courts might conclude there was no viable race discrimination claim.

Each of these approaches ignores a key aspect of Professor Hylton's potential employment discrimination claim. It is not merely whether the employer hired a black or Latina/o applicant, but whether the trigger for the discrimination she experienced was her interracial parentage. If so, then the employment decision was based on the impermissible use of race and should be actionable. Yet courts, stuck in their monoracial approach to race-based discrimination, are uncomfortable with claims brought by mixed-raced litigants wanting to assign the basis of discrimination to one race rather than to the interracial status of the claimant.

One possible solution would be to expand racial discrimination jurisprudence to include discrimination based on interracial parentage. On its face, this approach seems like a simple solution, but it ignores more than fifty years of race discrimination jurisprudence grounds in monoracialism. Judges, without specific guidelines, would look to this older body of race law for guidance, easily slipping back into the monoracial approach.

An alternative approach would be to create an entirely new cause of action that rejects the notion of racial immutability as a foundation for a discrimination claim recognizing intra- and interracial discrimination claims based on interracial parentage and colorism. Instead, the courts' focus would be on whether phenotype, ancestry, or cultural identity of a claimant was a factor in employment decision making. If so, then the inquiry would focus on whether consideration of these factors was permissible under the law.

But one problem with this approach is whether to retain the intent requirement for actionable race discrimination claims. Even though the type of discrimination Hylton experienced was intentional, as mentioned previously, much race-based discrimination today is unconscious and unintentional. Given the unconsciousness of much race-based decision making, in many cases, it may be impossible to establish intent to discriminate based on interracial parentage. Abandoning racial

---

[33] For a discussion of interethnic employment discrimination case law, see Tanya Kateri Hernández, *Latino Inter-Ethnic Employment Discrimination and the "Diversity" Defense*, 42 HARV. C.R.-C.L. L. REV. 259 (2007).

immutability as applied in race discrimination law would require a rethinking of antidiscrimination principles. This is a big agenda fraught with land mines.

CONCLUSION

In many ways, President Barack Obama's family reminds us of what the United States might have looked like had the politicians and courts of the late nineteenth and early twentieth century not worked so hard to enforce racial segregation, anti-miscegenation, and exclusion of nonwhites. His white mother, Ann Dunham, has a son who self-identifies as black, and a daughter, Maya Soetoro-Ng, who self-identifies as "hybrid": "half-white" and "half-Asian." Obama's sister sees nothing unusual about the fact that her brother "named himself" black and she named herself hybrid, reasoning that "[e]ach of us has a right to name ourselves as we will."[34] Further, Soetoro-Ng is married to a Chinese Canadian and has one child, so President Obama's two daughters have a first cousin with Chinese, Indonesian, and white ancestry. Adding more spices to the mix, Soetoro-Ng's racially ambiguous appearance causes her to be misidentified as Latina, so she learned Spanish. President Obama and his sister were raised in Hawaii, the most multiracial state in the Union, and their families and viewpoints reflect different attitudes about racial identity that twentieth-century-made laws are ill-equipped to handle.

We face a bumpy road ahead in developing more precise and searching definitions of actionable "race" discrimination; the old-formula labels are outmoded and no longer reflect the new direction in which the *Loving*-era children are taking us. The challenge in twenty-first-century America is to develop more flexible and realistic legal theories that allow people the freedom to choose their identities without being defined by them, while at the same time guarding against the pernicious and arbitrary use of ancestry to confer privilege or burdens on segments of Americans.

---

[34] Ellen Goodman, Op-ed, *Transcending race and identity*, Boston Globe, Jan. 25, 2008, at A19, *available at* http://www.boston.com/bostonglobe/editorial_opinion/oped/articles/2008/01/25/transcending_race_and_identity/ (last visited June 7, 2011).

12

Political Blackness

A Sociopolitical Construction

Angelique Davis

During the presidential campaign of Barack Obama, and his subsequent election to office, the public and the media consistently questioned whether or not he was black. This inevitably reopened the discussion of what, exactly, is blackness? The son of a white mother from the state of Kansas and a black, Kenyan father, President Obama, pursuant to the current U.S. Census definitions, is black and identifies himself as such.[1] Yet people continue to interrogate Obama's blackness. Is he black enough because he was the former editor of the *Harvard Law Review*? Was he too black because he attended Reverend Jeremiah Wright's church? Is he black because his mother is white and his father black? Should he be called multiracial instead? A 2009 survey by the Pew Research Center found that the answer to this question varies by race and ethnicity.[2] Because individuals such as President Obama are no longer constrained by Jim Crow laws in this post–*Loving v. Virginia* era, many choose to identify in ways that challenge the current census definition of blackness. This inevitably raises the question of whether or not our racial categorizations should reflect the modern realities of race. The answer to this question has important implications for a number of social, political, and legal matters.

To illustrate the complexity of this inquiry, let us examine the hypothetical situation of cousins Jason, Julia, and Sheila. They, like the majority of their generation born in the post–civil rights movement era, did not grow up with clearly delineated racial lines, and although they are subject to the forces of racism and oppression, they are often unaware of how it impacts their daily lives.

---

[1] Barack Obama, THE AUDACITY OF HOPE 227–69 (2006); *see also* Barack Obama, DREAMS OF MY FATHER (1995).

[2] Pew Social Research Trends Staff, *Blacks Upbeat about Black Progress, Prospects: A Year after Obama's Election,* available at http://www.pewsocialtrends.org/2010/01/12/blacks-upbeat-about-black-progress-prospects/ (2010); findings included that most blacks (55%) said Obama was black and conversely most whites (53%) said he was multiracial.

Jason and Julia are the children of Tasha, a light-skinned black woman, and Stephen, a blond white man. Both have fair complexions, light brown hair, and hazel eyes, but their hair texture and facial features are different. Jason's hair, which he wears in a small afro, has a kinky texture, and his nose and lips are full. In contrast, Julia's hair has loose curls, and her facial features are not as full as her brother's. When the siblings are out in public together, they are often asked if they are related because of their phenotypical differences. Most people assume that Jason is black, but often ask Julia what she is as they are not sure if she is Latina or something else. They are only certain that she is not white. Although they both self-identify as multiracial, they publicly acknowledge their black ancestry.

Jason and Julia have a cousin on the black side of their family, Sheila, who lives in a different state. Sheila is the daughter of Wyatt, Tasha's estranged brother. Sheila's complexion is light and she has hazel eyes, like her cousins', but the phenotypical similarities end there. Sheila's hair is naturally blond with a straight, but slightly wavy, texture. In addition, her facial features are similar to those of her white mother, Andrea. Sheila refuses to racially categorize herself and, because she lives far away from the black part of her family, no one in her social circle knows that she has black African ancestry.

Are these cousins "black"? Addressing this question allows us to interrogate not only the ways in which blackness is ascribed to multiracial individuals, but also the broader impact of multiracial identification on issues like affirmative action or reparations. Historically, the cousins would have been classified as black because of the "one-drop" rule[3] and, technically, fall under the census definition of black because of their African ancestry. In this post-*Loving* era, however, they can check more than one box to identify their race on the census, and many feel free to reject the traditional racial categorization of black.

Racial categorizations are a sociopolitical construct, which is made particularly evident in light of our nation's post-*Loving* demographic changes.[4] Exploring the current ascription of blackness provides a critical step toward developing a racial categorization that mirrors the contemporary sociopolitical nature of race. Toward that end, this chapter explores: (1) historical and current census definitions of blackness; (2) the post-*Loving* multiracial upsurge; (3) ambiguous cases of blackness both pre- and post-*Loving*; and (4) the need for sociopolitical definitions of race – that encapsulate its sociopolitical nature – such as Political Blackness.

---

[3]   F. James Davis, WHO IS BLACK?: ONE NATION'S DEFINITION 4–5 (1991).

[4]   Because of the complexities surrounding each of the racial and ethnic categorizations currently contained in the U.S. Census, the inquiry here is narrowed to an examination of the census definition of blackness.

CENSUS DEFINITIONS OF BLACKNESS

One way of gaining a deeper understanding of the current definition of blackness is to examine the ways in which the census has constructed its meaning. The U.S. Census Bureau currently defines black or African American as referring to "a person having origins in any of the black racial groups of Africa."[5] This definition essentially utilizes the one-drop rule to categorize individuals of black African descent. The one-drop rule has historically been used to categorize black Americans, and means that those who have even a single drop of black blood are considered black. It is also referred to as the "hypodescent" rule, meaning that "racially mixed persons are assigned the status of the subordinate group."[6] Utilized to subordinate those of black African descent, the one-drop rule perpetuated white domination when slavery was legal by defining mixed-race descendents of slave holders as black, and thus slaves. After the United States abolished slavery, several states continued to use the one-drop rule or other percentages of blood quantum to suppress those of African descent through the use of Jim Crow laws.

Census enumerations of individuals of African descent have undergone numerous permutations from the first U.S. decennial census in 1790 to the present.[7] Although the U.S. Census Bureau currently states that their racial categories "generally reflect a social definition of race recognized in this country and are not an attempt to define race biologically, anthropologically, or genetically,"[8] the historical and current practices for defining blackness belie these claims as they have consistently required some purportedly quantifiable amount of black African ancestry. The 1840, 1850, and 1860 censuses provided the undefined racial classification of mulatto. The 1870 and 1880 censuses defined mulattoes to include those with any perceptible trace of African blood. In 1890, census takers were instructed to record the exact proportion of visible African blood; the census itself included the categories of Mulatto, Quadroon, and Octoroon, and counted those with three-fourths or more black blood as black. In 1900, the census counted blacks and mulattoes separately. The current category, which formally incorporates the one-drop rule, was adopted in 1920, when the mulatto category was dropped and black was defined as any person with black ancestry, no matter how small the percentage. Under the current definition, the cousins would all be defined as black, even though they do not self-identify that way.

5 U.S. Dept. of Commerce, Bureau of the Census, Census 2010 Brief, Overview of Race and Hispanic Origin 2010, (2011).
6 Davis, *supra* note 3, at 4–5.
7 U.S. Dept. of Commerce, Bureau of the Census, Measuring America: The Decennial Censuses from 1790 to 2000 (2002).
8 U.S. Dept. of Commerce, *supra* note 5, note 7.

POST-*LOVING* MULTIRACIAL UPSURGE

Since *Loving*, our nation has seen a significant increase in the number of interracial marriages and births. This multiracial upsurge has gained national attention and shows no signs of waning. In 1960, the number of new black interracial marriages was, at most, 1 percent of total marriages; it was 8.9 percent in 2008.[9] That same year, the Pew Research Center estimated that among blacks who were newlyweds, an unprecedented 15.5 percent married someone of a different race or ethnicity.[10] Moreover, these marriage statistics do not take into account the number of individuals in interracial sexual or cohabiting relationships or the increased public acceptance of interracial relationships in general.[11]

These interracial unions that *Loving* fostered have led to various questions regarding racial identity and categorization. Over the past few decades, a number of first-generation multiracials and their parents[12] gradually formed the Multiracial Category Movement (MCM). Initially intended to address the identification of multiracial children in public schools,[13] many of these groups evolved and joined forces to advocate that the current racial categories utilized on public and private data collection forms do not adequately recognize the ancestry of multiracial individuals. The groups now seek to include a multiracial category on the U.S. Census and other public and private data collection materials.[14] To date, the movement has enjoyed only marginal success.

9   Paul Taylor et al., *Marrying Out: One-in-Seven New U.S. Marriages is Interracial or Interethnic*, Pew Research Center: A Social & Demographic Trends Report (2010) available at http://pewsocialtrends.org/files/2010/10/755-marrying-out.pdf; *see also* Angelique M. Davis, *Multiracialism and Reparations: The Intersection of the Multiracial Category and Reparations Movements*, 29 T. Jefferson L. Rev. 161, 162–64 (2007).
10 Paul Taylor et al., *Marrying Out: One-in-Seven New U.S. Marriages is Interracial or Interethnic*, Pew Research Center: A Social & Demographic Trends Report (2010) available at http://pewsocial-trends.org/files/2010/10/755-marrying-out.pdf
11 *See generally*, Sharon Sassler and Kara Joyner, *Social Exchange and the Progression of Sexual Relationships in Emerging Adulthood*, Working Paper Series 2010–12, Bowling Green State University: The Center for Family and Demographic Research (2010); Taylor et al., *supra* n. 10; and David R. Harris and Hironi Ono, *How Many Interracial Marriages Would There Be if All Groups Were of Equal Size in All Places? A New Look at National Estimates of Interracial Marriage*, 34 Social Science Research, 236–51 (2005).
12 Tanya Katerí Hernández, *"Multiracial" Discourse: Racial Classifications in an Era of Color-Blind Jurisprudence*, 57 Md. L. Rev. 97, 106–07 (1998); Carrie Lynn H. Okizaki, *"What Are You?": Hapa-Girl and Multiracial Identity*, 71 U. Colo. L. Rev. 463, 491–92 (2000).
13 Jon Michael Spencer, The New Colored People: The Mixed-Race Movement in America 18 (1997).
14 Tanya Katerí Hernández, *The Interests and Rights of the Interracial Family in a "Multiracial" Racial Classification*, 36 Brandeis J. Fam. L. 29, 29 n.2 (1998) (citing Linda Jones, *Mixed Race and Proud of It*, Gannett News Serv., Nov. 20, 1990). Some of the best-known organizations advocating for recognition of multiracial ancestry on census forms include AMEA (Association of MultiEthnic

Those advocating for a multiracial category want it to be defined in at least one of two ways.[15] The first would define the multiracial category to include a "person whose parents have origins in two or more of the above [American Indian or Alaskan Native, Asian or Pacific Islander, Black, Hispanic, or White] racial and ethnic categories."[16] This definition is problematic for racial justice efforts, because estimates indicate that between 75 percent and 90 percent of African Americans have mixed-race ancestry.[17] An alternate, and more restrictive, definition would limit the multiracial category for those whose parents are of different races.

Some in the MCM also argue that the multiracial category should be used to eliminate all racial categorizations. They argue race has become too fluid to monitor, and that creating a multiracial category will slowly efface all racial distinctions and, ultimately, eliminate racism. This position has generated support from right-wing conservatives, such as Newt Gingrich,[18] and has become an avenue to promote a color-blind agenda.

In 2000, the census included a "one or more" option that allowed individuals to mark whether or not they wanted to be identified as a person who belonged to one or more racial category. This change was made as a result of "evidence of increasing numbers of children from interracial unions and the need to measure the increased diversity in the United States."[19] Ten years later, in the 2010 Census, 2.9 percent of the population reported multiple races, with black and white comprising the most frequently reported multiple-race combination.[20]

Americans), *available at* http://www.ameasite.org; Project RACE (Re-classify All Children Equally), *available at* http://www.projectrace.com; and the MAVIN Foundation (*mavin* is yiddish for "one who understands"), *available at* http://www.mavinfoundation.org; see generally Rainier Spencer, Reproducing Race: The Paradox of Generation Mix (2011).

[15] John A. Powell, *The Colorblind Multiracial Dilemma: Racial Categories Reconsidered*, 31 U.S.F. L. Rev. 789, 797 (1997).

[16] Kenneth E. Payson, *Check One Box: Reconsidering Directive No. 15 and the Classification of Mixed-Race People*, 84 Cal. L. Rev. 1233, 1279–80 (1996).

[17] There are various estimates regarding the number of black Americans with mixed-race ancestry. Christine B. Hickman, *The Devil and the One Drop Rule: Racial Categories, African Americans, and the U.S. Census*, 95 Mich. L. Rev. 1161, 1204 (1997) (estimating that between three-quarters and four-fifths of blacks in America have white ancestors); *see also* F. James Davis, Who Is black?: One Nation's Definition 21 (1991) ("At least three-fourths of all people defined as American blacks have some white ancestry, and some estimates run well above 90 percent.").

[18] Letter from Newt Gingrich, Speaker, U.S. House of Representatives, to Franklin Raines, Director, Office of Management and Budget (July 1, 1997) (*available at* http://www.projectrace.com/hotnews/archive/hotnews-070197.php).

[19] U.S. Dept. of Commerce, Bureau of the Census, Questions and Answers for Census 2000 Data on Race (Mar. 14, 2001), *available at* http://www.census.gov/census2000/raceqandas.html (last visited June 8, 2011) ("Prior to this decision, most efforts to collect data on race (including those by the Census Bureau) asked people to report one race.").

[20] U.S. Dept. of Commerce, *supra* note 5.

The increased visibility and state recognition of multiracial identities has precip-itated a plethora of new legal and political issues. As noted by Michael Omi and Howard Winant, the "mark one or more" option now available on the census opens "up a Pandora's Box regarding self-identity and social location. Individual and group identities, access to political rights such as citizenship, and 'life-chances' are thrown into doubt more by state management of racial meanings and categories."[21] Thus, the examination of the creation of new multiracial identities and categories requires continued scrutiny; here, the examination of ambiguous cases provides insight.

AMBIGUOUS CASES: WHO IS BLACK?

The answer to the question of who is black is complex. Various factors such as appearance, blood quantum, documentation, and reputation have been considered in defining blackness. In an effort to explore the need for a census definition that includes the sociopolitical nature of blackness, this section examines the concepts of black multiracial identity formation, political affiliation, and the impact of being "regarded as" black on social location.

Identity Formation

A study of individuals with one black and one white parent by Kerry Ann Rockquemore and David L. Brunsma examined how they perceive their racial iden-tity and the social factors that influence them.[22] Rockquemore and Brunsma define identity as a "validated self-understanding that places and defines the individual; it establishes what and where an actor is socially."[23] Thus, an individual cannot have a realized identity without validation by others. The study classified the subjects into four groups based on their method of self-identification.

The first group, referred to as "border identity," included individuals whose iden-tity was "between predefined social categories."[24] These individuals did not consider themselves black or white, but instead incorporated both into their framework for self-reference. This was the most common category selected in the study: 58 percent of those surveyed defined their racial identity as separate from the traditional catego-ries of black and white. Of this group, 20 percent indicated that others validated their biracial identity. The rest of of this group indicated that they considered themselves

---

[21]   Michael Omi and Howard Winant, *Foreword: The Unfinished Business of Race* in Rachel Moran and Debon Carbardo, eds., RACE LAW STORIES (2008) at xi–xii.
[22]   Kerry Ann Rockquemore & David L. Brunsma, BEYOND BLACK: BIRACIAL IDENTITY IN AMERICA, vii–xi (2002).
[23]   *Id.* at 40.
[24]   *Id.* at 42.

multiracial, but that they experienced the world as black. In addition, more than 60 percent of the individuals whose identity was validated, and 62.5 percent of those whose identity was not validated, described their appearance as ambiguous. These responses indicate the impact of racial identity validation on the identity formation of biracial individuals. Both Jason and Julia fall under the border identity category because they self-identify as multiracial while publicly acknowledging their black African ancestry.

The second group, those with "singular identity," comprised only about 13 percent of the individuals studied.[25] This identity included those individuals who classified themselves solely as black or white. Of this group, 4 percent considered themselves exclusively white, whereas the other 9 percent defined themselves as exclusively black. Of the individuals from this group who considered themselves black, 95.5 percent indicated that others assumed that they were black. Although a number of these black-white, light-skinned individuals had a singular identity as black, none of these individuals considered themselves able to pass as white.

A "protean identity" was the third group in the study and included individuals whose racial identity shifts according to social context.[26] These individuals adjust their identity based on the expectations of others and the circumstances in which they find themselves. Only 4 percent of the individuals in the study selected this identity, and they were the individuals most likely to use a variety of self-labels. Most individuals in the study reported their appearance to be "ambiguous, but assumed black."

Rockquemore and Brunsma labeled the fourth group as those with "transcendent identity."[27] This group included individuals who choose to entirely opt out of racial categorization. Of individuals in the study, 13.8 percent classified themselves as transcendents. These individuals perceived themselves as detached outsiders, or strangers, considering themselves able to "objectively articulate the social meaning placed on race and discount it as a 'master status' altogether." For these individuals, choosing a racial identity on a form had no bearing on their self-identification. This identity was most common among those who appeared white.[28] For the most part, they accepted categorization as black because of the persistence of the one-drop rule, but this categorization did not impact their self-identification. Sheila falls under the transcendent category because she refuses to racially categorize herself or acknowledge her black ancestry.

This racial identification study found a strong correlation between the socially validated appearance of black-white multiracial individuals and their choice of

[25] *Id.* at 47.
[26] *Id.* at 47.
[27] *Id.* at 49–50.
[28] *Id.* at 99.

racial self-identification. It appeared that almost all of those in the study recognized their black ancestry, but did so in a variety of ways. The study confirmed that race is socially constructed and that this construction changes over time. It also demonstrated that despite the persistence of the one-drop rule, only a small percentage of the black-white multiracial individuals studied categorized themselves as exclusively black.

Political Affiliation

Although many of the individuals who comprise this multiracial upsurge have refused to identify themselves as singularly black, it is noteworthy that the majority of those with black African ancestry identify politically with their black monoracial counterparts. A study by Natalie Masuoka found that individuals who identified as multiracial develop political opinions that parallel their monoracial minority counterparts. Masuoka focused on the role of racial self-identification and its relationship between multiracial identities and political attitudes.[29]

Masuoka found that, even for those who did not identify with a traditional racial minority group, a minority identity continued to influence their political beliefs. She noted that

> [the] finding that minority identities frame multiracial political attitudes points to the persistence of the continued use of the one-drop rule and marginalizing treatment of individuals because of their racial background. Those with some degree of minority background will be considered and treated as if they are a racial minority, thus that minority identity influences their political worldviews.[30]

Interestingly, she noted that the choice to identify as multiracial demonstrates a racial identity distinct from white Americans and that even for those whose racial identities are flexible or ambiguous, race continues to structure their life chances. She also found that multiracial individuals, although influenced by their racial background, cannot be lumped together as one group.

Noteworthy is that there were no significant differences between the political attitudes of multiracial and monoracial blacks:

> [I]f multiracials were placed on the conceptual political attitudes scale, multiracials (regardless of racial background) fall somewhere between whites and blacks. There are two exceptions to this pattern: multiracial blacks have similar perspectives on race-based policy solutions as monoracial blacks, and multiracial Asians have similar

---

[29] Natalie Masuoka, *Political Attitudes and Ideologies of Multiracial Americans: The Implications of Mixed Race in the United States*, 61 POLITICAL RESEARCH QUARTERLY 253 (2008).
[30] *Id.*

perspectives on racial discrimination as monoracial whites. … [F]or multiracial blacks, racial group attachments are strongest when they consider public policies, but less so for the formation of their partisanship or views on discrimination.[31]

Further, Masuoka found that, even though black multiracial individuals identify as multiracial, they still adopt political attitudes with the interest of their minority racial group in mind. Her research demonstrates that even though black multiracials may not singularly identify as black, they often identify politically with monoracial blacks.

Racial Reputation: Being "Regarded as" Black

As history demonstrates, the racial reputation of being of black African descent impacts one's social location and legal status in the American racial hierarchy. Rogers Brubaker and Frederick Cooper explain that the concept of "identitarian theorizing" refers to "position in a multidimensional space defined by *particularistic categorical attributes*" such as race, gender, or ethnicity. Thus, the term "social location" refers to the individuals' identity in the eyes of others; the issue is not how these individuals understand or characterize their own identities – rather, it refers to the societal position in which they are placed.[32] Here, we focus on the social location of multiracial individuals with black African ancestry within the American racial hierarchy and whether or not they are regarded as black.[33]

As a result of the impact of having a black racial reputation on an individual's social location and legal status, many black and multiracial individuals chose to pass for white – completely disassociating themselves from their black family members in order to enjoy the privileges of whiteness. In contrast, others acknowledged their mixed ancestry. The following examples demonstrate the concept of racial reputation among three individuals of black African descent that appeared white.

Walter White

Walter White, former president of the National Association for the Advancement of Colored Persons (NAACP) and well-known civil rights activist, is an example of the impact of racial reputation on social location. In his essay, "Why I Remain a Negro," he states, "My skin is white, my eyes are blue, my hair is blond. The traits of my race

[31] *Id.* at 261.
[32] Rogers Brubaker & Frederick Cooper, *Beyond "Identity"*, 29 THEORY & SOCIETY 1, 7 (2000).
[33] *See generally*, Angela Onwuachi-Willig and Mario L. Barnes, *By Any Other Name?: On Being "Regarded As" Black, and Why Title VII Should Apply Even if Lakisha and Jamal Are White*, 2005 WIS. L. REV. 1283 (2005) (analysis of being "regarded as" black in the context of employment law).

are nowhere visible upon me." In this essay, he explores the paradox of the color line and why he chose to identify as black instead of passing as a white person. He tells a story from his childhood about a mob of white men with torches who went past his home in the middle of the night. One of the men yelled to burn down White's house because, "It's too nice of a house for a nigger to live in!" White wrote:

> In the flickering light the mob swayed, paused, and began to flow toward us. In that instant there opened up within me a great awareness; I knew then who I was. I was colored, a human being with an invisible pigmentation which marked me as a person to be hunted, hanged, abused, discriminated against, kept in poverty and ignorance, in order that those whose skin was white would have readily at hand a proof of their superiority, a proof patent and inclusive, accessible to the moron and the idiot as well as to the wise man and genius. ...
>
> Yet as a boy there in the darkness amid the tightening fright, I knew the inexplicable thing – that my skin was as white as the skin of those who were coming at me.[34]

After gunshots were fired at the mob by some neighbors, the mob disbursed and, fortunately, White's family was not injured. In the quiet that followed, White was gripped by the knowledge of his identity. White further described how, as an adult, white people were often confused when they found out that he identified himself as black. He said that after whites discovered his racial identity, they treated him as inferior and considered those who were not afraid to be seen with him as "nigger lovers." Thus, even though White looked like a white man, his reputation of being of black African descent negatively affected his social location.

Susie Guillory Phipps

Doe v. Louisiana[35] addresses to what extent one woman was willing to go to protect her white racial reputation. The plaintiff, Susie Guillory Phipps, who believed she was white, discovered that she was classified as black on her birth certificate. She made this discovery when she applied for a passport for a trip with her husband, a wealthy, white seafood wholesaler. Mrs. Phipps indicated that she was "flabbergasted and sickened" by her discovery.[36] She was so upset by this news that she told her husband that she was too sick to go on the trip, and was afraid to tell him about her discovery for five years. During this time, she used her "allowance" to pay for legal fees to try to change the racial designations of her parents, Simea Fretty and

---

[34] Walter White, *Why I Remain a Negro*, THE SAT. REV. OF LIT., Oct. 11, 1947, at 13.
[35] *Doe v. State*, 479 So. 2d 369, (La. Ct. App. Oct. 18, 1985).
[36] Art Harris, *Louisiana Court Sees No Shades of Gray In Woman's Request*, WASH. POST, May 21, 1983; Gregory Jaynes, *Suit on Race Recalls Lines Drawn Under Slavery*, N.Y. TIMES, Sept. 30, 1982.

Dominique Guillory, from black to white. She spent upward of $49,000 in legal fees to do this.

Along with her relatives, she sought a legal order that would compel the Louisiana Department of Health and Human Resources to correct this alleged error on her deceased parents' birth certificates. They also challenged the constitutionality of the former Louisiana statute that "provided that a person having one-thirty second or less of Negro blood shall not be described or designated as 'colored' by any state official."[37] The court, concluding that racial identity was permanent and unchangeable, found that there was no duty to change the racial designation of Phipps's parents.

Mrs. Phipps had been raised as white and was previously regarded as white in the community. She was willing to spend thousands of dollars to protect her white racial reputation, which demonstrates the property value of whiteness and the impact of being regarded as black.

Mary Catherine Walker

Ms. Walker was described as a "fair-skinned black woman with light eyes and aquiline features."[38] Her story differs from the others because her Kansas birth certificate indicated that she was white, yet, as an adult, she held herself out as a black woman. Her parents, both light-skinned blacks, had their children designated as white on their birth certificates in an effort to help them avoid discrimination. As a child, Mrs. Walker lived in a white community and her parents had the family hold themselves out as white. They did not allow their fourteen children to speak slang or to discuss their black African ancestry in public. One of Mary's childhood memories includes when "an older brother came home crying one day because someone had called him a nigger." This brother was darker than the rest of his siblings. Mary remembers her eldest brother calling all of the children together and explaining that they were black but that they were passing for white.

In college, she decided to no longer pass as white, which created a number of unique problems. For example, when she filed a discrimination complaint against an employer, she was accused of changing her race to get a job. In 1989, she successfully sued to have her racial designation changed from white to black; however, Kansas no longer put racial designations on birth certificates, so her race was only noted in confidential state files and used for statistical purposes. Thus, even though Walker looked like a white woman, she chose to have a racial reputation of being of black African descent.

---

[37] *Doe,* 479 So.2d at 371.
[38] Peggy Peterman, *After Growing Up Hiding Her Race, a Former Teacher Fights to Claim Her Ancestry in a World of Black & White,* St. Petersburg Times (Fl.), Sept. 15, 1989.

POLITICAL BLACKNESS

The current census definition of blackness fails to address sufficiently the sociopolitical nature of race. My concept of "Political Blackness" expands the definition imposed by law and emphasizes its sociopolitical nature instead of limiting it to a biological fiction. Instead of defining blackness solely upon having origins in any of the black racial groups of Africa, as currently required by the census, the expanded, sociopolitical definition would include the impact of being regarded as black on social location.

Under this definition of Political Blackness, Walter White, Mary Catherine Walker, and the twins Jason and Julia would be politically black, because they were regarded as black in their communities. Conversely, Susie Phipps, pre-litigation, and the twins' cousin, Sheila, would be politically white.[39] If the goal is to move away from biology, then the definition should recognize an individual's racial reputation and identity. Political Blackness would also include multiracial individuals who identify with multiple groups, but overwhelmingly acknowledge their black African ancestry and often share political beliefs with other black people.

[39] In the case of Susie Phipps, the publicity surrounding her case caused her to be known to have black African ancestry and, therefore, could possibly change her designation upon further inquiry as to whether this changed her racial reputation.

13

Finding a *Loving* Home

Angela Onwuachi-Willig and Jacob Willig-Onwuachi

Although *Loving* has forever changed the lives of interracial couples by allowing them to legally marry in every state, it has not led society to embrace all multiracial couples and families. More than forty years after *Loving*, 95 percent of all individuals marry a person of the same race. Additionally, interracial couples continue to face both physical and verbal threats to their existence, and they also continue to be largely invisible from the media, textbooks, and other types of communications.[1]

In other words, more than forty years since the Supreme Court decided *Loving*, we, a black woman and a white man who are married and reside with our three biracial children in Iowa, continue to live the legacy of *Loving*'s named plaintiffs, Mildred and Richard. Although we benefit from the Lovings' courage and courtroom victory through a range of legal privileges and protections that stem from the Supreme Court's recognition of their fundamental right to marry regardless of race, we also endure the legacy of their social lives. Even after the historic decision, the Lovings' lives were affected by both conscious discriminatory attitudes and unconscious biases.

Today, society and law continue to work together to frame the normative ideal of intimate couples and families as not just monoracial but also heterosexual.[2] In this chapter, however, we focus solely on the issue of race and the privilege of monoraciality among intimate couples and do not address the privilege of heterosexuality among couples, which is readily evident within our society.[3] As our primary focus,

---

[1] *See* Angela Onwuachi-Willig, *Undercover Other*, 94 CAL. L. REV. 873, 890–92, 898–905 (2006).
[2] *See* R. A. Lenhardt, *Beyond Analogy: Perez v. Sharp, Antimiscegenation Law, and the Fight for Same-Sex Marriage*, 96 CAL. L. REV. 839, 882 (2008); Melissa Murray, *Strange Bedfellows: Criminal Law, Family Law, and the Legal Construction of Intimate Life*, 94 IOWA L. REV. 1253, 1267–8 (2009).
[3] In this chapter, we address laws that are assumed to adequately protect interracial, heterosexual couples in a post-*Loving* era, but that do not provide such protection because they create no space for such couples in their language. We recognize that many of the privileges that attach to monoracial, heterosexual couples also do not attach to monoracial, same-sex couples; however, because antidiscrimination law generally excludes gay individuals from protection from discrimination based on

we analyze contemporary challenges that interracial couples, particularly black-white couples, may face in the public eye. First, we identify and explicate both the social and legal ways in which interraciality may affect and alter the treatment and recognition of multiracial, heterosexual couples and their families. Thereafter, we utilize housing discrimination law as one example of the way in which law can render multiracial couples and families invisible and thus fail to address fully the harms to such groups.

INVISIBLE KNAPSACK OF PRIVILEGES

All individuals in our society possess one or more invisible knapsacks of unearned privileges, whether they are based on race, color, class, sex, religion, sexual orientation, nationality, able-bodied-ness, marital status, or other identity categories. At the same time, however, individuals also may suffer or endure societal disadvantages that attach to one or more of their identity categories.

In 1990, Peggy McIntosh expounded upon this reality of simultaneous privilege and disadvantage based on identity categories in her paper, *White Privilege: Unpacking the Invisible Knapsack*.[4] There, McIntosh used her understanding of her oppression as a female to explore and understand her own privilege as a white person, a privilege that she had been taught from birth not to recognize. White privilege, she said, "is like an invisible weightless knapsack of special provisions, maps, passports, codebooks, visas, clothes, tools, and blank checks" that includes individual advantages, such as the following:

1. I can, if I wish, arrange to be in the company of people of my race most of the time.

2. I can avoid spending time with people whom I was trained to mistrust and who have learned to mistrust my kind or me.

3. If I should need to move, I can be pretty sure of renting or purchasing housing in an area which I can afford and in which I would want to live.

4. I can be pretty sure that my neighbors in such a location will be neutral or pleasant to me.

5. I can go shopping alone most of the time, pretty well assured that I will not be followed or harassed.

---

sexual orientation, the statutory language and law discussed herein is generally not seen as protective of same-sex couples. In other words, the hole in antidiscrimination law for same-sex couples is widely exposed, whereas it is not so easily exposed for interracial, heterosexual couples. Our hope is to expose this hole.

[4] Peggy McIntosh, *White Privilege: Unpacking the Invisible Knapsack*, INDEP. SCHOOL, Winter 1990, *excerpt available at* http://www.nymbp.org/reference/WhitePrivilege.pdf (last visited February 10, 2012).

Nearly twenty years later, in 2009, McIntosh's words ring equally true to us and speak to our experiences as both a privileged, heterosexual couple and an unprivileged, interracial couple. Just as we use McIntosh's words as a basis for examining our own invisible knapsacks of privilege, such as our unearned privileges as heterosexuals, we also use it as a basis for understanding and evaluating the ways in which our racial advantages and disadvantages as individuals are complicated by our marital union. Primarily, we use it as an avenue for understanding the ways in which our privileges – mainly Jacob's – disappear as a result of our marriage.

Much like McIntosh had been taught throughout her life not to recognize her white privilege, many heterosexuals have been conditioned to remain oblivious about their own unearned privileges based on sexual orientation. In general, heterosexual individuals and couples enjoy many social and legal benefits in our society. A few examples of heterosexual privilege include the following:

1. In all fifty states, intimate heterosexual partners can marry each other as long as they do not violate other marital restrictions, such as age or number restrictions, and can have their marriage recognized by every other state in the union.

2. Heterosexual couples can turn on the television or read the newspaper and see reflections of their cross-sex, intimate relationships widely represented.

3. So long as they are otherwise qualified, heterosexual couples can adopt children in all fifty states.

4. When out in public, the children of heterosexuals are presumed to "belong" to them as parents.

5. The children of heterosexual couples are given texts and classes that implicitly support their family unit.

This particular list of heterosexual privileges is not exhaustive, yet it illustrates McIntosh's point about how privilege can make insiders "feel welcomed and 'normal' in the usual walks of public life, institutional and social," and make outsiders feel unwelcome and without a home in those same areas.

Indeed, while this list of heterosexual advantages could be endless, the list of heterosexual couples that may enjoy all of these benefits is more restricted. Because of the interlocking nature of hierarchies in our society, not all heterosexual couples are treated equally. Every couple's experiences in the world can be complicated by other identity categories. Our society does not necessarily recognize and acknowledge interracial, heterosexual couples in all aspects of life. Instead, these couples' interraciality tends to complicate their ability to "enjoy" the full range of heterosexual advantages.

As Kimberlé Crenshaw illustrated in her seminal work on intersectionality, different groups of people may encounter varied forms of discriminatory behavior based on the intersection of two or more identity categories.[5] Intersectionality recognizes that power, privilege, disadvantage, and discrimination are influenced by interlocking spectrums of identity. For example, because the identities of black men and black women differ along the intersection of race and sex, black women and black men may have distinct vulnerabilities to violence and discrimination from black men.

Although Crenshaw's theory of intersectionality focused on black women and the ways in which they are uniquely oppressed based on the convergence of racism and sexism in their lives, her theory can be applied to other groups. For instance, while interracial, heterosexual couples may face discrimination based on a single identity category such as their marital status or socioeconomic class, they also may encounter discrimination at the intersection of race and family. As we, Jacob and Angela, have seen in our own lives, our interraciality tends to make our very existence as a couple invisible and places many of the privileges that generally attach to heterosexual couples and families outside of our reach. For example, although we enjoy the individual right to legally marry and have our marriage recognized in every state throughout the nation, no other privilege on the preceding list of heterosexual advantages falls within our realm of benefits as a couple.[6] Were we now to reconstruct that same list to comport with our own reality as a black female–white male couple, it would read as follows:

1. In all fifty states, we have the ability to legally marry each other, and every state in the nation has had to give full faith and credit to our marriage because of the *Loving v. Virginia* decision in 1967.

2. Heterosexual couples can turn on the television or read the newspaper and see reflections of their cross-sex, intimate relationships widely represented. But we do not see reflections of ourselves as a married, interracial, heterosexual couple widely represented in the media. Even when we do, the plot line nearly always ends in tragedy, spurred by the mixing of races.[7]

3. So long as they are qualified, heterosexual couples can adopt children in all fifty states. But even after the Multi-Ethnic Placement Act, we, as an interracial

---

[5] *See* Kimberlé Crenshaw, *Mapping the Margins: Intersectionality, Identity Politics, and Violence Against Women of Color*, 43 STAN. L. REV. 1241, 1242–43 (1991).

[6] *See generally* Adele M. Morrison, *Same-Sex Loving: Supporting White Supremacy Through Same-Sex Marriage*, 13 MICH. J. RACE & L. 177 (2007) (noting that "mixed-sex interracial couples" are "normative by being mixed-sex but non-normative by being mixed race").

[7] *See generally* Angela Onwuachi-Willig, *There's Just One Hitch, Will Smith: Examining Title VII, Race, and Casting Discrimination on the Fortieth Anniversary of Loving v. Virginia*, 2007 WIS. L. REV. 319 (analyzing the dearth of black-white interracial couples in film and television as a result of casting discrimination based on perceived audience preferences).

couple, would encounter difficulty in adopting children, especially children who were not of African descent.[8]

4. When out in public, the children of heterosexuals are presumed to "belong" to them as parents. But when we are out in public, together or separately, our children often are not presumed to be ours. For example, people frequently ask us, "Is that your child?" or "Are you playing big brother today?" Little children tell us that we do not "match" our children.[9]

5. The children of heterosexual couples are given texts and classes that implicitly support their family unit. But our children are not given texts and classes that implicitly support our family unit. Their texts almost never reflect or support the interethnic, interracial diversity of our family.

As our list demonstrates, different types of couples may have different experiences based on various intersections of identity categories. For example, unlike monoracial, heterosexual couples, we often suffer the daily microaggression of having our status as a family assumed away, even when we are out with our children. Other people rarely assume that we are intimate partners when we go shopping together in the grocery store. At best, store cashiers and other customers assume that we are friends, even with our rings on our hands and our children with us. At worst, clerks speak to Angela as though she were a random stranger throwing items into Jacob's basket. Jacob is always asked, "Is this together?" Similarly, other customers perceive us together as store clerk and shopper, often approaching Angela to ask if she will assist them as well.[10] Additionally, unlike white, heterosexual couples, fear of mistreatment plays a role for us when choosing public accommodations. We try to plan where we will eat, play, or stay overnight as a means of avoiding discrimination. At times, we even "game" the system, sending Jacob in first to scope out the premises, or to check us in at a hotel. We also have encountered difficulty in finding

---

[8] For a general discussion of the difficulties that interracial couples face in the adoption process, see *Interracial Couple Say They Were Denied Adoption Because They Had Not Suffered Enough Racism*, Jet, Aug. 16, 1999, at 23, *available at* http://findarticles.com/p/articles/mi_m1355/is_11_96/ai_55588159/ (last visited February 10, 2012).

[9] *See* Angela Onwuachi-Willig, *A Beautiful Lie: Exploring* Rhinelander v. Rhinelander *as a Formative Lesson on Race, Identity, Marriage, and Family*, 95 Cal. L. Rev. 2393, 2458 (2007); *see also* Rachel F. Moran, Interracial Intimacy: The Regulation of Race and Romance 155 (2001).

[10] Other interracial couples have documented similar experiences. *See, e.g.,* Erica Chito Childs, Navigating Interracial Borders: Black-White Couples and Their Social Worlds 40 (2005); Paul C. Rosenblatt et al., Multiracial Couples: Black and White Voices (1995). *See generally* Rashmi Goel, *From Tainted to Sainted: The View of Interracial Relations as Cultural Evangelism*, 2007 Wis. L. Rev. 489, 516–17 ("When faced with a mixed-race couple, people seem to ignore or disbelieve activity that – for a same-race couple – would be indicative of a relationship. People often express surprise at the existence of an interracial couple, asking in dumbfounded tones, 'Are you two … together?'").

neighborhoods where people approve of our household. Where possible, we have steered ourselves directly to integrated neighborhoods.[11]

While our experiences as an interracial, heterosexual couple are very real for us (and many couples like us), they cannot be generalized to all interracial, heterosexual couples. For instance, an Asian Pacific American male–white female couple may suffer the same discrimination as we do, but they also may experience a particular event differently than we would based on their own combination of race, gender, class, and sexuality. When out shopping together in a grocery store, an Asian Pacific American male, unlike Angela, is unlikely to be perceived as a store worker who is servicing a white female customer. Neither race nor gender stereotypes regarding Asian Pacific American men lend themselves to that type of imagery. Just changing the type of store, however, may alter the experience of both couples. For example, in an electronics store, racialized and gendered stereotypes may lead customers to believe that the Asian Pacific American male is a worker who is servicing a white female customer. Indeed, as one couple – a white woman and an Indian American man – has related to us, he is often approached by customers who believe that he is a store worker when they are out together in an electronics or computer store.

THE LEGAL INVISIBILITY OF THE INTERRACIAL FAMILY

The disadvantages of interracial couples are not limited to the social context alone. The law, too, plays its own role in reifying and reinforcing the normative ideal of coupling, marriage, and family as monoracial. This role is evident in the language and application of Title VIII of the Civil Rights Act of 1968, also known as the Fair Housing Act.[12] At this point, we use housing discrimination law as a tool for emphasizing the continuities between social discrimination against interracial, heterosexual couples and the failure to recognize interracial, heterosexual family units within the law. In so doing, we first describe the different methods for proving housing discrimination under federal law and then explicate how interracial couples that are victims of housing discrimination because of their status as an interracial couple alone remain unacknowledged as a family unit (at least in terms of expressive value) because they do not fit within any of the named legal categories.

[11]   Other interracial families have made similar choices. *See, e.g.,* Heather M. Dalmage, Tripping on the Color Line: Black-White Multiracial Families in a Racially Divided World 95 (2000) (asserting that black-white multiracial families "desire racially mixed neighborhoods because there they can have a sense of safety and comfort and not face repeated acts of border patrolling and racism"); Steven R. Holloway et al., *Partnering 'Out' and Fitting In: Residential Segregation and the Neighbourhood Contexts of Mixed-Race Households,* 11 Population, Space & Place 299, 319–20 (2005) ("All mixed-race household types are more likely to live in diverse neighbourhood settings than same-race households.").

[12]   Pub. L. No. 90–284, 82 Stat. 73 (codified as amended at 42 U.S.C. § 3604 (2000)).

Under Title VIII, only certain classes of citizens are protected from discrimination in housing. As enacted, Title VIII provided that "it shall be unlawful":

(a) To refuse to sell or rent after the making of a bona fide offer, or to refuse to negotiate for the sale or rental of, or otherwise make unavailable or deny, a dwelling to any person because of race, color, religion, or national origin.

(b) To discriminate against any person in the terms, conditions, or privileges of sale or rental of a dwelling, or in the provision of services or facilities in connection therewith, because of race, color, religion, or national origin. ...

(d) To represent to any person because of race, color, religion, or national origin that any dwelling is not available for inspection, sale, or rental when such dwelling is in fact so available.[13]

Under Title VIII, plaintiffs can prove discrimination with direct evidence, or through circumstantial evidence by using the burden-shifting model that the Supreme Court specifically developed for evaluating employment discrimination in *McDonnell Douglas Corp. v. Green.*[14] Applying this burden-shifting model to housing discrimination cases, courts have held that a plaintiff has to prove housing discrimination through three different steps. First, the plaintiff must establish a prima facie case of discrimination by proving the following four factors: (1) that she is a member of a racial minority; (2) that she applied for and was qualified to rent or purchase certain property or housing; (3) that she was rejected; and (4) that the housing or rental property remained available thereafter. Once the plaintiff proves each of these factors, the court draws an inference of discrimination and moves to the second step, where the owner or landlord must articulate a legitimate explanation for rejecting the plaintiff's application. If the defendant satisfies this burden, then, in the third step, the plaintiff must prove that the defendant's stated reason was a pretext for discrimination. The plaintiff can show pretext by demonstrating that the articulated reason was false, did not actually motivate the challenged conduct, or did not warrant the challenged conduct. However, even upon proof of pretext, a jury may still rule in favor of the defendant if it believes that a nondiscriminatory factor was at play. The ultimate burden of persuasion rests with the plaintiff at all times.

Additionally, a person discriminated against because of her association with an individual in a protected class can use the *McDonnell Douglas* framework to prove discrimination against herself. Recent court decisions have interpreted "because of race" in antidiscrimination law broadly, reasoning that an exclusion of discrimination-

---

[13] Civil Rights Act of 1968, tit. 8, Pub. L. No. 90–284 § 804, 82 Stat. 73, 83 (codified as amended at 42 U.S.C. § 3604 (2000)). Subsequent amendments have expanded the list of protected characteristics to include sex, familial status, and handicap, but the statute's protection is still limited to the characteristics specifically enumerated in its text. 42 U.S.C. § 3604 (2000).

[14] 411 U.S. 792 (1973).

by-association lawsuits would run contrary to the purposes of general discrimination law. According to these courts, plaintiffs in discrimination-by-association cases suffer discrimination because of their own race or protected class, not just because of their relationship to someone of another race or protected class. For example, in *Rosenblatt v. Bivona & Cohen, P.C.*, a white attorney at a law firm filed a lawsuit against his former employer, alleging that he had been terminated because he was married to a black woman.[15] In evaluating the plaintiff's claim, the district court noted other decisions that rejected discrimination-by-association claims for lack of standing, but then refused to adopt the same position. The court explained: "Plaintiff has alleged discrimination as a result of his marriage to a black woman. Had he been black, his marriage would not have been interracial. Therefore, inherent in his complaint is the assertion that he has suffered racial discrimination based on his own race."[16]

However, such statutory tools for filing housing discrimination lawsuits can be ineffective for truly combating the type of discrimination that interracial, heterosexual couples may face as a familial unit. Unlike the members of a monoracial, heterosexual couple who can assert the same factual allegations of race discrimination in their complaint and thus plead their claims together as a couple, the members of an interracial, heterosexual couple who are discriminated against because of their interraciality (i.e., because they have engaged in race mixing) have to make their individual races and family unit exclusive of each other in order to explain the factual basis of their discrimination claims.

Indeed, we encountered this very problem with housing discrimination law when we filed our own joint housing discrimination claim. While our lawsuit did not involve a claim of discrimination based on interraciality, we did confront the question of how interraciality would fit into our factual allegations, ultimately deciding to move forward with a more traditional and "recognizable" claim based on race. In what follows, we reveal a number of these complex issues in a hypothetical, which we hope exposes the unique harms that interracial, heterosexual couples may face and the law's inability to fully address these unique harms as written.

HYPOTHETICAL

Consider, for example, the hypothetical case of a married couple – Andrew Williams, a black man, and Jackie Owens, a white woman.[17] Andrew and Jackie live in a large

---

[15] See generally Rosenblatt v. Bivona & Cohen, P.C., 946 F. Supp. 298 (S.D.N.Y. 1996).

[16] *Id.* at 300.

[17] This hypothetical is loosely based on a lawsuit of ours, which was resolved to our satisfaction. We are unable, however, to discuss the specifics of that case and have altered the facts to protect the anonymity of the parties involved.

city on the East Coast, where Andrew works as a doctor at a prominent hospital and Jackie works as a high school teacher. Two years earlier, they had relocated from a large Midwestern city, where they lived in a suburban house that they owned jointly. Upon moving, they sold their house and rented an apartment in the bustling city-center, close to Andrew's new hospital. They enjoyed the experience of living in the city, but wanted to move to a quieter, more residential area. Because they planned to wait a few more years before purchasing their own house, they looked for another apartment or house to rent in a nearby suburb.

Andrew and Jackie found an advertisement for a two-bedroom apartment on a website with local rental listings. They called the landlord/owner to set up an appointment to view the apartment. Although the landlord could not meet them personally, he arranged a time for a rental agent to show Andrew and Jackie the apartment.

When Andrew and Jackie arrived for their appointment, they found the house attractive and well maintained, and they appreciated its location on a quiet, tree-lined street. While Andrew checked out the lawn, Jackie rang the doorbell and was greeted warmly with a handshake by the rental agent, Betty, who was white. When Andrew walked up behind Jackie and introduced himself as Jackie's husband, Betty's demeanor seemed to change. Betty greeted Andrew only verbally and quickly turned her back to begin the tour of the apartment. Both Andrew and Jackie noted Betty's odd behavior but quickly put it out of their minds as they toured the apartment.

As they viewed the apartment, Andrew and Jackie fell in love with it. Immediately after finishing the tour, Andrew called the landlord from the car to express their desire to rent the property. The landlord seemed very happy that they were interested, and he explained that he already had other applications for the apartment but had not yet made a decision. He instructed them to leave their application with the rental agent, with whom he would be speaking later that afternoon. The owner went on to say that, if they liked that apartment, he had another apartment just coming available for rent in a nearby house that they would surely like as well. The owner gave Andrew the address of the other house over the phone so that he and Jackie could drive by it. He concluded by requesting Andrew and Jackie call him later to schedule a time to see the other location. Once Andrew got off the phone, he and Jackie filled out an application and gave it to the rental agent. That evening, Andrew called the landlord to follow up about the apartments. He and Jackie were confident that the landlord would select them once he saw the strength of their application. During the phone conversation, the landlord told Andrew that he had their application and was speaking to the rental agent at the very moment, but that he would call Andrew back later. When Andrew spoke to the landlord again, the landlord told him that the first apartment was no longer available. Then, before Andrew could even ask about the second apartment, the landlord informed him that the second apartment, which Andrew understood as not even being on the market yet, was also no longer available.

The next week, Andrew and Jackie began to look on the Internet for rental listings again. They noticed that the same landlord had a new listing for an apartment for rent in that same area. They wondered if a third apartment had become available, if the renting of the second apartment had fallen through, or if (remembering Betty's odd behavior) the landlord did not want to rent to them for impermissible reasons. Andrew then e-mailed the landlord, reintroducing himself and inquiring about the apartment listing. Andrew wrote:

> Hello. I am writing to see if I can reschedule an appointment to view the apartment that you advertised on the housing.com website. You and I have actually spoken before on the telephone. My wife and I recently viewed the apartment that you had for rent at 34 Carson Road. I'm Andrew Williams, the person who called to tell you how much we liked the Carson apartment. At the time, you indicated that you had another apartment that we were sure to like (if we liked the Carson apartment) at 35 Eager Street. When we spoke last, you indicated that this apartment was not available.
>
> I was looking through ads on housing.com and saw your ad for another apartment in the area. Is this the apartment on Eager or a different apartment? Is it available? Can my wife and I set up an appointment to view the advertised apartment tonight or any other time? Thanks in advance for your quick response.
>
> Andrew Williams

In his reply, the owner indicated that the listing was in fact for the second apartment but asserted that it was still not available. He wrote:

> Dear Dr. Williams,
>
> This apartment, I thought was available, but for now it isn't. (We spoke about its non-availability earlier. The web ad shows a time-lag). Sorry for the confusion. I wish you good luck in your search.
>
> Best Wishes.

Two days later, at Jackie's request, a friend e-mailed the owner to inquire about the second apartment, which was still listed on the website. The landlord, who was not aware of any connection between the friend and Jackie, indicated in his response that the house was still available for rent and, in fact, suggested a meeting time with the friend to view the apartment. (The friend later cancelled the appointment.) Thereafter, Andrew contacted his brother, who is an employment discrimination attorney and is somewhat familiar with housing discrimination law. The brother told Andrew and Jackie that they had reasonable evidence to support a claim of discrimination.

Andrew and Jackie filed a complaint with the state discrimination commission, asserting discrimination because of Andrew's race. After all, they could easily prove the four factors of the prima facie case of discrimination under this construction: (1) that Andrew belonged to a minority group; (2) that Andrew, along with Jackie, had applied for and was qualified to rent or purchase the property at issue; (3) that Andrew, along with Jackie, was refused the housing despite being qualified; and (4) that the housing remained open thereafter, and the owner or landlord continued to seek or review applications from persons of lesser or similar qualifications outside of the protected (race) class.

During the preliminary investigation of the complaint, the owner provided his legitimate, nondiscriminatory reason for not renting the second apartment to Andrew and Jackie: that he had to go out of town a couple of days after speaking to Andrew on the phone and did not think that he could rent the apartment before he left. In fact, the landlord conceded that he did not enter into an agreement to rent the second apartment until two months after he first told Andrew and Jackie that it was not available. He also revealed that he had rented the second apartment to three unrelated women in their twenties. These women, apparently friends or roommates, had significantly worse credit scores than Andrew and Jackie, and a combined income that was less than one-third of Andrew and Jackie's.

Finally, the owner produced evidence that he had rented to white, black, and Asian monoracial families and couples in the past (although the black couple had begun their lease after the filing of Andrew and Jackie's complaint), which would make it harder, though not impossible, to prove a claim of discrimination based solely on Andrew's race. Still, the landlord provided no explanation for lying to Andrew on two separate occasions by telling him that the apartment was no longer available when, in fact, it was. Additionally, the landlord did not explain why he did not think that he could rent the apartment before he went out of town; after all, Andrew and Jackie had indicated a desire to rent either the first or second apartment immediately.

Based on the facts in this hypothetical, although Andrew and Jackie have persuasive (in fact, almost perfect) evidence of wrongdoing by the landlord under the *McDonnell Douglas* framework, they will encounter difficulty in explaining and detailing discrimination because of the identification of their protected class category. Although Andrew and Jackie arguably have a strong claim based solely on discrimination against Andrew, their strongest claim for discrimination lies at the intersection of race and family, not just on race or family alone. After all, the owner of the apartment in this hypothetical appears not to be discriminating against either

Andrew or Jackie based on animus toward their particular racial group, but rather against them together as an interracial couple. Yet, the law – here, housing discrimination law – fails to fully address their experience in the face of their "complex" familial identity.[18] No protected category under the law appears to include Andrew and Jackie's family as one interracial unit, a fact that not only complicates Andrew and Jackie's claim, but also redoubles their injury – at least with respect to dignity – by implicitly erasing the existence of their family.

Under current housing discrimination statutes, Andrew and Jackie cannot pursue an interraciality discrimination claim based on their "familial status," because housing discrimination statutes define "familial status" in relation to one's dependents. For example, Title VIII defines "familial status" to mean:

> One or more individuals (who have not attained the age of 18 years) being domiciled with –
>
> (1) a parent or another person having legal custody of such individual or individuals; or
> (2) the designee of such parent or other person having custody, with the written permission of such parent or person.[19]

Because the discrimination experienced by Andrew and Jackie did not result from having children in the family, they do not fit within the category of persons or families included in the term "familial status."

Additionally, assuming that Andrew and Jackie are in a state that provides protection for discrimination based on "marital status," Andrew and Jackie also cannot prove their claim based on "marital status" because that term generally refers only to individuals' status as either married or single.[20] For example, in *County of Dane v. Norman*, the Wisconsin Supreme Court made clear that, under Wisconsin's housing discrimination statute, "marital status" was defined as "being married, divorced, widowed, separated, single or a cohabitant."[21]

Most of all, as we noted earlier, Andrew and Jackie will encounter difficulty in factually asserting a joint claim of discrimination "because of" their interraciality as a family. Had the owner's actions against them simply been targeted at Andrew alone, Andrew and Jackie could just seek to plead and prove disparate treatment

---

[18] *See* Kimberlé Crenshaw, *Demarginalizing the Intersection of Race and Sex: A Black Feminist Critique of Antidiscrimination Doctrine, Feminist Theory and Antiracist Politics,* 1989 U. Chi. Legal F. 139, 140–50 (coining and explaining the term "intersectionality"). Of course, the owner's evidence regarding rentals to monoracial couples is not inconsistent with Andrew and Jackie's traditional race discrimination claim, because the lease of the monoracial, black couple began only *after* Andrew and Jackie filed their complaint.

[19] 42 U.S.C. § 3602(k) (2000).

[20] *See, e.g.,* Miller v. C.A. Muer Corp., 362 N.W.2d 650, 654 (Mich. 1984).

[21] 497 N.W.2d 714, 715 (Wis. 1993).

under the *McDonnell Douglas* burden-shifting framework by pleading racial animus against Andrew individually (as they did in this hypothetical). Because, however, the facts suggest that the landlord may have discriminated against Andrew and Jackie because of their interraciality as a couple, and not just because of animus toward Andrew's racial group, the couple will have to engage in wordplay to explain and prove the factual basis for their claim of discrimination against them as an interracial couple. Specifically, Andrew and Jackie will each have to assert discrimination based on the law of discrimination by association, claiming separately and individually that, but for the race of their spouse, they each individually would have been treated differently. In so doing, they will have to divide their family unit in their complaint allegations.

CREATING A SPACE OF THEIR OWN

Although courts arguably can (and certainly would) find discrimination "because of race" for couples like Andrew and Jackie under the analysis used in discrimination-by-association cases,[22] this method does not fully address the problem of housing discrimination against interracial couples based on their race mixing. Rather, it perversely maintains and reinforces discrimination. Specifically, while the discrimination-by-association analysis can technically offer such interracial, heterosexual couples redress through damages and other forms of relief under Title VIII, it fails to address the "expressive harms" or lack of dignity in the continued assumption of monoraciality among families in housing discrimination statutes.

Unlike in the employment context, where the law of discrimination by association has been applied to individuals, housing discrimination law is intended to recognize the family unit, as demonstrated by its protection of people based on familial status and marital status. Yet, in this particular context, the law implicitly presents all families and couples as monolithic – specifically, as monoracial (and heterosexual). It mandates that claimants in an interracial family split their individual races and family unit in order to factually assert a claim. In other words, it requires that the family unit be broken up, at least legally, in order to receive protection, and, in so doing, fails to fully recognize the unit's very existence.[23]

---

[22] The court may also recognize the claim without any analysis at all, as the Kentucky Court of Appeals once did. *See* Lexington-Fayette Urban County Human Rights Comm'n v. Metro Mgmt., Inc., No. 2002-CA001234-MR, 2003 WL 22271567, at *5 (Ky. Ct. App. Oct. 3, 2003) ("As an interracial couple, the Wilkersons are clearly members of a protected class.").

[23] *Cf.* Holning Lau, *Transcending the Individualist Paradigm in Sexual Orientation Antidiscrimination Law*, 94 CAL. L. REV. 1271, 1292 (2006) ("Exclusion [of same-sex couples in public accommodations] suggests that the business refuses to recognize the couple's legitimacy, striking a blow at the couple's collective dignity and self-respect. Those dignitary harms burden the couple's development.").

Importantly, the analysis in discrimination-by-association cases fails to acknowledge the true nature of discrimination against multiracial, heterosexual couples because of their interracial status. Such discrimination concerns more than pure race discrimination as it is based on the collective, not the individual. Specifically, it is based on interraciality and the particular stereotypes targeted at people who, together, intimately cross racial boundaries. As the hypothetical demonstrates, it is possible for an alleged discriminator not to treat individuals differently based on race, but to treat couples differently based on racial mixing. In other words, a landlord can choose to treat individuals and even monoracial families equally across many races, but may, if she finds interracial couples and multiracial families repugnant, treat them unequally. As the Michigan Court of Appeals once noted:

> Discrimination against interracial couples is certainly based on racial stereotypes and is derived from notions that the blood of the races should not mix. We believe that both the broad language of the civil rights act and the policies behind the act should be read to provide protection from discrimination for interracial couples.[24]

The need for changes in statutory housing discrimination law is growing every year. As the Equal Employment Opportunity Commission (EEOC) recently recognized in its initiative, Eradicating Racism and Colorism from Employment (E-RACE), "[n]ew forms of discrimination are emerging. With a growing number of interracial marriages and families ... racial demographics ... have changed and the issue of race discrimination in America is multi-dimensional."[25] If multidimensional discrimination against interracial, heterosexual couples is to be fully addressed in the housing context, legislators must offer the possibility of a more nuanced interpretation of such couples' experiences by specifically adding "interraciality" as an additional protected category in housing discrimination statutes. Such an addition is the only means by which the law may address the "expressive harms" or lack of dignity that can result from the current framing of family in housing discrimination statutes as monoracial.

Left unchallenged, the implicit requirement of monoraciality among couples in housing discrimination statutes works only to reinforce the normative ideal of a family that "looks" racially the same. As Crenshaw's theory of intersectionality highlights, broad interpretations of the words "because of race" cannot resolve this hole in anti-discrimination housing law, as such words fail to fully encapsulate the ways in which interracial, heterosexual couples are uniquely affected by the multiple intersections of race and family. As a consequence, broad readings still fail to address the problem of how an assumption of monoraciality in housing discrimination statutes pits the

---

[24] Bryant v. Automatic Data Processing, Inc., 390 N.W.2d 732, 735 (Mich. Ct. App. 1986).
[25] U.S. EEOC, WHY DO WE NEED E-RACE? (2008), *at* http://www.eeoc.gov/eeoc/initiatives/e-race/why_e-race.cfm (last visited February 10, 2012).

individual against the collective for interracial couples. Indeed, current protected categories under housing discrimination statutes essentially require individuals in interracial couples to make their individual races and family unit separable categories in order to pursue discrimination claims based on interraciality. To truly combat discrimination in all of its forms, legislators and courts need to reframe rights and protections in a manner that is inclusive rather than exclusive.

PART FIVE

Loving Outside the U.S. Borders

14

Racially Inadmissible Wives

Rose Cuison Villazor

The conventional narrative about the public regulation of interracial marriages is incomplete. Yet, as this chapter argues, state governments were not the only public actors who restricted the ability of individuals to marry their partners of choice. The federal government also played a crucial role in restricting interracial marriages. Specifically, during the decades before *Loving v. Virginia*, the U.S. government employed immigration, citizenship, and military regulations to operate like the federal counterpart of state bans against mixed marriages. Although the convergence of these laws did not formally prohibit interracial couples from getting married in the same manner that state antimiscegenation laws did, they collectively erected obstacles to citizen/noncitizen interracial couples who sought marriage and its benefits, rights, and privileges.

In uncovering the federal government's role in controlling interracial marriages outside of the U.S. borders, this chapter aims to complicate our legal and historical understanding of the overall public policing of racial lines through marriage. In particular, the chapter counters the long-held presumption that locates the regulation of interracial relationships and marriages within the domains of states. Indeed, the federal government actively participated in restricting mixed marriages, a practice that supported and perpetuated state-sanctioned racial subordination. This extended White supremacy beyond the borders of the United States. Such transnational regulation of interracial marriages shows that the promotion of racial subordination was far broader than originally perceived in legal history.

REGULATING INTERRACIAL MARRIAGES BEYOND THE U.S. BORDERS

To understand the federal regulation of interracial marriages, it is necessary to examine immigration and citizenship law in order to appreciate the ways in which this body of law affected marriages between citizens and noncitizens of color.

At the outset, racialized citizenship law rendered some persons racially inadmissible to immigrate to the United States. Between 1790 and 1870, only two racial groups were able to naturalize: "white persons," whose right to citizenship stemmed from the first naturalization act of 1790,[1] and persons of "African ancestry," whose right to citizenship was secured in 1870 after the Civil War.[2] Several noncitizens would later claim citizenship based on the grounds that they were "white," including Takao Ozawa, a Japanese man,[3] and Bhagat Thind, from Punjab.[4] In 1922, the U.S. Supreme Court rejected both citizenship arguments and held that Japanese and South Asian Indians were not white and thus unable to acquire U.S. citizenship by naturalization.[5]

The express racial restrictions on citizenship subsequently provided the basis for excluding certain noncitizens from gaining entry to the United States. In particular, Congress passed the Immigration Act of 1924, which expressly barred immigrants who are ineligible for naturalized citizenship from entering the United States.[6] The law specifically targeted Japanese – the only Asian group then still admissible to the United States. By grounding inadmissibility on one's inability to naturalize, the Act extended the ban against the entry of Asians to Japanese. Chinese had been deemed inadmissible since 1882[7] and all other Asians were already excluded in 1917 through a law that created the "Asiatic Barred Zone."[8]

The 1924 Immigration Act provided citizens with the ability to petition for spouses and other family members to immigrate to the United States. Yet, when the provision of family reunification in the 1924 Act was combined with the exclusion of those from the "Asiatic Barred Zone," it became evident that citizens who married those from Asia would not be able to petition for their entry into the United States.[9] Moreover, the 1924 Immigration Act officially created a permanent national origins quota system, which restricted the number of persons who could immigrate from a particular country. Notably, the law exempted those who were spouses and family members of U.S. citizens and those noncitizens from the Western Hemisphere. Unlike their

---

[1] See Act of Mar. 26, 1790, ch. 3, 1 Stat. 103 (1790).
[2] See Naturalization Act of 1870, ch. 253, 16 Stat. 254 (1869).
[3] Ozawa v. United States, 260 U.S. 178 (1922).
[4] United States v. Thind, 261 U.S. 204 (1923).
[5] See Ozawa, 260 U.S. at 179; Thind, 261 U.S. at 205.
[6] Also known as the Johnson-Reed Act, ch. 190, 43 Stat. 153 (1924) (repealed 1952).
[7] Act of May 6, 1882, 22 Stat. 58 (1882) (Chinese Exclusion Act); Ping v. United States 130 U.S. 581 (1889).
[8] Act of Feb. 5, 1917, 64 Pub. L. No. 301, 39 Stat. 874 (1917) (Immigration Act of 1917 or Asiatic Barred Zone Act). The Japanese government negotiated with the United States under the "Gentlemen's Agreement" to avoid an express prohibition against the entry of Japanese to the United States by agreeing to restrict the out-migration of Japanese from their country.
[9] Also known as the Immigration Act of 1917, ch. 29, 3, 39 Stat. 874, 877 (1917) (repealed 1952).

Asian counterparts, Europeans did not face any numerical limitations on how many noncitizens from those countries may immigrate to the United States.

World War II and the War Brides Act

Less than two decades later, the United States entered World War II. Millions of U.S. soldiers were deployed in various parts of the world, creating opportunities for international and interracial relationships – and ultimately marriages – to form.[10] Many military servicemen sought to bring their spouses to the United States. Yet, the process for immigrating under the nonquota system took a substantially long time, and the significant numbers of soldiers who had married and filed petitions on behalf of their wives to enter the United States compounded the problem. Indeed, by 1945, between 75,000 and 100,000 American military service personnel had married abroad, prompting Congress to pass legislation that would ease the entry of the spouses of these soldiers.[11] In particular, Congress enacted the War Brides Act in December 1945 to "expedite the admission to the [U.S.] of alien spouses and alien minor children of citizen members of the [U.S.] armed forces."[12]

The War Brides Act permitted members of the armed services to sponsor their spouses to immigrate to the United States.[13] Expressing that the Act would further the right of "service men and women [to have] their families with them,"[14] Congress intended that the Act would expedite the admission of these foreign spouses. By giving them nonquota visas, Congress virtually assured both military service personnel and their noncitizen spouses that their applications would be processed and approved at a faster rate. The majority of spouses who entered under the War Brides Act were women.[15]

Thus, both immigration and the War Brides Act cemented the foundation on which the federal government, through military regulations, relied to regulate marriage between citizens and noncitizens in foreign land.

The onset of World War II, however, and the deployment of service personnel in foreign countries led the War Department to issue "directives requiring prior

---

[10] *See generally,* Xiaojian Zhao, Remaking Chinese America, Immigration, Family, and Community, 1940–1965 (2002).

[11] *Id.*

[12] Pub. L. No. 271, 79th Cong., ch. 591, First Sess. (Dec. 28, 1945); 8 U.S.C. 232 (1945); 8 U.S.C. 204(a) (repealed 1952).

[13] *Id.,* at Ch. 591.

[14] H. R. No. 1320, 79th Cong., First Sess., Nov. 30, 1945, at 2.

[15] *See* Zhao, *supra* n.10, at 4. Out of the 119,693 noncitizens who entered the United States between 1945 and 1950, 114,691 were "war brides" and 333 were male spouses. *See* INS, Annual Report of Immigration and Naturalization Service, 1950.

permission for soldiers to marry foreign nationals."[16] Initially limited to a class of soldiers, the restrictions were later extended to include all military service personnel.[17] In particular, on June 8, 1942, the War Department issued Circular No. 179, providing that "[n]o military personnel on duty in any foreign country or possession may marry without the approval of the commanding officer of the United States Armed forces stationed in such foreign country or possession."[18] Failure to comply with this directive could result in a court-martial.

The Armed Forces adopted the restrictions for several reasons. Military regulation S.R. 600–240–5, which promulgated Circular No. 179 by explaining the policy and procedures for obtaining approval for marriage between a U.S. citizen military service personnel and noncitizens, addressed two of these reasons. One of these was the obligation that the military owed to the parents of young soldiers to "duplicate the wholesome influences of the home, family, and community."[19] Expressly stating that the regulations are not intended to proscribe marriage, S.R. 600–240–5 explained that the policy and regulations were adopted "to protect the individual from the possibility disastrous effects of an impetuous marriage entered into without a full appreciation of its implications and obligations."[20] Thus, from this perspective, the regulations furthered the military's desire to protect its personnel and maintain discipline and morale in the service.

The other reason addressed the mandate of federal immigration laws. Specifically, the U.S. armed forces sought to avoid potential marital problems that may be caused by the spouse's inability to immigrate to the United States. These problems included the "prospect of wholesale divorce and broken homes which would be the inevitable result if large numbers of alien wives failed to qualify for admission" to the United States.[21] Grounds for inadmissibility included ineligibility for citizenship, physical, mental, or character standards, and potential to be a public charge.

Indeed, S.R. 600–240–5 explicitly acknowledged the reliance on immigration law for the basis of approving a service personnel's application for marriage. It explained that the military's policy was to approve an application for marriage between a military personnel and a noncitizen would be given "due examination and consideration do not indicate that the alien fiancée would certainly or probably be barred from entry to the United States" under immigration laws. Importantly, S.R. 600–240–5 explains

---

[16] *See* Reese, 122 C.M.R. at 614.
[17] *See* Dana Michael Hollywood, *An End to "DEROS Do Us Part": The Army's Regulation of International Marriages in Korea*, 200 MIL. L. REV. 154 (2009) (examining the history of military directions that limited service personnel's right to marry).
[18] U.S. War Dep't, Circ. No. 179, Sec. 1 (June 8, 1942)..
[19] DEP'T ARMY AND AIR FORCE, S.R. 600–240–5, AFR 34–12, 3.
[20] *See id.* at 5.
[21] *See id.* at 3. The military seemed concerned also for the service personnel who might not be "aware of the probable inadmissibility" of their wives.

that "the screening of applications for permission to marry by the commander is *substantially similar to the processing of requests for entry of alien wives* and that lack of command approval is indicative of probably unfavorable action by the United States consul and the Commissioner of Immigration and Naturalization."[22]

As this evidences, commanding officers essentially functioned as both military supervisor and immigration officer. Under SR 600–240, the fiancee's anticipated inadmissibility constituted an "unnatural obstacle … to a lasting marriage" and required the commanding officer to reconsider an application for marriage at another time. By contrast, those whose applications have been approved by commanding officers received assistance from the military in securing visas and other immigration-related documents.

The formal requirements for obtaining approval for marriage were substantial. Applicants needed to take marriage counseling classes and interviews with a chaplain. They also needed to submit several documents including an affidavit of intent to marry, copies of financial statements, written consent of parents where appropriate, and character references. The commanding officer was required to examine all the documents submitted in support of the application for marriage and conduct a subjective assessment of the probable success of marriage before granting approval.[23]

Military Restrictions on Marriage and Interracial Relationships

In the play titled "Impressionism," the main character, Katherine Kennan, asks her friend, Thomas Buckle, "Do you see life as a realist or a impressionist?" Thomas replies, "As a realist." Kennan responds, "No, don't you see? Life is like an impressionist painting; only once we take a step back do we see what the true meaning is."[24] As invoked in this play, Impressionism offers a different way of viewing a work of art. To fully appreciate an Impressionist painting, one needs to examine the whole painting rather than its individual parts.

Similarly, to completely comprehend the ways in which the federal government regulated interracial marriage outside of the U.S. borders, particularly in Japan, it is necessary to take a step back and look at the big picture. The three distinct areas of law examined previously each had different legislative and regulatory aims that, on their face, had little to do with restricting mixed marriage. Yet by focusing less on the individual laws and examining instead their broad interactions with each other, one gains a complete understanding of how the federal government regulated marriages

---

[22] *See id.* at 4.d
[23] U.S. War Dep't, Circ. No. 179, Sec. 1.
[24] IMPRESSIONISM (Oscar Productions 2009).

based on race.[25] Specifically, viewing the three laws and regulations as a whole, one sees that they converged in ways that enabled them to prohibit interracial couples from marrying and thus enjoying the rights, benefits, and privileges of marriage. Formal restrictions on marriage facilitated the denial of marriage requests by military service personnel to marry racially inadmissible fiancées. In particular, commanding officers cited immigration inadmissibility rules to deny applications for marriage.

Thus, federal employees enforced the proscription against interracial marriages in foreign lands. The need to seek permission was akin to the ways in which interracial couples had to apply for and obtain a license to get married in a state. Records from the period indicate that many requests of soldiers on behalf of their "different race" spouses were rejected. In some instances, the military "punished" the soldiers by transferring them to another station, separating couples prior to their union.

Those who were able to get married faced the next obstacle to their union – the ability of the wife to immigrate to the United States. For the majority of spouses of European descent, admission to the United States was not a problem. Indeed, the majority of war brides came from Europe. In all, the War Brides Act facilitated the immigration of thousands of noncitizens. Between 1946 and 1950, more than 114,000 brides entered the United States. The majority of them (84,517) were from Europe, although there were also quite a number of Canadians (7,254) and Australians and New Zealanders (7,678) who were admitted as war brides as well.[26]

To be sure, the War Brides Act did enable Asian wives to enter the United States. By 1945, changes to citizenship law enabled some Asians to be admitted to the United States. Chinese nationals became eligible for citizenship in 1943, and Filipinos and South Asian Indians were allowed to become U.S. citizens in 1946.[27] Yet, eligibility for citizenship did not necessarily lead to significant immigration for Chinese, Filipinos, and Indians because of strict quota laws per country. Indeed, because few visas were available to Chinese nationals, Congress passed a law in 1946 that "place[d] Chinese wives of American citizens on a nonquota basis."[28]

Overall, Asian wives had among the lowest number of immigrant entries.[29] Between 1946 and 1950, only 9,246 Asians entered as war brides. The largest group

---

[25] As Melissa Murray has argued in a different context, by examining the ways in which laws (such as criminal law and family law) work together, we gain a deeper understanding of the ways in which our intimate lives are formed and shaped. *See* Melissa Murray, *Strange Bedfellows: Criminal Law, Family Law, and the Legal Construction of Intimate Life,* 94 Iowa L. Rev. 1253, 1257 (2009).

[26] CITE.

[27] 79 Pub. L. 482, 60 Stat. 416 (1946).

[28] Pub. L. No. 713, 79th Cong., First Sess., Aug. 9, 1945.

[29] Asian war brides were not the smallest group. There were only 907 from Africa. There were also 2,080 from Mexico. *See* INS Statistics, 1946–1950.

comprised of Chinese, which had 5,726 women. As Xiaojian Zhao has explained, however, many of these women were not "war brides" whose marriages were formed during World War II.[30] Most of them had been married to Chinese and Chinese-American husbands for several years prior to their husbands' service in the war. Indeed, some had been married for ten to twenty years. Thus, for Chinese women, the War Bride Act opened the door to the United States that was previously closed by the Chinese Exclusion Act.

Those married to Japanese encountered the most significant barrier to having their wives enter the United States. Japanese nationals continued to be ineligible to acquire U.S. citizenship and were thus not admissible to the United States. Accordingly, Japanese spouses were unable to enter unless some other legislation made it possible for them to do so.

The Promotion of White Supremacy Beyond U.S. Borders

The federal government's role in restricting interracial marriages reveals that the promotion of white supremacy through marriage restrictions was far broader than originally perceived in legal history. The combination of immigration law, citizenship, and military laws and regulations served at least two functions. First, it promoted white domination by extending the reach of antimiscegenation laws outside of the U.S. borders. Second, it reinforced the separation of interracial couples by seeking to exclude racially inadmissible Japanese at the border. Although Congress ultimately allowed Japanese wives and husbands to enter the United States, it did so for a limited period only, demonstrating the federal government's resistance to opening the borders to Japanese-White interracial couples.

In 1947, Congress amended the War Brides Act to lift the racial ban against the admission of Japanese to the United States.[31] In passing the amendment, Congress expressly stated that the "alien spouse of an American citizen ... shall not be considered as inadmissible because of race, if otherwise admissible under this Act."[32] Indeed, Congress recognized that the racial exclusion of Japanese affected not only interracial couples but monoracial couples as well:

> Those alien spouses, however, who are racially ineligible for citizenship are barred from admission to the United States for permanent residence. As an example, a number of United States citizen soldiers of the Japanese or Korean race have

---

[30] See Zhao, *supra* n.10, at 82.
[31] Act of July 22, 1947, Pub. L. No. 213, 61 Stat. 401 (1947) (amending the War Brides Act to allow spouses who are otherwise racially inadmissible to be admitted to the United States).
[32] *Id. See also* Sen. R. No. 501 (1947) (explaining that the purpose of the bill was "to permit the racially inadmissible spouses of United States citizen members of the armed forces").

married girls of their own race while serving in the Pacific. ... One court on the west coast ruled that a GB bride of the half-Japanese race should be admitted to the United States. However, the Department of Justice appealed that decision and the Circuit Court of Appeals for the Ninth Circuit sustained the appeal of the Department of Justice.[33]

The amendment to the War Brides Act thus lifted the ban against the entry of Japanese to the United States that Congress set into law in 1924. By allowing "racially inadmissible spouses" – albeit briefly – to enter the United States, the amendment to the War Brides Act constituted the first step toward overturning the racial exclusion of Japanese, which it ultimately did in 1952.[34]

It should be noted, however, that the amendment's scope was narrow. Congress imposed a date upon which the marriage had to have occurred.[35] The marriages had to have been entered into no later than thirty days after the passage of the law.[36] No such restrictions were imposed on marriages of any other couples. Notably, the imposition of a deadline on marriage was intricately tied to discouraging interracial marriages between White citizens and Japanese. Congress explained that the restriction was necessary "in order not to encourage marriages between United States citizen service people and racially inadmissible aliens."[37] A few years later, in 1950, Congress enacted yet another amendment to the War Brides Act.[38] Similar to the 1947 amendment, the 1950 change to the War Brides Act imposed a deadline, underscoring the law's ability to discourage interracial marriages.

CONCLUSION

In the 1957 film titled "Sayonara," Marlon Brando plays an Army officer, Major Lloyd Gruver, who falls in love with Hana-ogi, a Japanese woman, while Gruver is stationed in Japan during the Korean War.[39] Initially harboring reservations about interracial relationships between white soldiers and Japanese women, Gruver

[33] SEN. R. No. 501 (1947), at 2.
[34] Immigration and Nationality Act (McCarran-Walter) Act of 1952, ch. 477, tit. IV, 403(a)(23), 66 Stat. 163, 279.
[35] SEN. R. No. 501 (1947), at 2. In 1950, Congress passed yet another amendment that, notwithstanding "section 13(c) of the Immigration Act of 1924 [Japanese exclusion], alien spouses or unmarried minor children of United States citizen serving in, or ... honorable discharged ... if otherwise admissible under immigration laws, be eligible to enter the United States with nonquota immigration visas." Pub. L. No. 717, Aug. 19, 1950.
[36] Pub. L. No. 213, 61 Stat. 401, 80th Cong., 1st Sess., July 22, 1947.
[37] SEN. R. No. 501 (1947), at 2; H.R. Rep. No. 501 (1947), at 2.
[38] Act of Aug. 19, 1950, ch. 759, Pub. L. No. 81–717, 64 Stat. 464 (permitting the admission of alien spouses and alien minor children).
[39] The film was based on James A. Michener's novel, SAYONARA (1954).

eventually wants to marry Hana-ogi. Military policies, however, proscribe interracial couples from getting married and, as explained in the film, violation of the policy constitutes insubordination and can lead to a court-martial. Despite the policy, the film shows that interracial marriages did occur. Among the soldiers who defy the policy is Gruver's best friend, Joe Kelley, who marries Katsumi. When the military issues an official rule requiring the soldiers to return to the United States without their Japanese wives, Kelley and Katsumi become despondent about their eventual separation. Tragically, they commit double suicide. Their deaths lead the Army to change its antimiscegenation policy. The end of the film highlights Gruver and Hana-ogi's decision to get married.

Shown at a time when state antimiscegenation laws were valid, "Sayonara" boldly depicted barriers to marriage in a different context.[40] Race discourse in the 1950s focused primarily on Whites and Blacks, who were prevented from getting married in some states because of state antimiscegenation laws. "Sayonara" complicated this chronicle by illustrating how racial proscriptions against interracial marriages transcended state and, indeed, national borders. Specifically, the film underscored the ways in which the federal government implemented and thus reinforced antimiscegenation laws beyond the U.S. borders through the promulgation of military policies.

[40] The film's depiction of interracial romance received positive reception from film critics and moviegoers, having received five Academy nominations and two Academy Awards. This was a remarkable achievement from the perspective of race and the law. The film predated the Supreme Court case, *Loving v. Virginia*, which invalidated antimiscegenation laws, and another film about interracial relationships, "Guess Who's Coming to Dinner," both of which came out in 1967.

15

The Military and Interracial Marriage

Nancy K. Ota

This chapter supplements our historical view of restrictions on mixed marriages and relationships by exploring the impact of social norms and state law on the regulation of sexualized relationships in the U.S. military. The specific focus of this essay will be interracial, heterosexual, and transnational relationships from the Spanish-American War through the first half of the twentieth century, a period of significant economic and social change that included overseas military operations during the Spanish-American War, three major U.S. Marine Corps interventions in the Caribbean and Central America, World War I, and World War II. These operations led to interracial encounters between White GIs and local women of color in the Philippine Islands, the Caribbean, and East Asia, and between GIs of color and White women in the United Kingdom, Europe, and Australia. I call for a deeper exploration of the ways in which the military regulated sexual relations between male soldiers and foreign women, particularly women of color, in order to illuminate the varied ways that marriage was policed along racial lines.

This chapter begins by outlining the military regulatory framework governing private sexual conduct. It continues with a description of the social context and specific details about heterosexual encounters during overseas military operations prior to the Korean War. This section primarily focuses on interracial relationships and encounters involving marriage. The circumstances where these encounters take place involve the sometimes volatile mix of young men emerging from long periods of hypermasculine social isolation and young women ready to extend some form of hospitality. These circumstances created situations where policies about race, gender, class, nationality, and sex could potentially clash and force a shift in the underlying values. The incidents show how, instead of clashing, a neat alignment of values reinforced and upheld a particular view of American citizenship. Importantly, they illuminate the ways in which legal and cultural norms about interracial relationships within the United States affected the military's regulation of interracial relationships in foreign lands.

MILITARY DISCIPLINE AND PRIVATE SEXUAL CONDUCT

The military is "a specialized society separate from civilian society." Additionally, it has a jurisprudence that "exists separate and apart from the law which governs in our federal judicial establishment."[1] During the period at question, the military regulated offenses, such as private sexual conduct, through a three-tiered court-martial system in accordance with the rules set forth by the Army's Articles of War, the Articles for the Government of the Navy, and various orders.[2] One officer adjudicated proceedings at the lowest level – the summary court-martial – which limited punishment to confinement or solitary confinement for up to one month and forfeiture of two-thirds pay for one month.[3] The special court-martial involved at least three officers and allowed imposition of more severe punishment including up to six months confinement and forfeiture of six months' pay. General courts-martial were convened to handle more serious violations or charges against officers. A general court-martial required five officers. Depending on the violation, a court-martial could end with the imposition of the maximum penalty: capital punishment.[4]

At the heart of these regulations is military morale aimed at maintaining obedience and discipline – that is, a commander's ability or power to control his troops. At war, military leaders do not want troops to question orders; they just want them carried out. It is through discipline and obedience that this end is met. Military leaders achieve this discipline in a variety of ways. Most obviously, good conduct is rewarded with promotion and other rewards, and bad conduct is punished. In addition, and in contrast to the studio images of drill sergeants barking out orders, most military leaders maintain morale through "professional paternalism,"[5] uniformity, and routine, which generate the esprit de corps. Members of the armed forces must set aside their individualism for the military team, which stands ready to protect that individualism.[6]

The Armed Forces regulate private conduct including many aspects of military personnel's intimate relationships, over which civilians have near autonomy or are

[1] Parker v. Levy, 417 U.S. 733, 743 (1974). The Constitution bestows Congress with plenary power over the military. U.S. Const. art. I, § 8, cl. 14.
[2] In 1947, Congress consolidated the service branches under the Department of Defense, National Security Act of 1947, 61 Stat. 495, and in 1950, Congress enacted the Uniform Code of Military Justice, Act of May 5, 1950, 64 Stat. 107. Capt. Jay M. Siegel, Origins of the Navy Judge Advocate General's Corps: A History of Legal Administration in the United States Navy, 1775 to 1967, 2–5 (1997).
[3] *See, e.g.*, Edwin C. McNeil, *United States Army Courts-Martial in Britain: Judge Advocate Section, European Theatre of Operations, U.S. Army*, 60 L. Q. Rev. 356 (1944) (citing the Articles of War, ch. 227, 41 Stat. 789 (1920)).
[4] *See id.*
[5] Lawrence B. Radine, THE TAMING OF THE TROOPS: SOCIAL CONTROL IN THE UNITED STATES ARMY 75 (1977).
[6] NEW SOLDIER'S HANDBOOK 254 (1942).

normally left unregulated. Regulating sexual relationships in the military is justified in order to maintain morale and discipline. Engaging in sexual relationships
with local women while posted in a foreign country often meant that military personnel had to maneuver around regulations governing marriage, prostitution, and
criminal activity such as rape. The military regulations did not officially condone
prostitution, rape, or marriage. Prostitution and rape were outside the boundaries
of legality, whereas regulations and commanders seriously impeded or discouraged
the marriage of sailors and soldiers.[7] The rationale for these measures was that service personnel would not be distracted by personal problems arising from marriage
or prolonged separation from family. In addition, the restrictions worked to prevent
rash decisions during periods of conflict.

Regulation of marriage and commercial sex among soldiers, sailors, and marines
was also effected through legal and social controls arising outside of the military.
The military regulations governing overseas relationships worked in tandem with
immigration laws and state marriage laws.[8] Immigration laws impeded many relationships because of the restrictions on migration from certain parts of the world.[9]
Even if the relationship could overcome the immigration law hurdle, couples also
had to deal with state marriage laws that prohibited interracial marriage and sexual relationships in more than half of the states.[10] In harmony with social taboos
against interracial marriage, the three legal systems operated to curtail the ability of
American soldiers, marines, and sailors to establish permanent legal relationships
with women overseas.[11]

MILITARY'S MARRIAGE RESTRICTIONS

Between the end of the nineteenth century through the Korean War, roughly 27
million men served in the various branches of the U.S. military machine. A large
proportion of them served overseas. Among these men, approximately 1.5 million

[7] *See* Roger W. Little, THE MILITARY FAMILY, in HANDBOOK OF MILITARY INSTITUTIONS 248 (Roger W. Little ed., 1971).
[8] I explore the regulation of overseas marriage in the military in Nancy K. Ota, Loving Off Base (unpub-lished manuscript) (available with the editors).
[9] Immigration exclusion laws focused on migration from Asia. For example, the Immigration Act of February 5, 1917 prohibited immigration from the Asiatic barred zone that included India, Siam, Indo-China, Afghanistan, Asian Russia, Asian Arabia, New Guinea, Borneo, Sumatra, Java, and other islands. Immigration Act of February 5, 1917, § 3, 39 Stat. 874.
[10] Thirty states had antimiscegenation laws on the books during World War I and World War II. Fourteen of these states prohibited marriage between Whites and Asians. See Ota, *supra* n.8.
[11] Maria Höhn, GIs AND FRäULEINS, 103–107 (2002) (discussing the social anxieties in postwar Germany arising from the American occupation and interracial sexual relationships among Black GIs and White German women).

were men of color.[12] Additionally, overseas duty included locations in countries populated primarily by people of color. The various military missions created occasions for sexualized relationships of which the U.S. military was well aware and regulated. The circumstances created opportunities for cross-national, interracial relationships involving American soldiers and women in Europe, Asia, Latin America, the Caribbean, and Africa. The relationships often took place within the context of a colonizer in the colony or of the liberator or protector of freedom in the freed or protected country. Also, the relationships took place in countries that did not have the de jure legacy of slavery found in the United States, namely Jim Crow and anti-miscegenation statutes.[13]

Until World War II, the military neither forbid nor encouraged marriage. In 1896, Brigadier General William Dunn noted that an order forbidding a soldier to contract marriage would be an unlawful command.[14] But in 1939, youthful officers were denied the privilege to marry.[15] The justification for the prohibition was that marriage was a financial burden, and preoccupation with the problem of supporting a wife decreased the officer's value to the government.[16]

Before World War I, marriages arising out of military presence in foreign countries appeared to be influenced most by social norms. Taboos against interracial marriage, reinforced by state laws and eugenicists' beliefs, created a strong case against interracial marriage. By the time of the Spanish-American War, the Supreme Court had weighed in against interracial relationships with its decision in *Pace v. Alabama*.[17] African-American soldiers reportedly married Cuban women and Filipinas,[18] but the

---

[12] Roughly 10,000 African-American soldiers served during the Spanish-American War. During World War I, approximately 12,000 Indians, at least 5,800 Mexicans and Mexican Americans, and 367,000 African Americans served. And nearly 1 million African Americans served in the armed forces through the Korean War. *See*, The New York Public Library American History Desk Reference 138, 149–51 (1997).

[13] Antimiscegenation statutes in many states not only covered interracial marriage, but also prohibited interracial cohabitation and fornication. For example, the Florida statute in question in McLaughlin v. Florida concerned interracial cohabitation. 379 U.S. 184, 186 (1964). This case marked the beginning of the Supreme Court's dismantling of antimiscegenation laws. The Court declined to extend its holding to cohabitation. Instead, it found that Florida's parallel law banning interracial marriage was unconstitutional and limited its decision to the law's effect on nonmarital sex. See id. at 195.

[14] *See* Lt. Martin Drobac, *Regulation of Marriage Overseas*, 15 Jag J. 183 (1961); see also Richard B. Johns, *The Right to Marry: Infringement by the Armed Forces*, 10 Fam. L.Q. 357, 359–60 (1977).

[15] *See* Act of July 25, 1939, 53 Stat. 1074 (1939). The Secretary of War was authorized to revoke the commission of any officer who married within one year after the date of receiving his commission.

[16] *See* Sen. Rep. 1190 to accompany S2380, 77th Cong. 2d Sess. (Mar. 23, 1942) (statement of Sec. of War Stimson commenting on a bill to suspend all prohibitions against marriage for the duration of the war).

[17] 106 U.S. 583 (1882) (upholding Alabama's statute punishing interracial adultery and fornication against an equal protection challenge).

[18] *See* Willard B. Gatewood, Jr., "Smoked Yankees" And The Struggle For Empire: Letters From Negro Soldiers, 1898–1902, 184 (1987) (at least two dozen Negro soldiers married "Cuban señoritas").

record is unclear about marriages for White soldiers. One might guess that very few marriages occurred between White soldiers and Filipinas because the "dark-skinned" Filipinos were viewed as savages, and according to one correspondent, "the White soldiers, unfortunately, got on badly with the natives."[19] In Haiti, all of the Marines were White, and other Americans treated the few who married Haitian women as outcasts.[20]

Approximately 140,000 African Americans would serve in France during World War I. Military officials did not actively prohibit marriage among GIs, but they did make it difficult for African Americans to socialize with the French. The Secretary of War and the Judge Advocate General expressed reluctance to prohibit marriages among French women and GIs, especially when the women became pregnant.[21] The Army did not keep statistics on the number of marriages, although one officer estimates that between 1,000 and 2,000 African-American soldiers married French women. I would speculate that some number of these soldiers returned to France. The combination of restrictions on social interaction, the improbability that a commanding officer would authorize marriage, the relentless humiliation inflicted by White Americans, the hostile social climate back home, and the relatively positive reception in France may have influenced a Black soldier to return to France and join the African-American expatriate community.[22]

The Army's position on marriage changed under the War Department's Operating Circular No. 179, which stated, "No military personnel on duty in any foreign country or possession may marry without the approval of the commanding officer of the United States Army forces stationed in such foreign country or possession."[23] Under this order, a commanding officer could and did forbid certain marriages.

The main justification for denying marriage under this order was the military's interest in maintaining discipline and morale. The military did not want its members distracted by personal problems that arise in military marriages, such as a lengthy separation from family. In addition, policy makers believed the stress of military service during war led to hasty and careless decisions. These decisions are more

---

Capt. Crumbley of the 49th Infantry wrote about business opportunities for African Americans in the Philippines and stated: "[a]s a rule they are well liked by the peaceable natives and many of them will ask for their discharges with a view of staying over here, and will marry native women as soon as they are free of Uncle Sam." *Id.* at 296.

[19] Willard B. Gatewood, Jr., BLACK AMERICANS AND THE WHITE MAN'S BURDEN 1898–1903, 280 (1975). Gatewood also quotes several other reports of racial prejudice among White soldiers who viewed and treated Filipinos the same as "niggers." *See id.* at 281.

[20] Hans Schmidt, THE UNITED STATES OCCUPATION OF HAITI: 1915–1934, 140 (1995).

[21] *See* Letter from Sec. of War Newton D. Baker to Hon. James W. Wadsworth, Jr., in Sen. Rep. No. 295, Marriage of Persons in Military or Naval Forces of the United States in Foreign Countries, 66th Cong., 1st Sess., Nov. 3, 1919.

[22] *See* Tyler Stovall, Paris Noir: African Americans in the City of Light 1–24 (1996).

[23] Op. Circ. No. 179, June 8, 1942, National Archives, RG 165 Entry 418 Box 470.

complicated when they involve cross-cultural or interracial relationships. Apart from the anticipated problems stemming from social and cultural differences, couples also encountered legal impediments to their marriages. Through World War II, thirty states had antimiscegenation laws on the books. Additionally, the military's marriage restriction served to protect the policy objectives of federal laws governing military benefits and immigration.[24] In the case of overseas marriage, restrictive immigration laws were formidable obstacles for many couples.[25]

After the implementation of marriage restrictions in World War II, one might expect that the number of marriages would have been relatively low. But the military would experience an explosion in the number of war-bride relationships because of the huge number of Americans who served overseas during and immediately after the war. Twelve million Americans served in the military during World War II.[26] The relationships developed in at least sixty-one countries spanning five continents. Estimates of the actual number of marriages range from 100,000 to 750,000. Most marriages occurred between GIs and women in Britain, Australia, continental Europe, China, the Philippines, and Japan.[27] The Immigration and Naturalization Service (INS) reported that nearly 150,000 Asian wives of U.S. citizens entered the United States between 1945 and 1970. Of these, more than 55,000 came from Japan and nearly 14,000 from Korea.[28]

War-bride marriages involved intra-racial relationships formed in Europe and Australia among White GIs and local women. In Europe and Australia, Black GIs had to overcome local intolerance to interracial relationships in addition to having to deal with White American GIs exercising Jim Crow social control. Violence and harassment from within the newly integrated ranks continued to plague soldiers of color and hampered their ability to interact with European women. Moreover, commanders who wanted to discourage interracial relationships from further development could simply transfer the soldier.[29] The Court of Military Appeals struck

---

[24] Military courts have upheld legal challenges to the marriage restrictions under the broad Constitutional authority delegated to commanding officers. See U.S. v. Parker, 5 M.J. 922 (1978); U.S. v. Wheeler, 30 C.M.R. 387 (1961); U.S. v. Levinsky, 30 C.M.R. 541 (1960).

[25] The primary provisions to have an impact on overseas marriage were the Asian exclusion and the quota restrictions. The impact of these provisions following World War II was diminished by the enactment of the War Brides Act. Yet, as Rose Cuison Villazor argues, restrictions on the entry of Japanese women continued even after the passage of the War Brides Act. See Rose Cuison Villazor, The Other Loving: Uncovering the Federal Restrictions on Interracial Marriages (unpublished manuscript).

[26] See N.Y. TIMES 1999 ALMANAC 149 (John W. Wright ed., 1997).

[27] See Ota, *supra* n.8.

[28] See INS Annual Reports 1945–1970.

[29] See Elfrieda Berthiaume Shukert & Barbara Smith Scibetta, WAR BRIDES OF WORLD WAR II 29 (1988) (discussing a Chinese-American soldier who was transferred because of his race after being denied permission to marry an Englishwoman he met in Manchester).

down rules with excessive requirements before permission to marry was granted.[30] Nevertheless, commanders had many reasons for denying permission to marry and could do so with impunity. In Europe and Asia, a commanding officer's, or in some cases a chaplain's, subjective assessment of the probable success of a marriage was the primary consideration before granting permission. The commanding officer's discretionary decision determined the viability of an interracial marriage and the ability of a foreign woman to assimilate into American society. The officer could determine that, based on antimiscegenation laws, the marriage would not legally survive.[31] Several of the western states with antimiscegenation laws barred marriages between Whites and Asians, and all of the states with antimiscegenation laws barred marriages between Whites and Blacks. Even if the GI was headed to a state without an antimiscegenation law, the officer or chaplain could project his own misgivings about interracial marriage and refuse permission because he did not believe the couple could survive the difficulties they would face at home. If the immigration laws would not allow the bride to immigrate to the United States, the commander could likewise determine the marriage had little chance of success. The key ground for inadmissibility affecting war brides was the Asian exclusion provision, but other women were barred from admission to the United States on the ground that they were security risks.[32]

DISPARITY IN MARRIAGE

Unlike prior military operations in countries populated predominantly by people of color, the war and occupation in the Pacific yielded a significant number of interracial marriages involving White soldiers. Although the military occupations of Haiti and East Asia occurred in distinct periods, the elimination of legal restrictions on interracial marriage was not yet viable by the time American military forces occupied Japan and Korea. At least part of the reason for the large number of marriages in Japan was the length of the occupation. However, comparing the seven-year occupation of Japan to the nearly twenty-year occupation of Haiti raises questions regarding White soldiers' willingness to intermarry with Japanese women and not with black women. The cultural gaps between Americans and Japanese were arguably

---

[30] See United States v. Nation, 26 C.M.R. 504, 508 (1958) (holding the requirements for marriage to be too broad and unreasonable to sustain the prosecution of a sailor for marrying a Filipina woman without permission). This case was decided outside of the time frame of this essay, but offers some guidance regarding the limits that a commanding officer could go to before infringing on military personnel's private right to marry.

[31] See, e.g., 24 Op. LA Att'y Gen. 240 (1949) ("A marriage in another state between a person of the White race and a person of the colored race who is domiciled in Louisiana is not recognized in Louisiana as a valid marriage.").

[32] See, e.g., United States ex rel. Knauff v. Shaughnessy, 338 U.S. 537, 552 (1950) (denying admission to the United States on security grounds).

wider than the gaps between Americans and Haitians. The deep level of hostility between the United States and Japan was not a factor preceding the Marine Corps' arrival in Haiti. Both of these factors would seem to facilitate a closer relationship between Haitians and Americans.

A few factors may explain the disparity in intermarriage. Foremost would be the numbers. The occupation troops numbered around 2,000 in Haiti and around 500,000 in Japan.[33] In addition, after the Marines gained control of Haiti and with the diversion of the Marines to Europe during World War I, their numbers dropped to approximately 600. The Japanese had suffered defeat at the American's hands and were not in the position to resist.[34] On the other hand, the Marine occupation of Haiti was more of an imperialist intervention in a country that had a history of anticolonial revolt, and a portion of the population committed to resisting the American intervention. Race differences also played a role. That is, the salience of race in marital relationships reflected in American antimiscegenation laws made it impossible for the Marines in Haiti to overcome the overwhelming repugnance of Black-White intermarriage.

The increase in the number of interracial marriages involving GIs following World War II does not, however, reflect a significant change in notions of the White privilege. In spite of the military regulations, immigration restrictions, and social stigma confronting interracial couples, thousands of GIs sought permission to marry Asian Pacific Islander (API) women.[35] Once granted permission to marry by a commanding officer or once married without permission, hundreds of GIs were forced to petition for private bills from Congress in order to bring their families to the states.[36] The private bills had a twofold impact: they enabled entry of Asian women otherwise banned from migrating to the United States, and the sheer volume of the petitions encouraged Congress to revise the exclusion law. The romantic sexual relationships portrayed in the petitions had a legitimizing force. That is, the approved petitions described relationships that promoted patriarchal nuclear family values and assured the continuation of the dominance of an American identity as White, heterosexual, male, and Christian.[37]

---

[33] J. Robert Moskin, THE U.S. MARINE CORPS STORY 177 (1982).

[34] William Manchester, AMERICAN CAESAR 116 (1978).

[35] Some of the GIs who married API women were African American or Asian American. These couples did not pose a threat to the racial order in the same way that White-Asian or White-Black couples might. *See* Ota, *supra* n 8.

[36] The private bill enacted a law granting a personal exemption from immigration restrictions. *See* Bernadette Maguire, IMMIGRATION: PUBLIC LEGISLATION AND PRIVATE BILLS 1–3 (1997). Private bills enacted by Congress were at their highest level in the early 1950s. *See id.* at 70. Most of the enactments concerned quota limitations and racial exclusion. *See id.* at 71–79.

[37] *See* Nancy K. Ota, *Private Matters: Family and Race and the Post-World-War-II Translation of "American,"* 46 INT'L REV. OF SOC. HIST. SUPP. 209 (2001) (discussing the private bill petitions).

CONCLUSION

GIs' intimate interracial relationships were affected by a web of laws governing marriage, the military, and immigration. The stated concern for social stigma and cultural differences was a transparent attempt to cover underlying racism. The power of White privilege in the formation of race in the United States is exemplified by Asian war brides' initial exclusion from the benefits of the War Brides Act and continues long after their exclusion was challenged. The private bill petitions that overcame the limits on the immigration of Asian wives demonstrate how, by pledging allegiance to American values, Asian women could be transplanted to the United States, thereby shedding some of their foreignness. The entry of Asians into the United States and their renewed entry into American consciousness in the late 1940s and early 1950s marked the beginning stages of the Asian-American journey to the "model minority" status. And even though Asian Americans continue to be perceived as foreign – that is, not American – they serve the purpose of a foil to African-American complaints of racism. More importantly, the success of the model minority bolsters a meritocractic domain where full citizenship rights that accompany substantive equality are available to those who can identify as not foreign and not Black.

Granting permission to immigrate should not lead you to conclude that the couples were welcomed with open arms when they settled in the United States. *See* Jan Breslauer, *Hues and Cries for Playwright Velina Hasu Houston*, L.A. TIMES, July 7, 1991, at 3 (noting that "[t]he society at large did not welcome the Japanese women").

16

Loving Across the Miles

Binational Same-Sex Marriages and the Supreme Court

Victor C. Romero

In May 2004, the *Los Angeles Times* reported a surge in travel to Massachusetts by many gay and lesbian couples, hoping to capitalize on that state's monumental decision to be the first to recognize same-sex marriages. At least one couple chose not participate in the mass nuptials: Austin Naughton, an American, and his partner of many years, a Spanish national here on a temporary non-immigrant visa, decided not to wed for fear that this act would signal an intent to permanently reside in the United States. Under the Immigration and Nationality Act ("INA"), noncitizen who are in the United States on a temporary basis would be considered in violation of their status if they manifest any intent of remaining in the country permanently. As Naughton put it, "If we marry, he could be deported."[1]

Like Naughton, U.S. citizen Richard Adams has a partner who is also a foreign national, but from Australia. This man, Tony Sullivan, has a long-expired visa, and so Adams and Sullivan are "fugitives" from the U.S. Immigration and Customs Enforcement ("ICE") bureau, which is part of the U.S. Department of Homeland Security, the federal agency that enforces the INA. If discovered, Sullivan would, most likely, be removed from the country and thus separated from Adams for several years. Accordingly, the couple keeps a low profile and lives quietly somewhere in the United States. More than twenty years ago, Adams and Sullivan had sued the predecessor to ICE, the Immigration and Naturalization Service (INS), arguing that their receipt of a marriage license in Colorado allowed Adams to petition for Sullivan's "immediate relative" status as his "spouse." The INA allows U.S. citizens and legal permanent residents (LPR) to sponsor their spouses to permanently immigrate to the United States. In affirming the INS's rejection of Adams's petition, the

---

[1] Elizabeth Mehren, *Massachusetts Begins Allowing Gays to Wed*, L.A. TIMES, May 17, 2004, at A10. As of this writing, only Massachusetts, Connecticut, Iowa, New Hampshire, New York, and Vermont give equal marriage rights to hetero- and homosexual couples; California and Maine remain battleground states.

Ninth Circuit in *Adams v. Howerton*[2] ruled that although the INA did not define the term "spouse," the INS's decision to limit its reach to heterosexual relationships was "rational."[3] As a consequence, Adams and Sullivan have never been able to fully receive the blessings of liberty that other American couples enjoy.[4] Sullivan attributes their present financial difficulties to his "outlaw" status: "We would probably own our own home. We both love to travel. We would have been able to travel. I would have been a professional of some kind."[5]

In this chapter, I explore the connections between the obstacles to both marriage and freedom of movement experienced by binational same-sex couples[6] because of both anti-same-sex marriage and immigration laws, and those encountered by Richard and Mildred Loving and other interracial couples as a result of antimiscegenation laws. As I explain more fully later in the chapter, the Lovings' situation is a story of migration. It is a border-crossing tale that parallels and sheds light on the struggles of binational same-sex partners today who face barriers to marriage and its attendant benefits and privileges. Specifically, I argue that the hardships faced by gay and lesbian couples who want to legitimize their relationships through state-recognized marriage mirror the struggles of interracial couples during the heyday of the civil rights movement. Both race and sexual orientation function as barriers to the freedom to marry, and the law uses these traits to limit free movement. Ultimately, it is this freedom of movement – this migration or immigration – that is the focus of this chapter, with particular attention paid to the Supreme Court's role in assessing this freedom. *Loving* reveals the extent to which the Court affirmed the couple's desire for unrestricted physical, legal, and cultural movement – to break barriers erected by the law that restricted their physical movement (they could not live in Virginia, their home state), their legal movement (they could not legally wed within Virginia), and their cultural movement (they could not wed outside of their respective races). Forty years later, Richard Adams and Tony Sullivan, as well as Austin Naughton and his unnamed Spanish partner, face similar physical, legal,

---

[2] 673 F.2d 1036 (9th Cir. 1982). In basing its decision solely on the text of the Immigration and Nationality Act, the Ninth Circuit did not reach the question of whether the couple's marriage was valid under state law. *Id.* at 1038–39.

[3] It is worth noting that, in its original denial of Adams's petition, the INS stated: "You have failed to establish that a bona fide marital relationship can exist between two faggots." Victor C. Romero, ALIENATED: IMMIGRANT RIGHTS, THE CONSTITUTION, AND EQUALITY IN AMERICA 154 (2005).

[4] Aside from the *Adams* case, Congress has also limited the federal definitions of "marriage" and "spouse" to only heterosexuals through the Defense of Marriage Act of 1996 ("DOMA"), providing yet another barrier to binational same-sex couples. 110 Stat. 2416 (1996).

[5] Joyce Murdoch & Deb Price, COURTING JUSTICE: GAY MEN AND LESBIANS V. THE SUPREME COURT 224 (2001).

[6] "Binational couples" refer to relationships in which one partner is either a U.S. citizen or LPR and the other is a noncitizen who does not have permanent legal status in the United States.

and cultural restrictions on their movement because of their sexual orientation. Describing the current difficulties posed by his relationship with Richard Adams, Tony Sullivan aptly put it: "We would have been able to *travel*."

I discuss these three aspects of movement – physical, legal, and cultural – starting with a brief discussion of physical migration in the first section of this chapter. After considering this *physical* aspect of movement, it is the *legal* context of migration that is explored in the second section. I examine the ways in which U.S. immigration law operates to erect barriers to movement that parallel the hardships the Lovings endured under Virginia's antimiscegenation statute. The third section will round out this migration trilogy by exploring the ways in which the Court has addressed the *cultural* migration that has occurred within sexual orientation discourse. Even though progress had been made on the issue of gay rights, the Court's recent decisions suggest that race and sexual orientation may be doomed to follow separate, and hardly ever analogous, paths. I conclude the chapter by offering some thoughts on pending Congressional legislation designed to unite same-sex partners and their families, situating the discussion within the context of the Obama administration's professed commitment to individual rights and the recent same-sex marriage gains in a number of states.

LOVING AS A STORY OF MIGRATION AND PHYSICAL BARRIERS TO MOVEMENT

Perhaps because it is most obvious, the parallel between the immigration struggles of binational same-sex partners and the physical travel engaged in by the Lovings requires little further explication: just as the Lovings were limited in where they could move to and reside, so, too, are Richard Adams and Tony Sullivan similarly limited in their physical movement today. In fact, Adams and Sullivan are in the same position now that the Lovings found themselves in immediately after their Washington, DC marriage and their return to Virginia: living in the shadow of the law, fugitives unable to reside as others would in their communities.

Although the law posed no physical restraint on either the Lovings or Adams and Sullivan, the punitive nature of the then-existing antimiscegenation law in *Loving* and the narrow reading of the immigration code's definition of "spouse" in *Adams v. Howerton* both serve as the functional equivalent of a physical obstacle. Indeed, in the Lovings' case, their violation of Virginia's law led to their incarceration – a palpable restriction of their freedom to move; similarly, should Sullivan's whereabouts be discovered, his deportation to Australia would constitute his physical removal from the United States against his will. The intangible wall of the law is as formidable a force as a tangible barrier, limiting these couples' movements between jurisdictions in much the same way.

LOVING AND LEGAL BARRIERS TO MIGRATION

Apart from examining how the antimiscegenation laws impeded the Lovings' physical travel, it is likewise important to understand how these state laws compare with the federal immigration statutes that limit the movement of foreign guests in our country. Ultimately, I demonstrate how the different doctrinal approaches between laws that implicate race and laws that govern immigration make it difficult for binational same-sex couples who wish to marry and remain together in the United States to achieve equality in marriage as the Lovings did.

Aside from their ability to restrict movement, Virginia's antimiscegenation statute and current immigration laws preclude couples from availing themselves of benefits bestowed upon similarly situated couples deemed to be validly married under the jurisdiction's laws. Virginia's ban on interracial marriages meant that the Lovings could not lawfully present themselves as a married couple for purposes of, among others, state income tax, inheritance, family, and insurance laws, while white couples could. Similarly, even if their civil union is recognized by Colorado, Adams and Sullivan cannot avail themselves of the myriad *federal* benefits that attach when a U.S. citizen is able to petition lawful permanent residence status for his spouse. The advocacy group Human Rights Campaign estimates that more than 1,100 federal benefits come with the legal status of marriage.[7] There are, therefore, measurable, pecuniary benefits that come with expanding the borders of marriage and immigration law that were denied to the Lovings because of their mixed-race status in 1967 and that continue to be denied to same-sex binational couples some forty years later.

Even as they work similar disabilities upon the couples, there are differences between the antimiscegenation laws at issue in *Loving* and the restrictive immigration laws at work today. Most important, they differ because one is a state law on marriage, whereas the other governs federal law on the movement of noncitizens between the United States and other nations. This basic difference has an impact on both the scope and status of the law in American jurisprudence.

As to scope, state marriage laws govern only their state's residents – indeed, that is why the Lovings traveled to nearby Washington, DC. They knew that the antimiscegenation laws of Virginia held no power over them in the District of Columbia. In contrast, because immigration laws are federal, they have a broader scope, reaching across all fifty states of the Union. Thus, even if Adams and Sullivan were legally

---

[7]   Lambda Legal, *Why Marriage Equality Matters*, at http://www.lambdalegal.org/our-work/ publications/facts-backgrounds/page.jsp?itemID=31988962 (last visited on June 21, 2006) ("Not only does [marriage] bring the stability of a committed relationship, but also more than 1,138 automatic federal and additional state protections, benefits and responsibilities designed to support and protect family life.").

married in Massachusetts, Adams's right to petition Sullivan to immigrate derives solely from his being a U.S. citizen and is, accordingly, governed by one uniform, federal immigration law.

A law's status follows its scope. As state laws, marriage laws are subject to the restrictions of the federal Constitution. Although the Rehnquist Court did much to limit federal power vis-à-vis the sovereign states, it has long been recognized that the Constitution limits what states can do within their own jurisdictions. As Chief Justice Marshall declared in *Marbury v. Madison*, the Constitution is the "supreme law of the land."[8] *Loving* can thus be properly understood as a case in which equality principles enshrined in the Constitution prohibited Virginia's marriage laws from treating U.S. citizens within its territory differently from others based solely on skin color. Federal immigration law, by contrast, enjoys a higher status than state law in American jurisprudence, not because it is superior to state marriage law,[9] but because the Supreme Court has seen fit to defer to Congress's plenary power to regulate immigration matters. Accordingly, the Supreme Court has found few constitutional bases for striking down otherwise discriminatory immigration regulation.

This second difference – the way in which the Supreme Court has treated state law matters less deferentially than immigration law under Due Process and Equal Protection analysis – is worth exploring in more detail. This difference ultimately persuades me that the Supreme Court will likely not find *Loving* particularly useful as a tool for understanding immigration restrictions on binational same-sex relationships.

From *Loving*, we learn that a state may not bless same-race marriages only because the U.S. Constitution forbids such racial discrimination against its citizens, even if they reside within that particular state. This principle has deep roots in an earlier nineteenth-century opinion demonstrating the Court's willingness to tamp down state-sanctioned racial discrimination, even if not facially obvious. In *Yick Wo v. Hopkins*, the Supreme Court used the Fourteenth Amendment's Equal Protection Clause to strike down a San Francisco ordinance that required all laundries to apply for an operating permit because the municipality clearly discriminated against all Chinese laundry operators, even though the ordinance itself was facially neutral.[10] Thus, *Loving* and *Yick Wo* teach us that the Court will not abide state-sponsored racial discrimination either in the writing or the enforcement of a statute.

In immigration law, however, the Court has taken a different path, as demonstrated by a pair of cases decided around the same time as *Yick Wo*. In *Chae Chan Ping v.*

---

[8] 5 U.S. 137, 180 (1803).

[9] Indeed, the doctrine of dual federalism recognizes that the federal and state governments and their laws stand on equal footing, although both are inferior to the U.S. Constitution. *See, e.g.,* Printz v. United States, 521 U.S. 898, 918 (1997) (discussing the doctrine of "dual sovereignty").

[10] 118 U.S. 356 (1886).

United States and *Fong Yue Ting v. United States*, the Court held that, within immigration law, the Supreme Court must defer to the political branches of government, because Congress, and not the Court, is in the best position to create a national policy on immigration.[11] At first glance, this deference seems quite reasonable. The Constitution requires Congress to make a "uniform rule of Naturalization," and immigration rules – those that govern when noncitizens may enter and must leave the United States – are certainly a rational outgrowth of that power.

However, both the *Chae* and *Fong* cases grew out of a national policy, born of xenophobia and economic nativism, that excluded Chinese immigrant workers. In 1882, Congress passed the Chinese Exclusion Act, aimed at putting an end to Chinese immigration that had begun much earlier for the purpose of supplying cheap labor to build the railroads out west. The *Chae* and *Fong* cases examined the scope of Congress's power under the Act.

Chae involved a longtime resident of the United States who, upon learning that he would be returning to China for a visit, obtained permission from the U.S. government to return. At port, Chae presented his credentials to the immigration authorities who, without hearing or adequate explanation, revoked them, excluding Chae from reentering the United States. The Supreme Court held that, as a sovereign nation, the United States had absolute authority to exclude any foreign citizen that it wanted, and that this power resided in the political branches of the federal government. Chae and other noncitizens had no right to be in the United States, and only enjoyed a privilege that could be revoked at will. Justice Field's opinion was replete with racial bias. After favorably describing America's magnanimity in allowing the Chinese to work in the United States, Field lamented that "they remained strangers in the land, residing apart by themselves, and adhering to the customs and usages of their own country. It seemed impossible for them to assimilate with our people, or to make any change in their habits or modes of living."[12]

Fong extended *Chae*'s holding by ruling that Congress had a plenary power to deport noncitizens that was not to be second-guessed by the judiciary. Under the Chinese Deportation Act of 1892, Fong was required to establish that he was a resident of the United States by producing a credible white witness to affirm his claim; he was unable to do so and was ordered deported. Arguing that the white witness provision violated Due Process norms, Fong challenged his deportation, but was rebuffed by the Court. Citing *Chae* extensively, Justice Gray had no trouble finding for the government:

---

[11]   Fong Yue Ting v. United States, 149 U.S. 698 (1893); Chae Chan Ping v. United States, 130 U.S. 581 (1889).
[12]   *Chae Chan Ping*, 130 U.S. at 595

The power to exclude or to expel aliens, being a power affecting international relations, is vested in the political departments of the government, and is to be regulated by treaty or by act of congress, and to be executed by the executive authority
according to the regulations so established, except so far the judicial department
has been authorized by treaty or by statute, or is required by the paramount law of
the constitution, to intervene.[13]

Although *Loving* and *Yick Wo* affirm the Supreme Court's commitment to racial
equality, *Chae* and *Fong*, which have been never overruled, highlight, within the
context of immigration law, the limits of that commitment. While it is true that, in
recent years, the Court has provided basic due process protections to noncitizens,
at least one lower court has recently held that Arab-Muslim plaintiffs who claimed
they have been detained longer than others based solely on their race and religion
may not pursue an equal protection claim for selective prosecution.[14] As in *Chae*
and *Fong*, the court specifically cited the federal political branches' plenary power
over immigration law to justify its dismissal of the plaintiffs' claim.

Because of how our constitutional jurisprudence treats state laws differently from
immigration laws, deferring to the second but not the first, binational same-sex partners will likely have a difficult time using *Loving* to curry favor with justices whose
precedents dictate a political rather than a legal solution to the thorny issue of immigration law. Long-standing precedents like *Chae* and *Fong* have rendered courts wary
of appeals to racial equality within the immigration context, despite being sympathetic
to such arguments when raised to challenge state laws. Indeed, even when litigants
have successfully challenged immigration law provisions that burden marriage, the
plaintiffs have been heterosexual couples, not homosexual ones.[15] Thus, even if the
Supreme Court applied the *Loving* analogy to state same-sex marriage bans, litigants
would still have to convince the Court to extend benefits to binational same-sex partners to overrule *Adams v. Howerton*, absent Congressional intervention. Given the
Court's historical unwillingness to entertain even race-based equality claims within
immigration law, it is unlikely that we will see the Court act ahead of Congress here.

---

[13]   *Fong Yue Ting*, 149 U.S. at 713.
[14]   Turkmen v. Ashcroft, 02-CV-2307(JG), Memorandum and Order, at 77–80 (June 14, 2006) (granting
       government's motion to dismiss plaintiff's equal protection claim regarding selective detention based
       on race and religion), available at http://www.nyed.uscourts.gov/pub/rulings/cv/2002/02cv2307mo-f.
       pdf (last visited June 10, 2011). This opinion is also available in the Westlaw database at 2006 WL
       1662663.
[15]   While some courts have held that immigration rules burdening bona fide spousal relationships violate
       the constitutional right to marry, none have held that the immigration ban against same-sex marriages
       is itself unconstitutional. *See, e.g.,* Manwani v. INS, 736 F. Supp. 1367 (W.D.N.C. 1990) (holding that
       INA's mandatory two-year foreign residence requirement as applied to lawful spouses is unconstitu-
       tional); *see also* Cynthia M. Reed, *When Love, Comity, and Justice Conquer Borders: INS Recognition
       of Same-Sex Marriage*, 28 COLUM. HUM. RTS. L. REV. 97, 99 n.6 (1996).

LOVING AND CULTURAL BARRIERS TO GAY MARRIAGE

Overall, as I contend in this part, much of the challenges to obtaining equality in marriage would require overcoming cultural barriers. Although marriage is a legal status, I treat the issue of race and same-sex marriages as cultural phenomena. Indeed, the Supreme Court appears to do this as well, as exhibited by its unwillingness to second-guess the dominant culture on issues involving sexual orientation. Even though gay-rights advocates have much to celebrate recently with more states recognizing same-sex marriages,[16] it is unlikely that the Supreme Court will take the lead on the issue of domestic or binational same-sex marriage anytime soon. My reading of the Court's recent gay-rights opinions suggests that, unlike the Warren Court that penned *Loving*, the Roberts Court prefers not to be a catalyst for cultural change.

Although its legal analysis in *Loving* focused on the Equal Protection Clause, the Court threw in a brief discussion of the Due Process Clause for good measure:

> Marriage is one of the 'basic civil rights of man,' fundamental to our very existence and survival. ... To deny this fundamental freedom on so unsupportable a basis as the racial classifications embodied in these statutes ... is surely to deprive all the State's citizens of liberty without due process of law.[17]

The thrust of Warren's due process opinion focuses on the right of all persons to marry as a basic, fundamental right that the U.S. Constitution protects. Whereas his equal protection analysis focuses on the unequal treatment received by nonwhites and their partners, Warren's due process analysis rests squarely on the idea that all persons in the United States have a right to marry, and that the decision, whether to marry or not, is an individual, *human* one, not to be interfered with by the state.

Unfortunately, whereas the promise of such due process analysis suggests that there are no rights that can be denied any person, and that race has been firmly established as a line that states may not blithely cross, the Supreme Court has not been so bold in the context of gay rights. Instead, it has opted to find only a minimum quantum of rights that gay and lesbian persons enjoy and that government is required to respect. The Court's decisions in *Romer v. Evans*[18] and *Lawrence v. Texas*[19] are but two recent examples of this approach.

At issue in *Romer v. Evans* was the constitutionality of Amendment 2 to the Colorado Constitution, passed by voters ostensibly to deny "special rights" to those

---

[16] In addition to the increasing number of states that have passed laws that allow same-sex couples to get married, there is also a high-profile lawsuit challenging the constitutionality of the federal DOMA.
[17] *Loving*, 388 U.S. at 12.
[18] 517 U.S. 620 (1996).
[19] 539 U.S. 558 (2003).

of homosexual or bisexual orientation. Responding to ordinances ensuring equal treatment for gays and lesbians, passed in cities like Boulder and Aspen, opponents sought to prevent this trend by way of a state constitutional amendment. Interestingly, the lead-up to the referendum was tinged with racial rhetoric in which proponents of Amendment 2 compared gays and lesbians to white males, arguing that neither group required special protection from discrimination, and that Boulder and Aspen were wasting scarce resources that should be conserved to battle true discrimination against minorities and women. In the end, it appeared that Coloradans were uncertain about the scope of the proposal. While the measure passed by a slim 53.4 percent to 46.6 percent margin, exit polls conducted by the *Denver Post* revealed that most Coloradans would have favored antidiscrimination laws to protect gays and lesbians in housing and employment.[20] Whether the Supreme Court was aware of this history when it voted is unclear, but the justices struck down Amendment 2 by a 6-to-3 vote.

Relying on an Equal Protection Clause analysis, Justice Kennedy viewed the measure as a clear example of unconstitutional animus visited by a hostile majority against a vulnerable underclass:

> Amendment 2 fails, indeed defies, even this conventional inquiry. First, the amendment has the peculiar property of imposing a broad and undifferentiated disability on a single named group, an exceptional and, as we shall explain, invalid form of legislation. Second, its sheer breadth is so discontinuous with the reasons offered for it that the amendment seems inexplicable by anything but animus toward the class it affects; it lacks a rational relationship to legitimate state interests.[21]

Although it would be tempting to read this case as a strong vote in favor of gay rights and against sexual orientation discrimination, one wonders whether the suit really was about a group's access to the political process. Unlike statutes or ordinances, a state constitutional amendment has a particular force that bypasses regular legislative processes and purports to convey fundamental ideals of its citizenry. If the *Post's* exit polls are to be believed and Coloradans actually favored some antidiscrimination laws for gays and lesbians, then maybe the Court's ruling was meant to remedy voter confusion by allowing them the opportunity not to be bound by a constitutional provision that did not accurately express their will. Put simply, Coloradans did not get what they thought they were voting for when they passed Amendment 2, and the Court's opinion in *Romer* corrected that error.

In *Lawrence v. Texas*, however, the Court made clear that *Romer* was primarily about animosity toward gays and lesbians rather than about access to the political

---

[20] *See* Evan Gerstmann, THE CONSTITUTIONAL UNDERCLASS: GAYS, LESBIANS, AND THE FAILURE OF CLASS-BASED EQUAL PROTECTION 99–105 (1999).
[21] *Romer*, 517 U.S. at 632.

process. Writing for the majority, Justice Kennedy cited *Romer* as one of two important cases that influenced his thinking about the constitutionality of antisodomy
statutes directed against gays and lesbians.[22] The majority struck down Texas's antisodomy law, finding that its terms criminalized conduct engaged in primarily by
gays and lesbians. As such, it overruled its decision in *Bowers v. Hardwick*,[23] finding
that the Due Process Clause guaranteed a floor of liberty for all persons to engage in
private, sexual conduct, free from government interference: "Persons in a homosexual relationship may seek autonomy for these purposes, just as heterosexual persons
do. The decision in *Bowers* would deny them this right."[24] In the majority's view,
moral disapproval of same-sex sexual conduct is never enough, standing alone, to
justify the state's penal encroachment on personal privacy.

   While the Court affirmed its *Romer* commitment to protecting gays and lesbians
from animus in *Lawrence*, the majority did not clearly set forth the limits of its holding, prompting both Justices O'Connor and Scalia to fill the gap. Justice O'Connor
chose not to join Kennedy's majority opinion, relying solely on an equal protection
analysis to conclude that the Texas statute bespoke animus against gays and lesbians.
She did, however, make clear that the antisodomy law was irrational in a way that
bans against same-sex marriage were not. The latter bans, she argued, were rational
because they were meant to preserve "the traditional institution of marriage."[25]

   In dissent, Scalia ridiculed O'Connor's analysis, claiming that there was no rational way to distinguish the moral basis for approving heterosexual marriages from the
moral disapproval of antisodomy laws:

> This reasoning leaves on pretty shaky grounds state laws limiting marriage to oppo-
> site-sex couples. Justice O'Connor seeks to preserve them by the conclusory state-
> ment that "preserving the traditional institution of marriage" is a legitimate state
> interest. But "preserving the traditional institution of marriage" is just a kinder way
> of describing the State's *moral disapproval* of same-sex couples. Texas's interest in
> [its antisodomy law] could be recast in similarly euphemistic terms: "preserving
> the traditional sexual mores of our society." In the jurisprudence Justice O'Connor
> has seemingly created, judges can validate laws by characterizing them as "preserv-
> ing the traditions of society" (good); or invalidate them by characterizing them as
> "expressing moral disapproval" (bad).[26]

From *Romer* to *Lawrence*, then, we can discern a positive trend to provide greater
protection for gay rights, despite the Court's reluctance to apply anything more than

[22] *Lawrence*, 539 U.S. at 574.
[23] Bowers v. Hardwick, 478 U.S. 186 (1986).
[24] *Lawrence*, 539 U.S. at 574.
[25] *Id.* at 585 (O'Connor, J., concurring).
[26] *Id.* at 601–02 (Scalia, J., dissenting).

the traditional rational basis test to strike down homophobic legislation. Because nothing in the *Lawrence* majority opinion specifically limits its holding to anti-sodomy laws, gay-rights advocates may conclude that, like Scalia, the justices may come to embrace *Loving* as persuasive precedent for finally outlawing state bans on same-sex marriages. Returning to the idea of traversing cultural divides, gay-rights advocates might actually take heart in the following words of Justice Scalia: "Today's opinion is the product of a Court, which is the product of a law-profession *culture*, that has largely signed on to the so-called homosexual agenda, by which I mean the agenda promoted by some homosexual activists directed at eliminating the moral opprobrium that has traditionally attached to homosexual conduct."[27] If Scalia is right, the day may not be far away when a majority of the Court may find that bans against same-sex marriage, like antisodomy laws and homophobic constitutional amendments, do not reflect the appropriate cultural norm. When that time comes, the Court will be able to make that cultural move, to travel that cultural divide, using *Loving* as its guide.

However, lest anyone is tempted to declare outright victory in the war against same-sex marriage bans, one only needs to read carefully the Court's latest statement on gay rights, *Rumsfeld v. FAIR*,[28] to conclude that any optimism growing out of *Romer* and *Lawrence* must be tempered with a dose of realpolitik. Decided in 2006, *FAIR* was a challenge to the notorious Solomon Amendment's requirement that law schools provide equal access to students for all employment recruiters, including the military, or else the schools would forfeit federal funding. The law schools sued, arguing that the law violated their free-speech rights by forcing them to promote the military's less-than-favorable view of gays and lesbians (as embodied in their infamous "don't ask, don't tell" policy) – a view that was contrary to the law schools' beliefs – at the risk of forgoing federal funding. A unanimous Court sided with the government, ruling that the Solomon Amendment's requirements did not violate the law schools' free-speech rights. At best, the law regulated conduct, not speech, by requiring the law schools to provide the military the same access to students as it did to other employers. If they disagreed with the government's stand on gays and lesbians in the military, schools were free to express that view to their students.[29]

For our purposes, what may be most interesting is Chief Justice Roberts's single reference to race in this case. Among other things, *FAIR* had argued that because law schools were forced to communicate military recruiters' information via e-mail

[27] *Id.* at 602 (Scalia, J., dissenting).
[28] Rumsfeld v. Forum for Academic and Institutional Rights, 547 U.S. 47 (2006).
[29] *Rumsfeld*, 547 U.S. at 60 ("The Solomon Amendment neither limits what law schools may say nor requires them to say anything. Law schools remain free under the statute to express whatever views they may have on the military's congressionally mandated employment policy, all the while retaining eligibility for federal funds.").

and flyer, the government was compelling them to speak in violation of the First Amendment. In rejecting this view, Roberts stated that such compulsion was merely an incidental infringement on speech pursuant to a valid regulation of the schools' conduct. To illustrate, his opinion used an example of an antiracial discrimination command: "Congress, for example, can prohibit employers from discriminating in hiring on the basis of race. The fact that this will require an employer to take down a sign reading 'White Applicants Only' hardly means that the law should be analyzed as one regulating the employer's speech rather than conduct."[30] What is unclear is why this illustration does not work in the law schools' favor in arguing for gay rights. If the law school has an acknowledged right to advocate against sexual orientation bias, why can it not require the military to have to modify its conduct by, for example, setting up temporary private recruitment facilities off-campus? Under this interpretation, the military would still be free to advocate and enforce its "don't ask, don't tell" policy, but it may not use law school resources to promote that view.

In rejecting FAIR's arguments, perhaps the Court is promoting two ideas: on the one hand, the difference between race and sexual orientation, and on the other, the difference between Congressional and private power. First, the animating force behind Roberts's analogy is that, culturally, society has come to accept racial equality as a given. Thus, it is no surprise that a federal government would properly be able to require employers not to discriminate against nonwhites. Our culture has largely made the shift from Jim Crow to integration – using our migratory metaphor, it has already immigrated to a better place of racial equality. No such migration has fully taken place with respect to sexual orientation discrimination.

Second, and evocative of our earlier discussion about Congress's power over immigration law, FAIR highlights the divide that the Court draws between public and private power. In assessing the Solomon Amendment, the Court cited Congress's plenary power over the military, noting that, while Congress chose to regulate military recruiting at schools through the Spending Clause, similar deference should be accorded the legislative decision on how to properly support the military. This deference to Congress in military affairs parallels the deference that the Court affords Congress over immigration law. It is not surprising, then, that when a political body, like Congress, attempts to legislate for the good of the United States as a whole, it will adopt policies most in line with what it perceives its constituents want. In the context of military recruiting, Congress and the military have taken a rather conservative line with respect to balancing the desire of gays and lesbians to serve in the armed forces against the corps' concern about perceived threats to morale and unit cohesion. Compared to military affairs, Congress is no less conservative in immigration policy: at the margin, it is unwilling to allow a lesbian U.S. citizen, married

---

[30] *Id.* at 62.

in the Netherlands, to petition for recognition of her Dutch partner as a spouse without fear of running afoul of national policy. (It is no surprise then that in 2006, the Senate voted on a proposed U.S. constitutional amendment to restrict marriage to a "husband" and "wife.") From a conservative viewpoint, moreover, the deference granted to Congress in military and immigration matters springs from a common point – the concern over national security. Perhaps unintentionally, Justice O'Connor highlighted this when she identified "national security" as a valid governmental interest while implicitly noting its absence in the *Lawrence* case.

I am less sanguine after reading *FAIR* than I was after studying *Romer* or *Lawrence*. While I hope that the unanimous opinion in *FAIR* may be due to the Court's commitment to a robust First Amendment right, as well as its view that law schools were free to reject the federal funding the law threatened to withhold, I think that the underlying message for our issue of cultural migration across the boundaries of sexual orientation and immigration policy is quite negative. *FAIR* supports the view that *Romer* and *Lawrence* are less about gay rights than they are about individual rights: *Romer* guarantees that all persons have equal access to the political process, and *Lawrence* preserves the privacy of all persons to engage in sexual relations within their homes. *FAIR*, therefore, becomes less about protecting gays and lesbians and more about respecting Congressional deference to military recruiting practices and ensuring their equal access to students.

To the extent that *FAIR* affirms the power of Congress, not only over military matters, but also over antidiscrimination initiatives (implicit in its reference to fair employment rules), and given what we have learned about Congress's concomitant power over immigration law, perhaps the (second-)best solution to the barriers to movement faced by binational same-sex couples today is via legislative action, and not by analogy to *Loving*.

I wish that the *legal* divide that makes Congress's immigration power different from state power over marriage law did not persist today. But perhaps the most realistic approach at this point is to advocate for the bridging of the *physical* gap that separates binational same-sex partners. First introduced in 2000 by Congressman Jerrold Nadler of New York, the Uniting American Families Act of 2009 ("UAFA")[31]

---

[31] S. 424, 111th Congress, 1st Sess. (Feb. 12, 2009). Here is a summary of what the bill attempts to accomplish:

Uniting American Families Act of 2009 – Amends the Immigration and Nationality Act to include a "permanent partner" within the scope of such Act. Defines a "permanent partner" as an individual 18 or older who: (1) is in a committed, intimate relationship with another individual 18 or older in which both individuals intend a lifelong commitment; (2) is financially interdependent with the other individual; (3) is not married to, or in a permanent partnership with, any other individual other than the individual; (4) is unable to contract with the other individual a marriage cognizable under is designed to allow U.S. citizens and lawful permanent residents to petition their foreign same-sex partners to immigrate on the same grounds as heterosexual couples, except that these benefits will have no broader effect on state or federal laws referencing marriage. Although it will surely not bridge all the legal and cultural divides that treat same-sex marriages differently from heterosexual ones, the UAFA will eliminate the physical barrier that effectively separates foreign same-sex partners from their U.S.-based counterparts. At the same time, it leverages Congress's plenary power over immigration to effect a significant, if incomplete, change to the immigration law so that same-sex partners, while not the same as marital spouses, may reap the same immigrant benefits.

As of this writing, Congressional support for the bill is far from overwhelming. This is not surprising, given the large number of other important issues in immigration law that Congress and the president have had to grapple with recently, including debates in both houses during consecutive spring sessions in 2006 and 2007 on comprehensive immigration reform. Despite the presumptive salience of these issues to our current president, the biracial son of a binational couple, as of this writing, Barack Obama's administration has been relatively quiet on gay rights and immigration reform. In fairness, a large part of this may be a matter of prioritization, with the economy, health care, the environment, and education taking precedence. Or it may well be that our politically savvy chief executive understands that the forces of xenophobia and homophobia, even if primarily unconscious, might make passage of this bill untenable despite the recent positive momentum among the states. One need only recall that, in the year following *Lawrence v. Texas*, thirteen states amended their constitutions restricting the definition of marriage to unions between a man and a woman;[32] a similar backlash may yet be in the offing.

Nevertheless, my hope is that just as *Loving v. Virginia* captured the imagination of the nation forty years ago, at some point in the not-too-distant future, the United

this Act; and (5) is not a first, second, or third degree blood relation of the other individual. Defines a "permanent partnership" as the relationship existing between two permanent partners.

    See Congressional Research Service Summary of S. 424, *available at* http://www.govtrack.us/congress/bill.xpd?bill=s111-424&tab=summary (last visited on June 10, 2011). In 2011, Senator Patrick Leahy submitted S. 821, which is an updated version of S. 424. *See* Congressional Research Service Summary of S. 821, *available at http://www.govtrack.us/congress/bill.xpd?bill=s112-821* (last visited on February 10, 2012).

[32] *See, e.g., Group Drops Bid To Ban Same-Sex Marriage*, N.Y. TIMES, Dec. 29, 2005, at A24. Eleven of the thirteen passed these amendments in November 2004: Arkansas, Georgia, Kentucky, Michigan, Mississippi, Montana, North Dakota, Oklahoma, Ohio, Oregon, and Utah. *See Voters Pass All 11 Bans on Gay Marriage*, MSNBC.COM, Nov. 3, 2004, *at* http://msnbc.msn.com/id/6383353/ (last visited June 10, 2011). Missouri and Louisiana voters approved similar laws in August and September of 2004, respectively. *See* Monica Davey, *Missourians Back Amendment Barring Gay Marriage*, N.Y. TIMES, Aug. 4, 2004, at A13; *Gay-Marriage Ban Passes in Louisiana*, N.Y. TIMES, Sept. 19, 2004, §1 at 24.

States will recognize the injustice that it visits upon the more than 40,000 binational same-sex partnerships in America today.[33] Just like the Lovings, today's couples – from Adams and Sullivan to Naughton and his Spanish partner – are being forced either to migrate from their homes to other, more hospitable lands, or to remain fugitives from the law. This is not a choice they should be forced to make. In a country built on immigrants and the promise of family unity, the United States should clear the way to bring families together, not tear them apart.

[33] A 2006 joint report by Human Rights Watch and Immigration Equality estimates that there are more than 40,000 binational same-sex couples in the U.S. today. Human Rights Watch & Immigration Equality, *Family, Unvalued: Discrimination, Denial, and the Fate of Binational Same-Sex Couples Under U.S. Law* (Executive Summary, 2006), *available at* http://www.hrc.org/issues/6918.htm (last visited on June 11, 2011).

PART SIX

Loving and Beyond: Marriage, Intimacy, and Diverse Relationships

17

Black v. Gay?

Centering LBGT People of Color in Civil-Marriage Debates

Adele M. Morrison

Loving is a cornerstone of social, political, and legal arguments for, and against, civil marriage rights for same-sex couples. Same-sex marriage-rights advocates assert that restricting marriage to only one man and one woman[1] is similar to barring Whites from marrying non-Whites. Thus, barring two people of the same-sex from marrying violates the proposition that the fundamental right to marry is fully realized only if one can marry a person of her choice. Denying civil marriage rights to same-sex couples constitutes sex and/or sexual orientation discrimination, which parallels the race discrimination found unconstitutional in *Loving*.

Utilizing this 1967 decision to connect same-sex and interracial marriage has come to be known as the "Loving analogy," which generates a discussion of same-sex marriage as a civil rights issue. The state determines which relationships, and thus the people in them, may receive the blessings of marriage. Leaving same-sex couples out suggests that they, and lesbian, gay, bisexual, and transgender (LGBT) people in general, lack worth and are excluded from the 1,000-plus benefits, rights, and privileges of marriage.[2] Thus, LGBT communities have strong reasons to fight for access to marriage. Society as a whole benefits if adults in intimate relationships are allowed full access to marriage regardless of their race, sex, gender, or sexual orientation. All subordinated groups, who themselves have been excluded from full marriage rights at different times throughout history, should recognize that there are benefits to accessing marriage for all, even if there is personal disagreement over the purpose and meaning of civil marriage itself.

---

[1] *See* Defense of Marriage Act, 1 U.S.C.A. §7 (1996) (defining marriage as between a man and a woman for federal purposes and allowing states to refuse to give full faith and credit to same-sex marriages performed in foreign jurisdictions).

[2] U.S. Government Accountability Office, *Defense of Marriage Act: Update to Prior Report* (Jan. 23, 2004), *at* http://www.gao.gov/products/GAO-04-353R (as of December 31, 2003, our research identified a total of 1,138 federal statutory provisions classified to the United States Code in which marital status is a factor in determining or receiving benefits, rights, and privileges.)

At the intersection of the *Loving* analogy are people with multiple subordinated identities; in this case, LGBT people of color. LGBT people of color experience the multiple and material effects of racism and homophobia, and also religious, class, religion, and gender bias. However, as has been discussed by others,[3] LGBT people of color do not experience the effects of hetero-supremacy and White supremacy independently of each other; rather, the effects are experienced at the same time. A true understanding of the similarities of interracial and same-sex marriage requires a shifting of LGBT people of color "from margin to center."[4] It is this centering that can bring visibility to the common struggles of subordinated groups in challenging oppressions such as White supremacy and hetero-supremacy. Centering should also create the possibility of coalitions dedicated to people realizing equal access to all civil rights, including marriage.

Equality based on sexual orientation echoes *Loving*'s principles of freedom, anti-discrimination, and anti-subordination.[5] *Loving*'s principles are defined as follows: (1) freedom of choice means that marriage is a fundamental right that is only fully realized by being able to marry the person of one's choice, regardless of race; (2) antidiscrimination stands for the idea that prohibiting interracial couples to marry constitutes race discrimination; and (3) the anti-subordination principle means that

---

[3] *See generally* Kimberlé Crenshaw, *Mapping the Margins: Intersectionality, Identity Politics, and Violence Against Women of Color*, 43 STAN. L. REV. 1241, 1244–45 (1991) (coining the term "intersectionality" in the context of women of color and violence); Darren Lenard Hutchinson, *Out Yet Unseen: A Racial Critique of Gay and Lesbian Legal Theory and Political Discourse*, 29 CONN. L. REV. 561, 566 (1997) (arguing that the issue is much more complex than simple comparisons would have one expect and calling for the creation of a "multidimensional gay and lesbian discourse," a discourse that would include identities along multiple axes.); Angela Onwuachi-Willig, *Undercover Other*, 94 CAL. L. REV. 873, 875 (2006) (discussing the inaccuracy of the idea that gays, lesbians, and bisexuals can pass for heterosexual, undermining comparison to the struggle Blacks have because of their visible skin color).

[4] *See* bell hooks, FEMINIST THEORY: FROM MARGIN TO CENTER (South End Press Classics 2d ed. 2000) (1984).

[5] While I am arguing in favor of the applicability of the *Loving* analogy and I do find the argument comparing antimiscegenation laws to laws barring same-sex marriage compelling, I do not assert that racism and heterosexism are the same, or that they are indistinguishably harmful. I recognize and agree with Catherine Smith's critique of the "same as" argument in which she asserts that an argument that categorizes homophobia and heterosexism as "the same as" racism serves to divide rather than unite subordinated groups. *See* Catherine Smith, *Queer as Black Folk?*, 2007 WIS. L. REV. 379 (2007). It is not my intention to contribute to discourse that continues this problem. This essay does not compare or rank oppressions because, as Black feminist scholar bell hooks wrote, "Suggesting a hierarchy of oppression ... evokes a sense of competing concerns that is unnecessary." Attempting to further determine who is more or less oppressed is unproductive and divisive. hooks, *supra* note 6, at 35. My effort here is to argue that gay rights are civil rights and that certain rights that have been extended to, and that benefit, Blacks should be extended to lesbian, gay, bisexual and transgender (LGBT) persons for their benefit as well. I further argue that extending full marriage rights to couples whose partners are the same-sex, in the way *Loving* extended full marriage rights to interracial couples, also benefits people of color.

maintaining White supremacy, and thereby subordinating non-Whites – more specifically Blacks – is not a legitimate reason to bar persons from marrying. These principles prove three things: (1) The *Loving* analogy is valid; (2) there is a connection between interracial marriage and same-sex marriage; and (3) gay rights are civil rights, with the Black LGBT community at the intersection.

A LOVING ANALOGY

The *Loving* analogy has become less of a question of legal precedent and more of a question of the sameness or difference of "civil rights" and "gay rights." However this misses the point, which is that marriage equality in *Loving* speaks universally to core principles of fairness and equality in the context of intimate relationships. *Loving* invokes three principles: freedom, antidiscrimination, and anti-subordination. First, the case champions freedom of choice in the selection of a marital partner. But transferring the race issues of *Loving* to the different context of sexuality needs to be examined further. Second, sexual orientation discrimination and racial discrimination are interdependent. The intent of the antidiscrimination principle in *Loving* should be applied to same-sex contexts. Lastly, if *Loving* took an anti–White supremacy stance, this anti-subordination principle should apply to same-sex marriage. Successful same-sex marriage cases have espoused anti-hetero-supremacy as a reason to strike down bans on same-sex marriage.

Loving (Is) Freedom of Choice

Loving reasserted the court's determination in California's *Perez v. Sharp*[6] that the fundamental right to marry meant choice. The court in *Perez* stated, "[T]he essence of the right to marry is freedom to join in marriage with the person of one's choice."[7] The freedom-of-choice principle is employed in the pro-same-sex marriage context to argue that if the decision to marry does indeed mean to marry the person of one's choosing, then it should not be limited based on any identity-based characteristics. such as race, gender, or sexual orientation. *Perez* holds that because the fundamental right to marry is about freedom of choice, a law forbidding interracial marriages violates the Constitution. The *Loving* decision nationalized *Perez*'s "freedom to choose whom to marry," but it did not specifically state that making those decisions was limited to choices based on race. Thus, the freedom-of-choice principle is applicable in the same-sex marriage context because, arguably, the right attaches to the

---

[6]   Perez v. Sharp, 198 P.2d 17 (Cal. 1948) (en banc).
[7]   *Perez*, 198 P.2d at 21.

choosing itself, not to the identity of the person an individual is choosing to marry
or the identity of the person doing the choosing.

Loving (Is) Anti-Discrimination

LGBT marriage-rights advocates argue that anti-same-sex marriage laws discriminate
based on sex. *Loving* has been invoked to analogize the race-based discrimination
of antimiscegenation laws to sex-based discrimination. Same-sex marriage advocates
further insist that the heightened scrutiny applied to race and gender would defeat
same-sex marriage restrictions. However, there is no universally binding precedent
that classifies sexual orientation as a suspect classification, as in the case of race.
Individual states, however, have given it more weight. In *Varnum v. Brien*, the Iowa
Supreme Court found sexual orientation to be "quasi-" or "semi-suspect."[8] This echoed the Massachusetts Supreme Court in *Goodridge v. Department of Public Health*,
which treated sexual orientation as similar to race and gender.[9] *Goodridge* did not
use heightened scrutiny when evaluating the constitutionality of its state's marriage
law, but it did determine that individuals were being denied access to marriage based
on sexual orientation. Although the California Supreme Court did find that sexual
orientation was a suspect classification for purposes of its equal protection clause in
In Re Marriage Cases,[10] this victory was short-lived. Proposition 8, passed in 2009,
rendered the finding in *In Re Marriage Cases* moot by amending the California
Constitution to limit marriage to being between one man and one woman.

Different levels of scrutiny have yielded similar results. If *Loving* argues that there
was "patently no legitimate overriding [governmental] purpose" for barring access
to marriage based on race,[11] it should follow that there is no legitimate purpose to
restricting access to marriage based on sexual orientation. The Iowa Supreme Court
declared: "While the objectives asserted may be important ... none are furthered
in a substantial way by the exclusion of same-sex couples from civil marriage."[12]
Although *Loving* applies strict scrutiny and *Varnum* intermediate, both reject reasons to exclude interracial or same-sex couples from marrying. In *In Re Marriage
Cases*, the California Supreme Court applied strict scrutiny to conclude that, "we
cannot find that retention of the traditional definition of marriage constitutes a
compelling state interest."[13] Even when Massachusetts applied "only" rational basis
review in *Goodridge*, the court determined:

---

[8] Varnum v. Brien, 763 N.W.2d 862, 880 (Iowa 2009).
[9] Goodridge v. Dep't of Pub. Health, 798 N.E. 2d 941 (Mass. 2003).
[10] *In re* Marriage Cases, 183 P.3d 384 (Cal. 2008).
[11] *Loving v. Virginia*, 388 U.S. 1, 11 1967).
[12] *Varnum*, 763 N.W.2d at 904.
[13] *In re* Marriage Cases, 183 P.3d at 402.)

The marriage ban works a deep and scarring hardship on a very real segment of the community for no rational reason. The absence of any reasonable relationship between, on the one hand, an absolute disqualification of same-sex couples who wish to enter into civil marriage and, on the other, protection of public health, safety, or general welfare, suggests that the marriage restriction is rooted in persistent prejudices against persons who are (or who are believed to be) homosexual.[14]

A heterosexual couple may legally marry; a homosexual couple may not. Although this is discrimination based on sex, because a woman can marry a man but a man cannot marry a man, sexual orientation is implicated, because, as Professor Holning Lau has noted, "a gay couple can never get married even though a gay individual can."[15] Comparably, under antimiscegenation laws, neither Whites nor non-Whites were barred from marrying, but both were generally prohibited from marrying someone outside of their racial category (White or non-White), although sometimes the limitation was only on Whites marrying Blacks.

Loving (Is) Anti-subordination

The anti-subordination principle also confirms the validity of the Loving analogy. Same-sex marriage-rights advocates note that Loving struck down antimiscegenation laws based solely on racial animus, which meant that these laws were designed to support the doctrine of White supremacy. Although Loving specifically opined that maintaining White supremacy was not a constitutionally protected interest, the result has not been the eradication of White supremacy. In fact, it remains tenaciously intact and helps maintain a system of subordination of which hetero-supremacy is also a part.

Loving's anti–White supremacy holding can be viewed as foundational in the work to develop anti-subordination jurisprudence and counter the dominant/subordinate paradigm. So too is Goodridge's extension of marriage rights to same-sex couples in Massachusetts a monumental step forward on the path to equality; a judicial path down which California (although there was a subsequent setback) and a unanimous Iowa Supreme Court successfully followed. Also, the Iowa Court recognized that the particular same-sex marriage-rights case before it at the time was in a long line of Iowa anti-subordination decisions, from the case that ended slavery in the state to the one that admitted women to the practice of law. The Varnum case extended this anti-subordination trend while being on the leading edge of the same-sex marriage revolution.

[14] Goodridge, 798 N.E.2d at 968.
[15] Holning Lau, Transcending the Individualist Paradigm in Sexual Orientation Antidiscrimination Law, 94 Cal. L. Rev. 1271, 1321 (2006).

RETHINKING MARRIAGE IN A POST-RACIAL WORLD

The year 2009 may go down in history as the one in which the tide turned in favor same-sex marriage. Even though the passage of Proposition 8 in California banned same-sex couples from marrying, the resulting response galvanized those supporting same-sex marriage rights and added new voices to the movement. A string of "victories" in other states legalized same-sex marriage or recognized marriages performed in other states. Within the first four months of the Obama administration, the number of states legalizing same-sex marriage grew from one to five.

Through it all, there has been a particular focus on the Black communities. The notion has been that there is little support for same-sex marriage among Blacks, especially civil rights leaders. But this is not necessarily true. There is no more or less support for same-sex marriage rights within Black communities (if age and religiosity are controlled for) than in any other community of color. Even Mildred Loving herself came to support same-sex marriage rights. In 2007, during the planning of a commemoration of the fortieth anniversary of *Loving v. Virginia*, she – who was a plaintiff in the case that finally ended antimiscegenation laws – told a member of a marriage-rights advocacy group that she would make a statement supporting gay marriage. As Mrs. Loving was well into her sixties, the individual speaking with her wanted to be clear that she understood what she was doing. Mildred Loving was clear that she was supporting marriage rights for same-sex couples and is quoted as saying, "I understand it ... and I believe it."[16]

An argument often attributed to the Black clergy or Black civil rights activists is that there is no connection between Black communities and same-sex marriage. However, a recent study of "same-sex couples raising children in California" showed that those families are "more likely to be of color and that their median household income is 17 percent lower than the income of married couples with children."[17] Thus, communities of color who profess to be pro-family while standing against same-sex marriage are ultimately harming some of their own children. This exemplifies the interconnection of subordination and the counterintuitive perpetuation of dominant ideologies by subordinated communities.

---

[16] Susan Dominus, *The Color of Love*, N.Y. Times Mag., Dec. 28, 2008, at MM21, *available at* http://www.nytimes.com/2008/12/28/magazine/28loving-t.html?_r =1&pagewaned=print (last visited June 13, 2011).

[17] Tyche Hendricks, *Same-Sex Couples Raising Children Less Likely to Be White, Wealthy*, S.F. Chron., Oct. 31, 2007, at A-1, *available at* http://www.sfgate.com/cgi-bin/article.cgi?file=/c/a/2007/10/31/MNJET3CR3.DTL (last visited June 13, 2011).

Loving *Couples:*[18] *Extending Civil (Marriage) Rights*

Loving was, and continues to be, about more than marriage. It stands for the principle that White supremacy is not a legitimate or compelling governmental interest. It spelled the demise of dictating racial categories through the "one-drop rule" and determined that animus cannot be the reason for a law's existence. The *Loving* decision also endorsed marital and racial freedom by promoting better personal and intimate relationships through friendships, extended families, and children.[19]

Loving's principles of equality reveal the interconnectedness and interdependence of race and sexual orientation. Countering subordination should be a common goal of all subordinated communities. Communities of color need to deal specifically with issues of homophobia, and LGBT communities must work against racism. *Loving* should encourage communities of color, specifically Black communities, to see same-sex marriage as a civil rights issue. It should also compel LGBT communities to include issues specific to LGBT people of color as part of marriage-rights activism.

However, the full potential of *Loving* has yet to be realized. *Loving's* potential to eradicate cultural White supremacist attitudes – at least in the area of adult intimate relationships and family law – actually lies in the hands of interracial same-sex couples, even more so than interracial mixed-sex couples or monoracial same-sex couples. Interracial same-sex couples are gap bridgers and can bring together people of color and LGBT activists who understand that inserting discrimination against gays and lesbians into the law, through statutes or constitutional amendments, begins a slippery slope to backtracking on other civil rights gains. Interracial same-sex couples are those that most fully exemplify the *Loving* principles of freedom of choice, antidiscrimination, and anti-subordination if they are able to marry. Once the centrality of interracial same-sex couples is acknowledged, the movement for marriage equality can influence antiracist work and the potential of *Loving* can be truly realized. Same-sex marriage fully realizes the civil right of marrying the "person of one's choice."

---

[18] Thanks to Rashmi Goel for this phrase.

[19] *See generally* Maria P. P. Root, Love's Revolution: Interracial Marriage 287–95 (2001) (asking the question "Is love the answer," and answering with the following:

The old segregationist fear that integration would lead to "race mixing" was well-founded. Meaningful integration allows Blacks and whites to meet, to transcend the cultural and historical legacies that hinder healthy relationships, and to marry if they so choose. There is no question that interracial love will become more common and even more accepted as racial barriers erode in American society, but it will take more than love to break down those barriers. Old hierarchies must be dismantled for new attitudes about interracial love and marriage to flourish.

18

Beyond the *Loving* Analogy: The Independent Logic of Same-Sex Marriage

Rachel F. Moran

In recent years, there has been a renaissance of interest in *Loving v. Virginia* because of its role in the same-sex marriage debate. According to some gay and lesbian advocates, the Court's decision to strike down bans on interracial marriage provides a constitutional roadmap for undoing sex-based restrictions on the right to marry. Although the analogy to *Loving* has produced high-profile courtroom victories, these novel arguments also have yielded a number of defeats. Interestingly, recent litigation successes in the same-sex marriage campaign have turned on a new constitutional logic, one that does not depend on extensive comparisons to race. As important as this emerging logic is in addressing the historical exclusion of same-sex couples from marriage, the approach is but a first step in understanding fully what authentic liberty and equality mean in the realm of intimacy.

THE *LOVING* ANALOGY IN SAME-SEX MARRIAGE CASES

The *Loving* analogy has served several key purposes in the same-sex marriage movement. For one thing, the landmark 1967 civil rights decision demonstrates that courts can nullify even long-standing marriage laws, so long as they are rooted in irrational discrimination, whether that be racism or homophobia. In addition to this principle of equal treatment, the opinion makes clear that the freedom to marry is a fundamental right, one that cannot be burdened without a compelling justification. So, stereotypical images of interracial marriages as unstable and antisocial could not justify antimiscegenation laws, nor should misleading portraits of gay and lesbian relationships be used to uphold bans on same-sex marriage. Overall, then, *Loving* shows that tradition alone, whether of same-race or opposite-sex marriages, cannot be invoked to perpetuate exclusion and subordination.

That said, the appropriation of *Loving*'s reasoning in support of the same-sex marriage movement is something that the justices probably did not anticipate. At the time of the 1967 decision, there was no visible gay rights movement. Two years later, the Stonewall riots in New York galvanized gays and lesbians, mobilizing them as a civil rights constituency. In the early 1970s, a few same-sex couples sought to marry. Although gay-friendly churches performed the ceremonies, local registrars soundly rebuffed any efforts to obtain marriage licenses.[1] State courts perfunctorily dismissed the rare legal challenge to denial of a license.[2] In 1986, same-sex marriage advocates confronted a major setback. In *Bowers v. Hardwick*, the U.S. Supreme Court upheld a Texas law that criminalized homosexual sodomy between consenting adults.[3] The Court held that no fundamental right to privacy protected the defendants from prosecution, even though they had engaged in sex in their own home. In reaching this conclusion, the justices found that "[n]o connection between family, marriage, or procreation on the one hand and homosexual activity on the other has been demonstrated."[4] This decision, which contrasted illicit homosexual activity with protected rights to marry and procreate, seemed to doom gay marriage in the courts. Heeding the message, activists turned their attention to fighting antigay violence, combating discrimination in the workplace, and grappling with the emerging AIDS crisis.

Gay rights advocacy in the 1980s arguably helped lay the foundation for the revival of a same-sex marriage agenda in the 1990s. The battle against economic discrimination revealed just how large of a tax that gays and lesbians paid because they could not marry. Advocacy organizations would soon catalog the many advantages that accrued to spouses: workplace insurance and health care coverage, preferred tax status, social security benefits, standing to file wrongful death actions, and rights to inherit property under the laws of intestacy, among others.[5] The AIDS epidemic brought home the need for official recognition of gay relationships in a dramatic way. As Frank Rich would write in the *New York Times*, "in retrospect, [the AIDS epidemic] made same-sex marriage inevitable. Americans watched as gay men were turned away at their partners' hospital rooms and denied basic rights granted to heterosexual couples coping with a spouse's terminal illness and death."[6]

In 1993, the same-sex marriage issue took center stage when the Hawaii Supreme Court found in *Baehr v. Lewin* that a statute limiting the right to marry to heterosexuals discriminated on the basis of sex and therefore potentially violated the state

[1] William N. Eskridge, Jr. & Darren R. Spedale, GAY MARRIAGE: FOR BETTER OR FOR WORSE?: WHAT WE'VE LEARNED FROM THE EVIDENCE 16–17 (2006).
[2] *See, e.g.*, Jones v. Hallahan, 501 S.W.2d 588 (Ky. 1973) (citing to standard definitions of marriage in a brief opinion); Baker v. Nelson, 191 N.W.2d 185 (Minn. 1971) (citing common definitions of marriage, treating marriage as procreative, and rejecting the *Loving* analogy because antimiscegenation laws involved racial discrimination).
[3] Bowers v. Hardwick, 478 U.S. 186.
[4] *Bowers*, 478 U.S. at 191.
[5] *See* Evan Wolfson, WHY MARRIAGE MATTERS: AMERICA, EQUALITY, AND GAY PEOPLE'S RIGHT TO MARRY 13–15 (2004).
[6] Frank Rich, *The Joy of Gay Marriage*, N.Y. TIMES, Feb. 29, 2004, § 2, at 1.

constitution's Equal Protection Clause.[7] In reaching this conclusion, the majority in *Baehr* relied heavily on *Loving*. As the opinion explained,

> the Virginia courts declared that interracial marriage simply could not exist because the Deity had deemed such a union intrinsically unnatural, and, in effect, because it had theretofore never been the "custom" of the state to recognize mixed marriages, marriage "always" having been construed to presuppose a different configuration. With all due respect to the Virginia courts of a bygone era, we do not believe that trial judges are the ultimate authorities on the subject of Divine Will, and, as *Loving* amply demonstrates, constitutional law may mandate, like it or not, that customs change with an evolving social order.[8]

Despite a backlash that undid the Hawaii court's ruling, gays and lesbians took a renewed interest in pursuing marriage as a constitutional right at the state level.[9] In fact, the intense hostility to the decision cemented a belief that same-sex marriage must be a centerpiece of the gay rights agenda.

THE LIMITATIONS OF THE *LOVING* ANALOGY

As the battle over same-sex marriage continued in the courts, many of the lawsuits drew on the analogies to interracial marriage that had featured so prominently in the 1993 Hawaii decision; in some cases, this approach was successful.[10] Although

---

[7] Baehr v. Lewin, 852 P.2d 44 (Haw. 1993), *declared moot sub nom*. Baehr v. Miike, 1999 Haw. LEXIS 391 (1999) (citations omitted). Although the focus of this chapter is on the role of the *Loving* analogy in judicial decisions, it is worth noting that in recent years, legislative action also has played an important role in the same-sex marriage movement. For example, legislatures in Maine, New Hampshire, and Vermont recently have voted to allow gay and lesbian couples to marry. L.D. 1020, 124th Leg., 1st Reg. Sess. (Me. 2009) (amending ME. REV. STAT. ANN. tit. 19-A, § 650–51, 655 701); H.B. 436, 2009 Gen. Ct., 161st Sess. (N.H. 2009) (amending N.H. REV. STAT. ANN. § 457) (effective Jan 1, 2010)); S.B. 115, 2009 Gen. Assem., Leg. Sess. (Vt. 2009) (amending VT. STAT. ANN., tit. 15, § 8 (effective Sept. 1, 2009)). In Vermont, the state's high court forced the legislature to act, first through recognition of civil unions. Baker v. State, 744 A.2d 864 (Vt. 1999). The Maine statute subsequently was nullified by a popular referendum. Devin Dwyer, *Maine Gay Marriage Law Repealed*, ABC NEWS, Nov. 4, 2009, *at* http://abcnews.go.com/story?id=8992720&page=1 (last visited September 22, 2011).

[8] *Baehr*, 852 P.2d at 63 (citations omitted). Interestingly, gay rights organizations did not take a leading role in the Hawaii litigation because of internal divisions about the wisdom of pursuing the right to same-sex marriage. Wolfson, *supra* note 5, at 30. The case therefore was filed by a local civil rights attorney in Honolulu. *Id.* at 30–32. It appears that the *Loving* analogy was introduced in an amicus brief submitted to the Hawaii Supreme Court by Lambda Legal Defense and Education Fund. *See* Brief of Lambda Legal Defense & Education Fund, Inc. as Amicus Curiae Supporting Plaintiff-Appellant at 1–3, Baehr v. Lewin, 852 P.2d 44 (Haw. 1993) (No. 15689).

[9] Arakawa Lynda, *Gays Vow to Keep Fighting for Rights*, HONOLULU ADVERTISER, Dec. 11, 1999, at 1A.

[10] *See, e.g.*, Goodridge v. Dep't of Pub. Health, 798 N.E.2d 941 (Mass. 2003); *see also In re* Marriage Cases, 183 P.3d 384 (Cal. 2008) (relying heavily on the California Supreme Court's post–World War II decision in *Perez v. Sharp*, 198 P.2d 17 (Cal. 1948), a forerunner to the *Loving* opinion). As discussed

the analogy to *Loving* could be serviceable at times, it regularly failed to produce the desired results for same-sex marriage advocates. A number of decisions explicitly rejected the claim that classifications based on sexual orientation, like those based on race, trigger the strictest constitutional scrutiny. Instead, these courts applied the most lenient standard, the rational basis test, to statutes that prohibited same-sex marriage.[11] Although a judge occasionally declared the bans wholly irrational under this deferential level of review,[12] most decisions found that legislatures could limit access to marriage based on the goal of promoting procreative activity. Judges rejected the notion that laws forbidding same-sex marriage were motivated by nothing more than homophobia; in doing so, the opinions implicitly rejected any straightforward analogy to antimiscegenation laws, which the Court had treated as an artifact of the wholly discredited ideology of white supremacy.

Just as courts rejected clear-cut comparisons between race and sexual orientation in determining whether marriage laws were discriminatory, judges also were not always persuaded that *Loving* was relevant in evaluating whether the fundamental right to marry had been violated. Because the Court simply presumed that marriage takes place between a man and a woman, some judges concluded that conferring marital rights on interracial couples did not reconstruct the underlying institution of marriage. Observing that *Loving* referred to marriage as "fundamental to our very existence and survival," some state courts found that the case actually supported a legislative preference for procreative heterosexual unions.

These mixed results reflected some underlying ambiguities in the *Loving* analogy itself. This landmark civil rights case was rooted firmly in images of race and racism, so the work of determining how much protection to afford to other disadvantaged groups, including gays and lesbians, was left undone. In addition, *Loving* did not elaborate on the right to marry because Chief Justice Earl Warren addressed the issue only briefly at the end of his opinion. After scaling back the discussion to satisfy colleagues,[13] he had little to say about the nature of marriage and the reasons for its central place in a well-ordered society. In all likelihood, Warren did not believe that he was overturning traditional images of marriage. In fact, his colleague, Justice Potter Stewart, described Warren as sincerely believing in "eternal, rather bromidic platitudes" that included "motherhood, marriage, family, flag, and the like." These received traditions were the foundation for his jurisprudence.[14]

later, the California decision was overturned by popular initiative, and this initiative in turn prompted new legal challenges. *See infra* note 18 and accompanying text.
11 *See, e.g.,* Dean v. District of Columbia, 653 A.2d 307 (D.C. 1995); Morrison v. Sadler, 821 N.E.2d 15 (Ind. Ct. App. 2005); Conaway v. Deane, 932 A.2d 571 (Md. 2007); Andersen v. King County, 138 P.3d 963 (Wash. 2006); Singer v. Hara, 522 P.2d 1187 (Wash. Ct. App. 1974).
12 *Goodridge,* 798 N.E.2d at 961.
13 Ed Cray, CHIEF JUSTICE: A BIOGRAPHY OF EARL WARREN 452–53 (1997).
14 Bernard Schwartz, DECISION: HOW THE SUPREME COURT DECIDES CASES 88 (1997).

The limits of the *Loving* analogy were evident not only in these judicial defeats, but also in resistance encountered in the political arena. The African-American community did not uniformly embrace the notion that gay rights are civil rights. In fact, some black leaders expressed concern that gays and lesbians were wrongly appropriating a history of slavery and oppression to advance the same-sex marriage agenda.[15] Although civil rights leader Coretta Scott King described these forms of inequality as "irrevocably intertwined," Jesse Jackson differed and found the comparison between antimiscegenation laws and bans on same-sex marriage "a stretch." The fear that gays and lesbians were "pimping off the black movement"[16] produced some inflammatory rhetoric, particularly among the black clergy. The executive director of Florida's Christian Coalition condemned efforts "to ride on the heels of Martin Luther King and the civil rights movement" as "outrageous," and a black bishop insisted that the "analogy makes no sense" because "[t]here's been no wholesale enslavement of gays and lesbians."[17] Black churches played a key role in mobilizing civil rights activism, and religious leaders within these communities could chill efforts to analogize sexual orientation to race.

The tensions came to a head in California after a hard-fought battle over an initiative that banned gay marriage. In 2008, the California Supreme Court, relying heavily on comparisons to earlier bans on miscegenation, had declared a state statute limiting marriage to a man and a woman unconstitutional.[18] In November of that year, state voters passed a popular initiative that overturned the decision.[19] Political analysts contended that heavy turnout among African-American voters, who were supporting Barack Obama's bid to become the first black President, propelled the initiative to a slim margin of victory. Exit polls showed that 70 percent of black voters supported the proposition in contrast to just under half of white voters. Commentators subsequently questioned these claims, which pitted blacks against gays and lesbians.[20] New studies asserted that income level, education, party

---

[15]   Herbert C. Brown, Jr., *History Doesn't Repeat Itself, but It Does Rhyme – Same-Sex Marriage: Is the African-American Community the Oppressor This Time?*, 34 S.U. L. REV. 169 (2007); Randall Kennedy, *Marriage and the Struggle for Gay, Lesbian, and Black Liberation*, 2005 UTAH L. REV. 781, 792, 798–99. Indeed, opponents of same-sex marriage have cited the strong opposition to gay marriage as evidence that the *Loving* analogy is misplaced. Lynn D. Wardle and Lincoln C. Oliphant, *In Praise of Loving: Reflections on the* "Loving Analogy" *for Same-Sex Marriage*, 51 HOW. L.J. 117, 129–36, 144–53 (2007).

[16]   Kennedy, *supra* note 15, at 792 (quoting Alveda Celeste King, niece of Martin Luther King, Jr.).

[17]   Brown, *supra* note 15, at 197–98.

[18]   *Marriage Cases*, 183 P.3d 384.

[19]   CAL. CONST. art. I, § 7.5 ("Prop 8"). The California Supreme Court subsequently upheld the initiative in the face of a constitutional challenge. Strauss v. Horton, 207 P.3d 48 (Cal. 2009). The proposition is now being challenged in federal court. Perry v. Schwarzenegger, 704 F. Supp.2d 921 (N.D. Cal. 2010), *stay granted pending appeal*, 2010 WL 3212786 (9th Cir. 2010).

[20]   Matthai Kuruvila, *Singling Out Black Prop. 8 Vote Ignores Larger Issues*, S.F. CHRON., Nov. 16, 2008, at A1; *Overcome the Animosity*, L.A. TIMES, Nov. 18, 2008, at A26; Wendy Wilson, *Lawmaker: Don't*

affiliation, age, and religion accounted for more of the voting disparities than race.[21] Nonetheless, the conflict cast a pall over claims of a common struggle to make marriage inclusive.

Faced with resistance to the *Loving* analogy, some advocates began to call on gays and lesbians to emphasize an independent claim of right based on their own unique story of subordination and oppression.[22] In the 1990s and early 2000s, when the *Loving* analogy was yielding key victories, one queer theorist argued that this type of strategy was so central to any equality claim that abandoning it "would be like asking [proponents] to write their speeches and briefs without using the word 'the.'"[23] Later, however, the limitations of *Loving* suggested that even if it once had been a critical element of the syntax of the same-sex marriage movement, the time might be ripe to move beyond analogy.

SAME-SEX MARRIAGE CASES: AN EMERGING LOGIC OF THEIR OWN

Some recent decisions offer fresh insight into how same-sex marriage cases might develop an internal logic of their own. One signpost is the Connecticut high court's 2008 decision in *Kerrigan v. Commissioner of Public Health*, which built on powerful dissents, including a forceful one by Justice Judith Kaye of the New York Court of Appeals. These dissents rejected conventional approaches, including the *Loving* analogy, by insisting that the unique history and experience of sexual orientation be the central focus of any legal analysis.[24] Rather than make comparisons to interracial marriage, the Connecticut court applied a four-part test to determine whether

---

Blame Blacks for Proposition 8, CNN.com, June 12, 2009, *at* http://articles.cnn.com/2009–06–12/living/what.matters.bass.gay.marriage_1_ban-on-gay-marriage-gay-activists-lgbt (last visited June 21, 2011).

[21] Gary Emerling, *Same-Sex Marriage Activists Regroup; Political Reality Poses Hurdles*, Wash. Times, Dec. 5, 2008, at A1; Justin Ewers, *Poll: Black Voters Not Responsible for Passage of Same-Sex Marriage Ban in California*, USNEWS.com, Dec. 4, 2008; Gregory Rodriguez, *The Ugly Side of "Beyond Race,"* L.A. Times, Nov. 17, 2008, at A21.

[22] Rebecca Schatschneider, *On Shifting Sand: The Perils of Grounding the Case for Same-Sex Marriage in the Context of Antimiscegenation*, 14 Temp. Pol. & Civ. Rts. L. Rev. 285, 304 (2004).

[23] Janet Halley, *"Like Race" Arguments*, in What's Left of Theory: New Work on the Politics of Literary Theory 46 (Judith Butler et al. eds., 2000).

[24] 957 A.2d 407 (Conn. 2008). The *Kerrigan* decision drew on Justice Kaye's dissent in *Hernandez v. Robles*, 855 N.E.2d 1, 18, 27–29 (N.Y. 2006). In contrast to the Connecticut court, Justice Kaye used a three-part approach that did not include immutability as a factor. One commentator has described Kaye's opinion as "eloquent" and "persuasive." Barbara J. Cox, *"A Painful Process of Waiting": The New York, Washington, New Jersey, and Maryland Dissenting Justices Understand That "Same-Sex Marriage" Is Not What Same-Sex Couples Are Seeking*, 45 Cal. W. L. Rev. 139, 152 (2008). Earlier dissents that applied a similar approach include *Dean*, 653 A.2d at 344–55 (Ferren, J., concurring in part and dissenting in part); and *Andersen*, 138 P.3d 963 (Fairhurst, J., dissenting); *see also Baker*, 744 A.2d at 892–93 (Dooley, J., concurring).

provisions that discriminate on the basis of sexual orientation should be subject to heightened scrutiny. The *Kerrigan* opinion examined whether gays and lesbians have experienced a history of discrimination, whether sexual orientation is related to a person's ability to contribute to society, whether sexual orientation is an immutable trait, and whether gays and lesbians are a minority that lacks political power.[25]

Under this approach, the history of oppression of gays and lesbians as well as their capacity to be productive citizens and loving parents were the centerpiece of the decision. As a result, the emphasis was no longer on whether sexual orientation and race are sufficiently similar to merit comparable protection under marriage laws. In fact, the Connecticut court was willing to recognize discrimination against gays and lesbians, even if sexual orientation is dissimilar to race. For instance, race has been described as a fixed trait ascribed at birth, but the court expressed doubts as to whether sexual orientation is similarly immutable or simply "highly resistant to change."[26] Nonetheless, the *Kerrigan* decision concluded that:

> In view of the central role that sexual orientation plays in a person's fundamental right to self-determination, we fully agree with the plaintiffs that their sexual orientation represents the kind of distinguishing characteristic that defines them as a discrete group for purposes of determining whether that group should be afforded heightened protection under the equal protection provisions of the state constitution.[27]

In short, the court dispensed with an immutability analysis anchored in racial comparisons and instead focused on the propriety of subjecting people to coercive pressure to conform under the marriage law, given the unique nature of sexual orientation.[28]

When analogies were drawn, the Connecticut court made comparisons to both race and gender. So, when considering whether gays and lesbians lack political power, the Connecticut court noted that the group need not be wholly without influence but "the discrimination to which they have been subjected [must have] been so severe and so persistent that, as with race and sex discrimination, it is not likely to be remedied soon enough merely by resort to the majoritarian political process."[29] The court asserted that when judicial protections were extended to racial minorities and women, they likely had more clout than gay and lesbians. So, some limited success in the political arena did not preclude proponents of same-sex

---

[25] 957 A.2d at 426.
[26] *Id.* at 437.
[27] *Id.* at 438.
[28] *See* Kennedy, *supra* note 15, at 794 (rejecting the view that "it is less objectionable to deny rights on the basis of something a person can change" as a logic that is "hardly appealing").
[29] *Kerrigan*, 957 A.2d at 440.

marriage from seeking relief in the courts. Ultimately, the *Kerrigan* decision relied on the kind of heightened scrutiny associated with gender classifications, rather than the strictest level associated with racial ones, to strike down the official restriction on same-sex marriages.[30]

In 2009, the Iowa Supreme Court employed a similar analysis to find that gays and lesbians could not be denied the right to marry under the state constitution.[31] But perhaps the most striking example of an effort to forge an independent rationale for the right of same-sex couples to marry came in *Perry v. Schwarzenegger*, the first and only federal court decision to date that has struck down a gay marriage ban as unconstitutional.[32] There, the district court judge heard extensive expert testimony on the history of marriage, the nature of sexual orientation as an enduring form of personal identity, the stability of same-sex relationships, the parenting capacities of same-sex couples, and the harms inflicted on gays and lesbians by same-sex marriage bans. The growing body of research on these questions made it possible to move beyond analogies to interracial marriage in arguing for a constitutional violation. Indeed, the court's conclusions were heavily driven by these data. The court found that "[s]ame-sex couples are identical to opposite-sex couples in the characteristics relevant to the ability to form successful marital unions," and that gay and lesbian couples as well as their children would benefit from the ability to marry.[33] The court also determined that domestic partnerships did not afford gays and lesbians a status equivalent to marriage, that same-sex marriage would not undermine the institution of marriage, and that religious groups that opposed gay marriage retained their First Amendment right to refuse to perform church wedding ceremonies.

In the end, the judge found that marriage increasingly has been defined as a matter of personal choice and consent, as demonstrated by the demise of not only antimiscegenation laws but also the legal obligations that once rested on a gender-based division of labor. The district court's focus was on how this model of marital agency and autonomy should apply to classifications based on sexual orientation. The judge concluded that the most searching level of scrutiny should apply, but he also noted that the empirical support for a same-sex marriage ban was so thin that it could not pass muster even under the lenient rational relation test. The *Perry* decision is striking because its reasoning relies almost entirely on findings about sexual orientation with only passing references to race and interracial marriage.

By departing from the *Loving* analogy, the emerging logic of same-sex marriage cases allows courts to appreciate that not all forms of subordination need to replicate

[30] *Id.* at 480–81.
[31] Varnum v. Brien, 763 N.W.2d 862 (Iowa 2009).
[32] 704 F. Supp. 2d 921.
[33] *Id.* at 967, 969, 973.

Moran

a racial dynamic. Political scientist Julie Novkov argues that the *Loving* analogy has
rigidified legal analysis in ways that prevent a nuanced jurisprudential approach
to distinct histories and experiences of discrimination. In her view, this analogical
reasoning "appears more as a cautionary tale than as a model and guidepost" in
the same-sex marriage cases.[34] Moreover, a narrow preoccupation with how closely
race and sexual orientation resemble one another can divert the judiciary's attention
from other fundamental questions about the role that marriage plays in entrenching
inequality. As Novkov contends, "a more critical examination would open marriage
itself to questioning about its capacity to structure private relationships and to mobi-
lize potentially restrictive conceptions of family and gender roles."[35] If Novkov is
right, focus on same-sex marriage can obscure the ways in which marriage itself marginalizes a wide range of intimate relationships that are denied legal recognition.

BEYOND MARRIAGE: THE NEXT FRONTIER

Novkov's critique suggests that there is some irony in discussing how the same-sex
marriage movement has advanced an understanding of liberty and equality in intimate relationships. Skeptics contend that marriage itself is a highly assimilative
institution and that, by pursuing the right to marry with such unalloyed zeal, gay
and lesbian advocates are further entrenching a hierarchy of intimacy. Same-sex
marriage proponents certainly have recognized the privileged position of marriage.
Activists regularly catalog the hundreds of benefits that are available to spouses and
denied to unmarried gay and lesbian couples. For these advocates, recognition of
same-sex marriage is essential to achieve full equality, but others see this reform
effort as highly partial because it fails to embrace a diversity of intimate arrangements, all of which deserve recognition and legitimacy.[36]

For instance, because the legal dominance of marriage persists today, other care-
taking relationships are neglected. Single mothers who must rely on friends and
neighbors to provide an informal network of care and support have no way to protect or subsidize these relationships by law.[37] Adults who want to care for the grandmother who raised them cannot seek unpaid leave under the Family and Medical

[34] Julie Novkov, *The Miscegenation/Same-Sex Marriage Analogy: What Can We Learn from Legal History?*, 33 Law & Soc. Inquiry 345, 383 (2008).
[35] *Id.*
[36] For an excellent analysis of the limits of marriage in addressing changing patterns of intimacy in the United States as well as some initial reform proposals, see Nancy D. Polikoff, Beyond (Straight and Gay) Marriage: Valuing All Families Under the Law (2008).
[37] Rosanna Hertz & Faith I.T. Ferguson, *Kinship Strategies and Self-Sufficiency Among Single Mothers by Choice: Post Modern Family Ties*, 20 Qualitative Soc. 187, 204 (1997) (describing how single mothers build a "repertory family," defined as an "ensemble" comprised of friends and neighbors as well as relatives).

Leave Act of 1993.[38] Elderly widows who would like to share housing to save money find few legal guidelines and are forced to model their arrangements on prenuptial agreements.[39] As much as Americans prize the freedom to forge intimate relationships, there are precious few ways to acknowledge these connections and shelter them from adversity outside of marriage.

In 2001, the Law Commission of Canada released a report entitled *Beyond Conjugality: Recognizing and Supporting Close Personal Adult Relationships*. The Commission recognized that "[a] substantial minority of Canadian households involves adults living alone, lone-parent families or adults living together in non-conjugal relationships."[40] Noting the importance of a "family of friends," the Commission urged the government not to "rely too heavily on conjugal relationships in accomplishing important state objectives."[41] Instead, the report contended, officials should allow people to register relationships not limited to couples; by mutual consent, the parties would be subject to legal responsibilities and entitled to legal protections.

Today, there is little evidence that the United States will follow the Canadian example and attempt to broaden the scope of protected intimate relationships. If anything, courts, legislatures, and political leaders seem more intently focused on marriage than ever. As president, George W. Bush advocated the adoption of laws that promote marriage as a cure for welfare dependency.[42] States have considered covenant marriage statutes that combine premarital counseling with tougher restrictions on divorce.[43] Gays and lesbians have pressed for same-sex marriage as a way to enshrine the institution's symbolic power, while Congress and most states have responded by defending marriage as, by definition, an act between a man and a woman.[44] This longing for the respectability of traditional marriage makes clear that it retains its hallowed place, despite some calls for greater recognition

[38] Pub. L. No. 103–3, tit. I, § 2, 107 Stat. 6 (codified at 29 U.S.C. §§ 2601–54 (2000); 5 U.S.C. §§ 6381–6387 (2000)).

[39] *See* Jane Gross, *Older Women Team Up to Face Future Together*, N.Y. TIMES, Feb. 27, 2004, at A1.

[40] Law Comm'n of Canada, BEYOND CONJUGALITY: RECOGNIZING AND SUPPORTING CLOSE PERSONAL ADULT RELATIONSHIPS x (2001), *available at* http://epe.lac-bac.gc.ca/100/200/301/lcc-cdc/beyond_conjugality-e/pdf/37152-e.pdf

[41] *Id.* at xviii, x.

[42] *See* Admin. for Children & Families, U.S. Dep't of Health and Human Serv., *The Healthy Marriage Initiative (HMI)*, at http://www.acf.hhs.gov/healthymarriage/about/mission.html (last visited June 21, 2011).

[43] *See* ARIZ. REV. STAT. ANN. § 25–901 to –906 (West 2006); ARK. CODE ANN. § 9–11–801 to –811 (Michie 1987 & Supp. 2002); LA. REV. STAT. ANN. § 9:272 to :275.1 (West 2000 & Supp. 2007).

[44] Defense of Marriage Act, Pub. L. No. 104–199, § 3(a), 110 Stat. 2419 (1996) (codified at 1 U.S.C. § 7 (2000) and 28 U.S.C. § 1738C (2000)). For an inventory of states that restrict marriage to unions between a man and a woman, see Human Rights Campaign, *Statewide Marriage Prohibitions* (2010), at http://www.hrc.org/documents/marriage_prohibitions_2009.pdf (last visited June 21, 2011).

of single parents, extended family members, and cohabitating adults. As a result, moving beyond the *Loving* analogy in same-sex marriage cases will not necessarily enable us to see beyond marriage to other forms of intimacy that deserve respect and protection.

CONCLUSION

The same-sex marriage movement has questioned traditional assumptions about who should be eligible to marry. Concerns about access to marriage are significant, but the most profound questions of justice could turn on how we rectify the gap between those who choose to express their affection through marriage and those who do not. Without efforts to address these disparities, significant inequality will persist between the married and the unmarried, thereby chilling the liberty to choose among diverse forms of intimacy. The shift away from analogies to race allows advocates to address distinct histories of exclusion and marginalization, but the emerging logic of same-sex marriage cases cannot tackle profound questions of fairness that inhere in the privileged nature of marriage itself.

19

The End of Marriage

Tucker B. Culbertson

For better and worse, U.S. constitutional law has long expressed the opinion that marriage is essential to both individual and collective well-being. In the 1923 case, *Meyer v. Nebraska*, the Court ruled that the liberties protected under the doctrine of substantive due process included:

> the right ... to contract, to engage in any of the common occupations of life, to acquire useful knowledge, to marry, establish a home and bring up children, to worship God according to the dictates of his own conscience, and generally to enjoy those privileges long recognized at common law as essential to the orderly pursuit of happiness by free men.[1]

Sixty-five years later, the Court decided *Zablocki v. Redhail* and offered its most extensive exposition on the fundamental right to marry.[2] Unlike *Meyer*, *Zablocki* was decided under the Equal Protection Clause of the Fourteenth Amendment. In his majority opinion, Justice Marshall argued that:

> It is not surprising that the decision to marry has been placed on the same level of importance as decisions relating to procreation, childbirth, child rearing, and family relationships ... it would make little sense to recognize a right of privacy with respect to other matters of family life and not with respect to the decision to enter the relationship that is the foundation of the family in our society.[3]

These opinions exemplify the Court's problematic jurisprudence on marriage: *Meyer* simply assumes the fundamentality of marriage, whereas *Zablocki* irrationally presumes that marriage is coterminous with sex, reproduction, and family. Perhaps the most famous of the Court's marriage cases, *Loving v. Virginia*, shares

---

[1]   262 U.S. 390, 399 (1923) (quoted in Erwin Chemerinsky, Constitutional Law: Principles and Policies 768 (2d ed. 2002)).
[2]   434 U.S. 374 (1978).
[3]   *Id.* at 386.

these flaws, taking marriage to be fundamental because it wrongly presumes a connection between marriage itself and the beneficial ends that marriage is thought to facilitate. Moreover, *Loving* most clearly exposes why constitutionalizing marriage is not only erroneous, but also dangerous.

Loving addressed Virginia laws that civilly prohibited and criminally penalized marriage between Whites and non-Whites (with the absurd and spectacular exception of Pocahontas's descendants).[4] The Court found that Virginia's laws violated the Equal Protection and Due Process clauses of the Fourteenth Amendment.[5] Despite rightly denouncing the white supremacist laws at issue, and despite doing right by the Lovings and all interracial heterosexual couples, *Loving* perpetuates the very harms that it should have cured. It legitimates discrimination against those whose sexual and familial relationships remain unrecognizable under any civil marriage regime. Virginia's marriage laws disparaged not only heteroracial heterosexual coupling, but also homosexual, polyamorous, platonic, and other ways of living and loving. In renouncing such laws, the Court should have declared unconstitutional all government action that privileges civil marriage.

The Court should have condemned Virginia's civil marriage regime as an infringement on the Lovings' rights to *the ends of marriage*, such as erotic pleasure and reciprocal care (which, for ease of reference, I will call the rights to sex and family). Recognizing fundamental rights to sex, family, and the other ends of marriage would more broadly defend the liberty and equality that concern the *Loving* Court. Instead, Justice Warren, writing for the majority, declares marriage itself fundamental.[6] Without elaboration, Justice Warren suggests that mixed-sex marriage

4 *Loving v. Virginia*, 388 U.S. 1, 5 n.4 (1967).
5 On equal protection, *Loving* continues the general work and particular logic of *Brown v. Board of Education*, 347 U.S. 483 (1954), identifying any racial classification as dubious, and invidious racial discrimination as damned, under the Equal Protection Clause.
6 Justice Warren's opinion is also unsound because it is issued under the Fourteenth Amendment. He contends that marriage is a fundamental right because it is "one of the basic civil rights of man." Historically, this claim must mean that heterosexual civil marriage is among the practices imagined by certain revolutionary eighteenth-century North Atlantic writers as essential to human nature and happiness. Even if this claim is true, can "the rights of man" be so simply asserted as the content of the Fourteenth Amendment when that Amendment upends our national traditions of racial caste? Racial caste was historically at the heart of "the rights of man." The revolutionary United States Constitution, and subsequent interpretations thereof, of course explicitly and frequently instantiated racial caste. Indeed, racial slavery was one of only a very few individual rights mentioned in the articles of the revolutionary constitution. *See* U.S. CONST. art. I, § 9; U.S. CONST. art. IV, § 2; U.S. CONST. art. V. Hence the Reconstruction Constitution.
    The French "Rights of Man and Citizen" similarly excluded racialized and subordinated peoples. The Friends of the Negro, as well as various emissaries from the French colonies, argued that the "Rights of Man" should necessarily call for the full equality of multiracial persons, the emancipation of slaves, and an end to racial caste generally. *See* C.L.R. James, THE BLACK JACOBINS Ch. 2–5 (Vintage Press, 2d ed. 1989). The Revolutionary French National Assembly consistently ignored,

is fundamental to "our very existence and survival." He must have meant that marriage is a literal prerequisite for the continuation of the species through procreative reproduction. However, civil marriage is clearly neither necessary nor sufficient for procreative reproduction, let alone for the survival of offspring.

Because marriage is unnecessary and insufficient for any of its beneficial ends, it cannot logically be a fundamental constitutional right. Marriage is a governmental means for advancing individually meaningful or socially beneficial ends – for example, species reproduction, reciprocal promises of care, and intergenerational transferences of wealth – all of which might be achieved without a marriage, and none of which is guaranteed by the mere fact of a marriage alone. By mistaking a governmental means for a constitutional end, the Court in *Loving* avows the traditional privilege given to civil marriage at the same time that the traditionally White supremacist parameters of marriage are condemned as illiberal and unequal. As the Court condemned the Lovings' exclusion from marital privilege on the basis of race, it should have condemned the exclusive privileging of marriage as such, which does similar harm to those involved in other, unmarried forms of sexual and familial relationships.

As a political matter, because civil marriage is unnecessary and insufficient for its ends, discriminatory dimensions of such regimes (e.g., exclusions of heteroracial and homosexual spouses) should be represented and redressed in ways that transcend discussion about equal access to marriage. Expansions of marriage fail to remedy subordination; they also facilitate and legitimate it. The policing and punishment of unmarried African-American families, lovers, and other cohabitants in the wake of the Civil War, which Katherine Franke importantly recounts and theorizes, demonstrates a racially and sexually disciplinary regime that worked to reinforce and reproduce white supremacy.[7] This regime, however, did not operate by withholding, *but rather by expanding* the terms of civil marriage. As in Loving, such normative laws for family formation – the law of marriage – illegitimately and irrationally attaches to different ways of having sex and a family.

Reframing "The Marriage Question" as a reconstructive demand for equal sexual and familial liberty might enable our constitutional politics to be more than an incremental reformation of unconstitutional practices of governance. Many seemingly unrelated communities, injuries, and policies become obviously politically

repressed, rejected, or granted and retracted such extensions of the "basic civil rights of man" to non-Whites. *Id.*

As such, Justice Warren's excoriation of the rights of racial caste renders untenable his simplistic defense of heterosexual civil marriage as among "the 'basic civil rights of man.'"

[7] *See* Katherine Franke, *Becoming a Citizen: Reconstruction Era Regulation of African American Marriage*, 11 YALE J.L. & HUMAN. 251 (1999); *see also* Katherine Franke, *The Domesticated Liberty of* Lawrence v. Texas, 104 COLUM. L. REV. 1399, 1420–25 (2004), (discussing discipline and policing of African Americans in the postbellum South through marital licensing and other habitation regulations).

connected when we emphasize individuals' rights to the ends of marriage, including rights to enjoy sexual and familial relationships. These rights are regularly denied to: people in prisons;[8] people on public benefits;[9] children who hope to be adopted;[10] people who produce, sell, or use sex toys;[11] married people with sexual partners other than their spouse;[12] people with multiple partners or spouses (including religious minorities);[13] and people whose primary relationships and promises of care are

[8] Presently, prisoners' and detainees' visitation privileges may be restricted so long as such restrictions bear a rational relation to any penalogical goal. Turner v. Safley, 482 U.S. 78 (1987). *See* ACLU, *Know Your Rights: Visitation in Prisons, at* http://www.aclu.org/prisoners-rights/know-your-rights-restrictions-visitation. In particular, note the Supreme Court's recent decision in *Overton v. Bazzetta*, 539 U.S. 126 (2003) (establishing that recurrent violation of substance use policy justifies suspending visitation privileges for inmates). *See Champion v. Artuz*, 76 F.3d 483 (2d Cir. 1996), for the argument that conjugal visits may be constitutionally denied to prisoners and detainees.

[9] Consider the Bush administration's "Initiative for Healthy Marriage":
    Recognizing the widespread benefits of marriage to individuals and society, the federal welfare reform legislation enacted in 1996 set forth clear goals to increase the number of two-parent families and reduce out-of-wedlock childbearing ... President Bush has sought to meet the original goals of welfare reform by proposing, as part of welfare reauthorization, a new model program to promote healthy marriage.
    See Robert E. Rector et al., *"Marriage Plus": Sabotaging the President's Efforts to Promote Healthy Marriage*, HERITAGE FOUND., Aug. 22, 2003, *available at* http://www.heritage.org/Research/Welfare/BG1677.cfm (last visited June 16, 2011).

[10] Lofton v. Children & Family Servs., 358 F.3d 804 (11th Cir. 2004) (finding no fundamental right to homosexual adoption and a rational, legitimate purpose in allowing only heterosexuals to adopt).

[11] *See, e.g.*, ALA. CODE. §13A-12–200.2(A)(1) (2006), which states: "It shall be unlawful for any person to knowingly distribute, possess with intent to distribute, or offer or agree to distribute any obscene material or any device designed or marketed as useful primarily for the stimulation of human genital organs for anything of pecuniary value." The law was upheld by a three-judge panel of the Eleventh Circuit on February 14, 2007:
    The only question remaining before us is whether public morality remains a sufficient rational basis for the challenged statute after the Supreme Court's decision in *Lawrence v. Texas*. ... The district court distinguished *Lawrence* and held, following our prior precedent in this case, *Williams v. Pryor*, 240 F.3d 944 (11th Cir. 2001) (Williams II), that the statute survives rational basis scrutiny. Because we find that public morality remains a legitimate rational basis for the challenged legislation even after Lawrence, we affirm.
    See Williams v. Morgan, 478 F.3d 1316, 1317 (11th Cir. 2007).

[12] *See* Franklin Foer, *Adultery*, SLATE, June 15, 1997, *at* http://www.slate.com/id/1063/:
    The United States inherited English common law, which made adultery, as well as fornication (sex between unmarried people) and sodomy (oral and anal sex), punishable crimes. In the mid and late 19th centuries, when states wrote their criminal codes, they incorporated these sex laws. Twenty-six states continue to have anti-adultery laws on the books. These laws vary considerably. Some define adultery as any intercourse outside marriage. According to others, it occurs when a married person lives with someone other than his or her spouse. In West Virginia and North Carolina, simply "to lewdly and lasciviously associate" with anyone other than one's spouse is to be adulterous. ... Punishments also vary. Adultery is a felony in Massachusetts, Michigan, Oklahoma, and Idaho, and a misdemeanor everywhere else.

[13] *See, e.g.*, State v. Holm, 137 P.3d 726, 738–40 (Utah 2006), *cert. denied*, 127 S. Ct. 1371 (2007) (upholding criminal conviction for bigamy after the Supreme Court's recent invalidation of laws against "homosexual sodomy" in *Lawrence v. Texas*).

platonic rather than romantic.[14] Although there may be compelling exceptions, in these and other circumstances, U.S. government agents should, generally, neither punish nor penalize people's sexual or familial relationships, but rather enfranchise their experience of liberty through both sex and family.

Heteroracial and homosexual couples are emblematic, but in no way exhaustive, of the wide range of sexual and familial relationships injured by the privilege historically afforded homoracial heterosexual marriages. Challenges to "traditional" (e.g., White supremacist, homophobic, heterocentrist, and patriarchal) marriage regimes should call for two things. First, marriage should be constitutionally disestablished as a necessary or sufficient condition for benefits or burdens. Second, state and federal governments should protect and not infringe persons' formation of collective social units or their pursuit of sexual pleasure.

There is both explicit and implicit Supreme Court precedent for recognizing fundamental rights to sex and family. The right to cultivate and maintain family has been recognized by the Court in the context of marriage,[15] child custody,[16] child rearing,[17] and extended family.[18] The right to sex, by contrast, has been consistently unrecognized as such by the Court. Even Justice Blackmun's momentous dissent in *Bowers v. Hardwick* argues only that consenting adults, behind their own closed doors, are due the negative "right to be let alone," not that they have a right to want and get erotic pleasure.[19] Justice Kennedy, writing for the Court that overruled *Bowers* in *Lawrence*, was similarly unwilling to avow a right to sex.[20] As Katherine Franke discusses, *Lawrence* overrules a law against homosexual sex by constitutionally defending not sex in general, but rather private sex between two people, of either of two sexes, conducted in furtherance of an intimate, presumably monogamous, romantic, familial, and not exclusively sexual relationship.[21] As Justice Scalia notes in his dissent in *Lawrence*: "The Court embraces ... Justice Stevens' declaration in his *Bowers* dissent, that 'the fact that the governing majority in a State has traditionally viewed a particular practice as immoral is not a sufficient reason for

[14] *See* Laura A. Rosenbury, *Friends with Benefits?*, 106 MICH. L. REV. 189 (2007).
[15] Zablocki v. Redhail, 434 U.S. 374 (1978); Boddie v. Connecticut, 401 U.S. 371 (1971); *Loving*, 388 U.S. at 1.
[16] Santosky v. Kramer, 455 U.S. 746 (1982); Stanley v. Illinois, 405 U.S. 645 (1972).
[17] Parham v. J.R., 442 U.S. 584 (1979); Wisconsin v. Yoder, 406 U.S. 205 (1972); Pierce v. Soc'y of Sisters, 268 U.S. 510 (1925); Meyer v. Nebraska, 262 U.S. 390 (1923).
[18] Moore v. East Cleveland, 431 U.S. 494 (1977).
[19] 478 U.S. 186 at 199 (1986) (Blackmun, J., dissenting) (citing Omstead v. United States, 277 U.S. 438, 478 (1928) (Brandeis, Jr., dissenting)).
[20] Lawrence v. Texas, 539 U.S. 558, 578 (2003) ("*Bowers* was not correct when it was decided, and it is not correct today. It ought not to remain binding precedent. *Bowers v. Hardwick* should be and now is overruled.").
[21] *The Domesticated Liberty of* Lawrence v. Texas, *supra* n.7.

upholding a law prohibiting the practice."[22] However, the Court's "embrace" of this argument is insufficiently energetic or explicit, thus occasioning Justice Scalia's compelling dissent. Justice Kennedy's majority opinion should have acknowledged the profundity of erotic pleasure in many human beings' lives by recognizing the consequent importance of erotic pleasure to our constitutional conception of freedom. Moreover, the majority should have denounced state practices and national traditions that enfranchise sexual liberty only for an exclusive class of persons, preferences, and practices. Instead, Justice Kennedy perversely draws on traditional familial and sexual norms – including mixed-sex civil marriage – in order to deduce a constitutional right to not be jailed for sex traditionally deemed immoral.[23]

Similar to *Lawrence*'s repressed encounter with sexual liberty, the Supreme Court's jurisprudence on procreation, contraception, and abortion presumes, but does not pronounce, a right to engage in heterosexual intercourse and intentional family planning.[24] Rights to control or refuse reproduction could theoretically correspond to a duty *not* to have intercourse rather than a right to pregnancy prevention and termination. There is, in such cases, an implicit right to have sex and an explicit right to not have a family. This right to sex, however, is too cabined as to place, manner, and gender of pleasure, just as the rights to family mentioned earlier overly promote marital and biological forms of kinship. In *Griswold v. Connecticut*, the Court defended married couples' access to contraceptive technologies by reference to the fundamentality and privacy of marriage rather than the rights to have sex and manage family.[25] Shortly thereafter, in *Eisenstadt v. Baird*, single people

[22] *Lawrence*, 539 U.S. at 586 (Scalia, J., dissenting) (quoting Bowers v. Hardwick, 478 U.S. 186, 216 (1986) (Stevens, J., dissenting)).
[23] See *Lawrence*, 539 U.S. at 567. Justice Kennedy, writing for the majority, noted:
   To say that the issue in *Bowers* was simply the right to engage in certain sexual conduct demeans the claim the individual put forward, just as it would demean a married couple were it to be said marriage is simply about the right to have sexual intercourse. ... When sexuality finds overt expression in intimate conduct with another person, the conduct can be but one element in a personal bond that is more enduring.*Id.* at 567. The Court also stated:
   In our tradition the State is not omnipresent in the home. ... It suffices for us to acknowledge that adults may choose to enter upon this relationship in the confines of their homes and their own private lives and still retain their dignity as free persons. The liberty protected by the Constitution allows homosexual persons the right to make this choice.*Id.* at 562.
[24] See Skinner v. Oklahoma, 316 U.S. 535 (1942); Buck v. Bell, 274 U.S. 200 (1927); Eisenstadt v. Baird, 405 U.S. 438 (1972); Griswold v. Connecticut, 381 U.S. 479 (1965); Stenberg v. Carhart, 530 U.S. 914 (2000); Planned Parenthood v. Casey, 505 U.S. 833 (1992).
[25] See *Griswold*, 381 U.S. at 486. The Court explained:
   We deal with a right of privacy older than the Bill of Rights – older than our political parties, older than our school system. Marriage is a coming together for better or for worse, hopefully enduring, and intimate to the degree of being sacred. It is an association that promotes a way of life, not causes; a harmony in living, not political faiths; a bilateral loyalty, not commercial or social projects. Yet it is an association for as noble a purpose as any involved in our prior decisions.

were afforded the same access to contraception, overturning a Massachusetts statute that limited birth control to married couples only. However, fundamental rights were not even discussed by the Court's majority. Although the lower court found Massachusetts's contraception ban a violation of unmarried persons' fundamental rights,[26] the Supreme Court found the statute to be, in light of *Griswold's* defense of contraception for married couples, an unconstitutional imposition on single people under the Equal Protection Clause.[27] In all of these cases, clustered temporally around *Loving*, there is a consistent expansion of individual rights regarding sex and family. However, as in *Loving*, these expansions become reconfirmations of marriage, despite the neither necessary nor sufficient connection of marriage to procreation, sexual activity, or romantic attachment.

The naturalized propriety of civil marriage can, and should be, rejected. The status afforded to civil marriage is irrational, illegitimate, and violative of all unmarried people's fundamental rights to the ends of marriage. Avowing marriage as a fundamental right yields a jurisprudence that is logically untenable, politically unjust, and, ultimately, anticonstitutional. That which "marriage equality" movements oppose must indeed be undone by constitutional analysis. Similarly, the governmental structures challenged must not provide the core terms for such analyses if we are to fight unfreedom and inequality.

[26] Baird v. Eisenstadt, 429 F.2d 1398 (1st Cir. 1970).
[27] *Eisenstadt*, 405 U.S. at 446–55.

Afterword

Peter Wallenstein

On June 12, 1967, when the U.S. Supreme Court handed down its unanimous ruling that statutes restricting interracial marriage could no longer be enforced, something happened. But exactly what? And how does it matter, whether for understanding (1) U.S. history before 1967, (2) the developments of the decades that followed, or (3) social or policy issues in contemporary America? Specialized scholars continue to address these questions, as the illuminating essays in this volume illustrate, and everyday citizens work within their own understandings, wishes, and concerns.

What, during the long history of the antimiscegenation regime, was understood as "interracial marriage" anyway? States freely defined the term, always differing from other states and often changing their own laws. If Mildred Jeter had been "Indian," as she described herself on her marriage license, then she and Richard Loving could have married in Virginia – at least before 1924, before either of them were born. Even if she had African ancestry, the question would have been how much – until after 1924, when Virginia introduced the "one drop" rule to marriage. Her description of herself when she sought legal help as Mrs. Richard Loving in 1963 – as "part" Native American and "part" African American – had no legal significance under Virginia law at that time, which simply deemed her "colored."

The couple's wedding in 1958 in Washington, DC, put them at risk, as they had soon learned, of prosecution and imprisonment. The Virginia law treated their going out of state to marry, with the intent of evading the law that barred them from marrying within Virginia, as indistinguishable from violating the law by marrying within Virginia. No matter how she might be classified, by herself or anyone else, unless she was Caucasian, she could not, under Virginia law, return to her home state with her new husband.

For Mildred and Richard Loving, *Loving v. Virginia* divided the world between before and after – much as BC/AD for Christians or before and after emancipation for former slaves. Mr. and Mrs. Loving learned on that day that they, together with their three young children, could live thereafter in Virginia, unchallenged by the law of race and marriage. For most people, that single event has proven to be much less significant, and yet – one premise of this volume – its significance, historical and contemporary, surely outstrips the relatively scant attention it has attracted and the limited scholarship it has previously generated.

On June 12, 1967, the world turned for a good many people – including vast numbers who benefited from it only years later. When Mrs. Loving died in 2008, people wrote messages in an electronic guest book celebrating her life while expressing their views that her case had freed them in fundamental ways. People in Florida, Louisiana, and elsewhere across the South had, because of the court victory of Mr. and Mrs. Loving, been able to marry their other-race lovers. Even a woman writing from New York, while observing that she and her family would have had no problems with the law of race and marriage in their current state of residence, recognized that they would have been unable to move to Virginia or any number of other states before the Supreme Court ruled the way it did in the *Loving* case.

Not only did the end of the antimiscegenation regime enhance racial justice, it also initiated new possibilities for social discourse as well as in private lives. Echoes of *Loving* continue in the debates over same-sex marriage, which generate questions both similar and new about family structure. As the essays in this collection show, the new environment after *Loving* accommodates diverse intimacies that reflect the free right to choose an adult partner, whether for life or for a season, of whatever sex or race. This collection, by bringing together various issues of "loving" in a post-*Loving* world, shows us its effects on the law and in our everyday lives.

Permissions Granted

We thank the journals and authors that gave permission to have their work included in this book

Tucker B. Culbertson:
Previously published as Tucker Culbertson, *Arguments against Marriage Equality: Commemorating & Reconstructing Loving v. Virginia*, 85 Wash. U. L. Rev. 575 (2007).

Jason A. Gillmer:
Previously published as Jason A. Gillmer, *Base Wretches and Black Wenches: A Story of Sex and Race, Violence and Compassion, During Slavery Times*, 59 Ala. L. Rev. 1501 (2008).

John DeWitt Gregory and Joanna L. Grossman:
Previously published in *Howard Law Journal* Vol. 51, Issue 1 (2007).

Robin A. Lenhardt:
© 2008 by California Law Review, Inc. Reprinted from the *California Law Review*, Vol. 96, No. 4, by California Law Review, Inc.

Rachel F. Moran:
Forty Years After Loving: A Legacy of Unintended Consequences, 2007 Wis. L. Rev. 239 (2010). © 2010 by The Board of Regents of the University of Wisconsin System. Reprinted by permission of the *Wisconsin Law Review*.

Adele M. Morrison:
Adapted from an article, "*Same-Sex Loving: Subverting White Supremacy Through Same-Sex Marriage*," which was previously published in 13 *Michigan Journal of Race & Law* 177 (2007).

Camille A. Nelson:
Lovin' The Man: Examining the Legal Nexus of Irony, Hypocrisy, and Curiosity, 2007 Wis. L. Rev. 543 (2010). © 2010 by The Board of Regents of the University of Wisconsin System. Reprinted by permission of the *Wisconsin Law Review*.

Kevin Noble Maillard:
Previously published in the *Fordham Law Review*, Vol. 76, 2008, as "The Multiracial Epiphany of Loving."

Angela Onwuachi-Willig and Jacob Willig-Onwuachi:
"A House Divided: The Invisibility of the Multiracial Family," which was previously published in 44 *Harvard Civil Rights-Civil Liberties Law Review* 231 (2009).

Nancy K. Ota:
Adapted from an article, "Flying Buttresses," which was previously published in DePaul Law Review, Vol. 49, p. 693 (2000).

Carla D. Pratt:
Loving Indian Style: Maintaining Racial Caste and Tribal Sovereignty Through Sexual Assimilation, 2007 Wis. L. Rev. 409 (2010). © 2010 by The Board of Regents of the University of Wisconsin System. Reprinted by permission of the *Wisconsin Law Review*.

Victor C. Romero:
Adapted from an article previously published in *Howard Law Journal*, Vol. 51, Issue 1 (2007).

Rose Cuison Villazor:
Adapted from an article, *"The Other Loving: Uncovering the Federal Government's Racial Regulation of Marriage,"* which was previously published in New York University Law Review, Vol. 86, p. 1361 (2011)."

Leti Volpp:
This work, © 2000 by Leti Volpp, was originally published by *UC Davis Law Review*, Vol. 33, pp. 795–835, copyright 2000 by The Regents of the University of California. All rights reserved. Reprinted with permission.

Index

CPSIA information can be obtained
at www.ICGtesting.com
Printed in the USA
LVHW081023190919
631576LV00006B/146/P